WORKERS, NEIGHBORS,
and CITIZENS

WORKERS, NEIGHBORS, and CITIZENS

The Revolution in Mexico City

JOHN LEAR

University of
Nebraska Press

Lincoln & London

Portions of this book have been previously published as "Mexico City: Space and Class in the Porfirian Capital (1884–1910)," *Journal of Urban History* 22, no. 4 (1996): 454–92, copyright © 1996 Sage Publications, reprinted by permission of Sage Publications; "La XXVI Legislatura y los trabajadores de la ciudad de México (1912–1913)," *Secuencia: Revista de ciencias sociales*, no. 40 (January–April 1998); and "Del mutualismo a la resistencia: Las organizaciones laborales en la ciudad de México desde fines del porfiriato a la Revolución," in *Ciudad de México: Instituciones, actores sociales y conflicto político, 1774–1931*, ed. Carlos Illades and Ariel Rodríguez Kuri (Mexico: Universidad Autónoma Metropolitana, El Colegio de Michoacán, 1997).

Library of Congress Cataloging-in-Publication Data
Lear, John, 1959–
    Worker, neighbors, and citizens : the revolution in Mexico City / John Lear.
        p.   cm.
    Includes bibliographical references and index.
    ISBN 0-8032-2936-4 (cloth: alk. paper) — ISBN 0-8032-7997-3
(pbk: alk. paper)
    1. Labor movement—Mexico—Mexico City—History. 2. Working class—Mexico—Mexico City—Political activity—History. 3. Poor—Mexico—Mexico City—Political activity—History. 4. Mexico—History—Revolution, 1910–1920. 5. Mexico City (Mexico)—History—20th century. I. Title.
HD8116.L43 2001
972.08'16—dc21   00-059967

To Marena and Soroa,
who like my other stories

Contents

Illustrations

MAPS

TABLE

Acknowledgments

Some debts, too large and numerous to be repaid, can only be acknowledged. I owe a special debt to Tulio Halperín-Donghi, who taught me Latin American history while I was a graduate student at the University of California, Berkeley, and who has remained supportive throughout my professional meanderings. My interest in Mexico City and the Mexican Revolution began with conversations with John Womack while I was on a graduate school exchange program at Harvard. Diego Armus, Barry Carr, Joseph Collins, Denise Dresser, Linda Hall, Carlos Illades, Kass Lear, Curtis Martin, Graciela Schmilchuk, Emilio Zebadúa, and Eric Zolov all gave me encouragement when I needed it and shared many of the endeavors that led to this book. Jeremy Adelman, Jonathan Brown, Stephen Haber, Tulio Halperín-Donghi, Linda Lewin, Kevin Middlebrook, Suzie Porter, Mauricio Tenorio, and John Womack read the dissertation on which this book is based and gave comments that guided me through its several transformations. Richard Warren and Ann Blum offered valuable suggestions on a nearly final manuscript. Adrian Bantjes and William French provided careful, challenging, and insightful reviews for the University of Nebraska Press.

I am grateful to the many people who helped me track down documents and images, especially to scholars John Mraz and Ariel Arnal, to Enrique Cervantes of Mexico's Archivo General de la Nación, to Walter Brem of the Bancroft Library, and to Paula Barra Moulaín and Juan Carlos Valdés Marín of the Fototeca del Instituto Nacional de Antropología e Historia. I thank the staff at the University of Nebraska Press for guiding my manuscript through the publication process and Anne Taylor for her careful copyediting. My thanks also go out to Jason Neighbors, who provided the initial draft of map 3 for this book.

In writing this book, I benefited from the work of many other scholars of Mexico. Related studies by Rodney Anderson, Barry Carr, Fernando Córdova Pérez, William French, John Mason Hart, Alan Knight, María Dolores Morales, and Paco Ignacio Taibo II were initial inspirations and constant points of reference.

The Inter-American Foundation and the Organization of American States provided research grants to carry out the bulk of my research in Mexico. Its first incarnation as a dissertation took place while I was a Visiting Research Fellow at the Center for U.S.-Mexican Studies at the University of California, San Diego. I did much of the revision during a junior sabbatical from the University of Puget Sound and with a Fulbright Scholar award in Mexico during the spring of 1997. My Fulbright affiliation at the Universidad Autónoma Metropolitana-Iztapalapa provided me with an intellectual home in Mexico City. Colleagues at the University of Puget Sound cheered me on to finish this book and cut me slack from other professional duties at all the right moments. A grant from the University of Puget Sound also made possible the reproduction of the photographs that appear in this book.

My greatest debts are, of course, my most personal. Mine begin with my parents, who taught me respect for work and gave me models of strength and love. Marisela Fleites entered my life between archives and has since taught me all the meanings of *compañera*. Despite such creditors, all the shortcomings of this book are my own.

WORKERS, NEIGHBORS,
and CITIZENS

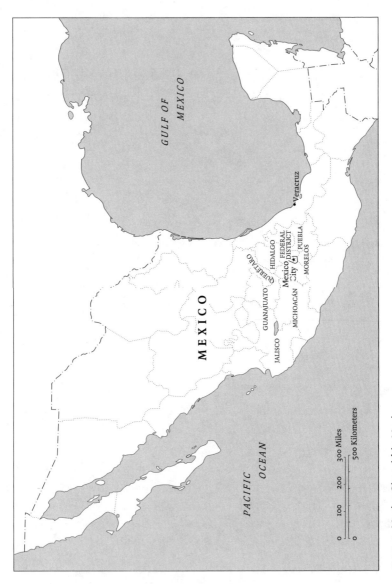

MAP 1. Mexico City within Mexico.

Introduction

As the most intense fighting of the Mexican Revolution came to a slow but certain end in the first half of 1916, the working people of Mexico City continued an extraordinary cycle of organization. On 31 July 1916 Mexico City awoke to a general strike. At four o'clock that morning the electricians' union cut off power, effectively closing down all production, transport, and commerce in the city. By midmorning, thousands of working people had gathered at Alameda Park near the city center to support their demands and to celebrate their ability to bring the city to a stop.

The general strike was notable on several levels. It culminated an intense cycle of organization among working people that dated back to the first days of the revolution. Among the strike leadership and rank and file were skilled and unskilled workers, and women as well as men. And strikers demanded fair prices as well as fair wages, a consumption demand that ensured the support of much of the poor urban population. Their challenge to government monetary policy also meant that their strike was as much a showdown with the generals of the newly triumphant Constitutionalist army as it was a conflict with employers and shopkeepers. Finally, workers suggested that, rather than an obstruction to the work of the revolution, their strike was an attempt to fulfill its promises.

Although the general strike had widespread support among working people, it was short-lived. First Chief Venustiano Carranza was quick to court-martial the strike committee and to impose martial law, strangling the strike within a few days. But the public presence the working people of Mexico City achieved during the previous years had become a permanent feature of urban life.

This book examines the origins, progress, and impact of the mobilization of the poor and working people in Mexico City from the eve of the 1910 revolution through the initial postrevolutionary settlement in the early 1920s. The mobilization of Mexico City workers during this period presents a paradox: during one of the greatest social upheavals of the twentieth century, urban workers and masses had a limited military role yet emerged from the fighting of the revolution with considerable combativeness and new significance in the power structure. To address this paradox, I explore three related processes: (1) the industrialization and urbanization that transformed work and community in Mexico City at the turn of the century and helped to undermine the legitimacy of the prerevolutionary order; (2) the cultural transformations and collective action that occurred among poor and working people before and during the revolution; and (3) the development of relations between urban workers and the Mexican state from the breakdown of the "old regime" through the initial consolidation of a postrevolutionary order.

This book shows that although the actions of the urban workers and masses rarely paralleled the armed insurrection of much of the Mexican peasantry during the revolution, the changes of the Porfiriato (the extended rule by President Porfirio Díaz, 1876–1911) and the events of the revolution transformed workers in ways that greatly enhanced their role in local and national politics. The prominence of labor after the revolution was not the result of a top-down populism imposed by revolutionary military leaders but rather the product of a continuous cycle of largely autonomous urban mobilization that began years earlier. Although the general strike that began in July 1916 ended in repression, it was part of a series of popular challenges by which working people helped shape the postrevolutionary order and pushed labor unions to unprecedented prominence. The broad possibilities and the limits of mass urban participation were outlined in the conflicts that climaxed in 1916 and that continued in the decade that followed, as contending actors and institutions, each with their own vision of urban society, created alternative, relatively autonomous, and often democratic organizations.

Of course the emergence of organized labor and popular urban sectors in the early twentieth century was not unique to Mexico. In the first decades of the twentieth century, crises of export-oriented growth and political authoritarianism brought mass sectors onto national stages throughout Latin America in both familiar and new ways. But the depth of those crises in Mexico during the decade of the revolution made urban mobilization there particularly precocious and significant.

The Mexican Revolution and the Labor Movement

A brief summary of the Mexican Revolution will help situate this book within the broader narrative and scholarship of the period. The Mexican Revolution began in 1910 when a crisis over political succession exploded into an armed revolt against aging dictator Porfirio Díaz, who had presided for thirty-four years over the rapid but unequal growth of the country fueled largely by agricultural and mineral exports and Euro-American investment. Francisco Madero, a wealthy liberal reformer from the northern state of Coahuila, unsuccessfully challenged Díaz in fixed elections before leading an armed revolt. Supported mainly by country people, Madero triumphed in a few brief months of fighting in the spring of 1911. But as president, Madero could not contain for long either the factions of the Porfirian elite and foreigners who opposed change or those groups, largely peasants and rural workers, that pushed for far deeper reforms than those advocated by Madero and middle-class politicians. In February 1913, his presidency was overthrown by conservative sectors of the Porfirian military led by Gen. Victoriano Huerta. The subsequent assassination of Madero and Huerta's militarized regime spurred another round of popular rebellion throughout much of the country. Over the next eighteen months, guerrilla and more formal armies throughout the country rallied to defeat Huerta and the remaining elements of the Porfirian army.

Within months of Huerta's fall, the revolutionary forces that defeated him divided into two factions: the northern-based Constitutionalist forces headed by Venustiano Carranza and his key general, Alvaro Obregón; and the Convention forces, whose bases were in the peasant armies of Emiliano Zapata in the southern state of Morelos and in the more diverse northern rural constituency led by Francisco Villa.

The revolution was fought primarily by peasants and rural workers from different regions of the country, though it was often led by alienated elements of the upper and middle classes. While much of the countryside experienced continuous armed rebellion, urban workers rarely responded to the political vacuum and social upheaval by taking up arms or taking over factories. Rather, they furthered their organizational attempts by initially embracing the possibilities of electoral politics. When that failed, they organized mutual aid societies, unions, and even regional federations. One of the most coherent of these was founded in 1912 and involved a variety of craft, service, and unskilled workers in Mexico City who gathered under the auspices of the anarchist-inspired Casa del Obrero Mundial, or House of the World Worker. The Casa initially abstained from formal politics while increasingly confronting employers and displaying their working-class solidarity in citywide demonstrations.

In February 1915, as the civil war between Constitutionalists and the Convention deepened, a majority of the Casa leadership finally abandoned their position of neutrality and marched out of the capital city along with General Obregón, providing Carranza with six "Red Battalions" of around five thousand soldiers in return for the right to organize workers throughout Constitutionalist territory. Thus the principal participation of workers in the armed movements of the revolution was more in the nature of an alliance, or "pact," than an insurrection. The debate around the strategic and symbolic importance of the Casa-Constitutionalist Pact has dominated much of the literature on workers in the revolution, greatly overshadowing events such as the 1916 general strike or the pattern of organization that preceded and followed the pact. While providing some clear benefits to the Casa membership, the alliance was subjected to immediate stress, evident only six months later when Carranza ordered the demobilization of most of the Red Battalions soon after the Constitutionalist victory over Villa's troops at Celaya.

The return of the adherents of the Red Battalions to Mexico City in August 1915 fortified continuing organizational activities and led to escalating confrontation of workers with employers and Constitutionalist officials, culminating in the general strike that began on 31 July 31 1916. The military faction that repressed the general strike in 1916 would in turn succumb to pressures from popular sectors, domestic rivals, and the United States, finally yielding in 1920 to a new group, led by General Obregón, that was able to negotiate with popular sectors, including the labor movement, as well as with the United States.

Populisms, Revisions, and Microhistory

The orthodox, populist view of the Mexican Revolution emerged in the 1930s and was closely identified with historian Frank Tannenbaum.[1] Writing during the period of the great Cárdenas reforms, Tannenbaum portrayed the revolution as a peasant and nationalist revolution that arose from the injustices of the old regime and gave rise to a revolutionary government dedicated to social justice and a national development of Mexican resources—in short, the victory of the people.

In the 1960s, in the context of the more radical Cuban Revolution and after the Mexican army massacred student protesters in Mexico City in 1968, the orthodox view came under attack. Revisionist historians emphasized continuities between the Porfirian and the postrevolutionary periods, in particular, unequal capitalist development, economic dependence on the United States, and state manipulation of the masses from above. Peasants and social mobilizations almost disappeared from many revisionist narratives.[2]

Since the mid-1980s, historians have attempted to salvage elements of the populist view of the revolution. Alan Knight and John Mason Hart are among those who have tried to restore the central role of the mobilization of peasant masses to the revolution while acknowledging the interplay between mobilizations from below and the cooptive and sometimes repressive manipulation of these groups from above by the Mexican state.[3]

But all historians agree that the Mexican Revolution definitely was not a revolution of urban workers. Studies of labor and the revolution often use events in Mexico City to generalize about the working class in Mexico. When urban workers are discussed in the literature of the revolution, the focus is usually on the brief period in 1915 when the Casa took up arms to support the military faction that eventually triumphed. Thus the workers of the Red Battalions are celebrated in the orthodox view for their support of the faction that eventually won the revolution and are condemned in the revisionist view for the same reason.[4]

Like the first generation of labor history in the United States, Mexican labor history focused first on militant minorities, usually anarchist or communist, on particular unions, or on particular dramatic moments, such as strikes, to the exclusion of other aspects of the lives of working people and other types of conflicts and mobilizations.[5] Important and pioneering studies by revisionist labor historians, writing after the Mexican Labor Confederation (Confederación de Trabajadores Mexicanos, or CTM) endorsed the government crackdown on students in 1968, tended to focus primarily on the relations of unions and their leaders to the postrevolutionary state, relying largely on corporatist paradigms borrowed from political science.[6] Just as peasants had been lost from the revisionist narrative of the revolution, workers had very little historical agency in these histories. At best, unions and the working class they represented were seen as dependent instruments of the state or of the prototypical revolutionary factions that were destined to form a new state.

The "dependency" school predominant in much of the study of Latin America during the 1960s and 1970s tended to fortify this view. When labor was considered at all, the emphasis remained on external, international factors and the consequent adjustments made by the domestic ruling elite at the cost of the working class. Ironically, in this view workers were seen as the key to revolutionary change, yet under dependent capitalism their agency in national histories was structurally limited. Like the authors of revisionist and corporatist literature of the revolution, those writing from a dependency perspective neglected concrete studies of the historical experience of working people.[7]

For similar reasons, much of Latin American labor history has focused until recently on factory workers and workers in export sectors such as mining, to the exclusion of artisans and other groups of urban workers who far outnumbered factory workers and whose political participation was often vital. For example, Charles Bergquist, in his excellent study *Labor in Latin America*, places workers in export industries at the center of their national histories. While his paradigm is suggestive, it does not fit well for Mexico, where the diversity of exports deprived

any single export of sufficient strategic dominance and where strong artisan traditions close to the center of political power made urban workers important actors.[8]

A related challenge is that of achieving a balance or synthesis between
the study of the everyday experiences of working people, common in
much of North American social history, and the focus on economic
structures (reinforced by dependency theory) and union-state alliances
(inspired by studies of populism) that has characterized much of Latin
American labor history. In the context of twentieth-century Latin America, where the state has had a fundamental role in the process of economic development and the mediation of class differences, the everyday
experiences of workers cannot be divorced from an understanding of
the larger structures of economic and political power and conflict.[9]

The study of a single urban community provides advantages in perspective that, after thirty years of the publication of regional histories of
the Mexican Revolution, should be evident. It is ironic that, while many
microhistories of the revolution rejected the view from the "center" for
that of specific regions, until recently few studies have looked closely at
local structures, political cultures, and ongoing organizational processes in Mexico City during the revolution or its immediate aftermath.
Of course the political center of gravity shifted from Mexico City to rural
areas and the north during the years of greatest revolutionary conflict.
But the size of the capital city and the extreme centralization of Mexican
political life before and after the revolution made events there national
in importance, particularly as they concerned the relations between
working people and political and economic elites. During the revolution, the working people of Mexico City participated in defining moments of urban mobilization. While Mexico City may not be paradig-
matic of all urban and working-class mobilizations in Mexico in this
period, it is a good place to begin to better understand these urban dynamics nationally and comparatively.

Assumptions and Organization

Although the narrative of the mobilization of Mexico City workers in the
Casa del Obrero Mundial may be known from general histories of the

revolution and of labor, this book attempts to tell this and related stories in new ways. It draws from many of the insights of the "new social history" to examine the urban rhythms of daily life of working people and their experience of the revolution. These social historians have stressed the relation between work and the social and cultural spheres of workers' lives and the effect of industrial and urban change on rural, ethnic, and religious traditions. These traditions often provided working people with powerful moral bases to resist and reshape aspects of capitalist change. In many of these studies, community itself is understood as a basis for collective action.[10]

Class formation and mobilization were not simply products of economic structures, material conditions, and workplace experiences; they also were rooted in the creation of a working-class community. A working-class community emerged in Mexico City from the development of a geographical and cultural separation between broadly constituted elite and popular sectors and from different networks of sociability and identification at the level of tenements, bars, markets, and neighborhoods. Networks that joined and distances that separated gave significance to space in the urban setting and led to a series of conflicts over its use. This book explores popular mobilizations and conflicts that occurred in the streets, markets, and plazas as well as in the workplace. Through their collective actions, working people asserted their public presence, demanded political change, and protested a variety of consumption as well as workplace issues.

The working-class community was more diverse than the factory workers and even the skilled artisans, who until recently have dominated labor histories. Unskilled workers with precarious positions in the labor market far outnumbered skilled and factory workers, and recent rural migrants made up a large percentage of the urban population. Women, too, were central to class formation through their migration to Mexico City, their participation in the work force, and even their fulfillment of traditional domestic roles. In fact, working-class women frequently found that fulfilling their traditional domestic roles required them to participate as public and political actors.[11] This book considers these diverse groups that constituted the working-class community and their distinct and common modes of mobilization.

Similarly, economic structures influenced but did not determine political identity and behavior. This book attempts to understand the identity and actions of working people in terms of their historical experiences, their gender, local and national traditions, and their embrace and transformation of different political discourses, such as liberalism and anarchism.

Workers and urban masses in Mexico City were first formed by their experiences during the Porfiriato and only later were galvanized by their experiences of the revolution. The first section of this book (chapters 1 and 2) outlines the economic and social changes in the capital city during the late Porfiriato that shaped the city as well as people's lives. Chapter 1 traces the beginnings of the geographical separation of the city by class at the turn of the century. The very space of the city was transformed as different areas became more specialized in function, as wealthy and middle-class families built their houses on the west side of the city, and as poor and working people were pushed into crowded central tenements or into working-class neighborhoods and squatter settlements on the eastern and southern periphery. This geographical separation by class was reinforced by attempts to regulate the appearance and behavior of the poor when they ventured near the city center.

Chapter 2 creates a portrait of the working people of Mexico City on the eve of the revolution. It examines changes in production and work during the Porfiriato and considers the origins of different types of workers, the relation of skilled and unskilled, male and female workers to the labor market, and the opportunities for and limits of organization among various types of workers.

Transformations of the city and the workplace brought new identities that went far to undermine the legitimacy of the government of Porfirio Díaz. Workers and the popular classes began to elaborate a new sense of community based on new networks, and their collective demands after 1910—whether to local authorities, employers, or landlords—made them difficult to ignore and threatening to the larger order.

The second section (chapters 3, 4, and 5) considers working-class cultures, organization, and demands from the last years of the Porfiriato through the most intense years of the revolution. Chapter 3 delineates working-class cultures and mutualist forms of organization during the late Porfiriato as well as attempts by officials and middle-class reformers to shape working-class mores and to influence organization in Mexico City in the face of contrary popular traditions and an emerging opposition among workers to their economic and political subordination. During the presidential election of 1910, a significant portion of workers in Mexico City rejected Porfirian paternalism and backed the candidacy of Madero, in the process drawing on and elaborating further a type of "popular" liberalism that emphasized the historical role of workers in building the nation.

Chapter 4 follows the organizational path of workers in electoral politics after the fall of Díaz and the transition from mutual aid societies to unions. The possibilities for political expression explicit in 1910 proved limited and frustrating during Madero's brief presidency and during the dictatorship of Victoriano Huerta, pushing urban workers to strengthen their own organizations in the workplace and in their own communities.

Chapter 5 explores the pattern by which working people confronted employers and made demands on government officials in increasingly assertive ways. The circumstances of the revolution allowed workers to move from spontaneous and sporadic resistance to elements of their dependence to intense confrontation with employers and to move from traditions of mutualism to the organization of independent political clubs, cultural groups, and unions. The new strength and unity of worker organizations became evident in new public rituals held in the heart of the city by which working people demonstrated their presence as a class.

Fundamental to any effective citywide popular mobilization were alliances between a minority of skilled and a majority of unskilled workers, those schooled in modern industrial values of progress and those rooted in preindustrial and paternalistic traditions. Various factors helped to bridge this gap during the revolution. Working people balanced anarchist ideas with notions of popular liberalism and other traditions that constituted their social order. Anarchist ideas served as a catalyst for working-class leaders to mobilize workers who had historically been separated by gender, skill levels, and cultural traditions.

The dire economic changes imposed by the revolution also helped to reduce cultural divisions among workers, often by pushing to the forefront consumption issues related to inflation and food supplies that affected the larger working-class community. The link between issues of work and consumption also encouraged the participation of women, who provided the initiative and primary participation for a series of mobilizations in Mexico City that ranged from the overtaking of food shops in order to administer a just exchange to the occupation of municipal and national government buildings in order to press demands for basic goods and services. Women mobilized in their own organizations and on their own initiative, but they also extended crucial or definitive support to male-dominated organizations, particularly when the link to consumption issues was clear.

The final section of the book (chapters 6, 7, and 8) delineates the labor movement's coming to terms with the national revolution, as the different military factions of the revolution in turn came to terms with the labor movement. Chapter 6 examines the relationship between the popular classes and workers of Mexico City and the revolutionary military factions that defeated the dictatorship of Gen. Victoriano Huerta during the period of 1914–15, the height of the military and social revolution. It analyzes both the factors that drove the Casa leadership and a portion of its membership to offer armed support through the Red Battalions to Carranza's Constitutionalist forces in February 1915 and the sustained pattern of popular mobilizations and labor conflicts that took place in the city under Convention control and during the absence of the Casa.

Chapter 7 begins with the series of riots and mobilizations around food issues that occurred in the summer of 1915, just before the Constitutionalists took definitive control of the city, and ends with the organization of the general strike of July–August 1916 around related issues. The cycle of organization that culminated in the general strike is notable for its combativeness, the growing unity among workers, and the increasing independence from and sharpening antagonism with the Constitutionalist leaders of the revolution.

Chapter 8 traces attempts by workers to create autonomous political parties and to reconstitute labor and community-based movements in the city and nation after the repression of the general strike and the enactment of labor guarantees in the 1917 constitution. These efforts were framed by rivalries between independent and officially supported unions and by the rise of the Mexican Labor Party to political prominence in Mexico City politics. The alliance of much of the labor movement with Gen. Alvaro Obregón in his political and military challenge to President Carranza in 1920 was a key moment in the restoration of a new order in which labor held an unprecedented, though subordinate, role. A final examination of patterns of organization among distinct sectors of working people in the early 1920s suggests the continued prominence of popular mobilization in Mexico City in the postrevolutionary period. The conclusion reflects on how the revolution transformed workers and how workers helped transform the revolution.

PART ONE

Making a Metropolis, Forming a Class,
1884–1910

MAP 2. Mexico City, 1910. Mexico City expanded dramatically at the turn of the century as wealthy and middle-class families built their houses on the west side of the city and working-class neighborhoods grew on the eastern and southern periphery. From S. G. Vázquez, *Guía Descriptiva* (Mexico City: Viuda de C. Bouret, 1913).

1 | THE SOCIAL GEOGRAPHY
OF THE PORFIRIAN CAPITAL

Foreign travelers to Mexico City in the 1880s were invariably struck by the provincialism of the capital, which could be a source of either disappointment or pleasure. A Frenchman in 1884 described the city as having a grand air from afar, with its white houses, bell towers, and domes, "but on penetration one is disappointed. The center is dirty and poorly kept, and the streets so badly paved that to take a stroll is far from a pleasure." Open sewers ran down the middle of streets, and when summer rains flooded the city center, *gente decente* ("respectable people") might even resort to hiring porters to carry them across streets and from carriages. A Mexican man of letters years later would remember the downtown area in the 1880s as "teeming" (*pululaban*) with Indians who could barely speak Spanish, many of them selling lottery tickets or produce from the outlying lakes and districts. An English-woman, Elizabeth Blake, found the city in 1888 to be "fortunately for the sentimental travelers still luxurious and lovely," but she speculated with a prescience many progressive Mexicans would have endorsed that "twenty years hence, no doubt there will be smoky piles of manufactories, teeming hives of tenement houses, noise and confusion of traffic and travail outside the City of Mexico."[1]

Two decades later, when sundry foreign dignitaries, journalists, and tourists arrived for the 1910 Centennial of Mexican Independence, they sang praises to that epitome of modernization and progress, the city of Mexico. Those who had visited before marveled at the changes. An Italian engineer remarked upon arriving that, since his first visit in the 1890s, "only the 2260 meters of altitude are the same as before." First-timers remarked on the "modernity" rather than the progress. A new sewer system seemed to solve the centuries-old problem of flooding and waste disposal, and a new water distribution system was almost complete. A relatively dynamic manufacturing sector, often using the latest factory machinery from Europe and the United States, provided consumer goods. In a flurry of public works, streets had been paved and widened and new monuments and public buildings had been erected, in what one observer termed the attempt of Mexico's longtime ruler Porfirio Díaz to "take the city of mud he acquired, and leave a city of marble."[2]

By the turn of the century the city's most enthusiastic boosters, native and foreign, would regularly liken the city to Paris and extol its high society and cultural events. Affluent visitors could stay at new hotels with all the modern comforts off Alameda Park, and wealthy Mexicans could travel from their suburban homes to shop at large, downtown department stores and be entertained at any of eighteen theaters, a circus, and at least six large cinemas.[3]

A more astute observer in 1907 realized that the comparison of Mexico City to Paris was not simply in physical layout: "The City of Mexico represents progressive Mexico. In it is concentrated the wealth, culture and refinement of the republic. It is the political, the educational, the social and the commercial centre of the whole country. It is to Mexico what Paris is to France. In fact it would be Mexico as Paris would be France. The same glare and glitter of a pleasure-loving metropolis are found here." Nor was the transformation as complete as some visitors assumed. In a brief afterthought, the same visitor observed that "within the same boundaries may be seen the deepest poverty and most abject degradation."[4]

Exactly one year before the Centennial of Mexican Independence, a new workers' newspaper pointed out in its inaugural edition that "until today nobody has shown concern except for the public boulevards, believing with that they fool the foreigners that visit us." The editorial speculated that, by contrast, foreign-born employers who visited their workers' houses would most likely first take elaborate precautions for hygiene and defense, "such is the disgust and fear inspired by the tenements workers live in." The editorial ominously warned the "*señores burócratas*," the positivist-inspired group of technocrats known as *científicos*, and the corrupt paid press that now "the people have awakened."[5]

During the last years of the Porfirian regime, the city underwent profound changes in its physical layout, leading to a pattern of great inequality between sections of the city and a redefinition of geographical class relations. Technological innovations, most important electric tramways, connected railroad stations to each other and to the historic downtown center. Broad central avenues were laid out, deliberately patterned on those of Paris, that increased the circulation of people and goods from one part of the city to another. Different areas of the city thus became more specialized in function.

By 1910, three trends were evident. First, many of the elite and middle classes abandoned the traditional multiclass downtown for the more exclusive residential neighborhoods on the western periphery of the city. Second, the core colonial downtown area—once characterized by its mixture of housing for wealthy and poor residents and production in the form of commerce and trades—became increasingly devoted to commerce and finance. Third, high rents and deliberate policies of demolition pushed many workers and urban poor from the core downtown area to a dense fringe of tenements nearby and to working-class and poor neighborhoods on the southern and eastern edges of the city.

These trends were, of course, not unique to Mexico City. Nineteenth-century European and North American cities underwent deep changes as industrialization and technological changes in transportation and urban infrastructures transformed the use of public and private space and differentiated the residential areas of poor, wealthy, and ethnic groups within the expanding metropolis.

Recent literature on Latin American cities has shown that related urban transformations were filtered through the regional experience of peripheral development as well as through particular national contexts. Urban modernization in Latin America occurred somewhat later than in Europe or the United States, coinciding with the export-driven economic booms of the late nineteenth century. Like the rural railroads, mills, and credit that made the export of agricultural products and minerals possible, urban infrastructure was shaped largely by foreign investment and technology and often by foreign design.[6] Moreover, the transformation of Latin American cities was premised on far greater inequalities than those experienced by the cities of western Europe and the United States.

The turn-of-the-century national capitals of the principal countries of Latin America presented dazzling showcases of modernity to the North Atlantic countries that provided capital and markets for their export products; but these cities in turn offered stark contrasts within national boundaries. In the countryside, the boom in export agriculture often consolidated large estates and reinforced servile and coercive labor relations. Similarly, in most Latin American countries, export-led growth reinforced the administrative and political dominance of the capital, thereby intensifying its traditional primacy over the countryside and secondary cities.[7]

National elites, obsessed with their international image, grafted European ideas of the city and structures on to their own. French architectural facades were plastered on public buildings that had more humble or traditional interiors, while broad elegant boulevards were cut through farmland or crowded tenement districts. But the seeming prosperity of such Belle Époque capitals as Rio de Janeiro and Mexico City, with their monumental public buildings and fashionable new neighborhoods, provided a thin veneer to the mass poverty of inner city tenements and emerging squatter settlements. Often, contradictory notions of modernity and national sovereignty led elites, inspired by positivism, to practice the forced "civilization," or removal of embarrassing signs, of traditional cultures and impoverished groups such as Indians, Africans, and poor immigrants, even as they elaborated sanitized versions of their indigenous past.[8]

Ultimately such superficial modernization made Latin American cities particularly vulnerable to social upheavals that brought workers and the urban poor into conflict with modernizing elites. In virtually all of the primary cities of Latin America, tensions increased and conflicts, ranging from consumer riots to general strikes, often shook the foundations of elite modernization projects.[9] But for the most part, national political elites managed to politically marginalize the urban poor until the populist experiments of the 1930s and 1940s.

Porfirian Mexico City fits roughly within the historical pattern for Latin American capital cities, with two important differences: far from any
port, Mexico City's administrative and political functions were privileged over its exporting function; and the indigenous makeup of Mexico
meant that immigrants were far less important in the formation of the
urban labor force than they were in cities such as Buenos Aires or Rio de
Janeiro.[10] Another difference is that perhaps nowhere in Latin America
before 1930 were the elite modernizing projects of nation and capital so
thoroughly challenged from below as in Mexico. In spite of the essentially rural logic of the Mexican Revolution, a variety of increasingly dis-
affected urban actors—from middle-class professionals to workers and
popular crowds—played important roles in toppling the Porfirian regime in 1910 and 1911. If these emerging social groups remained secondary to the military struggles of the decade that followed, their conflicts and organizations, shaped by the previous decades of urban
transformation, would ultimately be fundamental to the consolidation
of the postrevolutionary regime. Porfirian transformations in the capital
clearly suited the needs and desires of Mexico's economic and governing elites yet ultimately undermined their authority and set the tone of
later urban conflicts.

The Traditional Center

The perimeter of Mexico City changed little in the first half of the nineteenth century from that of the late colonial period. Although the center
of activities and wealth shifted west of the Plaza de la Constitución (pop-
ularly known as the Zócalo), most of the city proper remained within the
bounds of the old colonial city limits, while Indian suburbs retained
their precarious existence on the outskirts of the city. For example, in
1840 Fanny Calderón, the noted chronicler of the period, described her
recently built house bordering the now very central Alameda Park as
semirural.[11]

The city up to midcentury kept much of its traditional Hispanic organization centered around the Zócalo, which was in turn dominated by
the symbols of wealth and authority: the Cathedral and the National Pal-

ace. Carefully laid out, grid-pattern streets extended in all four directions, and a loose hierarchy of wealth began at the Zócalo and declined rapidly within blocks.

After midcentury the majority of the city's wealthiest families shifted their residences toward the west in the area between the Zócalo and the Alameda, which also contained the most important businesses. Occurring from 1850 to 1880, a period of very modest population growth, this shift reflected economic change rather than demographic pressures. The midcentury expropriation of urban church property, which in 1813 had accounted for half of the buildings in Mexico City, created a new market for urban real estate.[12] Considerable destruction and rebuilding took place over the following decades without a significant expansion of the boundaries of the city.

In the 1880s, many of the city's wealthiest residents lived along San Francisco Street (today Madero Street) and adjoining streets. For example, Martínez de la Torre occupied the ostentatious Casa de Azulejos, with the Escandóns on one side and the Zamora y Malo family on the other. While their mansions might be exclusive, their neighborhood was not. Foreigners, who usually stayed at nearby hotels, repeatedly remarked on the contrasts they saw in the same few blocks, such as a doorman living with his countless children, pigs, dogs, and turkeys in a small room underneath the stairs of a wealthy residence. Of two adjacent and identical colonial mansions, one might be carefully maintained by an elite family, the other transformed into a tenement (known as a *casa de vecindad*, or simply *vecindad*). In turn, a tenement might have a vertical hierarchy, housing lawyers in spacious quarters around a front patio and soldiers, washerwomen, and domestic servants behind.[13]

Many of the oldest colonial houses east of the National Palace deteriorated and were taken over by trades or converted to tenements. The *científico* Miguel Macedo described his own childhood barrio along Reloj Street (today Argentina Street), which extended north from the Zócalo. Once home to "the most comfortable families," by the 1870s the street contained a mix of public ministries, schools, and middle-class and poor housing. Macedo grew up in a second floor apartment above two shops "of the second order," a butcher and a shoemaker. On one side of his building were three identical patio houses, and on the other a crowded tenement.[14]

Another slow but marked tendency throughout the nineteenth century, one that coincided with the decline in artisan production, was the expulsion of small artisan shops from the historic center. At independence, pockets of both artisan shops and residences were still clustered throughout the increasingly privileged space between the Zócalo and the Alameda. The 1850 industrial census shows that artisan shops had already been pushed northward several blocks from the center to the Santa Catarina neighborhood as well as southward to the barrio San Juan, south of the Alameda.[15]

In spite of these shifts and the incipient specialization of productive areas, during much of the late nineteenth century the city maintained its traditional preindustrial mixture of residences and commercial and trade shops. As a result, different classes intermingled in what some foreign visitors disdainfully referred to as the "democracy" of the city center—referring not to the distribution of wealth or political power but to the sharing of public and residential space by rich and poor, white, mestizo (mixed race), and Indian alike.[16]

The Restoration of Mexico City's Primacy

Thirty years of "Porfirian progress" brought to Mexico City a particular type of development. Under the auspices of a federal constitution (1857), the authoritarian liberal project of Porfirio Díaz succeeded in reversing half a century of civil war, foreign invasion, and the "ruralization of power" to create a national government that could impose its interests on the rest of the nation. Soon after coming to power in a military rebellion in 1876, Díaz began to open Mexico to foreign capital, reducing longstanding restrictions on subsoil use and commercial transactions and initiating a period of unprecedented export-led economic growth. This pattern reinforced a centralization of all types of decision making and power in Mexico City—administrative, political, financial, commercial, and military.[17] Agricultural exports might move from the point of production in the states to the point of export without passing through the capital; but imports, with the exception of some capital goods, were much more likely to end up in Mexico City, a center of regional distribution and the major center of consumption for basic manufactured and luxury goods. Similarly, increases in the federal bureaucracy and government spending, and the presence of foreign banking and insurance companies, consolidated Mexico City's role as the country's center of administration and finance.

The most tangible boon to both Mexican economic growth and the dominance of the capital was the construction of a system of railroads with its focus in Mexico City. From 1873, when the first Mexican railroad was completed between the capital and the port of Veracruz, until 1910, nine railroad lines from different regions were built leading into six Mexico City railroad stations.[18] Railroads connected Mexican producers with international markets and unified domestic markets, thereby spurring economic growth and furthering the concentration of economic power among a small group of foreign and domestic elites. Control of transportation, once carried out by thousands of mule drivers, was consolidated among a few foreign companies and helped accelerate the eventual dominance of the commercial system in the hands of a few immigrant families.

In addition to promoting economic growth, railroads improved communication and mobility, which were essential to political consolidation. The national government could now dispatch troops to areas of agrarian revolt or areas where regional elites persisted in their hopes of political autonomy. The large-scale mobilization of regional armies—the source of much of the political instability of the early nineteenth century—was made obsolete by a federal army and the famous *rurales* (rural police). Though seemingly ubiquitous, the *rurales* were based primarily in the capital and in the surrounding valley, with access by railroad to much of the country.

Railroads also gave mobility to prospective residents of the capital. Suddenly it became feasible for regional elites to spend part of the year in the capital and maintain a residence there. For example, Pablo Escandón could devote his business efforts to running his sugar hacienda in the nearby state of Morelos, serve as that state's federal deputy and even governor, yet spend virtually all of his time among metropolitan high society. Even the Chihuahuense Enrique Creel could serve as foreign minister while remaining an important link between the business interests of his father-in-law, Gov. Luis Terrazas of Chihuahua, and the *científico* circle of the capital.[19]

The railroad system further facilitated the movement of massive numbers of poor and middle-class migrants from Mexican provinces to work in the rapidly growing bureaucracy and urban economy. As a result, Mexico City grew at an unprecedented rate, from 300,000 in 1884 to 471,000 in 1910.[20]

The Transformation of Space

In the years leading up to the centennial celebration, the government initiated construction of a new congressional palace, which was to be a huge domed neoclassical structure. By the time of the celebration in 1910, its incomplete frame towered above the wealthy new suburbs of the western side of the city. The project, never to be finished, seemed to articulate the political alliance between the Porfirian political elite and the financial elite that had transformed so much of the new space of wealth and power, the axis that ran from the old Zócalo, past the Alameda, and through the elegant Paseo de la Reforma (see map 3).

If Mexico City lacked its equivalent of Baron Georges Eugène Haussman, the prime planner behind the remaking of Napoleon III's Paris, the political and financial class that willed, financed, and profited from the transformation of Mexico City was far more cohesive than its Parisian counterpart, even if the transformation proved less complete. A small group of powerful merchant-financiers, primarily European- and American-born, controlled much of the industry, commerce, and real estate of Mexico City and therefore of the nation. Investments were often held jointly among them, so the same merchants—such as Thomas Braniff, Adolfo Prieto, José and Julio Limantour, or Sebastian Robert— sat repeatedly on the same company boards. These deals created a type of monopoly power over production and commerce that was often paralleled in terms of real estate speculation. Their proximity to the political elite, indeed their direct overlap, allowed them to manipulate the state to support their interests. From this alliance emerged their dual project of transforming Mexico City into the center of consumption and state power. At the same time they differed from an older class of urban magnates, whose fortunes had rested almost entirely in real estate speculation.[21]

A final measure that completed the union of financial and political power was the 1903 Law of Municipal Organization. After two decades of gradually losing power, the elected city councils (*ayuntamientos*) of Mexico City and surrounding towns were officially stripped of their property and considerable revenues and reduced to a minimal "advisory" role in running the government of the Federal District, the federated zone that contained them. Real power passed into the hands of the Superior Council of the Government of the Federal District, which consisted of the governor, the president of the Council of Public Health, and the director general of public works, all offices appointed by President Díaz and funded by the federal government. The subordination was completed one month before the gala celebration of the Centennial of Mexican Independence, when it was decreed that in the future all public appearances of the Mexico City city council had to be made in conjunction with and subordinate to the governor of the Federal District.[22]

In fact, after 1903 the new Federal District posts were occupied by many of the same men who had been elected to the city council; Guillermo Landa y Escandón, for example, had been president of the city council up to 1903, when he was appointed governor of the Federal District and president of the Superior Council of the Government of the Federal District, positions he maintained right up until he fled the country in 1911. But unlike the city council, the government of the Federal District had no pretense of political representation or democratic process.

Not only was the city council made largely ceremonial, but the working classes lost what representation they had been allowed. Although a very imperfect elected body, the city council had incorporated reformist working-class leaders as councilmen during the early years of Porfirian rule. For example, in the 1880s and 1890s the president and vice president of the moderate workers' organization, the Congreso Obrero, both sat on the city council and were responsible for the council's Commission of Artisan Development. In 1903, the Commission of Artisan Development disappeared, and no representatives of any worker organizations were elected to the city council until the revolution.[23]

The newly organized government of the Federal District consolidated power in the hands of a few like-minded men who could decide where to provide public services, what public works to build, and which buildings to demolish, often benefiting themselves. Landa y Escandón, for example, sat on the board of several key industries based in Mexico City. In 1910, he represented the National Railways of Mexico before the national government, was the director of the Mexican Commercial and Industrial Bank, and was a member of the board of directors of the Bank of Construction and Real Estate. This overlap helped consolidate the Porfirian vision of Mexico City administered by and for the nation (embodied in the *científico* slogan "limited politics, lots of administration") at the expense of municipal democracy. The latent popular desire for municipal autonomy would reemerge with the revolution, leading to a brief restoration of the autonomous faculties of the city council from 1915 to 1928.[24]

Undoubtedly the most important improvements to the city itself took place along the Paseo de la Reforma. During the French occupation of Mexico in the 1860s the emperor Maximilian had carved out this broad avenue in direct imitation of those of Haussman's Paris. Starting on the northwestern corner of the Alameda, then the edge of the city, it extended four kilometers west through the forested grounds of Chapultepec Palace. When the city underwent rapid growth during the Porfiriato, the newly widened, paved, and illuminated Paseo de la Reforma became a major impetus to the direction of growth, articulating centers of transport, commerce, and residence (see fig. 1).[25]

If wide avenues made these areas more accessible, new forms of technology also helped to reshape new areas of the city. Tramways and railroads initiated regular commuting as early as 1857 between the city and the outlying towns of Tacubaya, La Villa, and Tlalpan, which were centers of leisure, worship, and manufacturing. A round trip to San Angel by carriage had previously taken half a day, whereas by tramway it took only forty minutes one way.[26]

By the 1880s mule-driven tramways also formed a network joining all six train stations, the Zócalo, and much of the city and suburbs. This made it possible for elite families to move permanently to the western suburbs while maintaining easy access to the financial, commercial, and social heart of the city. The increasing convenience and declining fares of the electric cars used after 1896 would also make it more feasible for professionals of more moderate means to move to the suburbs. Tramways were used to move furniture to new homes, to haul freight, and even to bring coffins to the cemeteries.

Fares in 1910 ranged from five centavos around the city to thirty centavos for a trip to Tlalpan. Second-class fares were 30 to 50 percent less than first-class fares. Although tramways made daily commutes possible from outlying suburbs, the cost of daily trips remained prohibitive for many wage earners, given that the wage for an unskilled day laborer in 1910 was around fifty centavos, which at the time was the equivalent of one-quarter of a U.S. dollar. According to the *Mexican Year Book*, of the sixty-five million passengers carried in 1907, the great majority (72 percent) paid first-class fares, suggesting that those of greater means were still the primary users of the streetcars. In addition, tramway lines were built at the discretion of private interests and installed where they would prove most profitable. The eastern zone of the city depended on only two lines, although it was by far the city's most populated area. Working-class and popular suburbs were thus very much underserved in contrast to the more lucrative lines that served the city center and wealthy western suburbs.[27]

This network of transport systems was fundamental to the reorganization of space in the city, allowing for different neighborhoods to move toward specialization by function and class. The six railroad stations connected Mexico City to the flow of passengers and consumer and capital goods from the rest of the country and abroad. They became key poles orienting urban growth, particularly the Buenavista station, around which many of the new northwestern neighborhoods sprang up. The railway stations were in turn linked by the tramways and the Paseo de la Reforma, together facilitating the flow of people and goods through the center of the city.

The possibility of getting on a streetcar and having the city and its hinterlands a few minutes away changed the way residents viewed their city and their own relationship to it. An office worker in Manuel Gutiérrez Nájera's turn-of-the-century short story, "La Novela del Tranvía," gazes out of a streetcar window and declares, "No, the city of Mexico doesn't begin at the National Palace, nor end in the Paseo de la Reforma. I give you my word that the city is much larger." Such a new vision of the city must have affected even members of the popular classes who still could not afford the daily commute from home to work. In a period of unemployment, a family from Tlalpan might send a daughter by streetcar to sell tamales or bootleg pulque, the mildly fermented drink of the lower classes, in the central market, La Merced. A family from the tenements around La Merced might aspire to an occasional outing by streetcar to the floating gardens of Xochimilco.[28] Even as the city became increasingly segregated by class, new forms of transportation helped unify a vision of the growing city and its environs.

The Segregation of Wealth

While the first wave of growth in Mexico City after the 1856 Reform Laws was internal and relied on the absorption of much church property, the second wave, which began in the 1880s and accelerated rapidly in the 1890s, moved primarily outward and westward. For a variety of reasons upper- and middle-class *capitalinos* (residents of the capital) in the late nineteenth century increasingly began to abandon the Zócalo and center to move permanently to the higher lands west of the city. Instead of simply displacing the center westward and leaving it for the most part sociologically intact, as had happened early in the nineteenth century, this exodus initiated a process of permanent separation by class of residences into rich and poor *colonias* (divisions).

The *colonias* were constructed on public land, private haciendas, and Indian corporate land. The bulk of land entered the market only after the anticlerical 1856 Reform Laws, when the Ley Lerdo privatized a large quantity of church land as well as other corporate holdings surrounding the city. Selling municipal lands became a form of political patronage and a ready source of revenue for a city council constantly in financial crisis. For example, in the 1850s Francisco Somera used his connections with the city council and the governor of the Federal District to wrest the area known as the Potrero de la Horca, on the western edges of the city, from its longtime renter. Similarly, by 1910 the Indian communities of Tenochtitlán and Tlatelolco had lost their centuries-long battle against the encroaching city.[29]

Before the 1880s, there was very little movement of the population onto these newly available lands. The highest concentration of the city's population lived within the area extending east to the National Palace and west to the eastern edge of the Alameda. As late as 1890, these blocks held 65 percent of the total population of the city.[30] When expansion west did occur during the 1880s, the density of the areas immediately north and south of the Alameda remained relatively low, as speculation in land markets, encouraged by the ready delivery of municipal services to favored speculators and by new transportation possibilities, initiated a diffuse pattern of settlement on the fertile and sloped lands farther to the west and southwest of the city. The early colonias of Santa Maria and Barroso were formed in the 1860s but would have limited growth until years later. Colonia Guerrero, northwest of the Alameda, was formed around 1880 from the old San Fernando convent lands adjudicated to Rafael Martinez de la Torre.[31]

While the number of building constructions during the 1870s roughly doubled that of the previous decade, they more than tripled over each of the next two decades. Much of this growth came in the form of the twenty-seven official colonias formed between 1884 and 1910, although the size, class of residents, and official status of each varied greatly. Colonias Guerrero and Santa Maria grew along each side of the Buenavista train station, the first attracting a largely working-class population (especially carpenters and mechanics) and the second increasingly attracting the clerks and bureaucrats of the new Porfirian middle class.[32]

From 1900 on the most spectacular physical growth of the city came in the westernmost District Eight, where wealthy suburbs began to form around the Paseo de la Reforma. This avenue and the smaller diagonals that fed into it became the privileged areas of municipal investment. Old obstacles to transportation and social interaction, such as the colonial aqueduct, were torn down. Other projects were undertaken to improve the pavement, lighting, and public sculptures, largely under the sponsorship and guidance of Finance Minister José Ives Limantour and Gov. Guillermo Landa y Escandón, both of whom had spent part of their youth in Haussman's Paris. In the late 1880s the Paseo de la Reforma became the new fashionable promenade for affluent Mexicans, and land values on adjacent properties increased dramatically as wealthy Mexicans and foreigners fled the center and began to build their houses near it. Lands directly north of the Paseo de la Reforma skyrocketed in value and attracted a wealthier class of inhabitants, such as former president Manuel González and Governor Landa y Escandón himself.[33]

A handful of men from Mexico's elite made not only their residences in these neighborhoods but also a part of their fortunes. For example, Thomas Braniff, the U.S.-born railroad manager who became one of Mexico's most dynamic entrepreneurs, had over 20 percent of his property invested in urban real estate in these new wealthy *colonias* at the time of his death in 1906. He owned 45 percent of the land bordering both sides of the Paseo de la Reforma in Colonias Juárez and Cuauhtémoc. By ceding one-tenth of this land to the city in 1903 for the widening of the Paseo de la Reforma, he assured himself or his heirs phenomenal returns.[34]

The most exclusive *colonias* were carved from the hacienda Teja along the southern and western edges of the Paseo de la Reforma in the 1890s and 1900s and became the *colonias* of Cuauhtémoc and Juárez. Only slightly less affluent were Colonias Roma and Condesa, south of Colonia Juárez along the route to Tacubaya and built around the newly fashionable racetrack. The European-style traffic circles and diagonal boulevards that mirrored the Paseo de la Reforma divided the new western neighborhoods.

The decision of the municipal government to spend or withhold scarce resources and services had a great effect on land values in new *colonias*. In effect, the government only provided services if they thought they could recuperate costs from taxes on the resulting properties, a condition only the wealthier *colonias* could meet. Speculation in real estate was largely in the hands of a small group of men such as Braniff and the foreign companies in which they participated, including the Bank of London and Mexico and the Anglo-American Chapultepec Land Company. Land values in Colonia Juárez increased from three U.S. dollars per square meter in 1890 to fifty U.S. dollars in 1909.[35]

The move to such *colonias* as Juárez and Condesa reinforced a rejection of much of the traditional culture associated with the old center of the city, similar to the adoption by the Porfirian elite of the dress, sports, and recreational activities of North Americans and Europeans.[36] The greatest contrast between the *colonias* and the old center was in the houses. The mansions and houses of the suburbs were quite different from the traditional patio houses of the center. The norm was no more than two families in the same building, and tenements were few or temporary. According to the 1900 census, the ratio of households to houses in Districts Seven and Eight, the westernmost districts of the city, were 3.3 and 1.7, far below the city average of 5.5 and the citywide high of 7.7 residences per building in District Three. Fenced-in houses provided the affluent or middle-class family one further degree of removal from the shared buildings and multiclass neighborhoods of traditional Mexico City and from the traffic, business, and pockets of poverty of the city center.

One of the ironies of this flight to the suburbs is that wealthy and middle-class families brought with them a multitude of servants. In wealthy District Eight, for example, servants comprised 14 percent of the population, compared to 9 percent for the city at large. The desire for status and comfort thus imposed a certain inevitable degree of cohabitation across classes.[37]

The Remaking of the City Center

By 1910, the tendency for the elite and middle classes to abandon their residences in the city center for the wealthy suburbs to the west of the city was well advanced, if not yet complete. The center and Zócalo still held their allure for the wealthy. But by the early twentieth century observers would view such aristocratic families as that of Antonio Cervantes, who still lived two blocks from the Zócalo in the Palacio Cervantes, or President Díaz, who lived a few blocks from the National

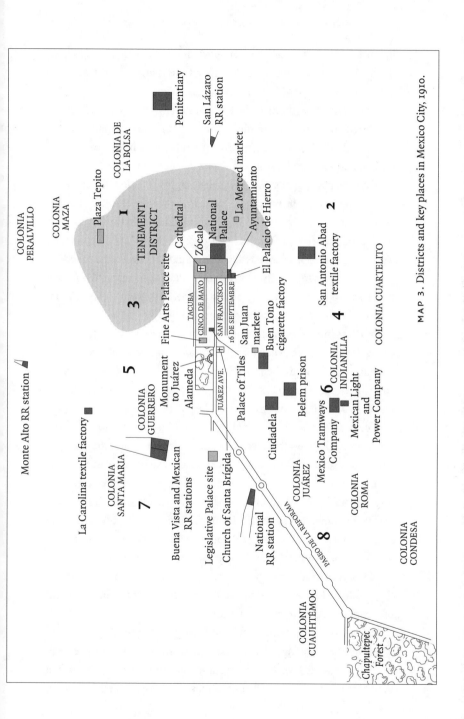

MAP 3. Districts and key places in Mexico City, 1910.

Palace on de la Cadena Street, as conspicuous exceptions.[38] Increasingly, the new dynamic bourgeoisie abandoned the center as a place of residence to the more traditional, pre-Porfirian elite.

At the same time, the historic center of the city reinforced its financial dominance over the city and the nation. Not only was the pull from the residential suburbs strong, but rising land values in the center also pushed many to seek housing elsewhere. In 1901 real estate on the principal streets of the center cost as much as eighty U.S. dollars per square meter. The district in which the historic center was located, District Four, actually lost twenty-five hundred inhabitants between 1890 and 1921, dropping from 15 percent to 7 percent of the city's population, while the population of the city as a whole almost doubled and other districts grew dramatically. By contrast to the decline in District Four, District Eight to the west grew by nearly 300 percent, from eighteen thousand to seventy thousand between 1900 and 1921.[39]

As real estate values in the center rose, many large patio houses on the central avenues were divided into shops and smaller residences. Entire colonial palaces were taken over as banks, hotels, and offices of foreign companies. The Palacio Iturbide was converted from an aristocratic residence to a hotel and then to a bank. The palace of the Conde de Valparaiso became the Banco Nacional. A detailed insurance map of the city center in 1907 shows few dwellings and no tenements on the principal streets of Cinco de Mayo and San Francisco, extending west from the Zócalo. The few blocks surrounding San Francisco Street, referred to by English journalist T. Philip Terry as the "nerve-center of American activity," were dominated by banks, insurance offices, railroad offices, and such social clubs as the Casino Español and the Jockey Club. According to a survey of commercial tax data for the year 1900, the top 23 of 501 city blocks paying commercial taxes were all within the few blocks between the Zócalo and the Alameda, and together they accounted for 50 percent of the total tax paid by city businesses.[40]

Many of the small shops that lined these streets were unable to compete with the huge, new department stores, such as El Puerto de Veracruz, El Palacio de Hierro, and El Centro Mercantil, all started by French immigrants. Similarly, small crafts shops had long been pushed out of the center into neighborhoods south of the Alameda and south and northeast of the Zócalo or else were completely replaced by factories on the outskirts of town. Exceptions to this pattern were the fashion industries by the west side of the Zócalo—jewelry shops, tailors, and seamstresses, many of whom sewed in workshops or their homes for the big department stores—and the small print shops that remained clustered on streets immediately southwest of the Zócalo.

Just as the Porfirian bourgeoisie had closely intertwined investments in banking, manufacturing, commerce, and real estate, their concentration of financial power oriented the use of space in the center. Many Porfirian banks existed primarily to finance real estate transactions. As such, banks remained subordinate to the merchant-manufacturers who controlled them, while helping them to dominate urban real estate and construction. Merchants such as the Swiss-born Sebastián Robert or the French-born Signoret family not only dominated the big commercial establishments in the center of town but also owned controlling shares of the banks and the local and national factories that provided cotton goods to their department stores.[41] Their huge, Parisian-style department stores came to dominate the Zócalo and its proximity, rivaling even those traditional symbols of power, the Cathedral and the National Palace (see fig. 2).

Renewed private and public construction further changed the use of space in the traditional center. Many churches, convents, and charities that had once dominated much of the center fell to real estate interests and government imperatives of sanitation or public works. Old buildings were destroyed as four- and five-story structures went up in their place. Foreign companies introduced new building techniques and designed and directed construction of a few "skyscrapers" that exceeded the previous structural limit of five stories.

Although commerce set the pace and style for new construction, public building came in a flurry before the centennial celebration of 1910. Progressive Mexicans were particularly sensitive to the perceptions of foreigners, and the various national delegations that were to attend the centennial provided an opportunity for Mexico to assert its claim to membership among modern nations.[42]

The Federal District government undertook to pave central streets and, whenever possible, make their width and nomenclature regular. They lit main avenues with electric lamps, and a regular system of drainage and water supply was functional in the city center by 1910. In 1895 the city tore down several portals throughout the city at considerable expense, both to eliminate the often seedy market stands that proliferated under their arches and to widen adjacent streets. Dead-end alleys, which often hid tenements and underused valuable space, were closed off and built over by developers. After 1898, the city government destroyed the National Theater and adjacent tenements in order to extend Cinco de Mayo Avenue.[43]

In the first ten years of the century, various hallowed edifices of traditional corporations fell to make way for progress. In 1910 the city closed the three hundred-year-old university, located at the southern edge of the National Palace. The long-secularized convent Santa Isabel and numerous tenement houses on the Puente de San Francisco were razed by the city in order to build the new Fine Arts Theater (Bellas Artes), which was planned as the cultural showpiece of the Porfirian regime. The government also razed two colonial hospitals in the center of town (on Terceros and San Andres Streets) to build the neoplateresque central post office and the Secretary of Communications. These symbols of state power and culture went up, as with the never completed congressional building, in the immediate proximity of the Alameda.

Among the new public buildings and institutions constructed by the Porfirian government in this period were those directly concerned with the "social question." The Porfirian government reluctantly accepted a degree of responsibility for public services that had previously been provided by the church. A new public hospital for the poor was constructed on the southern edge of the city, by the Belém prison. Similarly, in 1905 the government destroyed the old Hospicio de Pobres across from the Alameda on Juárez Avenue and replaced it with a new orphanage on the southern outskirts of town. Separate correctional schools for girls and boys went up in the suburban towns of Coyoacán and Tlalpan respectively.[44] Perhaps no public work better symbolized the paternalistic reforming impulse of the Pofirian government than the construction of the model panopticon Lecumberri penitentiary on the eastern edge of the city.

Porfirian public welfare was defined around limiting notions. On inaugurating the new orphanage in 1905, the government stressed its determination to avoid the creation of long-term dependencies by insisting that the new orphanage filled a temporary need to supplement private institutions, but that caring for the poor "is not the primordial function of the state." While restricting the responsibilities of the state, the Porfirian government built the new edifices of reform in a monumental scale and style and with considerable promotion, in an attitude that Ann Blum calls "conspicuous benevolence."[45] Yet most striking in the great flurry of public works is the apparent attempt to physically displace from the city center the prisons, tenements, hospitals, and orphanages—and therefore the populations associated with them—which detracted from the Porfirian vision of progress. The increase in urban land values certainly put pressure on the government to move public welfare institutions to more marginal land on the periphery of the city. But also evident is the tendency among Mexican elites and their government to address the so-called social question by putting these high-profile institutions at a physical distance from the modern center. Similar to the flight to the suburbs, the intense campaign to reconstruct the city center reflected the specific social criteria of the progressive Mexican elite.

This monumental public construction was provided at considerable expense by the federal government and the financially strapped city governments.[46] It followed the same logic as the provision of services to the wealthy western suburbs—serving primarily those areas of greatest commercial importance and public display and leading to a pattern of great inequality between sections of the city. As the center of the city was gradually transformed into an international showpiece and the nerve center of national finance and commerce, and as wealthy Mexicans moved into residential suburbs on the west side of the city, the eastern and southern quarters became increasingly the realm of workers and the popular classes, including the marginal, the destitute, the sick, and the incarcerated.

Tenements

Mexico City's center had been notable in the 1880s for its provincialism and social diversity. By 1910, visitors might be shocked to see a peasant driving a flock of turkeys to market down the elegant San Francisco Street, because such scenes were increasingly rare in the center of town and they contrasted with the showpieces of Porfirian civilization. In a 1913 speech to the Mexican Society of Geography and Statistics, the architect Gonzalo de Murga remembered that "in this City of Palaces not too many years ago . . . there were Indians living in courtyards in places as central as Ancha Street." Though some might "believe that such embarrassments no longer exist," he insisted, "we can still find hundreds of the 'casas de vecindad' that are begging loudly to the minister of governance for the demolisher's pickax or the purifying torch." After some twenty-five years of progress, the remnants of the traditional city (and problematic elements of the new) contrasted and on occasion conflicted strikingly with its veneer of civilization. Tenement houses and their occupants were gradually pushed out of the most exclusive avenues of the commercial center to a dense fringe of settlements that encircled the center to the north, east, and south. But no matter how much the Porfirian elite sought to remove the poor and their tenements from the city center, the very structure of commerce and production and the persistent claim of the poor on the "moral" center of the city limited their success.[47]

Tenements had long existed as a form of low-income housing in Mexico City. In 1895 an estimated one hundred thousand occupants (out of a population of 330,000) lived in tenements, and tenements became even more important as the population swelled. A keen U.S. observer estimated in 1921 that one-quarter of the city's population lived in tenements. Many were formed from old colonial-style patio buildings that previously had housed a single extended family and servants. By dividing rooms, adding rooms to the internal patio, and renting each room separately, a landlord could increase his returns without major investment. With as many as ten people in a single room, some tenements reportedly housed as many as eight hundred people (see fig. 3).[48]

A labor inspector described the tenements in which tailors lived and worked as "an alley like a jail, with tiny quarters on either side, or a patio in quadrangular form surrounded by rooms. In one case after another the lodging for workers of few resources, like tailors and seamstresses, is made up of a room of 25–30 cubic meters, with only one door and lacking windows for the circulation of the air. A patio of five or six square meters in which you find a minuscule roof under which food is prepared and the washing basins and toilets for the whole *vecindad* is what the worker about whom we are talking has access to for his home life."[49]

Many of the same traditional families that had once lived in the colonial mansions retained ownership of the converted tenements. After conducting a survey of housing conditions in 1920, the Department of Labor issued a statement to the press, denouncing that "within a few meters of the Zócalo and the Fifth of May [avenue] can be found houses in ruins where dozens of families sleep exposed to the weather or among hundreds of rats or decomposing vegetables." The report added that "the majority of these ruins and centers of sickness are owned by wealthy and well-known people" and then went on to name various of these "millionaires," men almost all from the traditional elite.[50]

Densely populated and poorly maintained tenements brought landlords easy profits and provided workers with the only available form of cheap lodging close to their work. Wages were insufficient and too irregular for most workers to afford to rent or buy a house in respectable working-class suburbs like Colonia Guerrero. Even moving from one tenement to another posed problems. When a labor inspector asked a tailor whose room was consistently inundated by urine and fecal material from the tenement toilet why he did not move, the tailor responded, "because the houses in which my family could be modestly lodged are beyond my resources, because it would be necessary to pay rent in advance, a guarantee from a commercial establishment if the tailor's shop where I work wouldn't support me, and fill lots of other requisites, not to mention what the move would cost me, and that, even though it wouldn't be much, for me is a lot."[51]

Another obstacle that prevented the working poor from living in the suburbs was the distance from their sources of work. Given the service orientation of much of the Mexico City economy, the center of the city continued to be a major source of work, and the nature of this employment meant workers had to be close by, since their wages could not sustain the cost of daily commutes on the tramways.

However, for rich and poor alike, having access to the center did not mean living directly in the center. As late as 1920, inspection reports listed a few tenement houses on such central streets as Uruguay Street, in the heart of the city's commercial district. But rising real estate costs and "the demolishing pickax" had pushed most tenements outside of the area of five main streets between the Zócalo and the Alameda that was the heart of the commercial district.[52] Instead, tenements were clustered in the blocks immediately east of the Zócalo, primarily southeast near the area of La Merced, the sprawling produce market of the city, and northeast around the Plaza Tepito (see map 3). In these areas many buildings were designed and built specifically as tenements rather than converting older buildings to serve as tenements.

The rhythms of market delivery, public construction, and restaurant and hotel service and the subcontracting of much of the work of the clothing industry made it necessary for a cheap, flexible labor force, available on short notice, to be tied closely to the center. With the putting out of work, the middlemen and clothing shops displaced the costs of renting workshops onto the seamstresses, who often lived and worked in the same room. The high price of rent in turn forced them into high-density tenement houses.[53]

Some form of tenement house went up in every area of the city, even in posh District Eight, which included Colonia Juárez. But the greatest concentration of tenements was in Districts One and Two, which included the entire city east of the Zócalo.[54] The relative isolation of these inhabitants from the residences of wealthier classes made it less likely that such services as running water and closed sewer systems extended to these areas. Though the city water system was eventually extended into these districts, residents had to pay to be hooked up to city water pipes, which were often several blocks away. If not hooked up, they depended on the public faucets and the water carriers for water well into the twentieth century. Predictably, these underserviced areas were constant breeding grounds for sickness and disease, particularly dysentery, tuberculosis, and cholera. Districts One and Two repeatedly had the highest reported mortality rates in the city, with fifty-five and eighty deaths respectively per ten thousand inhabitants in 1906, the latter figure more than double that of District Eight.[55]

Attempts at regulating the conditions of tenements had limited effect. The lax conditions of the sanitary code of 1891 were easily ignored or challenged in court by landlords who opposed any government interference. The Federal District government was reluctant to intervene where private property and markets were concerned, much to the frustration of some of the city's architects and engineers. Suggestions for regulations requiring a space between tenement buildings, as was the practice in U.S. and European cities, went unheeded. Improvements to tenements made by landlords or resulting from city services usually led to higher rents, which in turn eventually displaced the poorest occupants to more crowded areas of the city.[56] Thus, at least in the central commercial streets, market forces were more effective than government health and building regulations at solving the problems of tenements, by displacing them.

Since it was forbidden to sleep in the streets and parks, those who could not pay for even the crowded conditions of the tenements had the option of living in the *mesones*, or flophouses. Twelve of the seventeen *mesones* registered in the 1900 census were in District Two, the rest in District Three. A 1912 city council report counted thirty-nine *mesones* throughout the city. The 1900 census included 658 inhabitants of *mesones* among the population of the city, although such a transient population is invariably undercounted. *Mesones* had traditionally been the temporary lodgings of mule drivers or peasants who briefly visited the city to sell goods in the market. The American muckraking journalist John Kenneth Turner estimated in 1908 that as many as twenty-five thousand people passed the nights in *mesones*, many of them recent migrants and the chronically underemployed. Such a high number seems less improbable if it included the free "public dormitories," which according to one newspaper housed over six thousand people. Turner vividly described the conditions of these flophouses: "To the *mesones* the ragged, ill-nourished wretches from the city's streets come to buy with three precious copper centavos a brief and scanty shelter—a bare spot to lie down in, a grass mat, company with the vermin that squalor breeds, rest in a sickening room with hundreds of others . . . In one room I have counted as high as two hundred . . . (and) in not one of the *mesones* that I visited was there a separate room for the women and girls."[57]

The architect Murga condemned the crowded tenements for reasons of health and virtue. A lot of people in close quarters made tenements incubators of disease and promiscuity ("antechambers for brothels"). But what most horrified Murga was the way in which the conditions of the crowded tenements forced people "out on the streets . . . or into the gaming rooms," bringing the fallen woman or the near naked peasant in contact with the dandy in Parisian clothes, juxtaposing the traditional Indian in his morally decadent urban transformation with the modern buildings and cultural trappings of San Francisco Street.[58]

Since liberal *científico* doctrines limited the government's willingness to support cheap housing or effectively regulate tenements, efforts at re-form passed from regulating private spaces—residences—to controlling public spaces and behavior, interventions more easily reconciled with the positivist dictum of "Order and Progress." Government intervention was not directed at the root of the problem—crowded, unhealthy housing—but at the result, which was to "throw people out on the street."

Starting in 1893, two years after the ineffective attempt to regulate tenements, a flurry of city ordinances regulating public appearances was passed, clearly aimed at the poor and more traditional elements of urban society. Porfirian officials required all males to wear pants rather than the simple peasant *calzón* (a loose wraparound cotton garment), and they made repeated attempts to control street vendors. Similarly, various groups of employees such as tramway conductors and newsboys were required to wear uniforms, a rule that eventually initiated more than one strike. Many popular festivals that were considered coarse, disorderly, and occasions for outbursts of popular discontent, such as the symbolic burning of Judas effigies held on Holy Saturday, were banned from the center of the city in favor of officially organized events such as flower parades that reinforced the civic order.[59]

Other measures were aimed at eliminating what the *científico* Miguel Macedo identified as "the deleterious environment of the lost classes: cheap eating houses, taverns, public dances, gaming houses and brothels." The major figure behind much of the reforming legislation was Gov. Guillermo Landa y Escandón. His principle targets were *pulquerías*, taverns specializing in the fermented drink produced from the maguey cactus, which were increasingly controlled through restrictions on new licenses and by the early closing decree, which shut down *pulquerías* by six o'clock in the evening. Such efforts went hand in hand with the increasing monopoly on pulque of the Compañía Expendedora de Pulques, since no new *pulquerías* were permitted to open in the center. At those that remained, mostly in the hands of the *compañía*, the price was raised almost 30 percent, as the company explained, "in order to reduce drunkenness." Among the officers and principal stockholders of the pulque company were key members of the *científico* group, including Francisco Bulnes, Pablo Macedo, and Fernando Pimentel y Fagoaga, the latter serving as president of the company as well as of the city council. According to one account written after the fall of Díaz, Governor Landa y Escandón himself had bought up many of the city's *pulquerías*.[60]

In an address on crime in 1897, Macedo urged stronger penalties and enforcement of laws regulating street crimes and made clear that the greatest criterion for culpability should be the visibility of immoral behavior rather than the previous criterion of scandalous behavior. Thus he argued that, while drinking in itself was legitimate, "being drunk in public should be considered a crime; it damages by example and damages sentiments of decency and morality of those who observe it." City ordinances in the next years forbade public drunkenness, sleeping in the streets or parks (a loosely defined vagrancy), and begging. Other ordinances tried to impose similar controls on prostitutes through registration, forced medical checkups, and the segregation of brothels into "tolerance zones." Additional targets of Landa y Escandón were religious holidays (which provided the popular classes with ready occasions for drinking), unhygienic dress, and the bathing habits of the poor. For example, on the eve of the centennial celebration in September 1910, the governor installed bathhouses at police commissaries throughout the poorer sections of the city, so that "a large number of poor people can be cleansed in one day."[61] All these measures were clearly intended to coerce the lower classes into orderly domestic and private lives or, if that proved impossible, to hide their excesses and shortcomings from public view.

If these were the targets of intervention, the instruments of enforcement were also put in place with attempts to modernize the police force and jail system. By the late Porfiriato, the city's police forces consisted of 422 mounted police, 1,872 gendarmes on foot, and a corps of secret police, all under the command of Col. Felix Díaz, the nephew of the president. Such a legion of policemen gave vagrants, beggars, prostitutes, and others defined as criminals a run for their money. In 1910 street venders and beggars (*pordioseros*) could still be seen on the main street of San Francisco, but as one visitor observed, they were wary and ready to flee upon detection: "beggars sidle up to one and solicit alms—*un socorro por el amor de Dios!*—the while keeping a watchful, flounder-like eye on the vigilant gendarme stationed at the street-corner." Such vigilance was rarely extended to poorer neighborhoods, where according to one visitor the residents "looked on the police with little sympathy."[62]

Such attempts at "civilizing" the poor in the city center dated back to the colonial period and would continue, with limited success, well past the fall of Díaz. Like previous and later reforming campaigns, the Porfirian project of ridding the center of the poor and of controlling their behavior proved contradictory and ultimately unsuccessful. Those in government wished to eliminate the presence of the poor so close to the corridors of power and wealth and feared the problems of health and morality generated by the tenements as well as their potential for internal solidarity and mobilization. Yet the presence of these poor and working people was fundamental to the needs of the urban economy. As a result, they repeatedly returned to the center, not only to look for work but also to pass their leisure hours in ways that elites now defined as criminal.[63]

Colonias Populares

At the turn of the century, squatter settlements, or *colonias populares*, initiated a period of rapid growth that would continue throughout the century. Guerrero, one of the first *colonias* of the city, was inaugurated as a workers' project with much fanfare in 1874 by President Lerdo de Tejada. But in fact, the sale of lots was left entirely to real estate developers. Colonia Guerrero did grow to have a strong working class component, largely because of its location immediately adjacent to the Buenavista train station, but workers lived primarily as renters in tenement houses rather than as homeowners. In spite of periodic proposals by developers and politicians to sponsor formal working-class neighborhoods, the government made no serious attempt to encourage them until the 1920s.[64]

To buy a house, a worker needed to save sufficient money to make the down payments on the lot and the construction of the house. Because the title was given only upon the final payment, the death of the main wage earner, a period of unemployment, or the bankruptcy of the developer of the *colonia* could mean the loss of lot, house, and savings. Only the most skilled worker with stable employment could aspire to own or even rent his own house in one of the more prosperous *colonias*.[65]

The elite and middle-class *colonias* that covered the best lands of the west did have their counterpart. A series of working-class and popular *colonias* formed to the south and east of the city. On the marshy land to the northeast, the *colonias* Valle Gomez, Maza, Del Rastro, La Bolsa, Romero Rubio, and others grew up around such centers of employment as the new slaughterhouse, the new penitentiary, and the four train stations on that side of the city. To the south, the main working-class and industrial *colonias* were Indianilla, Hidalgo, Cuartelito, and La Viga. This area included the station of the Tlalpan railroad, several hospitals and charities, the major factories of the city, and the warehouses and repair shops of the streetcar company.

Some of the textile and cigarette factories in Mexico City provided limited housing for a minority of their workers, but this was far less common than in factory towns such as Orizaba and even the factory towns sprinkled throughout the Federal District. Even when companies in the city provided houses or tenements, such as the Buen Tono cigarette factory or the Mexican Telephone and Telegraph Company (Compañía Telefónica y Telegráfica Mexicana), they almost never housed more than one-fifth of the work force, and company housing often went to the better paid employees.[66] At any rate, company housing also proved a constant bone of contention, since employers sought to control the visitors and leisure activities of their employee-tenants. Working-class housing in Mexico City was left for the most part to market forces, which—for all the deficiencies in the quality of market-based housing—at least allowed working-class culture and community life to develop beyond the control of employers.[67]

Taking advantage of remaining barren or agricultural land and the urgent need for housing created by rapid migration into the city, small land speculators proceeded to divide and sell private land unofficially. Referring to the illegal settlement of El Cuartelito in the south of the city, the newspaper El Imparcial observed:

> An entrepreneur buys a piece of land, badly situated, without ventilation, drainage, or anything to rid it of its terrible unearthliness. Within the enclosed limits he traces alleys and raises barracks, puts together in the least possible space 150 to 200 shacks of adobe or wood, and there you have something that for the authorities the owner classifies as a private residence, and for his renters he calls it a "charitable colonia." There within a space of 1,500 to 2,000 square meters you have a total population of 800 to 1,000 people who haven't a single sewer . . . or outhouse. Naturally . . . it doesn't take long to convert the rambling residence into a hospital.[68]

The city government was reluctant to approve a prospective colonia to which they would eventually have to provide services. Proprietors of poorer colonias were usually required to accept entire responsibility for paving the streets and providing drainage, as in the concession of Colonia Maza. Quite often the city government would deny the request, or the proprietor would reject the terms of the concession, and the sale of lots or rental of rooms would occur anyway. Such was the case with Colonias La Bolsa and Valle Gomez. In the case of Colonia Cuartelito, later known as Colonia Obrera, the municipal government periodically distributed a poster in 1899 and subsequent years disclaiming any responsibility to provide the colonia with municipal services (particularly water and sewage). The owners, they insisted, would therefore have to provide these services according to municipal health standards. Colonia Chivatito was registered with the city as a rancho, ineligible for services and beyond the provenance of regulations, yet in 1900 it had 232 inhabitants, more than those living in the officially recognized Colonia Maza.[69] Municipal services were systematically denied to these areas of popular settlement.

Most of these colonias populares perched on the eastern edges of the city and were contained in Districts One and Two, where wealthy Mexicans rarely had occasion to visit (see figs. 4 and 5). This was particularly true when the Jockey Club finally moved its race track from the poor Colonia Peralvillo to the fashionable neighborhood of Colonia Condesa (in District Eight) on the southwest side of the city.[70]

The guidebook Terry's Mexico counseled travelers that such "slums" as the Colonia de la Bolsa were "to be avoided . . . as it is the plague and ghetto with dirty and microbic streets, repulsive sights and evil smells." One adventurous visitor to La Bolsa was appalled at the absence of pavement and sidewalks, the presence of a dead, rotting donkey in the middle of the street, and the abundance of pulquerías. He warned of "the most ferocious fights . . . terrible vengeances, and . . . the most horrible crimes" that occurred in the almost complete absence of police.

The best dwellings in these colonias were made of adobe. But, besides basic tenements, the main type of dwellings were simple huts, or as one contemporary described them, "little shacks formed from badly joined boards and shingles." The 1900 census lists the highest number of "huts and shacks" on the eastern fringe of Districts One and Two.[71]

If the popular neighborhoods of the eastern half of the city had a reduced claim on the city's resources, the illegal colonias often had no claim at all. Colonias that were never recognized by the city government, like La Bolsa, escaped services but not always interference. Rather than granting services or recognition to La Bolsa, the city government instead threatened emptily to "stamp out this foul region which is just as offensive to intelligent Mexicans as it is to foreign visitors." Inspectors and visitors encountered great hostility when visiting these *colonias*, since the government had little recourse other than demolition to force landlords to make improvements.

At the same time poor *colonias* became shelters from the municipal authorities. Jesus Negrete, the notorious bank robber and womanizer whose escapades were exalted to heroic dimensions in the popular press, was nicknamed "the Tiger of Santa Julia" after the popular *colonia* that sheltered him. Similarly, traditional celebrations that were banned from the city center could be celebrated with impunity in the outskirts of the city.[72]

$\star$ $\star$ $\star$

The *científico* Miguel Macedo observed that the lower classes in Mexico City lived so much unto themselves that respectable people had "the profound consciousness that they would never be touched by the dangers and evils of other classes with whom they haven't any ties of community, not even of contact, except that related to commanding and obeying, serving and being served." This perceived separation of classes was not just physical but also "material, intellectual, and moral."[73]

During the late Porfiriato, Mexico City underwent profound changes in the organization of space and class. Broadened avenues increased the circulation of people and goods from different areas of the city. Technological innovations and public investments allowed people of the comfortable classes to move their residences away from a center increasingly devoted to commerce. Different areas of the city thus became more specialized in function: the commercial center, the industrial south, the upper-class residential suburbs of the west, the *colonias populares* to the east. The old multiclass neighborhoods of traditional Mexico, while still present, were less discernible in the face of overarching changes: wealthy and middle-class families built their houses on one side of the city; working class and the poor were pushed into crowded central tenements or into working-class neighborhoods and squatter settlements on the eastern and southern periphery.

These transformations of urban space to a large extent followed flows of national capital, emanating primarily from a small group of merchant-industrialists based in Mexico City, as well as local market forces in real estate. Capital flows and market forces were guided and encouraged by political elites with whom this group had very close ties, particularly a small group of *científicos* who envisioned Mexico City as above all the modern capital of a modernizing nation. The subordination of Mexico City, the community, to Mexico City, the national capital, required in turn the subordination of the elected city council to a governor of the Federal District, directly appointed by the president, thus making even traditional local municipal politics obsolete after 1903.

One result was the creation of a mosaic of neighborhoods where workers and popular classes increasingly lived, worked, consumed, and socialized far from the wealthiest classes, which set the stage for a growing assertiveness of workers and urban poor after 1910 that overcame previous patterns of respect for wealth and political authority. Poor and working-class Mexicans formed new identities not with the multiclass community of the past but rather with their tenement houses, their *colonias populares*, in short, the "other" Mexico that grew up in the shadows of Porfirian glitter. From spaces of exclusion, workers and the urban poor began to elaborate a new sense of community based on working-class and popular neighborhoods. While their alienation from the "gilded" Mexico City and their reorientation around new, working-class communities did not in itself determine an oppositional movement, it helps explain why and how working people responded to the opportunities for oppositional mobilization that multiplied around and after 1910.

Soon after the centennial celebration, progressive Mexicans and their applauding foreign guests were to discover that, in spite of their great pride in the considerable accomplishments of the Porfiriato, the modernity they had willed was far from complete. What had occurred was an initial differentiation of class and space, which, without completely eliminating old patterns of class and residence, gave rise to a nascent articulation of a working-class community. This would in turn bring an unexpected aspect of modernity—conflict between classes.

With the outbreak of the revolution, the Porfirian project was contested from not only the countryside but even closer to home, as the "other" Mexico City began to assert itself. New formative communities attempted to reassert themselves in public areas, particularly in the city center, by denouncing or supporting political leaders; by pressing their complaints against employers, landlords, or government policies; or by parading triumphantly with their new organizations. Their collective demands after the outset of the revolution, whether to local authorities, employers, or to landlords, made them difficult to ignore and often a threat to the urban order.

Though the geographical separation of classes was partial, its emerging logic is apparent. Without these changes, the Mexican Revolution might have bypassed the city with little more than the standard hardships that had characterized the capital during the national upheavals of the nineteenth century. Instead, these changes facilitated broad alliances among a formative working-class community that was shaped, in turn, by the changing worlds of work.

2 | WORLDS OF WORK

The electric light arrives
Illuminating the city,
And its great spotlight spreads
With its light, its liberty,
Like the sun that can't be denied.

HIGINIO VÁZQUEZ SANTA ANA,
"Corrido de la luz eléctrica"

Esther Torres arrived in Mexico City from her native city of Guanajuato in 1910 to join her younger sister and her recently widowed mother. She was thirteen and had just finished the third grade. Why move to Mexico? According to her mother, the only men to marry in Guanajuato were miners and mule drivers. And now that her miner husband was dead and she needed to support her family, the only work in Guanajuato for her or her daughters was as domestic servants, earning one and a half pesos a month and most likely living and working in separate households. Esther explained years later that "as far away as there [Guanajuato] the news arrived that in México City there was a factory where women worked." Indeed, right off the train in the Buenavista station, Esther's mother approached a woman in a tortilla shop to ask where she could find work. The next day, the tortillera's niece brought her to meet the maestra of La Cigarrera Mexicana, who immediately hired her. When Esther arrived, her mother found work for her and her sister in the same factory, the first of many similar jobs they held in the city before forming a seamstress union in 1915.[1]

Jacinto Huitrón was born in a tenement house near the center of Mexico City in 1885 of parents who had migrated years earlier from towns in the central states of Hidalgo and Mexico. His father, a respectable cobbler, died when Jacinto was seven, and in order to get by his mother opened a tiny variety store in the north of the city. After finishing primary school, Jacinto was apprenticed to a blacksmith at a peso a week while taking four years of classes at the government trade school on San Lorenzo Street. After 1900, he worked as a carriage maker, a mechanic, a blacksmith, and an electrician. In 1909, he became a mechanic in the Federal District railroad workshops at Nonoalco, where he also joined the Union of Mexican Mechanics (Union de Mecánicos Mexicos). The next year he was laid off, and after a brief stint of work and opposition politics in Puebla, he returned to the capital to work as a mechanic and plumber in several of the city's big workshops, while fully engaging in the vibrant political and labor activities of the decade.[2]

The lives of these two working people who rose to prominence in the labor movement during the revolution serve to illustrate broader patterns of work and class formation in turn-of-the-century Mexico City. This chapter examines the changes of industrialization and work that helped shape class formation in Mexico City at the turn of the century. Although the discordant urban growth and industrialization of Mexico City from the 1940s on might suggest otherwise, recent historical studies have shown that rapid urban growth and industrial change had their roots in the late nineteenth century.[3] As the capital and largest city, Mexico City was important to early industrialization, but its political dominance and demographic growth fed a particular kind of metropolitan industrialization, characterized by the expansion of urban infrastructure and the production of consumer goods in factories and semi-mechanized workshops, often through investment by foreign capital or immigrant entrepreneurs. Economic growth brought both displacement and opportunity for skilled workers while perpetuating the demand for unskilled workers (those without acknowledged skills) and thereby sustaining a huge casual labor force. Any inclusive working-class movement would need to incorporate not only the demands of skilled workers, like Jacinto Huitrón, but also the demands of a majority of workers who were less skilled or in weaker positions in the labor market, like Esther Torres, her mother, and sister. And in order to include workers in more informal sectors of the economy, who were often women, an ef-fective working-class movement would need to address the consumption demands of the broader working-class community.

Examining the structure of this formative working class provides an important part of the framework for understanding the patterns of collective action that unfolded after 1910.

The Peopling of Mexico City

In the 1880s and 1890s, Porfirian peace and the introduction of foreign capital and technology began to spur the migration of people to Mexico City and transform the nature of work there. The rapidly expanding railroad, which joined city to countryside and both to the rest of the world, provided a symbol and an engine for the transformation of the capital as well as the country. Railroads were constituted by and led the way for the flow of massive amounts of foreign investment and technology into manufacturing and urban infrastructure, which included substantial investments in electric power companies, tramways, and factories in Mexican cities. Railroads helped to create national markets for food and to connect Mexico to international markets for its silver, copper, coffee, and other exports. A secondary aspect of this development was the creation of large-scale consumer industries serving relatively weak domestic markets, owned largely by foreign-born merchant-financiers or foreign investment companies and protected by direct and indirect tariffs and close ties to the Porfirian political elite.[4]

Railroads similarly linked and extended labor markets; for many Mexicans, working to construct, maintain, and conduct the railroad was their first experience with wages and led to their eventual incorporation into a growing and dynamic labor market that moved them back and forth along the railroad lines, from the U.S. border through northern mining enclaves, central textile regions, and coastal oil towns. For those already born into an urban wage economy, like Jacinto Huitrón, working on the railroad provided valuable training with machines and industrial discipline that they could readily apply as machinists, mechanics, or managers in the factories and workshops of Mexico City. Many of these same skilled workers, like Jacinto Huitrón, gained their first involvement with workers' organizations while working on the railroad.[5]

For many others migrants to the city, like Esther Torres, the railroad was simply the vehicle that physically transported them between their provincial past and their new life in the metropolis, while allowing for continued family ties and the flow of information between city and pueblo. Opportunities, information, and mobility helped create a veritable army of potential workers—women as well as men, peasants as well as experienced textile workers, craftworkers, mechanics, and so forth—who moved along the industrial and railroad axis that stretched north to Querétaro and south to Puebla and Veracruz.[6]

As a result, Mexico City grew at an unprecedented rate. The first national censuses taken in 1895, 1900, and 1910 are of dubious precision but give a useful indication of general trends. After barely doubling in the first eighty years of the century, in the fifteen years after 1895 the city grew by more than half, from 300,000 to 471,000. From 1900 to 1910, the annual growth rate of Mexico City was 3 percent, less than that of such northern boomtowns as Torreón and Cananea. Yet the increment of 126,000 people that Mexico City absorbed constituted 36 percent of the total national urban growth of the period and was equal to the 1910 population of the next largest city, Guadalajara. During the turmoil of the revolution, from 1910 to 1921, Mexico City would absorb an additional 145,000 people, many of them refugees from fighting.[7]

Although it extended over a mere 5 percent of the larger territorial unit that surrounded it, Mexico City dominated the Federal District. By 1900, 68 percent of the residents of the Federal District lived in the capital city, and the physical growth of the city was already beginning to blur boundaries with surrounding towns. The subordination of the various city councils to the Federal District government after 1903 made political distinctions between the capital and such contiguous towns as Tacuba and Tacubaya largely nominal. Railroad and streetcar systems further incorporated the surrounding area into the economic and residential spheres of the city, and the largest towns became intermediate stopping points for rural migrants. Several nearby towns, such as Tlalpan, Coyoacan, and Necaxa, had access to streams and cheaper land prices and began to specialize in particular types of production, such as textiles, paper, armaments, and electricity.

Migration far outpaced natural increase, particularly in the boom years at the end of the 1890s. According to the 1900 census, 66 percent of the total Mexico City population had been born outside of the Federal District, and at least 6 percent had moved there in the previous year. The percentage of those actually born in the city as opposed to the larger Federal District (a distinction not made on the census) would be even lower than 44 percent, since the move from the towns and countryside of the Federal District to Mexico City was made by many. By 1910, the Federal District as a whole absorbed over 28 percent of all internal migration in Mexico, and almost half of its inhabitants had been born outside of the Federal District.[8]

As might be expected, the largest source of migrants was the state of Mexico, which bordered the Federal District on three sides. In 1900, residents born in the state of Mexico totaled 28 percent of the population of Mexico City. Other states with significant migration to the capital were, in descending order, Guanajuato, Hidalgo, Querétaro, Puebla, Michoacán, and Jalisco. In 1900, 52 percent of the residents of Mexico City were from these densely populated states in central Mexico. A variety of factors combined to draw this surplus population from the central valleys of Mexico: the expansion of large agricultural estates, high population density, and the decadence of traditional areas of mining and artisan manufacture in the face of new areas and forms of production. The decline in the highly urbanized Bajío was particularly acute; for example, the population of the city of Guanajuato dropped from fifty-two thousand in 1884 to thirty-six thousand in 1910.[9]

The number of people who came from rural or urban areas is not obvious from census data, but all the major feeder states except Michoacán were relatively urbanized. Census data do reveal other important characteristics of the population of Mexico City in general that suggest a strong presence of people with relatively urbanized origins. The literacy level of the entire Federal District in 1910 was registered at 51 percent, far higher than the national figure of 21 percent or that of any other state.[10]

The 1921 census, the only modern census to include a category of "race," registered a population of 19 percent indigenous, 55 percent mixed race, and 23 percent white for the entire Federal District. But the criteria used are unclear, and many of those registered as indigenous lived in a few surrounding southern and relatively rural municipalities, such as Milpa Alta and Xochimilco. By contrast, the 1900 census registered barely three hundred residents in Mexico City proper who spoke an indigenous language.[11]

Not surprisingly for a city of migrants, who are most likely to move during their most productive years, the population was relatively young. In 1900, 56 percent were between the ages of sixteen and forty-five, compared to the national figure of 45 percent. Women were a slight majority of both the overall and migrant population, approximately 53 percent, a figure that varies little between 1895 and 1910. This percentage is high compared to the northern states that were also net receivers of migrants. Yet the nature of the labor market, dominated by services and the manufacture of consumer goods (as opposed to the cattle and mining industries of the north), explains much of the attraction of Mexico City for female as well as male migrants.[12]

The capital also had the highest concentration of foreigners in the country, mostly Spanish, followed by North American and French. Their numbers grew dramatically, from nine thousand in 1895 to almost twenty-six thousand in 1910, but the latter figure constituted a modest 5.5 percent of the city's population, far less than, say, Buenos Aires at the same time, where immigrants were nearly half the population. Still, the presence of foreigners loomed far larger in the popular imagination than their numbers might seem to warrant, a factor of their prominence as merchants, managers, manufacturers, and labor organizers. The eminent Porfirian statesman Andrés Molina Enríquez observed that "the racial element placed at the top, the superior caste, is in reality now the unassimilated foreign element, and within that element, divided as it is in two groups, the North American and the European, the North American is superior." Like many Mexican elites, Molina Enríquez understood economic success in racial terms; but even so, he, like growing sectors of Mexico's middle and working classes, began in the last years of the Porfiriato to link the dominance of foreigners to investment and tax laws that privileged foreign over Mexican business.[13]

The Nature of Work

While the industrial transformation of Mexico City during the Porfiriato inspired repeated comments from foreign and national observers, the effects of industrialization were somewhat less dramatic there than in other areas of the country. In the southern sugar-producing state of Morelos, new technology and markets radically displaced patterns of labor and land use, leading in turn to one of the most coherent peasant uprisings of the revolution. The northern city of Monterrey, home to the largest steel mill in Latin America in 1910, had less than one-fifth of Mexico City's population but by that year surpassed it in the value of its manufacturing output. Similarly, the mining town of Cananea, Sonora, was a single-industry urban center that ballooned from a previously insignificant town; the coastal port of Tampico by 1920 was dominated by oil, and in Orizaba, Veracruz, one out of every four residents was employed in textile factories.[14] By contrast, industrialization and the related transformations of work and class in Mexico City were directly connected to its role as the political, financial, and commercial capital of the country.

Bureaucrats, Merchants, and Gente Decente

The new elite and emerging middle classes of Mexico City benefited from and worked for the recently consolidated national state. In recovering political hegemony over the country, Mexico City required a significant caste of bureaucrats and professionals whose numbers grew steadily at the turn of the century. The number of state employees surpassed five thousand on the 1910 census, a 77 percent increase over that of the 1895 census.[15] Perhaps more than any other group, public employees helped constitute the aspiring, if somewhat precarious, middle class. With considerable exaggeration, turn-of-the-century novelist Angel de Campo called office employers "invalids of the [labor] army . . . the poor of the great offices . . . many of whom don't die from hunger because la Patria, that immense nursemaid . . . gathers them up in her fecund breast with maternal philanthropy." Campo himself depended on public employment to support his family and his writing and vividly described in his fiction the struggles of this group to make ends meet and keep up all the public appearances of respectability, such as proper clothes, maids, club memberships, and restaurant meals.[16]

The military presence, closely tied to the political dominance of the capital, hovered between five thousand and six thousand, of whom roughly one-fifth were officers. While military recruits and police were notoriously underpaid and were usually from the poorest classes of society, officers were an important part of an aspiring middle class.[17] Teachers in Mexico City, the majority of whom were employed by the state, almost doubled in number between the 1895 and 1910 censuses, to more than three thousand. To this social stratum should be added such growing professional groups as lawyers, doctors, and especially engineers, many of whom were at least occasionally employed by the state.

Porfirian educator Jorge Vera Estañol described this expanding middle class as "*gente o personas decente*" (respectable people), often mestizos, who were "intelligent, instructed and . . . ambitious," who sought to "mix with the rich and comfortable classes, to dress like them," and who felt a repulsion against all manual or mechanical work. This view was echoed by northerners, who resented what they saw as the political parasitism of Mexico City, a view later articulated by northern revolutionaries like Venustiano Carranza and Alvaro Obregón.[18] But in spite of the political centralization of the Porfiriato and the demographic primacy of Mexico City, its bureaucratic character shaped but did not predominate over its commercial, manufacturing, and service sectors.

Commerce expanded prodigiously, a pattern reinforced by the confluence of railroads in Mexico City and the development of a culture of consumerism among a growing middle and working class. Over 25 percent of declared commercial sales in the country in 1910–11 occurred in the Federal District. Merchants remained the largest single census category outside of domestic service, increasing steadily from nineteen thousand in 1895 to thirty thousand in 1910; but their situations diverged dramatically. At the very top of the merchant hierarchy, and indeed among the wealthiest men in the city, were the French-born owners of El Palacio de Hierro, El Puerto de Veracruz, and El Centro Mercantil, department stores that one visiting Frenchman claimed "wouldn't be out of place in the most beautiful neighborhoods of Paris."[19]

Indeed, commerce became the most common path to fortunes that would eventually extend to finance and industry, and one paved most often by European immigrants. For example, Enrique Tron used his connections to merchants and investors in his native France to import goods and establish a commercial empire in Mexico City that culminated in the opening of the huge and elegant El Palacio de Hierro in 1891. Along the way, he became a prime investor in the Société Financière pour l'Industrie au Mexique, a French and Swiss banking group that financed some of the modern textile factories of the Compañia Industrial de Orizaba, as well as the premiere cigarette factory in the country, the Buen Tono in Mexico City. Similarly, Thomas Braniff, a U.S. citizen who helped construct Mexico's first railroad in the 1860s, used government concessions that were meant for importing basic goods for railroad employees instead to import and sell luxury goods. Profits from contraband eventually allowed Braniff to invest throughout the country in mines, banks, railroads, and haciendas and to invest in urban real estate in the capital, where he resided. These examples illustrate two patterns common in Porfirian Mexico City: foreign-born merchants often used their success in commerce to become financiers and industrialists, and economic opportunity often depended on close ties with powerful political figures in the Porfirian regime. Indeed, company boards often included key administration figures or their close family members, such as Julio Limantour, the treasury secretary's brother, or Porfirio Díaz Jr.[20]

Other merchants carved out more modest empires. The grain mills of the Spaniards Braulio Iriarte and Cordova y Arrache produced much of the flour and bread consumed in the city, allowing them ownership or indirect control of most bakeries. Similarly, the Compañía Expendedora de Pulques, constituted by such powerful men of politics and wealth as Pablo Macedo and Fernando Pimentel y Fagoaga, came by 1910 to own over 90 percent of the city's retailers of pulque. Medium-sized merchants included German owners of hardware stores and crystal shops and French owners of fashion shops and drug stores. Near the bottom of the commercial hierarchy, though well above market and street vendors, were the hundreds of mostly Spanish and some Mexican owners of grocery stores and pawnshops, often women, who clung precariously to their share of commerce and their claim to middle-class status. A 1920 commercial census done by the city council registered 201 Mexican-owned and 351 Spanish-owned grocery stores. The Spaniard Julio Sesto noted the profusion of these "changarros" in Mexico City, tiny shops with names like La Providencia and La Guadalupana, and speculated that "some of these little shops, that sell soap or contraband alcohol, prosper, others only produce enough to maintain a family or a widow."[21]

A 1901 guidebook of the city noted that "monopoly, which was a completely unknown plant on our soil, today is cultivated on a grand scale and is beginning to take control of exactly the basic necessities that are indispensable to survival." While many small businesses continued to proliferate and come into conflict with monopolies, they steadily lost political influence, social status, and control over their shops as they competed with large department stores and made their discontent known. The deterioration in the status of small shopkeepers led them at times to exploit their workers even harder or, as sometimes happened during the years of the revolution, to make common cause with their workers against the control wielded by big, largely foreign merchants.[22]

In sheer numbers, these groups of upper and middle classes were a significant presence by 1910, constituting a substantial 22 percent of the labor force.[23] In these groups lay much of the demand for the consumer goods that were the focus of Mexico City industry, and their leisure activities and consumption habits in turn shaped the work force and gave Mexico City much of its air of modernity. In addition, many of these middle-class groups, particularly professionals, would provide leadership and an important base for political opposition to the Porfirian regime.

Factories and an Urban Proletariat

A type of metropolitan industrialization transformed Mexico City in dramatic, subtle, and diverse ways that drew people like Esther Torres from the provinces and changed the way natives of Mexico City worked. One of the changes most remarked by Porfirian elites and foreign visitors to

the capital was the rise of factories. Factory-scale production involving
heavy machinery and large numbers of operators occurred primarily in
two industries, textiles and tobacco.

The formation of most large textile factories in the Federal District
coincided with the construction of railroads in the 1870s and 1880s. Because of large energy demands and the need for cheap land, factories
were usually built in the surrounding towns, such as Tlalpan and Contreras, which were close to the water sources necessary for power and
were accessible to the city by railroad. An industrial census of the Federal District in 1877 included six textile factories that employed roughly
900 men, 300 women, and 220 children.

The introduction of electricity in the late 1890s by various companies,
soon consolidated in the Anglo-Canadian Mexican Light and Power
Company, made it possible for more and larger factories to be set up,
many within the city limits. By 1910, the Federal District had twelve textile factories, employing some 5,088 workers, and production had increased fivefold. In that year, 16 percent of the nation's textile factory
workers lived in the Federal District, compared to 25 and 22 percent in
Puebla and Veracruz.[24]

With the rapid rise in real estate prices, setting up factories in Mexico
City proved expensive. But Mexico City provided two clear advantages:
proximity to the country's largest consumer market and abundant, inex-
pensive, and relatively experienced labor. As a result, factories were built
on the southern periphery around the Ciudadela barracks and the Cuartelito and Indianilla neighborhoods and to a lesser extent on the eastern
edge of the city. Mills in Mexico City produced not only the basic coarse
clothes increasingly worn by peasants and workers but also finer quality
woolens, linens, and silk. Some companies combined the production of
textiles with the actual cutting and assembly of clothing, a natural link-
age given the importance of merchant capital in textile production.

It is difficult to find uniform statistics on Mexico City textile factories
for any given year, but sporadic and uneven data collected by the Labor
Department during the decade after 1912 give a rough sense of the size
and composition of the labor force in textile factories. Of the fourteen
textile factories registered in the city in 1921, seven employed over two

hundred people, and only one, the modern La Carolina factory, employed more than one thousand workers, making it the largest textile factory in the Federal District. Even such operations as La Carolina were dwarfed when compared to the more than three thousand workers employed at the Río Blanco mill in Veracruz.[25]

The largest industrial establishment in the city, however, was the Buen Tono cigarette factory, founded in 1875 and incorporated in 1894. As it expanded in the next decade with state-of-the-art technology, it became the showcase of Mexican industrial progress for foreign visitors and in international industrial expositions. By 1910, French founder and director Ernesto Pugibet claimed Buen Tono to be the largest cigarette producer in the Americas; it employed as many as two thousand workers, primarily women, and had a daily production of ten million cigarettes. A smaller local rival, Tabacalera Mexicana, employed between four and five hundred. By importing and installing automated cigarette machinery, these two firms came to control over 60 percent of the national market. As a result, the number of traditional cigarette factories in all of Mexico dropped by more than half from 1900 to 1910 and in Mexico City by more than two-thirds (from forty-three to fourteen establishments).[26]

The number of Mexico City factory workers, mostly in tobacco and textiles, rose 355 percent from 1895 to some ten thousand in 1910, one-third of whom were women. In textile factories, women averaged 20 percent of the work force in the Federal District, though their presence was greater in factories that incorporated the sewing of garments. In tobacco factories, women were a slight majority, and the largest factories in the city employed children for about 10 percent of their labor force. Women and children were generally relegated to lower paid jobs involving the preparation and finishing of textiles and, as was true for Esther Torres and her sister, the manual packing of machine-made cigarettes.[27]

In spite of the growth of urban labor markets, hiring continued to depend largely on personal networks of family and friends, a pattern that applied to management as well as workers. As in colonial times, foreign merchants and industrialists not only married among the creole daughters of their countrymen, they often hired immigrants from their native countries, particularly from France and Spain, as high-level managers. For example, in the textile factory La Carolina, founded by the Spaniard Constantino Noriega, as late as 1921 all twenty-six salaried employees were foreign born.[28]

Managers in turn seem to have depended on personal and informal networks to hire unskilled workers rather than using classified advertisements or placement services such as those offered by the Labor Department after 1912. Factory managers often hired on Mondays, in the hope that workers would at least work through the week. Personal references of *"enganches"* gave managers some assurances of reliability and meant that family members or friends would help familiarize new workers to factory tasks and work discipline. Such references helped managers assure control over the hiring process and screen for potential "agitators." Workers often complained that factory managers kept a blacklist of troublemakers who were to be denied employment.[29]

Textile workers in the Federal District were a work force in the making. Many were country people from rural villages in the Federal District and the state of Mexico. This was particularly true of the factory towns surrounding Mexico City proper, where rural networks from the surrounding area helped feed the factories' labor force. As a result, workers in these towns would after 1910 occasionally try to incorporate *campesinos* in their organizations or include demands for land in their petitions to government officials. Of course, migration to these factory towns also came from urban areas with manufacturing traditions. According to one study of the 1870s, the largest contingent of workers in textile towns of the Federal District came from Mexico City, followed by a large contingent born locally (though not necessarily from rural settings), with workers from distant cities like Querétaro not far behind.[30]

By contrast, Mexico City factories almost certainly had a much higher percentage of workers born in urban areas, as suggested by higher literacy rates and the relative stability in the work force. Other factory workers had artisan backgrounds, though little data is available to determine how large a group this was for Mexico City. For the Santa Rosa textile factory in Veracruz in the same period, over one-third of factory workers had had previous experience as craftworkers, most importantly as weavers.

More obvious is that new modern factories drastically undercut the existence of artisan weavers and tobacco workers, whose numbers in the city dropped by over half from 1895 to 1910 (to sixteen hundred and seven hundred respectively) and by similar numbers nationally.[31]

Even so, the persistence of artisan weavers and cigarette makers in the face of modern industrial production was in itself remarkable. As late as 1916, a given household might send a son or daughter to work in a textile factory while the mother continued to weave commercial cloth by hand in the home. At least in Mexico City, the number of new factory positions exceeded the number of artisan cigarette and textile workers lost. So the displacement of artisan workers was probably less dramatic than in other areas of the country, such as León, or rather was manifest in the stream of migrants from traditional artisan zones to the capital. At the same time, the "agony" of the process by which artisans were proletarianized was further mitigated by the demand for a minority of highly skilled and well-paid workers within factory settings, such as mechanics and carpenters. These skilled workers were more likely to retain a broader sense of a departmentalized work process, and their cooperation was crucial to the functioning of the factory as well as to any organizational initiative by workers. In addition, factory production of textiles created job opportunities outside the factory, such as the burgeoning growth of seamstress work.[32]

But for all the importance of the rise of modern factories in a relatively short period, factory workers still comprised only 4 percent of the Mexico City work force in 1910, roughly equivalent to the combined total of government employees and military men.[33] Overall, while the emergence of a factory proletariat in Mexico City was important, factory workers were neither numerically nor organizationally the most important sector of the working class.

Shrinking Crafts and Expanding Workshops

Of greater significance in shaping the working class of Mexico City than the introduction of modern factories was the reorganization of the traditional manufacturing crafts and the growth of new skilled occupations rooted in new urban infrastructure and services. Artisan production had deep roots in the colonial capital and had survived intact through much of the nineteenth century, in spite of the tentative openings of free trade and the elimination of colonial guilds. But starting in the 1880s, new machinery and the reorganization of tasks within expanding workshops began to transform the nature of work, making many journeymen and master craftsmen redundant in the face of medium-sized, semimechanized workshops, often owned by foreign corporations or immigrants. The elimination in 1896 of the regional *alcabalas* (taxes on commerce between states) reduced protection for regional markets and further undermined artisan production.[34]

While factory production made inroads in some sectors, such as textiles, in others work was reorganized around expanded, semimechanized workshops that relied as much on the delegation of authority to overseers and on an increasing division of labor as they did on technology. Electrical power, new machinery, and new workshop organization incorporating unskilled workers into repetitive tasks resulted in large-scale production and the consequent displacement and deskilling of many traditional artisan groups. This transition to semimechanized production, a pronounced tendency at mid-nineteenth century in the United States, occurred in Mexico City much later and in a much shorter period, often under the impetus of foreign capital.[35]

Industrial data gathered during the 1910s and 1920s give a general sense of the size of workshops established during the Porfiriato, since most industrial capacity in existence before 1925 had been installed in the decades before the revolution and survived the decade of turmoil intact.[36] A Labor Department directory in 1923 listed over two thousand manufacturing establishments in Mexico City, most of which were no more than modest workshops engaged in, for example, construction (200), printing (80), or hat making (80). In the first published national industrial census in 1930, over 87 percent of manufacturing firms in the entire Federal District employed fewer than twenty workers. But even if small workshops were more numerous, 43 percent of all workers in manufacturing were employed in establishments of over one hundred employees, and over 30 percent were employed in workshops of between twenty and one hundred workers. While small and medium-sized workshops continued to exist, a few companies that organized around large, semimechanized workshops increasingly dominated many crafts—particularly those producing finished articles such as shoes, food products, and clothing. The overall effect was a drop in the relative importance of manufacturing employment in Mexico City, from 37 percent of the labor force in 1895 to 33 percent in 1910.[37]

A typical example is the shoe industry. Throughout most of the nineteenth century, shoemaking was the largest profession among Mexico City artisans, but by the end of the Porfiriato, the profession had been radically transformed. In some cases, workshops grew to be virtual factories, such as the Excelsior Company in nearby Tacubaya. Started by Carlos Zetina, a merchant and tanner, the Excelsior grew to combine departments of tanning, cutting, and assembly of shoes under one roof and by 1911 employed eight hundred workers. More modest workshops were the Eclipse Shoe Company and the United Shoe and Leather Company, each of which employed around two hundred workers. These new firms, a small percentage of the 160 shoemaking workshops listed in the city in 1923, put great pressure on the small workshop and traditional artisan shoemakers, many of whom moved from making shoes to repairing shoes.[38]

As a result, cobblers—men like Jacinto Huitrón's father—dropped in numbers by one-third from 1895 to 1910, a period when the population of the city grew by half. Other traditional trades, such as those of bakers, hat makers, and tannery workers, experienced similarly dramatic drops in numbers. Of course, this pattern was not uniform, and workers in many trades held their own in numbers, such as printers and metalworkers (see table).

The *Economista Mexicano* observed the increasing polarization between small workshops and expanding industries at the beginning of the century: "Industry in Mexico manifests itself in two distinct ways: one an industry that is small, disorganized, anarchic, weak, that of a poor country, and another one organized, with the rules of great manufacturing, solid, technical."[39]

New food industries such as soft drinks and beer were established after 1900 and employed large numbers of men and women in centralized settings. But these new industries did not keep the overall number of workers in the food industry from dropping, primarily because tedious occupations such as corn grinder (invariably women) fell sharply in the face of rudimentary mechanized mills.

In spite of the often basic technology involved, the food industry tended toward a high concentration of ownership, related in part to links to the nation's most commercialized haciendas. An example are the corn mills that produced the masa used by poorer Mexicans to make tortillas: in 1921 the Spanish-owned Compañía Mexicana Molinera de Nixtamal employed 130 men and 290 women throughout the city in ninety-one mills and outlets, an average of five workers per mill. According to a 1915 study of food problems, the company owned 100 of 130 total corn mills in the city; a Labor Department inspector observed a few years later that the company could set the price of masa in the city at will.[40]

A similar concentration and deskilling occurred in the city's bakeries. Wheat consumption in Mexico City grew dramatically, while the number of workers employed as bakers remained stable. In 1921, seventy-three bakeries throughout the city employed an average of twenty-five workers. Bakery owners in 1907 warned striking workers that they could easily be replaced, since with new technology, "In a few days the unskilled worker can know as much as the long-serving craftsman."[41] The level of deskilling is suggested by a 74 percent illiteracy rate among a sample of bakery workers in 1913. Concentration occurred primarily through the control of flour mills by a handful of merchants, in particular the Spaniards Braulio Iriarte and Arrache y Cordova and the Mexican Pedro Laguna, whose mills reached near industrial proportions. The Compañía Manufacturera de Harina employed 270 in its principal mill and supplied flour to its own bakeries and to virtually all others in the city. In times of scarcity after 1910, small bakers, bread distributors, and bakery workers tried to organize to break the hold of these merchants, who also became the targets for angry rioters.[42]

Even in crafts like metalworking, where workers retained much control over the productive process, the tendency was toward an increasing concentration of production in larger foundries that began to mass-pro-

Changes in Selected Occupational Census Categories for Mexico City, 1895–1910

	1895	1900	1910	% CHANGE 1895–1919
Bankers	21	17	48	129
Lawyers/Doctors	1,667	1, 896	2, 989	79
Merchants	19, 218	24, 808	30, 484	59
State employees	3,009	2,795	5,320	77
Professors*	1,645	2,074	3,119	90
Engineers	507	754	1,153	127
Military officers	1,264	1,080	943	-25
Mechanics	1,206	2,364	4,101	240
Tailors	3,057	3,140	3,562	17
Typographers	1,302	1,411	1,481	14
Lithographers	281	392	803	186
Electricians	NE	NE	917	—
Machinists	NE	NE	212	—
Metallurgy	3,632	3,533	3,617	0
Factory workers	2,299	6,443	10,465	355
Cigarette makers*	1,712	1,113	686	-60
Bakers	1,719	1,619	1,772	3
Tortilla makers*	3,763	2,604	1,813	-52
Shoemakers	5,562	5,581	3,770	-32
Seamstresses*	5,531	6,328	7,387	34
Dressmakers*	779	1,220	2,132	174
Laundresses*	5,815	6,559	6,635	14
Weavers	3,530	2,189	1,638	-54
Bricklayers	5,027	6,273	6,240	24
Carpenters	5,769	6,073	6,558	14
Plumbers	361	433	1,168	224
Painters	1,374	1,846	2,696	96
Mule drivers	130	34	38	-71
Porters	1,702	1,651	987	-42

Changes in Selected Occupational Census Categories (*continued*)

	1895	1900	1910	% CHANGE 1895–1919
Motorists	NE	NE	135	—
Military troops	3,794	5,181	4,299	13
Water carriers	249	66	38	-85
Agricultural workers	6,639	9,943	13,182	99
Domestic servants★	34,331	33,473	42,138	23
Concierges★	2,429	1,529	2,718	12
Private servants	6,693	10,871	21,006	214

NE No Equivalent

★   Majority women

Source: Elaborated from census data in Dirección General de Estadística. *Censo general de la República Mexicana*, 1895 (Mexico City, 1897–99); *Censo general de población por entidades, 1900, Distrito Federal* (Mexico City, 1901–7); *Censo población de los Estados Unidos Mexicanos*, 1910 (Mexico City, 1918–20).

duce nails, wire, and metal articles for construction. In a 1877 survey, only two mechanized foundries were registered in the entire Federal District and together employed one hundred men and children. An interview with one artisan included in the survey was probably typical of the trade: he identified himself as a metalworker rather than a businessman, worked out of his house, and employed two journeymen (*oficiales*) and three apprentices. When asked about his concerns for the profession, he complained that workshops such as his were caught between individual metalworkers who worked for little more than their food and foreign-owned workshops with access to capital and cheap imports. In 1895 a similar survey counted eight foundries and 104 blacksmith shops in the city. The population census that year showed a total of 3,600 employed as metalworkers, a figure that remained constant over the next fifteen years. By 1921, the gap between foundries and blacksmiths had grown. Of twenty-one metal foundries in the city, the largest three employed 330, 235, and 88 men. The first two were incorporated companies with English names, and the owner of the third was named Phillips. These enterprises relied on organizational innovations and new equipment such as electric ovens and metal lathes. Much of the old organization remained—a handful of master craftsmen handled the most delicate foundry operations aided by journeymen and minors who were still called apprentices. But well-paid mechanics and electricians maintained the new equipment, while the majority were peons and "*operarios*" (operators) who fulfilled less-skilled tasks. In terms of scale, these operations were far more modest than the integrated operations of Pittsburgh or, closer to home, the Fundidora of Monterrey, with its two thousand workers toiling round the clock. The remaining eighteen foundries surveyed resembled more closely the traditional artisan workshop. All were apparently owned by Mexicans, who were often maestros themselves, and had an average of seven employees. Owners of these modest workshops complained of being on the verge of closing in the face of competition and economic downturns, and many were reduced to making repairs.[43]

The printing industry underwent a similar transformation starting in the 1870s, spurred by technical innovations such as the rotary press and photolithography and by the expansion of a consumer market for the news and commercial ads offered by multiplying newspapers and magazines. While printers also maintained many of the craftlike aspects of their profession, the rise of large book companies, modern newspaper plants, government printing offices, and printing departments within factories, as at Buen Tono, all changed the setting in which most printers worked (see fig. 7). The number of printers increased slightly from 1895 to 1910, while the number of lithographers grew rapidly.

At the top of the scale were big workshops such as the American Book and Printing Company, with a capital investment of almost half a million pesos and over two hundred workers, half of them women and children working as binders. Newspapers founded in the 1890s, such as El *Popular* and El *Imparcial*, identified themselves as "modern dailies" due to their scale, content, and use of the latest imported technology. El *Univer-*

sal, founded 1916, employed over 150 in production by 1922. Of course, small, semiartisanal workshops that combined traditional and modern techniques, generally with start-up costs under two thousand pesos, persisted. Through the penny press, pamphlets, religious stamps, and song sheets, this *"periodismo ínfimo"* gave great vitality to the cultural ferment of turn-of-the century Mexico. A notable and perhaps typical example was the print shop of Antonio Venegas Arrollo on Santa Teresa Street, a block east of the Zócalo, which published many of the broadsides illustrated by José Guadalupe Posada. In 1921 the shop employed seven men, two women, and one child. But printers who worked in such small workshops were increasingly a minority of the profession.

Of course, printers were exceptional craftsmen in many ways. The trade continued to require a high degree of skill and training, and the nature of the printers' product made literacy almost obligatory. High levels of literacy even extended to the tasks done by women and children, such as binding books. And given the continual censorship and forced closings of newspapers throughout the Porfiriato, those who printed words and images shared many of the political risks of editors and reporters. As a result, printers remained among the most articulate and politically engaged of craftworkers.[44]

In some trades, the number of workers grew rapidly. Construction workers increased from fourteen thousand in 1895 to eighteen thousand in 1910, or 8 percent of the reported labor force. With the exception of a few large furniture shops and the huge public projects, such as the construction of the Palace of Fine Arts and the new sewer system, intermediaries continued to organize the building trades on a modest scale, with limited investment in machinery. Skill levels varied from basic bricklayers to highly paid plumbers, but wages and literacy levels suggest that, overall, construction workers were among the least skilled of the traditional trades. Accounts of the period describe thousands of day laborers (*jornaleros*) or peons who were periodically absorbed in construction and probably did not even appear on the population censuses under building trades.[45]

At the end of the Porfiriato, craftworkers continued to have considerable importance in the occupational structure of Mexico City, and even greater organizational weight, but only a small percentage were artisans in the classic sense of the word. While small workshops remained numerous, in most manufacturing sectors they were no longer the predominant form of production in terms of their share of production or even in terms of the number of workers. As a result, the existence and market share of many craftworkers in small workshops became more precarious. And in larger workshops, the circumstances of their employment were significantly different from those of nineteenth-century artisan settings, even where the introduction of new technologies in manufacturing increased the demand for skilled workers or where workers retained a high degree of control over the work process, as in printing and foundries. Craftworkers in 1910 were more likely to receive wages than to offer their goods on the market; shops were increasingly separate from their owners' homes; and ownership was increasingly based on capital rather than skill. Indeed, in the largest shops, owners were often corporations rather than individuals. And while traditional titles of maestro, journeyman, and apprentice lingered in many workplaces, access to these positions and their meanings were now very different. Already by the 1860s, "maestro" in many crafts was more a title of ownership than of skill.[46] By the turn of the century, the term "maestro" often was used for foremen within large workshops or for the middlemen who put out work to people working out of their homes. The term "journeyman" was often replaced with "operator" or simply "worker" (obrero), and men in this position had limited chance to aspire to become a foremen, let alone an owner; "apprentice" was often a euphemism for child labor, often girls, and less a position for learning skills. One labor inspector attributed the decline in male apprenticeship in the tailoring trade to "the aptitude of the maestro to not pay the apprentice, as well as the facility in the Metropolis to earn a salary without previous apprenticeship."[47] As a result, the rhythms, technique, and compensation of workers were transformed.

The growth of the urban economy degraded many crafts but also created new opportunities. The numbers of mechanics in the city more than doubled in the last fifteen years of the Porfiriato, growing from twelve hundred to over four thousand, exceeding the number of shoemakers. People like Jacinto Huitrón, who thirty years earlier might have pursued his father's profession of cobbler, instead moved from one trade to another as boundaries between many traditional crafts faded and new ones were created. For example, the business card that he used in 1913 as treasurer of the Casa del Obrero Mundial had the following printed on the back: "I do all types of work, plumbing, welding, forging, mechanical, inventing, fine machinery, installation, and all kinds of repair."[48] These were all tasks much in demand in Mexico City, though they required some education and craftlike abilities. Many artisans and their children probably became the "*obreros calificados*" needed in industrial settings. Machines and migrants reduced the skill and cultural boundaries between trades that had existed before among skilled workers and, by breaking down specific craft subcultures, facilitated involvement in working-class politics and the broad-based working-class organizations that emerged after 1910. Within a given workplace, the success or failure of a strike often depended on the leadership, or at least the acquiescence, of the most skilled and strategic workers, those who repaired the machines.

The introduction of modern urban infrastructure such as electricity and electric streetcars also entailed the creation of new skilled and semi-skilled occupations. Railroads, electrical plants, and tramways all demanded mechanics, conductors and electricians, people able to operate and maintain expensive machinery. The Anglo-Canadian electrical company that monopolized energy production in the Federal District, the Mexican Light and Power Company, employed one thousand workers. With the introduction of electric streetcars in the 1890s by the same Anglo-Canadian holding company, repair shops and warehouses on a scale as large as any factory in the city were built in Indianilla, near the southern industrial district of the city. Mule drivers and the carriers who worked the train stations almost disappeared in the face of new forms of transport. The streetcar company employed around seven thousand workers between 1910 and 1914, though during the construction of new suburban lines the payroll could expand to twenty thousand. Similarly, the railroad repair shop at nearby Nonoalco employed twelve hundred people. Want ads in El Imparcial and the Mexican Herald sought English-speaking mechanics and furnace men and offered salaries of up to three hundred pesos a month. Until the revolution, top management and technical positions as well as higher wages went mostly to foreign workers; for example, the streetcar company employed three hundred foreigners in management positions. Of course, many of the workers in these companies were unskilled peons—they made up one of every four workers in the streetcar company. But skilled positions abounded, and the streetcar company prided itself in offering a sliding scale of wages to skilled workers "to encourage industrious and capable men to remain with the company."[49]

The cost of their equipment and the importance of their work to the smooth functioning of the urban economy gave these skilled workers an importance far beyond their considerable numbers in the work force. By gathering together large numbers of workers, these new industries facilitated a high degree of consciousness among workers. And their sense of themselves as workers and of their relation to the city extended beyond the workshops and garages, spreading like the electrical wires and streetcar tracks that joined the city and the Federal District. Furthermore, the control of these industries by foreign capital and managers, almost always North American or English, helped create a fierce nationalism among them. Workers in these industries acquired tremendous strategic importance, starting with the first streetcar strike in 1899 and especially after 1911, as streetcar and electrical strikes could bring the city to a standstill and thereby required the immediate attention of municipal and national authorities.[50]

The type of metropolitan industrialization that occurred in turn-of-the-century Mexico City meant displacement as well as opportunities for factory, skilled, and strategic workers. In large-scale settings it set the stage for direct confrontation between labor and capital, while among workers in small workshops it created significant resentments over both the monopoly control of large producers and merchants and their often foreign origins. Not surprising, much of the organizational initiative in Mexico City after 1910 came from these three groups: textile factory workers, skilled trade workers in rapidly changing industries, and strategic workers in new infrastructure and transport industries. After

1911, alliances between these groups occurred relatively easily. But together they comprised barely 12 percent of the labor force.[51]

The process of industrial change in Mexico City resembles that of many European and U.S. cities in the nineteenth century, but there were a few significant differences: first, industrialization in the form of investment and technology came to Mexico City late and rapidly, in a period of barely two decades after 1885. Second, changes led to a very high concentration of production and commerce in a few hands, and third, those hands often belonged to a few foreign companies and foreign-born entrepreneurs. A fourth difference is that this modernization was very incomplete and left the majority of the labor force engaged in casual and unskilled labor.

Unskilled and Casual Labor

In spite of the increasing number of factory workers, and the strategic and cultural importance of skilled workers in traditional trades and new urban infrastructure, far and away the majority of the city's population worked in unskilled manufacturing and especially in service occupations. The type of economic growth that occurred in Mexico City perpetuated and even expanded the need for unskilled, "sweated," and casual labor. For men and women, work in domestic service, commerce, sweatshops, hotels, restaurants, street sweeping, or the generic categories of peon and day laborer constituted the great bulk of the urban labor market.[52] Most rural migrants were likely to be employed in these occupations, as were many poorer *capitalinos*.

The numerical predominance of unskilled and casual labor is clearest in the way women participated in the work force. In spite of middle- and working-class ideals that women should work only in the home, women made up 35 percent of the remunerated work force in Mexico City in 1910, far above the national average of 12 percent. A few lower middle-class women benefited from new opportunities as teachers, government secretaries, or telephone operators and continued to work as store clerks. But the vast majority of female jobs were restricted to unskilled, often short-term work in manufacturing and services that were extensions of household tasks. According to the 1910 census, 65 percent of the women employed in Mexico City worked in domestic service, laundry, or the food and clothing industries. Esther Torres and her sister, for example, learned to sew on a sewing machine in their home in Guanajuato, and when they left their first Mexico City jobs in the cigarette factory in 1911, this skill allowed them to work as seamstresses in a variety of sweatshops. When Esther was blacklisted from sweatshops after 1916 because of her organizing work, she sewed out of her home.[53]

The clothing industry suggests a broader pattern of informal work in manufacturing. Transformation came not through the factory system but rather by the division of production and the use of simple machinery, namely, the sewing machine, which allowed for the reduction of highly skilled labor to only a few aspects of production, such as cutting pieces of garments that in turn would be sewed by others. Tailors grew modestly in numbers as the consumer market for upscale clothing in Mexico City expanded, but like other traditional craftsmen, they faced pressure from the increasing domination of a few fashion houses, which either hired tailors directly or used intermediaries to subcontract with individual tailors and smaller workshops. Further pressure came from the rise of ready-made clothing sold in the new, modern department stores. All these manufacturers took advantage of the fast-growing pool of women willing to work at very low wages. From 1885 to 1910, the number of seamstresses in Mexico City rose by 34 percent and of dressmakers by 174 percent. These two groups combined almost equaled the number of industrial factory workers in the city by 1910. The largest of the European-style department stores, El Palacio de Hierro, employed over one thousand workers in their downtown stores, many of them clerks, and almost six hundred seamstresses in their sweatshop on the outskirts of Mexico City. After servants, this group of workers and all its variations (girdle makers, hemmers, and so forth) appear most in demand in the classified ads of the period. Wages for most women in these positions were low and usually paid by the piece, although some seamstresses earned wages comparable to those of skilled tailors.[54]

Commercial houses maximized their flexibility by employing a core of regular seamstresses on the premises and, during periods of excess demand, putting out jobs to women working out of their homes. One labor inspector in 1921 estimated that over ten thousand men and women did commercial sewing out of their homes. Much of this putting out was directly or indirectly undertaken for a dozen big commercial establishments, though most of the fifty-seven fashion shops throughout the city in 1914 put out a part of their work.

Work put out to women was usually "ready to wear" rather than made to measure and usually consisted of pants, shirts, and underwear rather than more highly paid suits and coats. Working in their homes gave women and some men some flexibility and control over their labor, but they also absorbed the costs of workspace as well as long periods of unemployment. According to one observer, they "always have someone to help them in their labor: sometimes family members, apprentices, or neighbors." They usually owned their tools and were required to pay for their own thread and to leave a deposit with contractors for materials received and against untimely return of finished pieces.

This dynamic of sweating and putting out often pitted primarily unmarried women working in sweatshops against married women or single mothers working out of their homes. After 1911, seamstresses working in shops often complained and even went on strike when contractors tried to reduce costs by putting more work out to seamstresses working out of their homes, and workers in the garment industry, led by organized tailors, began to articulate a critique of the system of subcontracts that allowed the big commercial houses to continually push down the price of labor. During the worst years of fighting, one of the few work possibilities for seamstresses was sewing military uniforms for contractors.[55]

The type of economic growth that occurred in Mexico City perpetuated and expanded the need for servile labor. Domestic servants were by far the largest single occupational category in Mexico City, as had long been the case. The census category "domestic work force" grew by half from forty-three thousand in 1895 to sixty-six thousand in 1910, to constitute almost 30 percent of the total work force of both sexes. Over thirty-five thousand women, or 43 percent of all employed women, worked as domestic servants. These percentages are almost identical to those of the 1848 Mexico City census, suggesting a remarkable persistence.[56]

Growth in the number of domestic servants was due to demand as well as supply. The growing army of clerks, professionals, and merchants aspired to a lifestyle that included an increasing variety of common and specialized domestic servants, and the abundance of recent migrants from the countryside made such middle-class aspirations affordable. For a lower-middle-class family or even some working-class families, to hire a servant was not only feasible but a necessary sign of respectability. Most women who worked as maids, servants, concierges, or laundresses had few employment opportunities beyond domestic service. Common maids received little monetary compensation beyond room and board and sometimes, particularly in the case of extended family members from the provinces, were absorbed into a household for no wages at all. At best, domestic service provided young rural women with a transitional job to ease them into city life and a better situation, perhaps a stint in a factory, and then marriage. At worst they remained domestic servants all of their lives, and some were seduced or raped and thrown out of their jobs.[57]

Domestic servants were almost impossible to organize as workers, and it is difficult to identify their participation in the various community mobilizations that occurred in Mexico City. Yet antagonisms were inherent in the sharing of the homes of the wealthy and middle classes that their profession entailed. Employers constantly complained or brought charges against servants they felt were stealing from them or who walked off the job from one day to the next. Indeed, short stories that featured the moral shortcomings of domestic servants became almost a subgenre among writers of literature of manners of the Porfiriato. Stealing and quitting were among the few types of resistance available to servants. City officials before and after the revolution tried to regulate domestic servants, "that class of society overwhelmed with defects," as one councilman put it in 1911, with projects that invariably obliged domestic servants to carry an identity card and passbook that included comments from past employers.

Akin to domestic service in the minds of employers and city officials was the occupation of prostitution. The city government repeatedly tried to impose similar controls on prostitutes, through registration, forced medical checkups, and the segregation of brothels into "tolerance zones." Indeed, domestic service and prostitution were often linked in public discourse, a connection due as much to the frequent movement of poor women from one type of work to the other as to the unique and threatening access both types of workers had to the intimacies of the idealized middle-class family.[58]

In a 1906 study based on official municipal statistics, the physician Luis Lara y Pardo made the astounding claim that the city had almost ten thousand prostitutes. This number, he pointed out, far exceeded the four thousand prostitutes believed to work in Paris, which was five times larger, and meant that 5 percent of the women of Mexico City practiced prostitution, or 10 percent of women between the ages of fifteen and thirty. Lara y Pardo's high estimate of prostitutes may reflect his own exaggerated perception of the moral decadence of poor women in the city or of the excessive zeal of police, but his data do suggest other characteristics of this group of women. Like Santa, the corrupted innocent of Federico Gamboa's popular 1903 novel, many prostitutes came from the countryside, and most were born in the provinces. They were often illiterate and indigenous and practiced prostitution primarily between the ages of fifteen and thirty. Most also worked when possible in other occupations, such as, in order of importance, domestic servant, garment sewer, and clothes washer, although a significant number were registered as "without a profession." Porfirian sociologist Julio Guerrero noted the relation of prostitution, or rather the loss of female virtue, to poverty and the labor market: "In women's work, salaries have been so reduced that in many cases of misery, the virtue [of women] survived because the offer of virtue was greater than the demand for pleasure." Besides the moral and material criteria by which contemporaries explained prostitution in Mexico City, it may have also been, as Katherine Bliss argues, "a common route of urban assimilation, quickly absorbing women who moved into the urban world of free time, expendable cash and freedom from moralistic family structures." Prostitution, like related lines of low-status work, thus served as part of the life cycle transitions of many young women.[59]

Other services constituted a significant portion of the labor market, such as the growing numbers of men, women, and children who worked in hotels, restaurants, and places of entertainment. Classified ads under "servants" in El Imparcial were more extensive than any other employment category and included a variety of positions from doormen, nannies, and maids, to cooks and waitresses, to vaguely defined "boys," "mozos," and "youth." And for many, particularly women, selling bric-a-brac, tamales, or bootleg pulque in the streets was a last alternative to destitution. One French visitor remarked in the last years of the Porfiriato that "few cities of the world are as infested with street vendors as Mexico City. In spite of the public markets, they sell all over the street, and if some vendors are useful, many are a real bother."[60]

Work in these sectors could vary dramatically from one season to the next or from one recession to another. Industries such as construction and garment making alternately absorbed and laid off large numbers of workers from one job and season to another. The census category of "profession unknown" included sixty-three thousand in 1900, and the number of rural peons in Mexico City grew from six thousand in 1895 to twelve thousand by 1910. These shifting categories suggest a floating population of underemployed who moved according to seasonal and economic cycles from one brief service job to another.

Visitors to the city often commented on the contrast of signs offering work and crowds of the unemployed. They assumed a shiftlessness among what they perceived as lumpen paupers (pelados) who rejected seemingly abundant jobs. The Spaniard Julio Sesto claimed that the construction industry potentially solved the labor problem, since anyone could walk into the street and find work: "If it's not to his liking, the next week he can go somewhere else." But in spite of incessant cries among employers of lack of labor much of the work available was brief and poorly paid and employers gained little advantage by offering these workers the wages or long-term security that would allow them in turn to demand regularity and discipline. Julio Guerrero credited the seeming laziness of unskilled workers to the overabundance of labor, which meant that those who did find work would linger over their tasks because they "were afraid to finish it, since often the following day they would not have had work." Thus the simple right to work, and in a secure job, loomed large among unskilled workers' aspirations.[61]

During the 1907 recession, and again during the most intense years of the revolution, unskilled and even skilled work became scarce. North American journalist John Kenneth Turner probably exaggerated numbers but not the general trend when he claimed that tens of thousands sought work every day in Mexico City, spending the night in flophouses or else wandering back out to the surrounding villages at night. The presence of this population of casual laborers and the attempt to criminalize popular behaviors made Mexico City one of the main urban centers for *enganchadores*, the ruthless labor contractors who used cash advances, alcohol, and force to recruit plantation workers for the Yucatán and the Valle Nacional of Oaxaca. The underemployed would similarly be the constant target of military drafts. For many, work remained precarious while the occupations they were forced to pursue remained numerous. The overabundance of the underemployed made for a constant downward pull on wages and considerable structural obstacles to organization.[62]

Mechanization increased wages for some groups and reduced or maintained low wages for others. A basic mechanic or metallurgical worker in 1910 earned two to five pesos a day, while adult factory workers in textiles and tobacco generally earned around one peso. The standard wage for unskilled workers in Mexico City in 1910 was between seventy-five centavos and one peso a day for men and as low as twenty-five cents a day for women. Children worked for as little as ten centavos a day and often worked unpaid in workshops and factories helping their parents do sufficient piecework to constitute a livable wage. As one foreign observer commented, child labor in areas where few skills were necessary or acquired was often disguised by the euphemistic title of "apprentice."[63]

Porfirian statistics suggest that wages increased in urban areas in the 1890s and then began to decline relative to the cost of living. The decision in 1905 by Finance Minister José Ives Limantour to move Mexico to the gold standard led to a dramatic rise in prices, while wages stagnated and even dropped. The United States' recession of 1907–8 further eroded employment and wages, and adverse weather undermined food production. Even the jobs created by the extensive public works in Mexico City in preparation for the 1910 centennial celebration could only partially absorb the rising number of urban unemployed. According to economic statistics compiled by the Colegio de México, the real value of industrial wages in the central region of the country that included Mexico City dropped by 38 percent from 1898 to 1908, with the biggest drop in 1905. The price of basic necessities such as corn and beans in the Federal District doubled, and the price of wheat rose by half during this period.[64]

Family Strategies

With the cost of living in Mexico City rising after 1900, it became impossible for an unskilled worker to support a family. One U.S. observer carefully estimated the annual income and minimal cost of living for an unskilled worker in 1910 and remarked on the resulting gap: "It seems, in contemplating the cold figures of the city peon's budget, as if it were impossible for him to exist, and yet exist he does, even though his children die like flies and his wife grows old at thirty." Of course, the answer to this mystery—besides periodic recourse to credit from pawnshops and corner stores (at rates between 20 to 40 percent a month)—was clear from his calculations: in most working-class families, women and surviving children entered the work force regularly. In the many cases where the nuclear family could not be sustained in such circumstances, extended households of relatives were formed to send multiple workers into the labor market to make ends meet.[65]

Even within marriages or common law relationships, the majority of poor and working-class women could rarely afford to withdraw permanently from the labor market. A cost-of-living survey done by the Labor Department in 1913 found that among working-class families "almost all the women are occupied, in addition to domestic chores, in jobs such as seamstresses, sandal making, etc., bringing to the sustenance of the family from 40 centavos to one or 1.4 pesos daily." When income from two working parents was not enough, the inspector went on, "the result is that we have a swelling number of children selling newspapers, shining shoes, delivering messages, etc."[66]

Women often moved in and out of the work force and through a series of different occupations, depending on their age, their marital status, and the availability of work for themselves and members of their family. For poor women, domestic service, sewing, and even occasional prostitution served residual functions, and their participation in the labor market often depended on whether they had husbands, fathers, or sons who could find work. One can get a sense of the transience of women's work from Elena Poniatowska's oral history of Josefa Bórquez in *Hasta no verte, Jesús mío*. Josefa was wrenched from her rural Oaxacan village when she followed her father, who joined up with a group of revolutionaries. After her time as a *soldadera*, she landed in Mexico City and worked on and off as a domestic servant for the next fifty years, with occasional stints working in box factories, cantinas, and a tobacco factory.[67]

In a world marked by the ideology of separate spheres for men and women, for women to work outside of the private, domestic sphere presented a moral dilemma for many families. Parents, middle-class reformers, labor inspectors, and even the working-class press frequently saw factories and shops as centers of disease and moral corruption for women, particularly where men and women worked together. At the same time, some employers who depended on female labor, such as Pugibet, the French-born owner of the Buen Tono cigarette factory, insisted that their factories were virtual finishing schools of useful skills and good behavior for young women. Just as important, wives or daughters who worked outside the house were a challenge to male authority over the family. In Verena Radkau's oral history of a textile worker, her subject, Doña Justa, reminisced about her father's refusal to let his wife work outside the home or to let his daughters even attend school: "Not a chance that I could even go out in the street!" Only after her father was drafted into the military and killed in the revolution did Doña Justa start working in a textile factory in Tlalpan in 1916. Similarly, Esther Torres, as well as her mother and sister, migrated to Mexico City and began working only after the death of her father.

If the workplace was seen as a site of potential moral corruption for women, it could also be a place where fallen women might find refuge, one probably more common than the brothels of the middle- and working-class literary imaginations of the period, where most famously Gamboa's fictional Santa fled after being seduced by a soldier and thrown out of her house. Doña Justa remembered "a woman [who] went down the wrong path and her parents threw her out of the house. And she came here [the factory], and she stayed forever." If necessity often drove women into the work force, many, like Doña Justa and Esther Torres, felt a certain pride in the income they brought to their family and enjoyed a freedom from traditional constraints on their activities.[68] The city and its sources of work could fulfill dire family needs but also provide unprecedented opportunities for women, both independence from the demands of male-dominated family life and a new sense of female sociability beyond the traditional spheres of home, tenement, and community.

★ ★ ★

With the changes of the late Porfiriato, Mexico City strengthened its dominance of the country, which resulted in a rapid growth of the metropolitan population, primarily through migration, and a variety of changes to its occupational structure. Its role as the political, financial, and commercial capital of the nation helped to expand and consolidate a privileged class of property owners, Mexican and foreign merchants, financiers, and industrialists and a growing number of professionals and government employees. These groups together provided the city with a bourgeois veneer and a stimulus for the growth of services and the manufacture of consumer goods.

The proportion of the work force involved in traditional manufacturing declined from 1890 to 1910 as new forms of organization and technology began to displace many skilled and unskilled workers. Although Mexico City never took on a predominantly industrial character, the number of factory workers grew, primarily in textiles and tobacco, while elsewhere, new machinery and organization transformed traditional crafts in more modest but still profound ways. The once considerable number of shoemakers, weavers, cigarette makers, and corn grinders dropped drastically as new machinery and shop organization made many workers, journeymen, and master artisans redundant in the face of cigarette and textile factories and medium-sized, semimechanized shops, often of foreign ownership.

Change not only displaced workers but also provided new opportunities. Many skilled craftworkers, men like Jacinto Huitrón, held their own in numbers over the late Porfiriato. The increasingly modern infrastructure of the city also required a small but strategically important group of new workers. Many men found work in skilled occupations that resulted from the proliferation of new printing techniques, the need for mechanics to service factory machines, and the introduction of streetcars and railroad engines. Many of these new industries, besides their importance to the everyday functioning of the city, were organized around large, foreign-owned monopolies that brought together and socialized thousands of workers.

For unskilled workers, many of them migrants like Esther Torres, continuities stand out more than changes. Some women benefited from the increase in teaching and clerical positions, but most entered the work force primarily as domestic servants, and many women worked in large numbers in factories and as seamstresses, in sweatshops and at home. Qualitative data give a sense of the extreme informality of work for many residents of the turn-of-the century capital.

Thus, industrialization transformed the Mexico City work force in ways that divided workers by gender and between the skilled and unskilled. This dichotomy went beyond the workplace to include both social and cultural aspects. Skilled workers were more commonly from urban backgrounds. They were far more likely to be literate and were often versed in liberal and radical thought. Among a sample of 230 workers convicted by judges in Mexico City in 1913, all ten printers were literate, and six had been born in the Federal District. For example, Jacinto Huitrón finished six years of primary school and then entered the Escuela Obrera, where part-time for four years he read classics of Mexican history and culture and thrilled at Mexican poet Salvador Díaz Mirón's ode to Victor Hugo. Inspired by liberal and anarchist thought, he would even name his children Anarcos, Acracia, Autónomo, Libertad, and Emancipación.[69]

By contrast, unskilled workers were more likely to have rural origins. In the sample of convicted workers, only 19 percent of bricklayers were literate and only 32 percent had been born in the Federal District. Esther Torres had barely been able to finish the third grade in her native city of Guanajuato before entering the labor market, and even this minimal education distinguished her from many unskilled workers. Unskilled workers, men in particular, were more prone to drink heavily and honor "San Lunes" (Saint Monday) by nursing hangovers at home. And in spite of the much more secular environment of the city, religious belief and veneration for the Virgin of Guadalupe remained important, especially for women. For example, Huitrón's wife, Refugio Castañeda, demonstrated her own rebellion by leaving her anarchist husband and raising their five children as Catholics.

Skilled workers had maintained a deep-rooted yet changing tradition of corporate organization, mainly mutual aid societies, and of political participation dating back to the nineteenth century. In Huitrón's case, he joined the Union of Mexican Mechanics in 1909 while working for the railroad, and during a brief stay in Puebla he became involved with the revolutionary shoemaker Aquiles Serdán and the anti-Porfirian opposition. For Esther Torres, as with many unskilled workers, unionization and political participation would come during the most intense years of the revolution and with help from skilled and educated workers like Huitrón. As William Sewell argues for nineteenth-century French artisans, "serious involvement in working-class politics required a level of information, organizational experience and commitment, and a freedom from the most pressing material wants." Such a pattern described a small but growing minority of Mexican workers but excluded the vast majority.[70]

The dichotomy in the work force meant that, for effective citywide mobilization to occur, alliances across genders and between the minority of skilled and the majority of unskilled workers were necessary. The organizational link between these groups could be made around universal demands for improving basic work conditions, even though those work conditions might differ dramatically among skilled and unskilled. But skilled and unskilled workers often lived in close proximity, and they shared a resentment of the presence of foreigners, whether as employers, managers, or shopkeepers, as well as of the increasing physical inequalities apparent in the city itself. Thus broader issues of consumption and community could help bridge the dichotomy between skilled and unskilled and male and female workers, particularly in times of political crisis and organizational freedom. While organizational leadership usually came from skilled workers, the participation and demands of unskilled workers often shaped the course of mobilization. The process by which working people as different as Esther Torres and Jacinto Huitrón came together in organizations and mobilizations during the revolution is central to the narrative that follows.

FIG. 1. The elegant Paseo de la Reforma extended from the old historic city center to the wealthy new residential suburbs on the western side of the city. Courtesy of Conaculta-INAH-SINAFO-Fototeca del INAH.

FIG. 2. El Palacio de Hierro and the Cathedral, bordering the Zócalo, in the 1930s. The historic city center lost residences but remained the financial and commercial center of the city and the nation. Courtesy of Conaculta-INAH-SINAFO-Fototeca del INAH.

FIG. 3. Children in the patio of a *casa de vecindad*. Densely populated tenements to the north, south, and east of the historic center provided workers with lodging close to their sources of work. Courtesy of Conaculta-INAH-SINAFO-Fototeca del INAH.

FIG. 4. *Colonias populares* of tenements, shacks, and huts grew around the penitentiary, train stations, and factories on the eastern edge of the city. Courtesy of Conaculta-INAH-SINAFO-Fototeca del INAH.

FIG. 5. Squatters staked out lots and built minimal shelters on the fringes of the city. Courtesy of Conaculta-INAH-SINAFO-Fototeca del INAH.

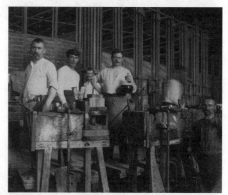

FIG. 6. Skilled craftworkers in a bottle factory. Courtesy of Conaculta-INAH-SINAFO-Fototeca del INAH.

FIG. 7. Printers maintained many of the craftlike aspects of their profession, even as print shops grew in size and incorporated unskilled workers. Courtesy of Conaculta-INAH-SINAFO-Fototeca del INAH.

FIG. 8. Worker in a brush factory. Much manufacturing work continued to use limited technology and require limited skills. Courtesy of Conaculta-INAH-SINAFO-Fototeca del INAH.

FIG. 9. Seamstresses under male supervision in a cramped clothing shop. After domestic service, the growing clothing industry provided the greatest amount of work for women. Courtesy of Conaculta-INAH-SINAFO-Fototeca del INAH.

PART TWO

Political Cultures and Mobilization

3 | WORKING-CLASS CULTURES

I admire the heroic echo of work
Which is a hymn in the Fatherland.
FERNANDO CELADA, El Paladin, 29 March 1914

Bossism rules from January to January,
From border to border, from foreman to worker.
ANONYMOUS, El Ahuizotito, 13 December 1908

In September 1910, Mexico City workers participated in the month-long centennial celebration of national independence in limited but symbolic ways. Typical was the Parade of Allegorical Floats of Commerce. While President Porfirio Díaz and foreign dignitaries observed from the balcony of the National Palace overlooking the Zócalo, flowery floats "alternated with groups of workers from the factories of the capital, bicyclists, charros and many industrial and commercial delegations." The float of the Centro Mercantil, a department store owned by a French-born merchant, featured French and Mexican flags over busts of national heroes Miguel Hidalgo, Benito Juárez, and Porfirio Díaz, all presided over, according to the official chronicle, by a "proud" woman representing la patria, the fatherland. Behind the float marched representatives of the mutualist society Employees of Commerce.[1]

Workers were also choreographed into the parade of the Great Civic Procession and were even given their own events in the centenary, such as the homage of mechanics and railroad workers to the heroes of independence. On the southeast edge of the city, Valbuena Park for Workers was dedicated as a modest working-class counterpart to the elegant Chapultepec at the opposite edge of the city. Both parks were the joint projects of Finance Minister José I. Limantour and Gov. Guillermo Landa y Escandón of the Federal District.[2]

On the last day of the month over twenty mutual aid societies and unorganized workers from various factories participated in a special "oath to the flag for workers of the capital" at the base of the newly erected Column of Independence. Governor Landa y Escandón, described in the official press as the "affectionate friend of the workers," asked those assembled to work for the prosperity of Mexico and to solemnly swear to follow and defend the flag, the "symbol of the law," even at the cost of their lives (see fig. 10). Similarly, the subsecretary of education, Ezequiel Chávez, intoned, "we need nothing to live and prosper as much as being united . . . we will be workers for the glory of the fatherland."[3]

Such rituals could be read as a demonstration of the strength of the renewed ties of Mexico and its former invaders, the close partnership of government and business, especially foreign, and the subordinate but public role of workers. Less obvious was the clear hierarchy of space in the celebration for observers as well as the observed: *pelados* without shoes or peasants in traditional manta garb were prohibited by police from the city center, while even "respectable" workers were denied access to events in the exclusive Chapultepec Forest. The patriotic orchestration of events was briefly disturbed at its climax when moments before Díaz initiated the *grito* of independence in the overflowing Zócalo, a localized crowd shouting "¡vivas!" to Francisco Madero, the exiled opposition presidential candidate, was dispersed by police gunfire.[4]

The participation of Mexico City workers in the centennial was symbolic of the effort to put a smooth facade over the cracks of Porfirian social policy. In each of these events, government officials manipulated symbols and rituals to create a vision of national and local unity in which differences of class, or rather the conflicts that arose from such differences, had no place.

This chapter examines the basic tenets of working-class cultures that were transformed into a nascent sense of class among working people during the transformations of the Porfiriato. The centennial celebration proved a final and, in retrospect, unconvincing show of unity between rich and poor, capital and labor, and workers' organizations and the Porfirian government on the eve of the revolution. In the context of the contested presidential election of 1910, whose formal conflicts were played out just months before the centennial, working people found meaning in the traditional historical struggles of liberalism. At the same time, they transformed rituals and symbols of national unity, debating their meanings in the newspapers, meeting halls, and streets of Mexico City. Ultimately, workers reshaped liberal discourse to give it significance to their own struggles in the workplace and in the community.

Working-Class Cultures

Identity among Porfirian workers in Mexico City was shaped but not determined by the changing structures of work and space. Also important were social origins, the experiences of family and neighborhood, preindustrial traditions and beliefs, and daily interactions with members of other classes and the government. Just as the skill level and social background of workers varied, so too did their cultural experiences. In this section I outline some broad patterns of divergent and shared cultural and political meanings among working people. While many of these meanings overlapped with those of Mexicans of various classes, they provided working people with a sense of distinctness from other classes that gave purpose to their actions during the Mexican Revolution.

Many unskilled and casual laborers still had strong ties to the countryside, and the persistence and transformation of rural traditions helped to shape their identity. As noted, over half of the residents of Mexico City at the turn of the century were migrants, whose origins were both rural and urban. Historians have tended to emphasize the gap that existed between city and countryside in Mexico at the time of the revolution, a gap generally perceived in terms of economic and material distinctions or of cultural differences between traditional rural and modern urban societies. Certainly the material changes were significant. Market relations and wage dependence predominated in Mexico City, in contrast to the countryside, where subsistence production and coerced labor systems remained strong. Although some migrants returned to rural areas after periods of work in Mexico City, for most, the economic break with the countryside was definitive.[5]

But if the move to the city meant immersion in a market economy, the break with cultural traditions dominant in the countryside—such as habits of work, leisure, religion, and drinking—was less clear. Many rural traditions were sustained by the continuous influx of rural migrants, many of whom joined family members or former village neighbors who had previously migrated. Adaptation to urban life was not simply a matter of modernization: many rural cultural traditions lingered or were transformed into aspects of urban popular culture shared by many city-born workers.

With the economic and social transformations of Mexico City, the habits of the working and popular classes became a central concern to employers, officials, intellectuals, and the rising middle class. Determined to create a disciplined and productive work force, employers sought to incorporate workers with rural and craft backgrounds into a culture of industrial discipline with an ever-accelerating pace of work. Middle-class reformers, many echoing the concerns of Porfirian officials and employers, sought to civilize the urban masses by remaking them in terms of their own self-image of a moral and modern middle class.[6] While many workers treated their bosses with deference and the humility due social superiors, the battle over their behavior in the shop or in the streets led to quiet struggles and open conflicts. In the process, workers and the popular classes elaborated a working-class culture that was distinctive and resistant to that imposed on them by employers and middle-class reformers.

A central aspect of working-class culture was the continued importance of religion. Certainly at the extremes of religious belief there was a "gulf between the enlightened urban worker and the obscurantist peasant," exemplified during the revolution by the contrast between the devout peasant followers of Zapata and the anticlerical leadership of the Casa del Obrero Mundial. The influence of the Catholic clergy over believers so common in many rural areas was greatly attenuated by the urban environment, by the presence of Protestant sects, and by a modest enforcement of legal restraints on the Catholic Church's public activities. Another attenuation was economic: religious observance in rural communities often entailed continuous donations of money, goods, and alcohol to the cults of specific saints. Among the hardships that Esther

Torres remembered from her native Guanajuato was leaving ten centavos of every peso for the festivals for the Virgin of Guanajuato.[7]

Even so, religious belief remained important to many of the urban popular classes. Porfirian intellectuals viewed the religious practices of the urban poor with suspicion. Manuel Gamio described in 1916 a spectrum of religious observance among Mexicans that ranged from the pagan superstitions of peasants and the popular barrios of Mexico City to the pious, secular, and nationalistic beliefs of the middle classes. Church ceremonies and institutions continued to provide an orienting community as well as occasional charity to recent migrants and down-and-out residents. This role was reinforced by the revived social mission and mild Catholic critique of capitalism rooted in the 1891 papal encyclical *Rerum Novarum* of Leo XIII, which appealed to many workers.[8]

Pervasive religious observance did not necessarily translate into regular attendance at mass. Still, foreign visitors to Mexico City commonly noted the private and public enthusiasm for religious symbols and ceremonies: the candles and icons in homes and workplaces and the popular observances of the feast of the Virgin of Guadalupe, Holy Week, or the blessing of the animals in San Antonio in the streets and churches of the capital. According to one report, more than 120,000 people went to confession on Good Friday in Mexico City in 1910. Many of the urban poor continued, though probably at reduced levels, to undertake religious financial obligations to support celebrations of the Virgin or pay for miracles granted.[9]

In the workplace, religion could provide common ground or a point of conflict between workers and employers. Pious employers perceived religion as a moralizing force on workers whom they regularly described as woefully lacking in moral character. Factories in Mexico City, such as the Buen Tono, contained chapels on their premises, and employers sometimes used religious organizations within the factory to limit worker activities and prevent the organization of more autonomous organizations.

Religion was one element of the attempt by industrialists to extend the totalizing and paternalistic organization of the hacienda. Wallace

Thompson observed in 1921 that foreign and Mexican managers had learned from the hacienda owner that "the most satisfactory way of handling labor in Mexico is to attach it to the industry by personal bonds with owner, manager, or superintendent." While industrialists tried to inculcate workers in modern values and insisted that wages be determined by market forces, they relied at the same time on traditional methods of paternalism and authoritarian control within the workplace. For example, factory owners often distributed clothes or other goods to workers on holidays. The streetcar company prided itself in the gymnasium, library, and billiard room that it offered its most skilled workers. As late as 1920, the director of the Buen Tono cigarette factory explained to a labor inspector, in the face of union demands, that "the Buen Tono, more than a cigarette factory, could very well be called a philanthropic society, for the many benefits that workers receive and because the administration does everything possible for the good of its workers." Religion thus supplemented the benefits, celebrations, and acts of charity by which industrialists sought to elicit loyalty and submission among workers.[10] For many workers, especially women, the space provided for religious observance in the workplace provided assurances against fears of a factory environment seen as morally corrupting.

But religious observance could also be a source of conflict. Workers demanded or simply took time off from work for religious holidays, among other reasons, while employers sought predictability and increased productivity by reducing the number of religious holidays observed each year and fined or fired workers for their absences. For example, over half of the workers of the Fábrica San Idelfonso were fired in June 1912 for abandoning work after lunch to honor Corpus Christi. On the other extreme, Protestant and organized workers in some factories complained that their jobs depended on continued membership in Catholic religious organizations or that charges for religious observance were discounted from their pay.[11]

The persistent observance of religious holidays provided workers with opportunities for rest and celebration, both of which often involved drinking, which was a central point of conflict with employers. Workers drank pulque at home, during their lunch break, and in and outside of the workplace. Drinking patterns were often rooted in craft and rural traditions, where workers had greater control over their time. Porfirian criminologist Julio Guerrero observed in 1901, certainly with some exaggeration, that "artisans suspend their tasks each hour or half hour to go to the pulquería." Foreign observers and government officials concerned with the condition of the working class estimated that workers consumed between 10 and 17 percent of their meager monthly income on alcohol, usually pulque. A typical comment by the Spaniard Julio Sesto suggests the common association many middle-class observers made between drinking and other working-class problems. Of the salary that common laborers might earn, explained Sesto, they "drink half of it daily in pulque or alcohol, and the rest of it they drink in one sitting on Saturday. When any is left over, they give it to their women: when there isn't, they give her a beating."[12]

Though employers saw drink as the scourge of the working class, many felt obliged to serve modest amounts of pulque to workers on breaks rather than have them indulge outside the premises, and they could face open resistance from workers if daily servings were eliminated. At the same time, employers used the paradox of impoverished workers who spent their earnings on alcohol to justify low salaries. Why pay more, they asked, if workers would simply work less and drink more?[13]

In spite of periodic government attempts to restrict the sale of alcohol, it remained readily available, in part because taxes on alcohol were central to municipal revenues. Guerrero counted in the Federal District in 1896 some 458 stores that sold alcohol and 1,761 pulque outlets, or one establishment for every 149 inhabitants, not including clandestine stands run out of houses and on street corners. Alcohol was consumed at public dances as well as gambling houses, brothels, and religious celebrations. Workers generally received their pay after work on Saturday, and many drank through Sunday, taking "San Lunes" off to recuperate. Middle-class writers often lamented the tradition of "San Lunes, pretext for laziness, the beginning of domestic disasters and moral catastrophes in which everything drowns, even one's honor." Even some working women went after work to pulquerías, several of which had separate rooms where women could drink.[14] Degrees of devotion to pulque and the Virgin of Guadalupe might vary greatly by sex, but for the most part, many working men and women continued to exalt in both customs, and both habits distanced them somewhat from skilled workers as well as from employers and middle-class reformers, who lamented the environment of drinking, prostitution, and fighting that they felt prevailed in the streets of many of the working-class neighborhoods of Mexico City.

As historians of the daily life of workers have observed, such patterns of behavior among workers attest more to the strength of working-class culture than to the moral decadence observed by middle-class reformers. Many workers shared a code of honor with deep rural roots that identified virility with the capacity to drink large amounts of alcohol. As William French has argued for the case of Chihuahuan miners, the occasions and places at which drinking occurred were important autonomous spaces of sociability in the lives of working people, places where the "working class imposed their own schedule and rules of behavior," which included fighting over slights of honor. In Mexico City, where workers lived separate from their place of work and company housing was limited, the supervision of bosses rarely extended beyond the factory or workshop. Cantinas, pulquerías, cinemas, and popular theaters allowed for an environment in which "working people fashioned an independence from the patriarchal claims of their employers." Such spaces of sociability could also become places of organization, as cantinas, cafes, cinemas, and the patios of tenement houses often doubled as locales for regular meetings of working-class organizations.[15]

At the same time, many of Mexico City's skilled craftworkers and service workers and some factory workers rejected the values of "culto y cantina" and shared many of the modern or developmentalist values of thrift, sobriety, education, and hard work advocated by employers, officials, and middle-class reformers. The Great League of Carpenters (Gran Liga de Carpinteros), for example, promised in its statutes to fight against the custom of "San Lunes." The weekly San Lunes, purportedly "by and for workers," continually urged its readers to "work in peace, obey the laws, and abandon the vice of drinking." Skilled workers were usually literate and enthusiastically absorbed secular ideas rooted in individualism, rationalism, and respect for the rule of law. Outside of the workplace, they took pride in, and strained their family budgets in order to wear, the suits and ties of "*gente decente.*" A small but growing percentage opted for one of the Protestant sects that, according to Jean-Pierre Bastian, offered Mexican workers who faced industrial change "an ideology that justifies displacement and centers its discourse on self-discipline and the values linked to industrial work."[16]

To the extent that religious beliefs remained important to skilled workers, they did not necessarily contradict or compete with workers' allegiance to aspects of liberalism such as the separation of church and state or their devotion to anticlerical heroes such as Juárez. Mutualist organizations traditionally avoided extreme anticlericalism while insisting on religious tolerance in their statutes. Mutualist ceremonies and marches beginning in the Restored Republic of Juárez began to blend the religious and the secular. Indeed, the Virgin of Guadalupe was to some extent nationalized and secularized—inextricably and deliberately tied to representations of Mexican nationhood through the figure of Father Hidalgo, hero of Independence Day, and through the state-sponsored coronation of the Virgin of Guadalupe in 1895.[17]

Distinct from the paternalism that often bound employers and unskilled workers, many skilled workers saw industrialists as their equals and counterparts within the productive classes. The affinity of workers with industrialists is suggested by the veneration some workers held for Esteban de Antuñano, who first introduced mechanized cotton looms in the 1830s and later fell in battle against the occupying French army. Pascual Mendoza, a key textile leader from Puebla during the 1907 textile conflict, named his workers' society the Esteban de Antuñano Workers League (Liga Obrera Esteban de Antuñano) and further honored the industrialist in his poetry.[18]

These workers often expressed a deep faith in progress that incorporated a secularized religious imagery. The minor poet and working-class leader Angel Montalvo, in his 1909 poem "El Artesano" (The artisan), called the artisan the "priest of work" and went on to proclaim, "blessed is he who professes faith in the religion of work." What distinguished these workers' faith from that of other progressive Porfirians is that they elaborated and transformed developmentalist ideology in a way that put workers at the center of national progress, on equal or even superior footing with the other part of the industrial classes, the bosses. This aspect of working-class culture is most apparent and eloquent in the writings of Fernando Celada, a printer and poet of humble origins and a frequent contributor to many Mexico City working-class and opposition newspapers. Celada's popularity among workers during the Porfiriato earned him the title "the poet of the proletariat" (el cantor del proletariado). In Celada's poems the progress of workers, integral to that of the nation, became a religion, with hard work being its prayers and penance and the machines and tools of work being its icons, as in these verses from "En la fábrica" (In the factory):

The machinery clatters with sovereign echoes
and, over the grandeur of that giant altar,
the noble pueblo raises with its million hands,
the hosts with which it returns diligently home.

Oh struggle of the poor! Oh battle of the arts!
your vigor is progress, your progress is an altar:
every open factory, for you is a bulwark,
every worker a soldier, every loom a triumph.[19]

At the same time that Celada evoked the progress of labor, he summoned workers' patriotism and a sense of their historical role as Mexican citizens. The poem "En la Fragua" (In the forge), published in the working-class paper El Paladín in the midst of Madero's 1910 election campaign, evokes the heat, sparks, and masculine exertion of an artisan in his foundry. The blacksmith and the metal under his hammer become metaphors for the nation. In the poem, the molten mass of metal speaks to the smith, reminding him that in the past he (the metal) had been forged into instruments of destruction (daggers and enslaving chains). But now that "the insolent foreigner no longer traffics with the Fatherland"—a reference to mid-nineteenth-century interventions by the United States and France—he commands the smith to "make of me a plow, a rail, a hammer, wire, a locomotive; / Make me a creative force for universal progress." In the final verse the metal warns that, if the Fatherland suffers any treachery, the smith should once again "forge me into a battle arm, an arm of liberty!" In this double metaphor, the worker becomes in the smith the powerful laborer for progress and in the molten iron, the raw material of nation building. Implicit in this imagery is a kind of symbolic repositioning of urban workers at the center of the nation's history. Both chords—that of worker and citizen—struck a deep note in working people.[20]

As suggested by Celada's poems, the public historical memory of workers often included references to the role of the pueblo in defending the liberal 1857 constitution and helping to expel the French in the 1860s. Given the image of workers as the central component of *el pueblo*, the implication, at times fairly direct, was that workers played a central role in defense of the nation and liberal reforms. To what extent this memory was based on the actual mobilization of Mexico City workers—whether as workers or citizens—is unclear. Justo Sierra wrote in 1900 that Mexico City workers had viewed the reform wars of the 1850s with hostility, not because of any defense of the Catholic Church or conservatives on their part, but because the wars had deteriorated employment and living conditions in the capital and the liberals had conscripted a good portion of the population by force. There is some evidence of mobilization among urban workers in the fight against the French intervention in the 1860s, particularly in some of the factory towns of the Federal District.[21] But given that the liberal republican order was established previous to the industrial changes that created a significant urban working class, the elaboration of such a historical memory among workers is in itself significant, apart from its historical accuracy.

From the assertion that they had helped consolidate a liberal republic against foreign intervention, workers derived many meaningful symbols and ideologies shared with the middle class and the Porfirian elite. Mutualist organizations throughout the Restored Republic and Porfiriato took the name of national heroes, celebrated national holidays such as 16 September (Independence Day) or 5 May (the defeat of the French at Puebla) within their organizations, and even chose the dates of key national holidays on which to found their organizations. Starting in the

1870s, government officials began to encourage the participation of workers' organizations in public parades to stimulate patriotism and devotion to liberal heroes and principles.[22]

The selective appropriation of liberalism by workers was in many ways similar to that of the countryside, where, as suggested by recent research, a powerful strain of "popular liberalism" coexisted and conflicted with both the doctrinaire liberalism of some intellectuals and the more conservative liberalism shared by many elites. While many skilled workers partook of a developmentalism and republican liberalism that was urban and somewhat middle class in nature, their struggles to assert themselves in the political sphere and the workplace led them to reshape liberalism in ways distinct from that of its middle-class proponents. This popular liberalism is clear in the concept of a "Republic of Work" elaborated in the 1870s by workers of the Gran Círculo de Obreros, who attempted to reconcile their roles as workers and citizens, seeking solidarity and collective representation within a liberal order that guaranteed, in theory, only the representation of individuals.[23]

Progressive industrial values and liberal republican symbols could be sources of loyalty or resistance to the existing order. One basis for such a shift was economic. Changes in the nature and concentration of production, slipping wages, long hours, unemployment, and frequent abuse led many Mexican workers over time to view the industrial system as one of great injustices in which their progress did not equal their efforts or expectations. Increasingly at odds with an industrial structure that they felt exploited them, many workers began to identify their own class interests as different from those of other industrial classes.

Elements of a critique of the Porfirian system can be traced in the media aimed at an audience of workers. Given the heavy censorship of the Porfiriato, criticism often came at an allegorical level. Again the poetry of Celada is suggestive and representative. Celada, like the popular engraver José Guadalupe Posada, was a reluctant rebel: he depended periodically on government employment and briefly edited in 1909 a newspaper that supported Vice President Ramón Corral against rival candidate Bernardo Reyes. But he also collaborated with a variety of opposition newspapers and, according to one biographer, spent time in jail for his ideas.[24] But the industrial morality and patriotism of Celada and of many skilled workers was different from that aggressively promoted by industrialists and politicians in their attempts to smooth the transition of workers to industrial discipline and to limit costly conflicts with workers.

A sense of moral betrayal of workers by the industrial system is clear in an early theatrical monologue written by Celada in 1898. In the extended monologue *En capilla* (In the chapel), an unemployed worker condemned to death for robbery and murder considers the motives and culpability for his crime from a prison chapel. Going from factory to workshop, he explains,

> I implored protection
> And there was no friendly hand;
> I asked for work, and in vain;
>
> . . . .
>
> And I became a murderer and robbed;
> My children had not eaten!
>
> . . . .
>
> The vile and stingy bourgeois thinks
> In his blind arrogance,
> That there must not be any honor
> Below the denim shirt.[25]

This worker is a victim of industrial change rather than a key protagonist in the nation's development. But rather than blaming himself, or by extension the perceived moral vices of all marginalized workers, Celada's character justifies the crime and puts the blame on a different class. The use of the term "bourgeois" in this poem and in other literary and journalistic writings suggests an emerging sense of difference between the interests of workers and those of other classes, in this case, industrialists. Such writings and the working-class press often denounced the rich in general, or more specifically the foremen, usurers, and policemen who abused and exploited workers. More systematic critiques attacked "monopolies" of production and distribution and frequently linked the exploitation of workers to the presence of foreigners in the economy, playing on the roots of Mexican patriotism in the fight against foreign intervention. For example, an anonymous working-class version of the Apostles' Creed, published in La Guacamaya, intoned faith in progress and denounced exploitation: "I believe in the all-powerful God of Work, creator of human happiness, and in Progress, his only son," who was "crucified, died and buried by the indolence of the exploiters of the proletariat" before rising up to "the heavens of industry." Pascual Mendoza, the Puebla textile worker who commemorated the industrialist Antuñano, also denounced in his poetry that "any foreigner oppresses with insolence" the worker who "suffers misfortune for a crumb of bread."[26]

It is worth noting the extremely gendered iconography of almost all of these male working-class poets. The factory or shop is a place of manly sweat and muscular exertion, and the patriotic callings of the worker-turned-soldier are similarly masculine. In Celada's celebration of work and popular patriotism, women are neither workers nor citizens but rather the wives and mothers for whom men have the responsibility of providing and protecting.

A relevant question is how extensively these poems reached working people. Skilled workers might be able to buy a weekly newspaper, as a labor inspector noted for many tailors, or attend meetings of working-class groups where such poems were discussed. By contrast, many unskilled workers were illiterate or newly literate and were much less likely to hear or read the formal poetry and denunciations of this group of working-class poets and spokesmen. However, a similar class-based perspective took shape in the burgeoning penny press at the beginning of the century, which with its widespread diffusion reflected or at least helped shape the views of large sectors of the working class. In her study of the Porfirian penny press, Maria Elena Díaz convincingly argues that this medium reflected the development of a working-class consciousness, "one, in effect, which narrowed its 'popular' constituency to an urban 'working class' by delineating this identity against other groups, by focusing particularly on issues related to that group, and by expressing

them in the language of that group." Satirical weeklies such as El Ahui-
zote, El Diablito Rojo, and La Guacamaya incorporated writers from humble
backgrounds, publicly identified with the working class, and wrote for a
working-class audience. La Guacamaya claimed a peak circulation of
twenty-nine thousand, compared to that of the major daily El Imparcial,
which ranged between forty thousand and one hundred thousand. In
these media, images were as important as the text, and even the verse
and prose captured much of the rhythm of street language, a stylistic in-
novation that often provoked the ire of the formal press. Illustrated by
men such as José Guadalupe Posada, these newspapers used satire to
denounce the abuses committed against workers in a way that was often
more biting than the allegory of working-class poetry or the cautious denunciations of the working-class press. Indeed, the sporadic publication record of these newspapers was as much a result of periodic forced
closings as it was of financial problems.[27]

Of course the penny press had its critics not only among the formal
dailies with close ties to the government, such as El Imparcial, but also
among more sober newspapers aimed at the working class. In 1909, the
mutualist El Obrero Mexicano denounced the penny press as "publications
that under deceptive masks hide grim ambitions, manifestos of pom-
pous fabrication and unhealthy ideas . . . that declare themselves em-
phatically organs of the working class . . . that introduce themselves fur-
tively in the temples of work and in the poor and honest homes of the
worker." While such statements probably reflect a real rejection of the
class perspective of the penny press by many workers who clung to mutualist ideas, that El Obrero Mexicano, which was closely tied to the governor of the Federal District, would single out the penny press for attack
suggests that the penny press was perceived as a threat and acknowl-
edges the increasing importance of a class-based perspective among
many sectors of the working class.

Together, the working-class and popular penny press developed a critique of economic and political aspects of the Porfirian system that,
while rarely challenging the basic premises of the economic and political order, allowed working people to articulate their interests as apart
from that of other groups. Inspired by a homemade version of a labor

theory of value, one that put them at the center of national progress, many skilled workers began to denounce the injustices in the economic system, often blaming speculators, monopolists, and foreigners.[28] An implicit assumption of this critique was that conditions for workers would improve if employers, the rich, or political authorities were made aware of their situation and learned to respect workers. "They [employers] should be conscientious in treating the worker," intoned Mendoza in one poem. Angel Montalvo, in a poem rhetorically addressed to the wealthy, insisted that they "be the friend of the worker," for he builds your palaces and brings you water when you are thirsty, and "is the only one that can give you what you desire." Many workers looked to government authorities to ameliorate abuses, an attitude effectively represented by a Posada print in which a worker in overalls stands before Porfirio Díaz in the presidential palace and points to a man beating workers in front of a factory. "You, great friend of the workers," he tells the outraged president, "Look at the fury of the slave drivers and the abuses of the foreman!" By contrast, a few working-class newspapers, such as El Diablito Bromista, publicly moved beyond attempts to enlighten bad employers and appeal to authorities and instead urged workers to organize and resist, even supporting strikes.[29]

If the tendency of workers to appeal to political authorities for justice remained strong, many of these media increasingly came to see many working-class problems as rooted in the corruption and abuses of political authorities themselves and linked the abuses of the economic system to those of the political system. This critique was usually aimed at generic, lower-level political authorities such as the local prefects (jefes políticos), rather than high officials, and almost never at Díaz himself. For example, a typical cartoon of the satirical newspaper El Ahuizotito in 1908 showed a humble barefoot worker, labeled "pueblo obrero," being kicked and beaten by a fat industrialist whose whip identifies him as the "cacicazgo de patrones" (tyranny of bosses). Gleefully watching by his side is a uniformed man whose hat reads "autoridad" (authority). The poem that followed began, "Bossism rules from January to January, From border to border, from foreman [jefe] to worker." The Spanish term "jefe" can refer to either local prefects or bosses, suggesting, along with the image, a close link between authoritarian abuse at work and in politics.[30] The emerging perception by many workers that many of the conditions and abuses they suffered were the result of political corruption helps to explain their response to Madero's liberal democratic challenge to the Díaz regime in the 1910 elections.

The critique that emerged from the working-class and penny press during the Porfiriato derived from, and was ultimately limited by, the dominant discursive context of a reformist democratic liberalism. By consecrating the 1857 constitution, workers accepted and defended a liberal republican order that guaranteed individual over collective rights. But while working-class political culture was rooted in an acceptance of a liberal democratic and capitalist system, workers attempted to transform liberal ideologies in ways that spoke to their own conditions and allowed them to critique aspects of the industrial and political systems. Some workers' groups and their newspapers, such as the railroad employees' Great Mexican League (Gran Liga Mexicana) and their biweekly El Ferrocarrilero, gave cautious support to the efforts of the exiled and increasingly anarchist-influenced leaders of the Mexican Liberal Party (Partido Liberal Mexicano, or PLM) to publish Regeneración in Mexico. These groups incorporated some of the vocabulary and demands of the PLM, though not its increasingly anarchist ideology or its call for armed rebellion.[31] The growing criticism of the government and the demand for justice, particularly among skilled workers, gained momentum during the last decade of the Porfiriato and provided a basis for their support of the liberal political opposition to Porfirio Díaz.

Though the move toward opposition was led by a minority of skilled workers and sympathetic writers and intellectuals, the mass of unskilled workers was neither unaffected nor left behind. Unskilled workers were also subject to the tensions between their values and those of the workplace and of larger society. Their reaction to the pace and organization of mass production often manifested itself in individual forms of resistance as well as collective actions and spontaneous strikes. Outside of the workplace or during periods of unemployment, members of these social groups clung to traditional moral norms concerning authorities, their social superiors, their public behavior, and the terms of their participation in the market economy. These norms were increasingly violated during the Porfiriato by the ostentation of the wealthy, the concentration of foreigners in commerce and manufacturing, the segregation of workers and the poor into their own neighborhoods, the abuses of political authorities, and the rising costs of housing and other market goods. Unskilled workers were given to riots and the traditional justice of the crowd, as well as more isolated street insolence, rebelliousness and attacks on authorities and the wealthy.

Of greater significance during the revolution were moments when this vernacular tradition of rebellion among unskilled and traditional workers infused or complemented the spirit of opposition led by "progressive" workers, when working-class organizations joined skilled and unskilled workers as a class and linked those imbued with industrial and traditional values. While this alliance rarely led to the type of insurrection that characterized much of the Mexican countryside, it challenged the urban social system through a variety of types of mobilization.

Mutualism

The type of worker organization most prominent and most tolerated in Porfirian society, as suggested by the centenary celebration, was the mutual aid society. Mutualist organizations provided an important form of sociability and identification among workers and remained the key vehicle for channeling their aspirations during the long transition from guilds to unions.

Mutualist societies emerged in the vacuum that resulted from the disappearance of previous colonial structures by which artisans had organized access to labor, markets, and security—namely guilds (*gremios*) and confraternities (*cofradías*). In the colonial period, guilds had allowed maestros, and to a lesser extent journeymen, a tight control over entrance into the different crafts as well as over the price of the manufactured goods. Their control was consolidated politically through organic ties to local government, in particular to the city councils. The confraternity was a parallel structure that provided space for religious worship outside of work and the traditional church hierarchy and often accumulated considerable property. Confraternities offered artisans and their families aid in times of unemployment, sickness, and death. Guilds were gradually undermined in the late colonial period by economic growth and liberalizing laws implemented by Bourbon reformers and reinforced later by republicans. Similarly, confraternities received their deathblow in the 1850s with the disentailment of church property.[32]

With liberal reforms, nineteenth-century artisans lost both their controls over the labor market and their direct links to political power. The liberal constitution of 1857 provided several guarantees that would become central to workers' perceptions of their rights from midcentury on, in particular the right as individuals to associate (Article 9), the freedom to work and receive the just fruits of one's labor, specifically ending forced or unremunerated labor and limits on the exercise of any profession (Articles 3, 4, and 5), and freedom from monopolies (Article 28). At the same time, workers' organizations remained weak in the absence of laws giving them formal legal identity (*personalidad jurídica*), which would give them stability and allow them to press collective demands within the workplace and in the judicial system.[33]

In this context, mutual aid societies emerged in the mid–nineteenth century shorn of most of the corporate and hierarchical structure of the guild yet limited in their possible actions. As voluntary organizations with no formal protection and with clear restrictions on their functions, mutual aid societies existed precariously in Mexico throughout much of the last half of the nineteenth century. In function they resembled more the colonial confraternities than the guilds, since their primary concern was to provide security for members in times of poor health, injury, unemployment, or death. Workers contributed a regular monthly quota, and in return they or their families received support in times of need. A few societies, generally among more skilled and better-paid craftworkers, established cooperative shops, consumer societies, and credit banks that allowed members to set up their own shops or work in cooperatives that might provide alternatives to the challenges of expanding mechanized industry.[34]

In addition, mutual aid societies took seriously the task of educating and providing cultural sustenance to their members, establishing their own classes or schools independently or in collaboration with the government. Just as important, these societies fulfilled an important function of sociability among workers, offering them and their families the opportunity to engage in sports and recreation, dances, and cultural reunions, where they could listen to and perform opera or corridos and recite the romantic poetry of European, Mexican, or their own working-class poets. Similarly, they undertook civic and patriotic celebrations within their organizations and participated in those organized by political authorities.[35]

The lack of clear financial regulations for mutualist societies, the reluctance or inability of members to pay quotas, the occasional embezzlement by officers, the fluctuating employment of many members, and periodic recessions, inflation, and epidemics that depleted sickness and unemployment funds all made the mutualist organizations notoriously unstable and subject to closings. Still, there were several organizations of exceptional longevity and others that reestablished themselves over time. At least one of these, the Mutual Society of Tailors (Sociedad Mutua de Sastres), claimed in 1912 continuous existence from 1864. At least sixty-two mutual aid societies existed in Mexico City in 1902.[36]

Traditionally, male workers of a particular or related skilled trade organized mutualist societies, a legacy of the old guild structure. The most successful and independent societies were those of skilled and relatively affluent craft, commercial, or clerical workers, since most others could barely squeeze their daily needs from their wages, let alone pay the monthly quota of one or more pesos usually required by mutual aid societies. For example, the small Society of Watchmakers, Jewelers, and Engravers (Sociedad de Relojeros, Joyeros y Grabadores), organized in Mexico City in 1901, was made up of a handful of men from each related branch. Each member paid 1 peso a month in dues and in return received between 1.5 and 3 pesos daily in case of sickness, or his family received 25 pesos in the case of his death. The Mutualist Society of Commercial Employees (Sociedad Mutualista Empleados de Comercio) was founded in 1892 and included as many as one thousand shop owners, employees, and traveling salesmen (*factores*), including such upper-level employees as the director of the Mexican Telephone and Telegraph

Company. In each of these societies, members might be owners of modest shops as well as paid employees, though many societies put limits on the capital investment of shops owned by members, since, according to one society, "the workers could not be at the side of the owners." Others brought together workers of a single workplace, most often the textile factory workers of the Federal District.[37]

In turn-of-the-century Mexico City, as the boundaries between traditional crafts were increasingly undermined by economic and technical changes and where workers might practice a variety of occupations during a short period, a single mutualist society often included workers from a variety of unrelated professions. For example, the "Unión y Amistad" of Bakers, founded in 1884, harbored tailors, carpenters, bricklayers, and others, in spite of its name. The main instrument of exclusivity of these societies, besides gender and moral character, was the level of the monthly quota. Other mutual aid societies might be made up of migrants born in the same state, friends (sociedad "Los Buenos Amigos"), residents of a particular neighborhood (precursor of the present-day *tanda*, or forced savings plan), or those based in church parishes, direct heir to the colonial confraternity.[38]

A few mutualist societies catered exclusively to women and emphasized their role as wives or mothers, such as the society "La Buena Madre," the mutualista "El Tesoro del Hogar," and the society for wives of members of "Unión y Amistad." The Catholic Church sponsored mutualist societies for specific groups of workers, in particular the Obreras Guadalupanas and the Association of Catholic Servants of Santa Zita (Asociación de Sirvientas Católicas de Santa Zita), groups that had clear evangelical motives. For example, the goals of the latter were the "moralization of women servants through the teaching of Christian Doctrine and the imitation of the heroic virtues of the celestial Patroness."[39] Other societies, such as the mutual-social society "Miguel Hidalgo y Costilla," routinely included women as members as well as men.

A few religious-based worker confraternities seem to have lingered on or been formed after the midcentury reforms, such as the Patriotic Religious Circle of Artisans (Círculo Patriotica Religioso de Artesanos), which was formed in 1887 to show that although workers had other defects they suffered no "lack of love for their fatherland and their religion." Mutualist organizations after the 1850s generally forbade formal church activities in meetings, but the Catholic Church was reluctant to cede its influence over workers. Inspired by the social mission of Leo XIII's *Rerum Novarum*, the Catholic Church began in the 1890s to aggressively recruit workers into church-based organizations, with some success. The Catholic Workers Center (Centro Católico Obrero) reported 1,255 members in various branches in the Federal District in 1912. Although these organizations duplicated many of the functions of mutualist societies, they created an atmosphere distinct from the more secular and democratic mutualist societies. For example, they transformed the traditional mutualist motto "One for all, and all for one" into "Some for others, and God for all." Similarly, the Catholic Workers Center was unconcerned with the practice or appearance of internal democracy: the church hierarchy itself filled leadership positions and provided most of the funds for mutualist programs, and members were "brothers" instead of "*socios*" and paid alms (*limosnas*) instead of dues. Though Catholic worker organizations were significant in Mexico City in the late Porfiriato, they were far more successful in such areas as Zamora and Guadalajara.[40] By contrast, Protestants rarely attempted to create exclusive religious worker organizations in Mexico City or elsewhere in Mexico, though many Protestant workers joined and even founded secular mutualist societies.[41]

Various attempts were made throughout the Restored Republic and the Porfiriato to centralize mutual aid societies regionally and nationally, bringing together a variety of artisans and waged craft and factory workers. One of the most important was the Gran Círculo de Obreros, formed in 1872, which represented in many ways the culmination of the golden age of mutualism. The Gran Círculo joined organizations of artisans and factory workers, including many outside the Federal District, in a tightly structured umbrella organization that, before its demise in 1883, veered from militant independence in its early years to a stance of relative moderation toward employers and political endorsements of officials. Its successors, the Congreso Obrero and closely allied Convención Radical, provided a far weaker but persistent structure among primarily craft-based mutualist societies in Mexico City until their dissolution in 1903. Both organizations remained largely under the influence of a handful of overlapping working-class leaders who dominated the board of directors, limited the active participation of affiliated mutualist societies, and maintained close ties to the government.[42] A final attempt to centralize mutualist organizations in Mexico City occurred in 1910, on the eve of the revolution, with the formation of the Great Workers League (Gran Liga Obrera) and the Mutualist and Moralizing Society of Workers of the Federal District (Sociedad Mutualista y Moralizadora de Obreros del Distrito Federal). But both organizations would soon be marginalized in the face of events and new forms of worker organization.

The traditional language of mutualism in Mexico invoked patriotism (usually linked to obedience to authorities), hard work, and moral behavior, values evidenced in the names of the societies. Although mutual aid societies sometimes sheltered anarchists and socialists who advocated struggle against employers and the state, the more dominant mutualist idiom, and the one strongly encouraged by officials and employers, spoke not only of unity among workers but also of unity between workers and their bosses. This language extended to areas increasingly dominated by large capitalist enterprises. For example, the symbol of a textile workers' mutualist organization, the Society of Free Workers (Sociedad de Obreros Libres), was two arms with hands clasped, one the suited arm of an employer, the other covered in the coarse cloth of a worker.[43]

Employers often encouraged mutualist societies, since their discourse was usually one of discipline and morality and their functions provided benefits to workers that might otherwise fall on the business itself. Some factory owners created their own mutual aid societies—in the case of the Excelsior shoe factory, the owner, Carlos Zetina, appointed his accountant to be the presiding officer of the factory's mutualist society and automatically deducted dues from workers' salaries. At the same time, employers, the church, and government authorities sought to discourage—in the words of the Great Workers League—any "rancor" (rencilla) or antagonistic feelings that might detract from national unity and progress. The financial dependence of many mutualist organizations on donations from employers and prominent political figures, who often became "honorary members," in turn limited their actions and ideology. When in 1907 the Mutualist Center (Centro Mutualista), a short-lived umbrella group for mutual aid societies throughout the country, repeated its motto "One for all, and all for one," they attributed the words to Jesus ("*del Mártir del Gólgota*"), invoking a different type of unity, between employers and employees, rather than that advocated by European radicalism. In spite of the support of many Porfirian elites for mutualist societies and their official discourse of morality and unity across classes, many shared the view of one observer that "although mutualism has achieved great advances in the last twenty years, it has still not managed to inculcate in its associates all the ideas of order, of morality, and of altruism that constitute the personal and collective happiness of some European peoples."[44]

Because of the ambiguities of the constitution and the civil code concerning workers' organizations and the strike, there was limited scope during the Porfiriato for workers' organizations that might operate as agents of negotiation or confrontation with employers. The liberal lawyer Guillermo Prieto argued in 1876, drawing from European socialist ideas of the time, that since labor is the worker's property, "the strike is the right of property of workers, protected by the right of association, to avoid the tyranny of capital."[45]

But owners of factories and shops and their political allies found ample leeway for denying workers this recourse. Abstract principles gave way to the realities of the power structure and local legal codes. The 1871 penal code of the Federal District, for example, provided for up to three months of jail and a fine of five hundred pesos for the use of "physical or moral violence with the object of raising wages of workers or impeding the free exercise of industry or work." Such arbitrary laws, often justified with liberal antimonopoly rhetoric, effectively limited the occurrence of mutualist-sponsored strikes.[46]

The limited capacity of mutual aid societies to mediate worker-employer conflicts was further strained by the changes in the economic structure of production and the urban labor force that occurred at the turn of the century. As a result, strikes and conflicts often occurred spontaneously, without or even in spite of the existence of a formal organization, as was probably the case in the famous Cananea strike of 1906. Still, mutualist societies occasionally provided a focal point and strike funds for worker discontent, becoming in effect societies of resistance during moments of conflict. This transformation occurred most frequently when mutual aid societies were based in a single workplace or industrial sector, particularly in textile factories or among large service and transport industries whose affiliated branches spread throughout the country. Such had been the case with the recently formed Gran Círculo de Obreros in the textile conflict of 1906–7 and with the Union of Mexican Mechanics in the railroad strike of 1906, in which key demands were the recognition of their organizations and the right to negotiate a collective work contract. In fact, ostensibly mutualist organizations in these sectors had for the most part outgrown mutualist forms and in their demands and actions resembled trade and industrial unions in all but name. The example of the Union of Mexican Mechanics may have in turn inspired Mexico City carpenters in 1908 and tailors in 1909 to form single "great leagues" of workers for each occupation.[47] In most sectors of Mexico City in 1910, mutual aid societies had limited success in satisfying the most basic security needs of workers and rarely made direct demands on employers. The need for new forms of organization and an explicit guarantee of the right of workers to organize and strike remained paramount.

Mutualist Politics: "The Strong Arm and Protecting Hand"

The view of Porfirian labor policy as one of uninterrupted repression, nakedly revealed at the strikes of Río Blanco and Cananea in 1906–7, was formulated by contemporary critics of the regime and later elaborated by those who looked back through the official lens of the revolution. But the Díaz government neither relied completely on repression nor left the relations between capital and labor entirely to the market. Throughout much of the late 1870s and 1880s, Díaz developed a series of strategies to encourage moderate labor organizations. His government provided subsidies and meeting places for labor organizations and political rewards to working-class leaders who supported the regime, in particular the Gran Círculo de Obreros, the Congreso Obrero, and the related Convención Radical in Mexico City, organizations that were coaxed and forced to abandon their initial militancy.

Early attempts to incorporate labor organizations into the Porfirian political consensus coincided with the political needs of Díaz to first achieve and then legitimate the military overthrow of the government of Juárez's successor, Lerdo de Tejada. Such policies were not random initiatives from above or entirely the products of political machines; instead, they were official responses to working-class claims in the workplace and on the new political order and to government fears of the potential appeal that militant leaders and ideologies might have for many workers. Government incentives succeeded in part because Díaz had genuine support among workers at the beginning of his regime in 1876. For many urban workers, the mestizo general, surviving hero of many key battles against the French, seemed to embody many of their aspirations of popular liberalism that were rooted in the constitution of 1857, not least of which were his initial promises of no reelection and rule by law.[48]

At the same time, the Díaz regime from its onset used repression to dissuade radical worker organizations and incentives to encourage moderates and channel their demands. Militant and anarchist-inspired workers who rejected all relations with the government were marginalized through imprisonment, military conscription, or a usually fatal stint of forced labor on plantations of the Yucatán or the Valle Nacional. If they were foreigners, they could be deported under Article 33 of the constitution. More moderate leaders of working-class organizations turned to public officials for support for their organizations and for help in mediating conflicts that arose in the workplace.[49]

In addition, the lack of a legal framework to legitimize labor organizations and negotiations with employers predisposed many workers to seek political protection. When the concerns of organized workers turned periodically from mutual aid to struggles against employers in the second half of the nineteenth century, their organizations pursued two distinct tendencies or strategies in their labor conflicts—one social, the other political. Some organizations, at least some of the time, chose to directly confront employers in a private, social struggle without the intervention of authorities. Other organizations, at least some of the time, turned to political authorities to mediate their conflicts with employers or to pass public laws to ameliorate working conditions. In return, political leaders looked to urban workers for political support. For example, in 1876 the Gran Círculo intervened in the presidential succession to support President Lerdo de Tejada, who was soon toppled by the military coup of Porfirio Díaz. After the Gran Círculo split in 1877, one faction began to collaborate with Porfirio Díaz.[50]

Carlos Illades argues that the juridical weakness of worker organizations in the mid-nineteenth century in turn shaped the nature of the political participation of workers. While most mutual aid societies officially rejected political participation, "the leadership of mutualist associations fulfilled the function of connecting civil and political spaces, the private with the public, previously unified and occupied by artisanal corporations." Political alliances allowed working-class leaders, often artisans, to regularly participate as electors in elections (still indirect) and to negotiate positions as candidates on tickets (planillas) headed by political bosses or factions, tickets that included workers but were never dominated by them. The result of this collaboration with labor leaders was "a type of patronage machine reinforced by the workers' press, calling on workers to vote." In the Restored Republic and beyond, this political machine allowed working-class leaders to regularly be elected as councilmen (regidores) on the city council, a presence that resembled the old organic link between guilds and the municipal government. In the 1880s and 1890s, Pedro Ordoñez, the president of the moderate Congreso Obrero, sat as councilman, as did at least two other labor leaders (Abraham Chávez and José Barrera). At least one working-class intermediary, the printer and director of El Hijo del Trabajo, Francisco de Paula González, even managed to be elected to Congress.[51]

At the same time, the ties of labor leaders to political power tended to reinforce antidemocratic practices within many mutualist organizations. In spite of democratic forms, directive councils commonly

"launched an official candidate" in internal elections, which perpetuated power in the hands of a single person or in a small group of leaders
with ties to political authorities. In the absence of secret balloting, voting outcomes tended to be extremely lopsided toward the official candidate.[52]

The détente between labor and the Porfirian state continued through
the early 1890s. In 1888, and again in 1892, amid substantial opposition
among liberal groups to the second and third reelection of Díaz, the
Convención Radical in Mexico City endorsed Díaz and applauded his fiscal policies. But support among workers as well as among other classes
for the government of Díaz ebbed after the first decades of Porfirian
domination, not least because of his failure to establish free elections
and the rotation of public office, the imposition of the *jefes políticos*, and
related abuses that coincided with the increasing centralization of the
federal government and its domination after 1895 by the *científico* circle
led by Finance Minister José I. Limantour. Worker participation in reelection rallies became less than spontaneous, to the extent that one foreign tourist who stumbled on a reelection parade was said to have in-
quired whether prisoners in Mexico were always accompanied by
music.[53]

In 1894 the proregime policies and the extended recess of the Congreso Obrero provoked a debate in the worker press over whether the
once powerful Congreso Obrero really existed. The short-lived newspaper El *Obrero Mexicano* questioned the role of the Convención Radical,
the affiliated Congreso Obrero, and the working-class leader and city
councilman Pedro Ordoñez: "What good are they? What do they do?
Nothing and nothing."[54]

Once the threat of labor militancy diminished in the 1880s, government support of moderate mutualist organizations tended to weaken, as
cooptive government paternalism gave way to a more laissez-faire policy. In its zeal to encourage investment and govern scientifically, the Porfirian government withdrew support from labor leaders and organizations and was less willing to negotiate conflicts between workers and
their employers. After 1896, the *científico*-dominated Unión Liberal took
charge of organizing the reelections of Porfirio Díaz around an oligar-

chic party structure, and the declarations and mobilizations of workers in such events became less important. When the aging labor broker Pedro Ordoñez died in 1903 (by then the owner of a glue factory), the city council did not replace him with another representative of labor. In that same year, when most functions of the city council were subordinated to the government of the Federal District, the municipal commission on artisan development that Ordoñez had headed disappeared and, within a year, so did his long-dormant organizations, the Congreso Obrero and the Convención Radical.[55] No similarly centralized structure of workers' organizations in the city would replace them until 1912.

In spite of the organizational vacuum, labor conflicts began to rise dramatically in the early twentieth century, in what the newspaper El Imparcial in 1902 called the "huelgamania" in the new "century of strikes." By 1905–6, they would reach a crescendo. Increased labor conflict in Mexico City arose in part from the transformations of production and community discussed in the previous chapters. At the same time, a new generation of workers began to organize, pushing the limits of the tight legal constraints, collaborationism, and limited results of mutualist organizations. Many were now a generation removed from the rural backgrounds of their parents and had been exposed to radical worker ideologies from abroad through contact with foreign workers in Mexico, such as Spanish craftworkers in Veracruz or Mexico City, and with U.S. railroad, mining, and oil workers on both sides of the Rio Grande. Similarly, the growing numbers and importance of foreign owners, management, and workers created nationalist aspirations and resentments among Mexican workers over wages, promotion, and treatment. And as noted, científico development policy had high social costs for urban workers due to falling wages and a rising cost of living, particularly after the 1905 adoption of the gold standard and the recession of 1906–7. Although the direct correlation of these changes to unrest or to the outbreak of the revolution itself is debatable, their contribution to increasing tensions between workers and employers is clear.[56]

In the face of a dramatic increase in working-class discontent, the Díaz regime was forced to shift its labor policy again to a position resembling its earlier policies. Rodney Anderson has convincingly shown that beginning in 1906, the year of such notorious labor conflicts as the Cananea miners' strike, the Díaz government abandoned its essentially laissez-faire policy for one of active intervention to ease conflicts between workers and employers as well as one of active repression.

The events leading up to the Río Blanco conflict are the best-known examples of this shift and so merit a brief review. In 1906, textile workers in factories near Orizaba, Veracruz, formed a new Gran Círculo de Obreros Libres. In a familiar pattern, radical leaders of the Gran Círculo, who identified with the exiled PLM, were soon arrested or scattered, while more moderate factions within the organization were recognized and supported by Díaz and local authorities. Months later, textile owners staged a national lockout of workers in response to the demands of the newly organized textile workers in Puebla. Porfirio Díaz reluctantly intervened to impose a settlement that, though considered by the Gran Círculo leadership to be favorable, led angry workers and their families in Río Blanco to burn down the company store and march on other buildings in the region. The riot was answered by federal troops under direct orders from Díaz, who responded with executions and massive arrests of suspected organizers.[57] The textile strike and Río Blanco massacre both resurrected and reinforced previous patterns of intervention and repression of labor organizations.

Landa y Escandón and the Mutualist and Moralizing Society

In Mexico City, the last years of the Porfiriato witnessed a series of government attempts to reconstruct mechanisms of control and consensus among urban workers that had been lost or neglected. These efforts were in part a response to the dramatic increase in strikes that occurred in the capital and the nation in the first years of the new century. Of course, in the last years of the Porfiriato, strikes actually dropped nationally from their dramatic peak in 1907, a drop that coincided with an economic recession that undermined the negotiating power of workers. But the earlier events left a legacy of resentment among workers and concern among industrialists and officials, and seven of the eighteen major strikes in 1909 took place in the Federal District, a greater percentage than in previous years.[58] Just as important, the political crisis that unfolded in 1909 around the reelection of Díaz and his vice president furthered the need for some semblance of popular support for the regime.

The most important of these efforts to incorporate workers was under the charge of Gov. Guillermo Landa y Escandón. In the last months of 1909, Landa y Escandón and his aides began to promote their vision of labor organization to industrialists and workers in visits to factories and in the worker press. Landa y Escandón was an unlikely populist. From the cream of the Porfirian aristocracy and a key member of the *científico* group, Governor Landa y Escandón sought to draw workers away from militant collective action and toward mutualist organizations, in particular to his Mutualist and Moralizing Society of Workers of the Federal District, which he began to plan and organize in mid-1909 and finally inaugurated in December 1910. The society differed from earlier attempts of the Díaz regime to coopt factions within already existing organizations, such as the Gran Círculos of the 1870s and 1906, and push them toward moderate demands. Instead, the society was remarkable in that the initiative came entirely from the governor and his coterie of aides and sought to bring together all workers in the city and Federal District.

The Mutualist and Moralizing Society was an attempt to channel general worker discontent in acceptable directions. Central to both its name and mission was its attempt to make workers moral. Landa y Escandón urged workers to strive toward self-improvement and personal regeneration from their own vices. These vices and individual failures, he argued, were what had denied workers regeneration and the social progress so evident elsewhere in Porfirian society, a message that echoed his attempts to regulate drinking, prostitution, and the bathing and dress habits of the poor in the city. This message was seconded by the Catholic Workers Center, which joined in the class struggle against "alcohol, sensualism, and tobacco, the three terrible enemies of the family."[59]

Corollaries to the moralizing mission of the society were the needs to educate workers through special schools and to provide them with wholesome recreational activities, such as theater, picnics, and trips to parks. These goals echoed self-improvement aspirations and social functions at the center of traditional mutual aid societies and craft organizations and probably appealed to many workers. In his effort to garner support for his initiative and propagate its ideals, the governor even collaborated to produce a series of free plays for workers with such titles as *La Huelga* and *El Señor Gobernador*. The first dramatized the grave consequences that strikes had for workers, and the second, presumably, the beneficial efforts of Landa y Escandón on behalf of workers' well-being. Similarly, Governor Landa y Escandón named a park in the Plaza Santa Catarina after Mexico's first official working-class martyr, the railroad worker Jesús García, who died conducting a burning train car of dynamite out of a Sonoran town before it blew up.[60] The official message of the "hero of Nacozari" was one of complete sacrifice by workers for community and fatherland.

As the plays suggest, the counterpart of the moralizing mission was to promote harmony between workers and their bosses and social superiors. This message was promoted in the weekly newspaper *El Obrero Mexicano*, which began as the project of the owners of the cigarette company La Tabacalera Mexicana before becoming the official organ of the society. Under Landa y Escandón's sponsorship, it reached a circulation of twenty thousand copies and at least initially was distributed free. One of the weekly's articles explained the role of their rich and powerful patron: "Señor Landa y Escandón has conquered the esteem of the powerful classes and the affection of the needy because he has known how to attend to one and the other, hear their complaints, sympathize with both, and remedy their problems. His leadership at the public rudder has thus been entirely paternal . . . he has sought with one jump to close the distance that separates the big from the little."[61]

In less personal terms, the weekly espoused the society's view that "capital without labor is simply impossible, and the latter, without the former, is simply illusory." Strikes, by disturbing this harmony, were harmful to national peace and progress and therefore were even unpatriotic. The newspaper used fictional dialogues and responses to letters from respectful but confused workers to argue that, even when successful, strikes would ultimately harm workers, since "it is not possible to raise the price of salaries without the price of goods increasing."[62] When conflicts occurred, Landa y Escandón personally sought to intervene on behalf of workers, particularly in the textile factories. For example, when workers from La Hormiga factory walked off the job after their wages were cut by one-third, they approached the governor with a list of their demands. Landa scolded them for not coming to see him before the strike and for resorting to a technique—the strike—that was only likely to harm the workers. While offering his negotiating services and often sympathizing with the problems of workers, especially women, Landa y Escandón proved unwilling to interfere directly in questions of wages, which he insisted should be determined by market forces and private contract.[63]

The first groups that responded to the governor's initial call to join the Mutualist and Moralizing Society in June 1910 were unskilled and semiskilled workers from large factories and shops, many of which employed primarily women, such as the garment industry, cigarette factories, and department stores. The structure of the society as designed by Landa y Escandón was to be loosely corporate, with different committees or boards of workers, owners, and government authorities. In order to join, workers needed a letter of good conduct from their bosses. At least one boss paid the dues of his employees, but the initial endowment, the considerable sum of one hundred thousand pesos, came from the governor. Many factories sent both management and workers as delegates, the former integrating the board of employers. At the first formal meeting in December 1910, members of the board of directors of the society were appointed by Landa y Escandón, and the treasurer was a member of the board of employers.[64]

The paternalistic reforming appeal for workers to remain sober and be good fathers must have had a clear attraction to women, who often suffered most from male drinking. Indeed, many craftworkers and other workers in their mutual aid societies pushed education and sobriety. The hours and work conditions of women were also a topic of primary concern to Landa y Escandón and the society (see fig. 11). But the organization envisioned the role of women as being even more passive and pliant than the role envisioned for workers in general and proved reluctant to reconcile the roles of women in the domestic sphere and the workplace. For example, an article in El *Obrero Mexicano* began, "Do you know what the sacred rights of women are?" At the top of a long list, devoid of any mention of work, was "the right to always have their souls open to good" and, at the end, "the right to forget oneself, to love and die for a loved one." In spite of the society's strong appeals to women workers and an initial membership that was almost one-third female, women were greatly underrepresented when the first assembly of delegates to the society was called in December 1910 (36 of 226 delegates) and were immediately denied the possibility of election to the board of directors.[65]

The society sought to assure workers that they too had a place in the Porfirian community "under the strong arm and protecting hand of Landa y Escandón." The name and style of Porfirio Díaz could easily be inserted in such turns of phrase, surely providing some irony to observers that one of the wealthiest and most Frenchified of the *científicos* should be dressed in the same populist rhetoric as the mestizo general from Oaxaca.

The paternalistic position of Landa y Escandón and other progressive elites contained a basic contradiction. In a period of rapid change in the urban economy, Landa and Porfirian elites saw poverty as the product of individual failure and vice. At the same time the working poor, and women in particular, were frequently referred to as the "unprotected class." Protection was to come not from workers' organizations but from the church, employers, and benevolent officials and was to be an act of charity rather than a legal obligation. But the contradiction of intervention in workers' lives and organizations and devotion to laissez-faire policies in the workplace was no longer possible.

Landa's top-down effort to centralize and control the organization of workers along mutualist lines sought to fill a real organizational vacuum in Mexico City since the demise of the Congreso Obrero. But after months of promotion in factories and in social events, the project faltered in mid-1910. A scolding article in El *Obrero Mexicano* pondered whether workers had ignored the governor's effort because of a lack of will. The founding of the short-lived Great Workers League in April 1910 may have constituted a rival centralizing organization, though it too clung closely to mutualist goals and sought government patronage. In addition, Governor Landa y Escandón shifted his attention to the July presidential elections and the organization of the September centenary celebration, both activities around which he managed to mobilize worker support, often using the same intermediaries and networks he had developed to support the Mutualist and Moralizing Society.[66] But the formal inauguration of the society would have to wait until after the unprecedented summer of political campaigns and the extravagant patriotic festivities of the centennial.

Workers in Opposition

The famous Creelman interview published in Mexico in February 1908, in which Porfirio Díaz declared to a U.S. reporter his intention to retire in 1910 and allow competitive political parties, provoked a free-for-all among groups vying for influence in the post-Díaz era that inevitably involved workers. Given the importance of popular liberalism to working-class culture and longstanding traditions of working-class political involvement, it is not surprising that working people became protagonists in national elections. Beginning in 1910, the organizational activities of many Mexico City workers shifted away from mutualist concerns and workplace organization and toward political involvement. While the political activities of those who sympathized with the efforts of Governor Landa y Escandón in support of Díaz resembled previous patterns in which workers had been mobilized on the caudillo's behalf, of greater significance was the large-scale mobilization of workers in support of the opposition. The presidential elections created an opportunity for workers to make their voices heard that was unprecedented since the 1870s. In the capital as elsewhere, workers were initiators as well as initiated, and the electoral campaign of 1910 was important to the patterns of independent worker mobilization that followed.

Reflecting on the revolution, conservative Jorge Vera Estañol bemoaned the emergence in the late Porfiriato of a "professional proletariat" that was "the only numerous contingent with which the opposition party could make their catechism." The result, he lamented, was "more

an immense demagogic explosion than a democratic practice." In response to the appeals of opposition parties to workers in the 1910 elections, one skeptical editorialist for the mutualist paper *San Lunes* observed, "this is the history of the Mexican worker; when he is needed,
when someone wants to make him the instrument of a passion or ambi-
tion, everything is praises or cries that he should be protected . . . that he
is admired. But when his work is needed, not for a machination, but to
build up capital or a factory with his effort, he is repressed and exploited
to the maximum."[67] The editor went on to accuse the opposition and excuse Díaz of such manipulations.

Within Mexico City, the clearest attempt to generate worker support
for Díaz came from those with close ties to Governor Landa y Escandón.
The proposed principles of the Mutualist and Moralizing Society prohibited its members from taking political positions, which may help explain why the governor postponed the formal founding of the society in
mid-1910, while channeling much of its momentum and infrastructure
toward the reelection of Díaz. In the months leading up to the elections,
the society's newspaper, *El Obrero Mexicano*, denounced "agitators" and
those who would deny the average citizen the "right to reelect their leaders." At the same time it sympathetically described such scenes as the
February visit of President Díaz to the celebration of the newly formed
Mutualist Junta of the Centenary, sponsored by Landa y Escandón ostensibly for workers to participate in the centenary activities. As part of the
festivities, two women workers symbolically jailed the president and his
vice president for the "august crime of having consolidated the fatherland . . . from now on you are prisoners of the fatherland and your
energies must be devoted to it." Both Díaz and his unpopular vice president, Ramón Corral, swore to accept the punishment imposed by the
people.[68]

The activities and discourse of the Mutualist and Moralizing Society
were not representative of all workers, nor were they left uncontested.
The response of many workers to the society was an increasingly overt
questioning of the political leadership of Porfirio Díaz that combined
with a growing assertion of their public rights as workers, even though
conflicts with employers do not seem to have increased significantly in

this period. These two perceptions were reinforcing and largely the result of a belief among workers that the government no longer defended their rights. Workers came to see their fight against the caciques or bosses of the factory in the same terms as the struggle against political caciques. In the past such a vision of conflict had been largely the realm of the satirical penny press and always couched in the parody and comic depiction of verse or cartoon.

The articulation of working-class opposition came in steps that echoed those of urban and largely middle-class opposition groups that rallied to support first Gen. Bernardo Reyes and then liberal landowner Francisco Madero. Rather than directly challenging Díaz, opposition groups first attacked his unpopular vice president, Ramón Corral, and played off divisions existing within governing elites between the *científicos*, who controlled economic policy, and traditional political elites and military leaders, who saw the necessity to restore a broader political base. Whoever was elected vice president would almost certainly succeed the eighty-year-old general Díaz at some time during the next six-year term and thus would determine the extent of reforms and continuities in the system created by Díaz. Ramón Corral, who had close ties to the *científicos*, was well known and disliked by the workers of Mexico City since he had been governor of the Federal District from 1900 to 1903 before becoming minister of the interior and vice president in 1904. In that year Corral had been chosen by Díaz to run for the newly created vice presidency as a compromise between the *científico* leader, José I. Limantour, and the leading military figure, General Reyes. Corral's main virtues were negative ones: he had no real constituency of his own by which to challenge Díaz, and he was considered less objectionable than Limantour to the army and the public in general.

In the months following the Creelman interview, various insiders jockeyed for position in the vice-presidential race. The alternative to Corral who generated the most support among various opposition groups was General Reyes, the popular governor of Nuevo León. What began as a factional dispute within the ruling elite soon incorporated middle-class opposition figures and eventually became, in effect, a popular movement.

Opposition support among Mexico City workers emerged to some extent among textile workers and even more so among craft-based workers, who formed their own political clubs weeks after the first clubs formed by middle-class Reyes supporters. Similar and perhaps even more vigorous groups of workers were formed in such strongholds of Reyismo as Guadalajara, Veracruz, and Monterrey. In June 1909, the Great National Workers Party (Gran Partido Nacional Obrero), a group primarily of six hundred craftworkers based in the Federal District, declared its support for Gen. Bernardo Reyes as candidate for the vice presidency.[69] In their newspaper, *México Obrero*, they explained their motivation in terms of a clear historical consciousness: throughout the nineteenth century workers had defended the nation in past struggles under the leadership of Juárez and then Díaz and returned to their homes to enjoy peace, resume their work, and leave public affairs to "their great Caudillo." But meanwhile conditions in the city had worsened for workers. Díaz was portrayed as a man of the people who had been misled by his advisors, the *científicos*. Now, they proposed, General Díaz had chosen to "shake the dust off the Reform Laws and put them into practice, so that the people can exercise their rights."

The redemption of Díaz remained central to this indirect challenge to the status quo, and there was no better way for Díaz to return to his popular roots than to choose another popular general as his running mate. Why, the editorial asked, should workers support Corral for another term as vice president? Corral was so closely associated with the technocratic group behind the country's economic and political model that the editorial shifted from the individual to the group in its denunciations: "The people that you threaten and insult daily señores '*científicos*' can never walk by your side. The people has never received any benefit from him and has only seen that he has worked on behalf of the aristocracy." The editorial went on to compare the "chalets" of wealthy neighborhoods of Mexico City to the crowded, dirty tenements of the poor, and the "Mexicanidad" of workers to the foreign nature of "those who would change their nationality for parchments of nobility." By contrast, the declaration explained, General Reyes was the only public figure who had shown concern for the people, the man who "understood, felt for, and protected the workers." The manifesto invoked his labor legislation while he served as governor of Nuevo León and his aborted attempt as minister of war to form popular militias as an alternative to the draft, a project that had rallied workers but greatly alarmed the *científicos*.[70]

Although they claimed to represent the working class in their support for Reyes, these workers incorporated only a very general denunciation of the increasing division between rich and poor, between the Mexican people and those who were foreign-born or emulated non-Mexican lifestyles. Their critique focused on the political order rather than on the nature of industrial production or even the need for workers to organize. Similarly, their vehicle of political change remained dependent on a caudillo who, like Díaz, owed allegiances to groups whose interests were often antagonistic to workers' aspirations. Their declaration of support for Reyes was studded with historical references to instances when such "illustrious plebeians" had been roused by *el pueblo*: Juan Alvarez, Benito Juárez, Porfirio Díaz, and now Bernardo Reyes. This imagery drew upon a tradition of popular *caudillismo* that had helped bring both Juárez and Díaz to power. The dependence on a strong political patron to defend workers' interests was still an essential component of their support for Reyes, one that historically had given them some political weight, though limiting their independence or ability to sustain their influence over time. In this sense, working-class Reyismo was not a dramatic break with personalistic working-class support for Governor Landa y Escandón or Díaz, though the mobilization of popular sectors on behalf of an increasingly open opposition was.

The main problem with Reyismo was Reyes himself, who hoped that public support would be enough to force Díaz to abandon Corral and bless him as his vice president and probable successor. But when Díaz responded instead with repression of Reyista leaders and demonstrations, Reyes proved reluctant to openly break with the regime he had been such a part of, let alone to head a popular movement of the type that he had often repressed as governor. In July 1909, with popular support growing fast, Reyes finally renounced any aspiration to the vice presidency and in November proved his submission and loyalty to the increasingly annoyed president by accepting a diplomatic mission to Europe and abruptly leaving the country. The Great National Workers Party collapsed, and its president, Abundio Romo de Vivar, soon defected to the now official Díaz-Corral ticket, though apparently without the remnants of the party. Many working-class leaders watched in disappointment as their caudillo fell from grace.[71]

When Díaz made clear that he would retain his running mate, Corral, the opposition was forced into direct contention for the presidency and soon unified around the Anti-Reelectionist Party under the leadership of Francisco Madero. Madero was the son of a wealthy Coahuilan family with limited political experience and no previous constituency outside of Coahuila. With little basis to portray himself as a popular caudillo, Madero and the Anti-Reelectionist Party based their opposition more solidly than the Reyistas on respect for the liberal laws of the nation as enshrined in the constitution of 1857. These purified liberal principles were elaborated in his book, *The Presidential Succession of 1910*, which circulated widely among opposition political elites, and were most effectively enunciated in Madero's revival of the slogan "a real vote and no reelection" (*sufragio efectivo y no-reelección*) and the demand for municipal autonomy.

Just as opposition leaders and middle-class supporters who had flirted with the Reyes candidacy shifted toward support for Madero and open opposition to the reelection of Díaz, so too did working people. As early as July 1909, the month Reyes renounced his aspirations to the vice presidency, among the Anti-Reelectionist groups active in Mexico City was the Anti-Reelectionist Club of Workers "Benito Juárez." With the departure of Reyes, the support of workers for the Anti-Reelectionist cause accelerated, culminating with the formation of several worker-based Anti-Reelectionist clubs in May and June 1910. For example, a condescending article in the *Mexican Herald* described the formation in June of one Anti-Reelectionist club by forty-two cab drivers, chauffeurs, streetcar workers, and teamsters. They met in a small room whose walls were covered with newspaper cuttings in a crowded tenement on the eastern edge of the city. The reporter described tongue in cheek the attempt of all attendees to escape when dues were collected, but in fact, the setting, participants, and amount of the dues (six centavos) suggest

how extensive and spontaneous political participation of workers on behalf of Madero could be.[72]

The shift of support that many workers made in 1910 from the vice-
presidential candidacy of Reyes to the presidential candidacy of Madero
was more than a switch from one patron to another. Rodney Anderson
has rightly argued that most workers in 1910 identified with Madero and
his professed liberalism rather than with more revolutionary ideologies
such as anarchism or the radical program of the Flores Magón brothers.
In his election campaign, Madero began to court workers in public appearances, particularly in demonstrations in the Federal District, Puebla, and Veracruz. Textile workers in Orizaba who supported Madero
not only attended his rallies but enthusiastically purchased copies of the
constitution. At the same time, Madero was careful never to elaborate a
specific labor program. In spite of the participation of workers in the
April convention, some of whom even gave speeches, the program of his
Anti-Reelectionist Party differed little from the efforts proposed by Governor Landa y Escandón and middle-class reformers: "to improve the
material, intellectual, and moral condition of the worker, creating work-
shop-schools . . . and combating alcoholism and gambling."[73] The major differences from the Porfirian regime were the program's brief mention of the need for laws on pensions and accident compensation and
Madero's advocacy of the application of existing liberal laws that allowed individuals to associate freely.

In an oft-quoted speech in Orizaba, Madero told a crowd of mostly
textile workers that "neither increases in wages nor decreases in working hours depend upon the government . . . that is not what you want
. . . You want your rights to be respected so that you will be able to form
powerful associations in order that, united, you will be able to defend
your own rights . . . you do not want bread, you want only freedom because freedom will enable you to win your bread." Madero's references
to basic rights and freedoms paralleled workers' own appeals to "the
constitution of 1857, to liberty, to regaining their lost freedoms and having their rights respected." The common language and symbols help to
explain the vast support Madero received from workers in his electoral
campaign. At the same time, Madero's project for workers also con-

tained a strong element of moralizing paternalism. At the end of the same speech, he referred back to the events of Rio Blanco in 1907, chastising the workers involved in disturbances for crimes that deserved punishment while condemning Díaz for executing guilty and innocent workers without distinction or judicial process. But Madero insisted that Díaz was correct not to force industrialists to raise wages. Besides respect for their rights as citizens, he told workers, "you desired guidance, and finally you desired schools."[74]

Liberal discourse denied legitimacy to the accumulated collective claims of workers within the political system, rejecting the validity of laws to regulate wages or work hours, to give legal personality to unions, or to allow for collective bargaining, none of which were mentioned in the Anti-Reelectionist platform. While workers rallied to common symbols and a discourse of respect for individual rights and an end to corruption, they also hesitantly transformed liberal discourse to give meaning to their own organizations and actions. While supporting Madero, many workers elaborated upon a type of popular liberalism that was distinct from that advocated by Madero, one that above all equated the struggle against tyranny in the political sphere with that in the workplace. In addition, workers selectively drew from liberal doctrine and invocations of past national struggles and heroes to condemn the role of monopoly and foreign capitalists and to reclaim the participation of workers in local and national politics. While this current of popular liberalism was identifiable in previous decades of the Porfiriato among a minority of organizations and the popular press, not until 1910 did it become the dominant voice among workers. After the fall of Díaz, the contradictions between the individual liberties proposed by Maderista liberals and the collective claims aspired to by workers would lead to greater demands and conflicts between these two groups. But in the context of the 1910 elections, the common ground of liberal discourse and the promise of liberal democracy proved sufficient to rally workers to support Madero.

The link workers made between politics and the workplace during the Madero campaign was rarely expressed directly as specific demands, probably a factor of the relative weakness of workers' organizations on the eve of the presidential election campaign and the unusual and tentative nature of the opposition political campaign. For the most part, the 1910 electoral campaign became an event around which working people organized rather than an event that attracted the interest of already organized workers' groups. Nonetheless, the link between workplace demands and political demands can be seen in a variety of associations made by workers in their activities and newspapers.

Typical was the workers' weekly *Evolución*, which debuted 1 May 1910. The craftworkers associated with *Evolución* proposed to organize first as workers and then as citizens. The first issue of the newspaper bore the lengthy subtitle "Independent Weekly published by a group of printers that propose to establish a league of workers of the various branches of the Graphic Arts." The printer Rafael Quintero, editor of *Evolución* and later leader of the Casa del Obrero Mundial, urged the formation of a union of printers as the first step toward the organization of all workers in a Gran Liga Obrera to "reclaim their rights and fulfill their duties as worthy citizens of a country that, freed from the pressures of personalities of doubtful patriotism, celebrates the triumph of democratic institutions."[75] But if the initial step expressed was to organize all workers of a particular trade, the broader goals and timing were clearly political, since the weekly debuted two weeks after the Anti-Reelectionist Party formally nominated Francisco Madero as its candidate for president and featured a photo of his running mate, Francisco Vázquez Gómez.

At the same time, the new workers' weekly minimized its support for particular personalities and instead proposed a protagonism among workers in the defense of citizenship rights. The very real possibility of repression forced critics of the government to use rhetorical, elliptical, and abstract arguments and above all to avoid direct attacks on President Díaz. *Evolución* announced its existence by rhetorically asking, "Where are the Cuauhtémocs, the Hidalgos, the Morelos, the Ocampos, the Juárezes, the Zaragozas, the Diazes . . . the defenders of Democracy and Liberty?" Most such heroes, the editorialist responded, had died, and those who were still around had seemingly ceased to be alive or feel. In the minds of many workers, Díaz had made the transition from defender to tyrant. Díaz "the hero" had "ceased to be alive," a postmortem similar in function to the *calaveras* (stylized skeletons) and epitaphs to the living that were common in the satiric penny press. In this vision, the strong-armed paternalistic leader was rejected as a tyrant, the principal enemy in the workplace and in the political sphere. In Mexico, *Evolución* declared, where the feudal lord has not yet disappeared, "authority is synonymous with tyranny." The role of heroes such as Juárez was by contrast seen as establishing and enforcing rights, not handing down favors to a passive constituency, as had been the dominant discourse among the officially sponsored mutual aid societies.[76]

Though their language was seeped in demands for citizenship rights and their attention focused on elections, their identity as workers was closely linked. Under cover of their support for Madero, a risky endeavor in itself, workers celebrated what was in many ways the first de facto May Day in Mexico, thus linking dissent in the workplace and dissent in the political sphere. The first edition of *Evolución* came out on the symbolic date of 1 May 1910, nineteen years after the first failed attempt by Mexico City workers to celebrate May Day as a day of protest. On that same day in 1910, over five thousand workers marched from their factories and neighborhoods to the Zócalo and then on to a gathering in front of Madero's residence in the elite Colonia Juárez, an unprecedented intrusion by the poor (see fig. 12). A designated worker even joined the Anti-Reelectionist leaders dressed elegantly in frock coats and tall hats on the balcony of Madero's residence and spoke on behalf of the workers of Mexico City. The workers' clubs that attended were frequently named after heroes of independence and the Reform such as Morelos and Juárez, patriotic figures that both appealed to workers and made repression somewhat more problematic for the government. Other clubs identified themselves with their occupation or their place of work. Since the celebration of May Day had remained prohibited, the significance of the march and the paper's debut, especially during the centennial year of the Hidalgo revolt, was not lost to participants or the pro-Díaz press. Photographs and journalistic accounts of the event reveal the social contrast between the Anti-Reelectionist leaders and their public, between the place of the demonstration and the origins of the demonstrators.

The Anti-Reelectionist paper *México Nuevo* celebrated the march of "sons of the workshop," while the *Mexican Herald* mockingly referred to the marchers as "the great unwashed" from Santa Julia, La Bolsa, and San Lázaro, all marginal neighborhoods on the edges of the city.[77]

By the time the fifth edition of *Evolución* came out on 29 May, the paper had formally endorsed the Madero ticket and had taken the subtitle "Political Weekly, Organ of the Workers' Anti-Reelectionist Clubs of the Federal District." Given the transcendence of the political moment, organization as citizens had taken precedence over organization as workers. For the brief period until the newspaper was closed down in mid-June, providing political support for Madero in the streets rather than organizing workers in the workplace remained the primary concern of *Evolución* and of workers' organizations in the Federal District. The relative facility with which such workers and their organizations moved from work-related initiatives into political participation is notable. Individuals such as Quintero and Jacinto Huitrón, both of whom enthusiastically supported Madero, were later involved continuously in anarchist-inspired organizations throughout the 1910s and 1920s, yet at crucial conjunctures such as 1910 and 1915 they supported middle-class reformers and revolutionary leaders. The political experiences of the 1910 Anti-Reelectionist campaign were key initiations in organizational activities for a whole generation of younger working-class leaders who emerged in 1910 and in the first years of the revolution and who would soon displace the previous generation of Porfirian labor brokers.

Similarly, the 1910 campaign incorporated women into the political process in significant though limited ways. An article in *Evolución* responded to reelectionist criticism of women for forming leagues to support the Anti-Reelectionists: partisans of Corral, it claimed, "deny women the right that they have to think and express their ideas." Women were to participate in politics by supporting and influencing men close to them, even though, the editorial went on, "it would be ridiculous for a señorita to present herself at the electoral urn to deposit her ballot: but never will it be laughable that a wife encourages her husband to fulfill his duty as a citizen; nor that a sister, mother, or friend do the same with their men."[78]

In spite of their lack of formal political citizenship, women gave considerable support to the Anti-Reelectionists, although few were apparently willing in 1910 to take the demand for "effective suffrage" enough to heart to demand the vote for women. Middle-class women of the capital joined in women's associations that supported Madero, such as the Liga Femenina Anti-Reeleccionista Josefa Ortíz de Domínguez and Las Hijas de Cuauhtémoc. Factory women also joined the Anti-Reelection effort, such as those who formed the group Hijas de Anáhuac, comprised primarily of textile workers from the factory towns of the Federal District.[79] Their participation suggests that, as with many workers, their concern was not simply with honest voting but with the broader social reforms and recognition of other types of political rights that a change of government might bring.

In the last days of the Madero campaign, workers participated prominently in the Anti-Reelectionist effort, boosted by flyers circulating in Mexico City that claimed, in spite of Madero's denials, that if elected, Madero would force employers to raise wages. Vera Estañol cynically reduced the variety of working-class aspirations in the elections to a verse circulating at the time: "Lots of money for little work, cheap beer—Viva Madero!" Certainly many workers must have seen in the prospect of democratic elections the possibility of specific material concessions. The stonecutter José Pacheco Vadillo, when asked years later whether his fellow construction workers were concerned with ideas before the revolution, remembered that "there were two or three that were aware of what was going on and developed something . . . I only listened, since I was never capable of developing any topic . . . I felt the need for a bit higher wages."[80]

In a huge 29 May rally sponsored jointly by workers' organizations and the independent press in the capital, workers' political clubs and mutual aid societies paraded alongside women's clubs and other components of the Madero coalition. After the event, the opposition newspaper *México Nuevo* observed that the considerable attendance of workers was a sure sign that the efforts of Governor Landa y Escandón "to distance workers from the practice of citizenship" had failed. The *Mexican Herald*, which catered to the colony of North Americans in Mexico, felt obliged—"considering the magnitude of American and other foreign interests here and the large amount of American and other foreign capital that has been invested in the republic"—to explain the popular support for Madero to its readers: many supported Madero because "Men in general are seldom content with their condition." But the editorial assured its readers that General Díaz "has the support of the immense majority of all that counts for anything in the country's population. Only the supporters of General Díaz and Mr. Corral are not exactly the class of people that are fond, on any pretext, of walking in procession in the streets."[81]

Indeed, by contrast the Díaz-Corral rallies were sparsely attended and notable for their lack of spontaneity and enthusiasm. In the first rally, on 25 April 1909, many who attended were textile workers transported from Puebla and Tlaxcala by loyal labor leader Pascual Mendoza. By the following year, the vast majority of workers in Puebla and Tlaxcala were firm supporters of Madero. In a second pro-Díaz rally on 2 April 1910, workers were organized under banners from their places of work rather than from mutualist societies or political clubs, and according to the (admittedly biased) *México Nuevo*, many of those present confessed that they had been sent by their bosses.[82]

The jailing of Madero on 4 June on trumped-up charges of inciting rebellion, just three weeks before the election, was followed by a series of arrests, forced exiles, and the closure of all clubs and newspapers that had dared to support his campaign. Workers were among the many jailed in the weeks of protest that followed. Tightly controlled elections took place on 26 June and produced predictably lopsided results in favor of the Díaz-Corral ticket; only 20 of the 301 polling precincts in the Federal District went to electors who supported Madero, many of them in poorer neighborhoods such as the eastern Colonia de la Bolsa. Of course plans for organization in the workplace, such as that of the *Evolución* group for a Confederation of Printers, were also suspended. Any attempts to create new workers' organizations besides those of the governor were automatically associated with the Madero opposition and subject to repression.[83]

When Madero was released from jail in October, he quickly fled to

Texas and issued his Plan of San Luis Potosí, which declared the recent elections void, repeated the minimal political program of the Anti-Reelectionist Party, and called for a national revolt on 20 November to depose Díaz. While his call to arms was aimed at the same urban groups that had supported his electoral campaign, the response came late and from other sectors. By early 1911, the most important groups to take up arms on behalf of Madero came from rural areas such as Morelos and Chihuahua.

In contrast to the extensive support of urban workers in Madero's electoral campaign, few rallied to his call to arms. In Puebla, a small group of armed craftworkers led by the shoemaker Aquiles Serdán were discovered and killed under siege by police on 18 November, but the many workers of Puebla who had supported Madero did not come to their aid. In some areas such as Tlaxcala, where many textile workers had recent and close links to the countryside, factory workers in small groups took to the hills to join rural-based rebels.[84]

One impediment to support among urban workers for Madero's armed rebellion was the military vigilance and repression evident in the cities, formalized in March 1911 by a "suspension of guarantees" passed by the Congress. The crackdown that followed helped abort the Tacubaya Conspiracy in the Federal District a few days later, a planned revolt against Díaz led by a mixed group of middle-class radicals, students, women, and workers under the leadership of former PLM member Camilo Arriaga. The movement's program recognized the legitimacy of Madero's claim to the presidency, but like the 1906 program of the PLM, the published Tacubaya document went far beyond Madero's Plan of San Luis Potosí to include demands for wage increases, the regulation of work hours, a minimum percentage of Mexican workers in foreign firms, and the regulation of urban rents and housing conditions of the poor. But the uprising failed, as key conspirators were arrested and police implemented a further crackdown on potential opposition activities in the capital.[85]

Certainly the very insertion of workers into the urban economy limited their response to Madero's call to arms. Unlike their rural counterparts, few urban workers had access to guns or horses. Moreover, the dependence of urban workers and their families on wages made abandoning work a difficult option, and any national violence that upset the functioning of the urban economy threatened their immediate livelihood. Finally, Madero's Plan of San Luis Potosí made vague promises of the restitution of illegally acquired land but otherwise made no mention of social demands that might rally workers to take up arms. For the workers of Mexico City, opposition to Díaz in the early months of 1911 was minimal.

While Madero was in jail, and opposition groups suppressed, the Porfirian elite pushed through their extravagant centenary celebration in Mexico City during the entire month of September 1910. In the weeks that followed, Landa y Escandón pressed on with his paternalistic Mutualist and Moralizing Society project for Mexico City's working class, just as the legitimacy of Porfirio Díaz among workers hit an all-time low. After election day, the society's *El Obrero Mexicano* congratulated workers on exercising their right of citizenship and on choosing the true path of democracy, "step by step rather than by jumps."[86]

When the first general meeting of the society took place in December, after almost two years of promotion by the governor, most of the large factories of the capital and Federal District were represented, even from places such as the textile mill La Carolina, where support for Madero had been strong. The society claimed to represent factories with a total of over twenty-five thousand workers, though a later questionnaire showed a maximum membership in 1911 of around four thousand. Even at the lower figure, no citywide organization had been able to claim so many members since the heyday of workers' organizations in the 1870s.[87]

In April 1911, as his regime crumbled in the face of revolt along the northern border, President Díaz attended the inaugural ceremony of the Mutualist and Moralizing Society, along with workers, factory owners, and other officials in the Teatro Hidalgo. His attendance suggests how important efforts to guarantee the support of workers, or at least keep them from joining the revolt, were considered by the ruling oligarchy. A few days later, on the 5 May anniversary of the defeat of the French at Puebla, engineer Carlos Peralta, secretary of the Junta de Patronato, proposed the formation of a battalion of workers to defend the nation in case of a foreign invasion, presumably that of Madero across the northern border. Although two training sessions were held before Díaz resigned three weeks later, it is unclear how many workers had volunteered or the extent of official support for the project, which, as in 1903, may have raised objections among *científicos* determined to limit popular mobilization. The idea of arming the urban working classes would reemerge and falter again in 1912, when the Madero regime came under siege, before taking definitive form with the Red Battalions in 1915.[88]

The society was an attempt from the heights of Porfirian society to restore a traditional model of paternalistic and harmonious relations between classes, relations that had become strained under the process of industrialization and the transformations of the urban community. What was both old and new was the intimate link between the government, in this case the de facto municipal authority, and the organization of workers, which vaguely resembled the colonial relation of guilds with the city government, and even anticipated elements of the postrevolutionary order. But after the experience of the 1910 elections, the formation of the Mutualist and Moralizing Society and rituals such as the centennial celebration were unable to restore the legitimacy of the old order or create a new one.

Popular Urban Classes and the Fall of Díaz

In spite of the apparent quiescence of organized workers in Mexico City in the last months of the government of Porfirio Díaz, the final days of his regime were marked by popular pressure to resign and a flurry of urban mobilization suggestive of patterns to come. In the first week of May 1911, a variety of groups of self-identified workers from Mexico City and other areas of the country demanded the resignation of Díaz. On 1 May, a year after thousands of workers had rallied in front of Madero's house in Mexico City, a group of "Mexican citizens, belonging to the *gremio obrero* of this capital," blamed the present state of violence on those "who helped to impose candidates that the people rejected, unaware of the force of this pueblo and the force of opinion," and demanded that the president resign. That 114 workers signed the letter suggests how emboldened the opposition to Díaz had become among some popular sectors in the capital. Another (anonymous) letter ended its plea for the resignation of Díaz by saying, "what the corps of workers [Cuerpo Obrero] of the Federal District asks for is National justice." Another group of women shop employees pleaded in more practical terms: the national conflict had paralyzed commerce and lost them their jobs, a situation that could only be remedied if "new minds and vigorous elements come to lead an evolution to the benefit of humanity."[89]

The press was also emboldened. The same week, the satirical journal *La Guacamaya* published a José Guadalupe Posada cartoon entitled "Political Epidemic" that reflected and predicted national events. In the center, Díaz sat in the presidential chair as a crowd of popular composition approached with a banner that read "request for resignation." On another plane, peasants pulled a state governor from his chair of authority. An adjoining poem spoke of the epidemic that was spreading as governors resigned throughout the country; the only sure cure for the sick fatherland, the poem declared, was for the president to resign.[90]

The Posada cartoon proved prophetic. Popular urban protest hardly brought down the Porfirian regime, but lower-class disturbances and the fear of them helped to shape the transition. On 19 May, the key border city Ciudad Juárez fell to the rebel troops of Pascual Orozco, and in the following two weeks, as negotiations dragged on, cities fell to Maderista troops throughout the country. Although the Treaty of Ciudad Juárez was signed on 21 May, the circumstances and date of the president's resignation remained in doubt during the following days. In the context of deep political crisis and the previous electoral mobilization of broad sectors of the urban population, the actions of the popular sectors of Mexico City took on new significance. On 23 May 1911, as the nation awaited the announcement of the resignation of Díaz, disturbances occurred throughout the city, leading to fifteen deaths. The next day, some fifteen thousand people gathered in front of the Chamber of Deputies in downtown Mexico.

Targets of popular disturbances were clearly political. Late in the afternoon, when it became clear that Díaz would not resign that day, a crowd briefly took over the Congress before marching on to the National Palace in the Zócalo with shouts of "death to bad government." As night fell, nervous policemen fired repeatedly on the crowd, killing several demonstrators and wounding dozens before the crowd dispersed in the face of bullets and rain. Another group encircled the private home of Porfirio Díaz on Cadena Street (a few blocks from the National Palace), where he remained trapped with various friends and colleagues. The crowd stoned the soldiers on guard, prompting them to fire into the crowd, killing several. Others attacked the key newspaper associated with the regime, El Imparcial. The next morning Díaz sent his resignation to Congress, and as the news spread, the protests of the crowds assembled in the streets of the center turned to jubilation, suggesting the limited and political nature of the goals of their collective protests.

Photographs and personal accounts of the makeup of the crowds attest to the strong presence of people from the popular classes, many of them barefoot and many of them women. At the same time, various versions hint that the crowd had its leadership. According to José Valadés, this "revolt of Mexico City" was led by such men as Mariano Duque, Adolfo Leon Ossorio, and Rafael Pérez Taylor, who functioned as important links between Madero and students, workers, and the city's popular sectors. An anonymous broadsheet distributed days after the event also made reference to vehicles "occupied by protesters of greater weight who apparently were those who directed the multitude."[91]

As argued by Ariel Rodríguez Kuri, the actions of the crowds from 23 to 25 May in Mexico City profoundly unbalanced the quarrel of political elites. Conservative Porfirian politicians Jorge Vera Estañol and Congressman Ramón Prida later referred to the riots respectively as "the commune about to explode" and "the orgy of democracy." Meanwhile, Maderista agents in the city Francisco Vázquez Gómez and Alfredo Robles Domínguez feared the potential storm of popular upheaval and so fabricated a telegram that was supposedly from Madero, reproduced in a broadsheet posted in the streets. It claimed that Madero instructed them to "order the people of the capital to stay calm, and if they don't obey, collaborate with the [Porfirian] military command to repress disorders with all energy."[92]

The spontaneous mobilization of popular sectors in the political sphere abruptly surpassed the previous acceptable limits of even the Maderista elites who had courted working people as voters, suggesting the potential dangers of harnessing popular sectors. While the immediate political goal of removing Díaz had been accomplished, in the days that followed the resignation of Díaz, spontaneous crowds and reconstituted Anti-Reelectionist clubs invoking democratic liberties made a series of attacks to depose "despotic and tyrannical" prefects, judges, and municipal presidents in the Federal District. Given the terms of the Treaty of Ciudad Juárez, which guaranteed a substantial degree of continuity for Porfirian officials in the postrevolutionary government, popular violence or the threat of it risked bringing on repression that was reluctantly sanctioned by Madero. But popular violence often proved more effective at removing hated Porfirian officials than more legalistic procedures. In the Federal District town of Xochimilco, a group of local residents succeeded in running the municipal president out of town and installing one of their own choice. By contrast, eighty-three male citizens of Coyoacán, a town on the outskirts of Mexico City, chose instead to petition the new government for the resignation of their prefect and proposed, unsuccessfully, their own candidate. Similar demonstrations to remove the city council proved unsuccessful, though Governor Landa y Escandón wasted little time in abandoning the city, stopping only to bid a brief farewell to the members of the Mutualist and Moralizing Society he had founded and inaugurated the month before.[93] These mass demonstrations symbolically conquered the Porfirian capital and overturned the carefully choreographed public rituals of Porfirian peace and order that eight months earlier had filled the city center during the centennial celebrations.

★　★　★

The variety of working-class cultures at the end of the Porfiriato reflected the rural and urban roots of Mexico City workers and the divisions between skilled and unskilled work. In spite of these divisions, many workers came to contest aspects of the transformation of work and society that occurred in Mexico City. They derived their critique from a transformation of liberal republican discourse into a type of popular liberalism that celebrated the historical role of workers in consolidating the republic, first through their participation in nineteenth-century struggles against foreigners and conservatives and second through their very work. Workers thus defined themselves both as central actors on the national stage and as conceptually distinct from other classes.

The opposition presidential campaigns of 1910 were hardly a mass movement led by workers, yet the mass involvement of workers in these campaigns, led mostly by dissident elites and middle-class professionals, allowed workers to assert themselves politically. While accepting the limited electoral reform agenda proposed by Madero, workers linked the critique of tyranny and corruption to abuses in the workplace and to the predominance of foreigners and monopolies in the economy. Although country people were the key social group that eventually rallied to Madero's call for armed revolt, urban workers made clear through their ordered and enthusiastic participation in the electoral campaigns of 1909 and 1910, and in their spontaneous mobilization in the streets on the eve of the Díaz resignation, that they were now a permanent fixture in the public political sphere of the capital that would have to be reckoned with.

4

MADERISTA POLITICS
AND THE RISE OF UNIONS

To the working and suffering people . . . make moderate and patriotic use of the liberty that you have won and have faith in the justice of your new governors; . . . since from the political point of
view your situation has undergone a radical change, passing from
the miserable role of pariah and slave to the august heights of citizen, don't expect your economic and social situation to improve as
rapidly, since that cannot be obtained by decrees or laws, but only
by a constant and laborious effort of all social elements . . . Know
that you will find your happiness in yourselves, in the domination
of your passions and the repression of your vices.

FRANCISCO MADERO, 24 June 1911

I, a worker like you, want to tell you from where our problems
come and what is the remedy.

JACINTO HUITRÓN, Lucha, 8 March 1913

Soon after the 1912 congressional elections organized under
the presidency of Madero, a plumber, two carpenters, and a tailor, "all
raised under the paternal government" of Gen. Porfirio Díaz, gathered
near Tepito Plaza to write a "humble" letter to their former president on
the occasion of his saint's day. "We all lament the ruin of our country,"
they wrote, "and weep for the lack of work and the misery and contempt
for our children." For this reason, they explained, they had decided to
write to the old general, "the father who no longer exists, who divided
the bread among all his children, and with the crumbs that were left over
the workers could live." Two tobacco workers in the Buen Tono factory
tapped a similar nostalgic vein when they wrote Díaz in his Paris exile on
his birthday (the day before Independence Day): "We, the sons of work,
those of callous hands . . . send you our humble but loyal and sincere

greetings because we feel that something is missing that was ours, something that formed a part of our being, and that something is you, Sir."[1]

The turn of phrase in the first letter is suggestive: the signers longed for a previous order, even one where workers had been clearly subordinate, receiving only crumbs from the loaf divided among the more legitimate Porfirian children, suggesting a meager but still important entitlement within the social hierarchy. The legacy of Porfirian paternalism was strong; the fears of instability and disorder, so ingrained in the discourse of Mexico's old ruling class, extended also to many of the lower classes, whose situation was in some ways worsened by the uncertainties that came with the revolution.

These workers were hardly likely rebels. But in spite of such fears, the social upheaval, the intellectual ferment, and the weakening of government patronage and repression during the revolution helped extend organization to an unprecedented number of the working people of Mexico City. Among them were those schooled in secular liberalism and radicalism as well as those raised in the moral obligations of paternalism.

This chapter traces the continued emergence of working people as key social actors in the city after the fall of Díaz. Working-class organization, while clearest among men and the most skilled and educated sectors of the working class, touched upon women and even the city's more humble "sons of work." Organization after the spring of 1911 would follow two linked but distinct paths: one rooted in local and national politics and the other in the workplace and working-class community. Since working people first mobilized in Mexico City in 1910 in political terms, it is not surprising that they continued, at least on the short term, to put their primary hopes in political reforms and to give political support to the largely middle-class Maderista reformers in elections. But Maderista reformers were more notable for their efforts to moralize the lower classes than to guarantee basic rights of workers and limit the worst abuses of employers. The limited results of political participation convinced many working people to strengthen working-class organizations and assert themselves more directly in the workplace and in their communities. Their new work-related organizations, particularly unions (*sindicatos*), went far to undermine the goals and forms of mutualism, which became subordinate to new patterns of mobilization in the city in the first years of the revolution.

After the Fall: Workers and Elections under Madero

According to Deputy Felix Palavicini, the 1912 congressional elections and the Twenty-sixth Congress that emerged from it were the freest and most democratic in Mexican history, a sentiment repeated, modified, and occasionally challenged by various historians.[2] The freedom and extent of participation in elections during the Madero presidency and the degree of effectiveness of the Madero administration and Congress in proposing reforms to the authoritarian system they inherited are all criteria by which to judge the potential of the revolution's initial, aborted experiment in democracy. One measure of the democratic nature of the elections might be the participation of different social groups in the electoral and political processes. While many historians have explored the limited attempts of President Madero and the Twenty-sixth Congress to address "the agrarian question," little attention has been paid to the relationship between elected officials and one of the most numerous sectors to support Madero in the elections of 1910–12: workers and the urban poor.

In his study of the Mexican Revolution, Alan Knight writes that "city workers were, in a sense, *disponible*, ripe for mobilization; but they were not, therefore, inert, malleable victims; on the contrary, with the revolution they displayed 'a very marked tendency to associate,' both politically and economically."[3] This quote captures two dilemmas that workers faced in their associational activities after May 1911. One dilemma was whether to organize in the workplace and working-class community alone or to choose "multiple action" that also pressed for change through political participation. A second dilemma for those who chose strategies of political participation was whether to pursue political strategies in which workers and their organizations might assert themselves as autonomous actors on the political scene—be it through civic demonstrations or the organization of working-class political parties—or else offer themselves as *disponibles*, clients seeking concessions from political bosses in exchange for their bodies at demonstrations, votes at urns, or even arms on the battlefield.

The fall of Díaz revived and accelerated the pattern of worker organization that had been cut off a year before with the arrest of Madero, and it initiated a series of tentative strikes that would test workers' newfound freedom and the strength of their alliance to the new ruling elite. While strikes and workplace demands are discussed more fully in the next chapter, two examples of strikes that occurred in the first months of the new era need brief mention, since they provided urgency to the "worker question" and helped shape the working-class movement in political and organizational terms.

In early July 1911, during the transitional government of Francisco León de la Barra, a strike of some three thousand streetcar workers closed down the tramway system for four days. The strike was notable for the militancy and near complete support of streetcar workers, the degree of solidarity from other groups of workers, and the general sympathy for strikers from the public, sectors of the media, and political circles. But like most strikes during the Porfiriato, the streetcar strike failed, in part because the streetcar workers had no organization previous to the strike or accumulated funds on which they could rely and in part because municipal authorities eventually chose repression over conciliation.

In late December 1911, barely two months after Madero's election to the presidency, textile workers in a Mexico City factory initiated a strike that soon spread to virtually all textile factories in the Federal District and to most of those in the rest of the country. In speeches and petitions, workers associated their newly recovered political rights with their exercise of rights as workers and demanded that the president they had elected intervene to support their demands. Madero responded by convening a textile convention under the auspices of the recently formed Labor Department to which both workers and industrialists sent delegates. As the outcome of these two strikes suggest, the ultimate success of many strikes would depend on either the previous existence of workers' organizations willing and able to confront employers or the willingness of workers to demand political support for their strikes and of government authorities to give it.

While considerable organization and conflict took place in the workplace, the first year after the fall of Díaz was more importantly one of political organization coupled with uneasy waiting among workers for political initiatives from the new national and local governments. Expectations were high among workers and popular classes that through elections for local and national office they would be able to elect workers, or at least progressive middle-class representatives, who would make the interests of working people a priority. In essence, they hoped that the new democratic order would help to close the gap between civil and political society that had existed throughout the Porfiriato. Three sets of elections in Mexico City raised hopes of democratic participation: the presidential elections of October 1911, the city council elections in December 1911, and the congressional elections in April 1912.

In the presidential election of October 1911, the victory of Madero was a foregone conclusion. It was not the result of a monopoly of coercion by Maderistas, since indeed much of the Porfirian army and political system remained intact, but rather of the tremendous popularity of the new caudillo of the triumphant revolution. Even so, in the months leading up to the elections Mexico City experienced an explosion of civic and political organization, and the organization of workers in general should be seen in this context.

The functions and membership of these new organizations were sometimes obvious from government registers or from newspaper letters or notices. They included neighborhood groups concerned with local improvements in public services or with ending abuses of political caciques; civic organizations of middle- and working-class groups oriented toward physical, moral, or intellectual improvement and exchange; specifically political groups whose aim was to participate in elections; and, of course, old and new mutualist organizations. The names of these organizations suggest continuities as well as changes brought by the revolution. In addition to taking on the usual nomenclature of nineteenth-century heroes, clubs were named after the heroes, dates, and documents of the revolution: the Club Libertador Madero, of course, and the Club 10 de Mayo, after the recent victory of Maderista forces at Ciudad Juárez, but also the Club Aquiles Serdán, after the working-class martyr who had died in the Madero uprising in Puebla, and Club Martyrs of Rio Blanco, in commemoration of those killed in the 1907 textile conflict. The working-class District One saw the formation of the Club Francisco Ferrer Guardia, named after the radical Catalan educator executed in Barcelona in 1909. Other new clubs were rooted in particular localities, such as the Club Político Popular del Séptimo Distrito.[4]

Among the various organizations involved in electoral politics, many of which included working people among others, some were made up exclusively of workers, who organized as workers to assert themselves in elections. Factory- and neighborhood-based political clubs were revived or created anew. One such club, the Great Workers League (Gran Liga Obrera), announced its intention to "assure that candidates be loyal [to workers] and defend their interests." The women's group "Las Hijas de Cuauhtémoc" changed its name to "Hijas de la Revolución" and continued to organize workers in the southern factory districts in support of Madero.[5]

While many of these workers' political clubs were continuations of Anti-Reelectionist clubs that had supported Madero in 1910, some were also formed by leaders or intermediaries of mutualist organizations that had previously either rejected a political role for workers or adhered to the Díaz-Corral ticket. Just as many Porfirian politicians survived the change in regime intact, so too did some mutualist leaders associated closely with the Porfirian regime. Examples are the engineer Carlos Peralta, who played a key role in Landa y Escandón's Mutualist and Moralizing Society, and Abundio Romo de Vivar, who made the transition from Reyista to Corralista to Maderista. But their influence would be greatly diminished in the face of a new generation of working-class leaders brought to the fore in both of Madero's presidential campaigns and in the cycle of workplace organization that occurred in the wake of the elections.[6]

Workers and their organizations mostly adhered to the platform of Madero's newly formed Progressive Constitutional Party (PCP), which replaced his Anti-Reelectionist Party of 1910. Other candidates who sought worker support, such as Francisco Leon de la Barra and Bernardo Reyes, were largely ignored or even violently rejected. Some public demonstrations against the opponents of Madero may have been manipulated by figures such as Madero's brother Gustavo, as claimed by Vera Estañol; but many demonstrations, such as those against the revived candidacy of Gen. Bernardo Reyes, probably reflected a visceral rejection of a figure who workers felt had abandoned them a year before. More than arbitrary violence, the demonstrations and parades by workers were a repeat of those they had undertaken a year earlier.[7]

But even among supporters of Madero there was considerable discontent among groups that felt workers' organizations and interests had been marginalized within the party and programmed out of the platform and convention. Complaints were rife among workers that Madero's key advisors had determined decisions about the platform and the vice-presidential candidate long before the actual convention, and indeed the efforts to court workers were relatively diminished compared to the 1910 campaign. Many workers supported the vice-presidential candidacy of Alfredo Robles Domínguez, who had been the key Maderista link to popular organizations in Mexico City in 1910, over that of Madero's choice of José Maria Pino Suárez. Madero and party leaders may have been indifferent because they felt that workers' needs would be fulfilled through the freedom to organize as workers and vote as citizens. It may also reflect their confidence in an electoral victory, their need to placate elements of the old Porfirian ruling coalition who still held office, and their fear of the consequences of mobilizing workers and popular classes, fears made worse by the riots of 24 May 1910 and the bitter strike of streetcar workers in July 1911.[8]

In spite of their political marginalization, workers' continued enthusiasm for Madero and for political change was demonstrated when they staged a huge rally during the PCP nominating convention in August. A month later, workers of La Carolina textile factory went on strike after their employer refused them permission to send a commission to the train station to greet the candidate Madero on his return to the capital. Ultimately, when citizens in Mexico City went to the polls in October in unprecedented high numbers, there was a broad consensus that extended to workers and popular classes over Madero's candidacy.[9]

In the weeks after the presidential election, a debate over worker participation in national politics took place in the pages of two newspapers oriented toward workers. The biweekly El Tipógrafo Mexicano, organ of the recently formed Confederation of Graphic Arts, responded to "a certain socialist periodical," probably El Radical, which had argued that it was better for workers to stay out of politics than to "serve as a toy for the petty politicians and opportunists that, singing hosannas to labor, repudiate all who wear over their clothes the stains of the machinery of the factories and workshops." El Tipógrafo Mexicano responded with considerable optimism though some vagueness about the ability of workers to articulate their political interests as a class: "The actual worker comes forth to the social arena with a precise notion of his rights and with the knowledge of the methods to exercise them. No longer will he be such an easy prey to petty politicians and opportunists. On the contrary, soon he will separate from them to the dictates of his class interests, and undoubtedly a party essentially of workers will arise that will conquer, with the unstoppable force of its solidarity, the part that corresponds to them in the treasure of social well-being that they accumulated in past generations."[10] But in the absence of significant workplace organization, the creation of an effective "party essentially of workers" would prove elusive.

The next elections of importance were those for the city council, held in December 1911. The restoration of municipal autonomy throughout the nation had been a key tenet of the Madero revolution, though one complicated in the case of Mexico City by its overlap with federal powers and the appointed position of the governor of the Federal District. Municipal elections were potentially important to workers, since throughout the nineteenth century and until 1903, the city council had provided the key entrée for workers into local politics. But both the restoration of municipal autonomy and popular participation in city government under Madero proved unattainable. In the months after the fall of Díaz, the city council as a body remained in the hands of Porfirian científicos and continued to be severely restricted in its power, as it had been since Díaz reduced its resources and authority in 1903. In spite of repeated public demonstrations by crowds in front of the City Hall to demand his resignation, longtime municipal president Francisco Pimental y Fagoaga refused to resign, giving up the post to a Porfirian colleague only when he joined other Porfirian politicians in Madero's cabinet.

In this context, the municipal elections held in December 1911 elicited limited popular participation and resulted in no worker representation. The structure of municipal elections and the limited power of the city council, both legacies of the previous regime, undermined popular participation. The sitting city council of *científicos* controlled the registration of voters as well as the selection of the voting booth monitors. The PCP and other parties repeatedly accused the newly formed Catholic Party, which had incorporated many incumbent Porfirian councilmen and appointed officials, of preparing for fraud, and indeed in the primarily working-class District One many potential voters did not receive credentials and were unable to vote.[11]

While the city council optimistically increased the number of ballots for the election dramatically over Porfirian levels, voter turnout remained low. The pro-Madero newspaper *Nueva Era* speculated that "the elections for councilmen had not awakened due interest in the public opinion because it is known that our city council has been . . . with hardly any functions and purely decorative." The conservative *El Diario* called the election a failure, since many of the balloting areas never opened or remained virtually empty, but did note the presence of the occasional "mailman, teamster, or electrical worker, and these were the ones who deposited their votes. The humble class of society provided the example of citizenship."[12]

An additional obstacle to popular participation was that elections were indirect and at large. Registered males voted for an elector from their section or neighborhood, and then those roughly one thousand electors met to select councilmen to represent each of the ten districts, through formal tickets, with half of the twenty seats renewed every two years. A workers' candidate from a well-organized or locally based party might have been able to win the majority vote in a single district, such as the largely working-class Districts One, Two, and Four, but he stood little chance of winning the vote of electors from throughout the city.

In spite of fears of fraud, the PCP managed to win over one-half of the electors, the Catholic Party one-third, and other smaller parties the rest. Since the second round of elections among electors involved at-large voting, the PCP majority was able to impose their candidates throughout the city, excluding the Catholic Party as well as any of the smaller parties from gaining any new seats. Although many local electors were self-described workers, none were included as candidates for city council seats on the PCP slate. Unlike in the 1870s and 1880s, working-class leaders were unable to bargain their way into any of the city council seats, which went primarily to well-known professionals and party leaders. Of course, among the new councilmembers were progressives such as Serapio Rendón, Felipe Gutiérrez de Lara, and Antonio Villareal. Villareal had been a founder of the PLM but by 1911 had abandoned his previous support for the party and the pro-labor provisions of its 1906 program. However, Rendón and Gutiérrez de Lara maintained close ties to working-class organizations and in the following year would participate in many of the events of the Casa del Obrero Mundial.[13]

Even if the at-large voting system favored the PCP slate, the victory was in some ways hollow. In spite of the PCP sweep of the city council elections, since only one-half of the seats were renewed, the Porfiristas maintained the balance of power in the city council and succeeded in electing one of their own incumbents as the new municipal president when the new city council was convened.

The attitude of the majority of the new city council toward the popular classes of the city was suggested by the inaugural speech of the new city council president, Pedro Lascuraín. The "worker question" he insisted, was one of the most urgent: "The new city council must, in a prompt and efficient way, attend to their moral improvement." In this, both Porfirian and Maderista councilmen seemed to be in agreement. The limited actions of the newly elected members of the city council aimed at working people did not go beyond attempts at moral reform, similar to those undertaken during the Porfiriato. Incoming councilman Carlos Patiño immediately submitted a version of the perennial Porfirian proposal to prohibit the wearing of the peasant *calzón* in public, a measure that the governor of the Federal District eventually tried to implement.

Patiño also submitted a proposal to register domestic servants in order to regulate the "abuses and crimes that they commit." The proposal by PCP councilmember Martin Reyes to move all "public women" out of the city center into a single "zone of tolerance" was particularly controversial, and the public reaction to it suggests the degree of popular resistance with which most of these measures were probably met. Many workers might have agreed with the intent to regulate prostitution, but few people of any social class or neighborhood could agree as to where the zone should be. When the governor endorsed the city council proposal and attempted to move all brothels to the contiguous southern barrios of Netzahualcoytl, Niño Perdido, and Cuahtemotzín—right in the middle of the city's densest industrial district—over two thousand factory workers and owners joined forces to oppose the measure, sending reams of signed protests to the city council and newspapers. The implementation of the measure was postponed indefinitely.[14]

These attempts at moral regulation echoed Porfirian mores and reinforced paternalistic decrees actually handed down from the Madero government. Madero accepted and gave almost messianic force to the progressive era urge to moralize the lower classes, speaking of the need to eliminate the "low passions of the *pueblo*" and the "repression of their vices." The president and the governor of the Federal District implemented such decrees as the closing of *pulquerías* in Mexico City by 6 P.M. and by noon on Sunday to keep workers from drinking and proposed the roundup of all beggars into asylums. Madero and the new councilmen seemed determined to outdo the moral reform campaign of exiled Governor Landa y Escandón.[15]

The moralizing actions of Maderista councilmembers should not be seen simply as the continuation and intensification of Porfirian efforts. They were also a reaction to the vigorous emergence of popular urban classes as social actors in the city with the upheaval of 1910–11. Already in the first year of Madero's government, notices abound in newspapers and the records of the city council of a rise of behavior seen as impudent or immoral by political authorities: members of the popular classes urinating in the streets of the city center or treating police officers with insolence; prostitutes soliciting in the Zócalo in ever greater numbers;

crowds challenging police over the arrest of presumed beggars or thieves; cinemas and popular theaters (*género chico*) taking greater sexual and political liberties in their shows and actors engaging in free and rowdy exchange with audiences of the popular classes. These behaviors demonstrated a liberty quite at odds with the attempted assertion of executive powers by the city council. In fact, the actions of the city council proved largely ineffectual, due as much to the strength of popular resistance to moralizing reforms as to the reality of the ambiguous responsibilities and powers of the city council. Both the appointed governor of the Federal District and the minister of the interior repeatedly reminded the councilmen that their faculties (in spite of Madero's electoral promises) remained exclusively consultative.[16]

The greatest shortcoming of the experiment in democracy in Mexico City was the failure of both the local and national governments to restore the municipal autonomy and authority to the city councils of the Federal District. Both Madero and the city council acknowledged that municipal autonomy remained a cherished objective of all classes. In February 1912 Madero established a commission that included Luis Cabrera and several councilmembers to elaborate a project that would restore to the city councils of the Federal District their "legal personality." But the process of elaborating a reform project was plagued by a variety of factors: most of those on the commission to restore the city councils were Porfirian politicians, as were the city council members and local prefects they consulted; and no attempt was made to incorporate or consult the new mosaic of social actors, such as the new political clubs and workers' organizations, that had multiplied in the city during the previous two years. As a result, proposals addressed the issues of political and fiscal autonomy, but none made any attempt to enlarge the vote or representation of popular sectors in the city councils, such as through direct elections or the elimination of at-large voting for councilmembers.[17]

Ultimately, in spite of the limited spectrum of proposals and the appointment of an additional commission, no reform proposal was ever sent to the Congress in the twenty-nine months between the fall of Díaz in May 1911 and the closure of Congress by General Huerta in October

1913. Because of the circumstances of the revolution, the December 1911 elections would be the last democratic city council election for seven years. Within months of Madero's assassination in February 1913, virtually all of the PCP councilmen had resigned, leaving General Huerta free to stage the next municipal elections Porfirian style in December 1913. From those poorly attended elections, which could not even muster half the normal number of electors, a council emerged that was made up primarily of former Porfirian councilmen. But in contrast to the elected council of 1911, the one established under Huerta included the perennial working-class interlocutor, engineer Carlos Peralta, and as alternate the self-described "worker" Angel Montalvo, both of whom had played important roles in Porfirian labor organizations. The restoration of municipal autonomy to Mexico City would come instead by decree from First Chief Venustiano Carranza in 1914 in the midst of civil war. Unable or unwilling to organize new elections, Carranza simply reappointed those councilmembers and several alternates elected in the December 1912 elections, before placing a military officer in charge of the city council in August 1915. Elections for the city council, restored for the next decade to its status of municipio libre, were finally held in December 1917, well after elected municipal government had been established in much of the nation.[18]

The last democratic elections held in the city under Madero were the congressional elections of June 1912. A law passed by the sitting Porfirian Congress in early 1912 allowed for congressional elections by direct vote, which encouraged popular electoral participation. In the months leading up to the actual elections, the PCP made a more concerted effort than they had in the previous two elections to include workers in its activities and to attract the working-class vote for its candidates. Nominating conventions were held in at least some of the Federal District delegations. But these efforts fell short of including specific worker demands in the party program or of running primary candidates for Congress in the Federal District with direct ties to the many worker political clubs. Some small political clubs of workers such as the Political Club of Workers (Club Político de Obreros) registered with City Hall separately but as "an integral part of the Progressive Constitutional

Party." Another group, which became the Club Político Serdán, was originally formed primarily by workers of the Mexican Light and Power Company as "a mutualist organization or league of workers." But the chair of the first meeting, engineer Ezequiel Pérez Jr., convinced those attending that work-related problems could be solved by meeting with bosses and that workers should instead "work to consolidate in whatever way possible the great work of the deserving chief of the revolution."[19] The incident suggests that some workers' organizations were divided between political and workplace organizing and that at least in the first year of the Madero revolution, middle-class intermediaries may have tipped the scale toward the political.

Several parties and some political clubs based in the electoral districts of the capital proposed candidates who were workers or had a clear worker-oriented platform to run within or outside the ruling coalition and managed somewhat to broaden the political debate. On the margins of the principal parties was the Socialist Workers Party (Partido Socialista Obrero, or PSO), founded in August 1911 by the German-born piano tuner Paul Zierold. While never acquiring more than fifty members or becoming a serious electoral force, it played an important role by introducing European social democratic ideas in Mexico and intellectually engaging a small group of Mexico City craftworkers, including Jacinto Huitrón, the tailor Luis Méndez, and the carpenter Pioquinto Roldán, who would all soon play a formative role in the workers' movement.[20]

The group remained in close correspondence with Socialist parties in the United States and Germany, and in its newspaper El Socialista and in the sympathetic pages of El Paladín, they advocated ideas out of synch with most Mexican radicals. For example, the PSO initiated a suggestive polemic by advocating women's suffrage, a position staunchly opposed by the Catholic Party. The debate may have been started by the hundreds of women who marched in public demonstrations and wrote to the provisional president, Francisco León de la Barra, during the summer of 1911 demanding the vote for women.[21] In the December city council elections, the Maderista press noted a conflict that occurred at a polling site when a sacristan who was a candidate for the Catholic Party tried to drag a woman affiliated with the Club Hijas de la Revolución to the police station. For the sacristan the issue was not the woman's distribution of PCP material in the proximity of the polling station but rather that "women shouldn't get mixed up in the practice of *civismo*." While the PCP accepted the support of women in electoral campaigns, they fell short of supporting their right to vote. One of the most progressive members of the PCP, Rafael Pérez Taylor, who developed close ties with workers' organizations, similarly denounced the proposal of the PSO as absurd. Workers should instead push for a general improvement in the conditions of male workers, "since the feminine sex depends on it, and helping the first, their consorts are directly helped as well." In spite of its role as an intellectual vanguard, the Socialist Workers Party remained isolated and without a social base.[22]

Workers joined the Popular Workers Party (Partido Popular Obrero, or PPO) in greater numbers when it formed just a month before the congressional elections. The PPO joined together many of the members of the pro-Madero mutualist organizations in the capital and managed to field their own candidates for senator and six of twelve deputies from the Federal District. Candidates included the engineer Ezequiel Pérez, who had briefly tried to mediate for workers in the citywide textile strike the previous January and who had urged electrical workers to choose political over workplace organizing. But the PPO was dominated by Madero's minister of the interior (*gobernación*), Jesús Flores Magón, and, except for its overtly political function, seems to have been largely in the mold of previous clientelistic labor relations.[23] Thus the two main political parties that claimed to represent workers were limited either by size (the PSO) or by overly close ties to the government (the PPO).

Small parties faced significant obstacles to even getting the names of their candidates on ballots. Since each party had to produce individual ballots for each of their candidates, the cost of printing could be significant. For example, the PPO, which ran candidates for only half of the twelve deputy seats in the Federal District, had to come up on its own with sixty-eight thousand ballots. The confusion created by this same system of separate ballots for each candidate also lent itself to accusa-

tions of fraud, since illiterate or uninformed voters could easily be manipulated if those attending ballot boxes did not give them all the available ballots.[24]

Of more electoral significance on the left of the PCP was the Liberal
Party (Partido Liberal, or PL), founded in August 1911 by former
members of the Mexican Liberal Party such as Juan Sarabia, Antonio
Díaz Soto y Gama, and Jesús Flores Magón. The PL was essentially an
amalgam of clubs from throughout the country, many tied to personalities, districts, and social sectors and all allied independently and somewhat critically with Madero and his official party, the PCP. With its roots
in the PLM and its 1906 program, the PL proved a much more vocal advocate of labor legislation than the PCP, including in their program an
eight-hour day for government employees and an end to preferential
wages for foreigners. But just as they alternated between critical support
and opposition to the Madero government during his brief presidency,
the PL wavered in their support of workers in labor conflicts. For example, in September 1911 many of the key radicals within the PL withdrew
their call for a public demonstration to condemn government repression of striking streetcar workers.

The bulk of the PL supported joint candidates with the PCP. The radical wing of the PL, already marginalized by the time of the party's April
convention, eventually ran its own independent candidates in several
districts of the Federal District. An example of the efforts of the radicals
was the independent candidacy of Felipe Santibañez in the primarily
working-class District Two of Mexico City, who had the support of Díaz
Soto y Gama, Juan Sarabia, and the "Advanced Group" of the PL. Santibañez was a lawyer, former PLM member, and one of the founders of the
PSO. Within the PL he had penned much of the party's position on
agrarian reform. He laid claim to workers' support through his Club
Obrero Liberal and their short-lived newspaper *Fuerza Obrera*. As with
most of the radical liberals, he was of middle-class background and—as
perhaps befitted the structure and social crisis facing the nation, if not
the campaign of a Mexico City candidate for Congress—his primary social concern was agrarian reform. In fact, under the outspoken leadership of Antonio Díaz Soto y Gama, even the radical wing of the liberals

had repeatedly pushed the need for agrarian reform over issues important to urban workers and moderated the labor demands made earlier in the 1906 PLM program and in the Tacubaya program. The neglect of labor issues helped undermine the brief political possibilities of a potential electoral alliance between middle-class radicals and workers in the capital.

The PCP and its allies in the PL, fearful of the strength of the Catholic Party in the capital as evidenced in city council elections, sought to assure themselves the majority of the electoral seats of the Federal District through awkward and eventually unsustainable alliances with conservatives closely associated with the Porfirian regime.[25]

A more traditional type of mutualist politics was undertaken in District Ten of the Federal District, in the suburban town of Tacubaya, where the right wing of the PL ran the industrialist Carlos Zetina. Zetina was an important financier and owner of a large Tacubaya shoe factory, where he had established, funded, and controlled a mutualist society among his own workers. He had been a firm supporter of Landa y Escandón's Mutualist and Moralizing Society and also represented industrialists in the textile convention that took place during the same summer as the elections. Zetina presented himself as the candidate not *of* the workers but *for* the workers, and his platform amounted to an extension of the philanthropic paternalism of the Porfirian governor of the Federal District, Guillermo Landa y Escandón. With the support of the party leadership and no doubt many workers—at least those of his own factory—Zetina won his seat as deputy from District Ten, while Santibañez lost badly in District Two. Months later Zetina headed the opposition in Congress to a Madero proposal that favored the regulation of the hours and wages of textile workers.[26]

The very working-class District Two was won by PCP candidate Marcos López Jiménez, who took pride in his past as a printer and would eventually become director of Carranza's Labor Department in 1915. But there is little indication that he ran a "labor" campaign, and as congressman, he remained marginal to the few debates on labor-related issues that occurred in the Congress. The labor activist who came closest to a victory was the journalist Rafael Pérez Taylor, who was elected as alternate from District Six on the PCP ticket and had been nominated at a district convention in which "the working element predominated."[27] Pérez Taylor had close ties with workers' organizations and would play an important role over the next two years organizing workers within the Casa del Obrero Mundial and in 1915 as an advocate of workers' rights in the Convention Congress of Villa and Zapata. But as an alternate, he would have no actual role in the Congress.

The workers of Mexico City were largely excluded from the formal political arena by the elections. To the extent that they had representation at all in Congress, they relied on a handful of radical middle-class leaders elected from other states, people like Heriberto Jara and Juan Sarabia. Heriberto Jara, who proclaimed his working-class roots on the floor of the Congress, was born into a middle-class family and had been a bookkeeper in the Rio Blanco factory. He had been involved in the Rio Blanco strike and was indeed elected with the support of the textile workers of Orizaba. José Natividad Macias, a lawyer, claimed to have been elected by miners from his native Guanajuato.[28]

National turnout for the 1912 congressional elections, which were probably the freest and most competitive in Mexican history, remained low, even in the Federal District. The two candidates who received the most votes for the Federal District senate seat, Francisco Leon de la Barra of the Catholic Party and Fernando Iglesias Calderon for the Maderista coalition, won a total of 4,431 and 5,061 votes respectively in the entire Federal District; their combined votes barely exceeded the total number of male workers in the textile factories of the Federal District. Marcos López Jiménez won the largely working-class District Two with only 696 votes. The *Mexican Herald* estimated that "the vote was a small one, not more than 20 percent of the voters in many places taking the trouble to go to the polls." The U.S. consul in Mexico City observed after the congressional elections that "while I saw many well dressed men, seemingly of the professional class, and those of the laboring class, I did not see any of the lower or 'pelado' class voting." The periodical *La Fuerza Obrera*, which supported Santibañez for the seat in District Two of Mexico City, lamented the effects of "the long political abstention of the immense majority of the Mexican people" under the Porfirian dictatorship.[29]

For the most part, the great, urban masses present at earlier Maderista rallies and at the fall of Díaz could not be mobilized to vote in congressional elections. Madero and the PCP proved unwilling to create a real party structure that could mobilize urban workers to vote by offering them representation and a meaningful political program. Workers on their own, and in the absence of strong union structures, proved unable to create viable political organizations, much less the "party essentially of workers" that El Tipógrafo Mexicano had predicted months earlier after Madero's election. The city council and congressional elections failed to incorporate or appeal to the "great unwashed" who had rallied to support Madero in public demonstrations in the previous two years.

After the elections, many members of workers' organizations became disillusioned with the possibilities for direct political participation and the support they could expect from elected officials of other classes. In the same month of the June 1912 elections, a series of political splits occurred that signaled this disillusionment. Many of the radicals within the PL left that organization, as if to acknowledge PLM founder Ricardo Flores Magón's reproach from the United States that elections would not solve Mexico's social problems. As James Cockcroft argues, by the time of congressional elections, "the moderate PL was in danger of forfeiting its claims of nonviolent, Leftist opposition against Madero to representatives of the ascending labor movement" in Mexico City.[30]

A similar split occurred within the small PSO, whose founder, Zierold, and core group continued to advocate a social democratic–style electoral role for workers' organizations. Craftworkers within the party, such as Luis Méndez, Jacinto Huitrón, and others, came to reject elections and lean more toward organizing workers exclusively in the workplace. In the next months, members debated the meaning of recent elections in the sympathetic pages of El Paladín. "What benefit have workers obtained going to vote?" asked Huitrón. They would be far better off, he insisted, if "the time employed by socialists in electoral battles had been dedicated to the organization of the productive classes." Several members left the PSO in June 1912 to form the anarchist-inspired cultural group Luz. Months later, the group formed around Luz along with the various groups of craftworkers and radical intellectuals who had left the PL, such as Díaz Soto y Gama, joined together to found the Casa del Obrero Mundial. The PSO gradually lost its few remaining members until it eventually was absorbed into the Casa del Obrero Mundial in the spring of 1913, where the dominant position was a rejection of electoral participation.[31]

Finally, a division occurred in the PPO, whose growing ties with the newly created Labor Department and the minister of the interior made it more and more dependent on government favor. In spite of these ties, the PPO declared the elections to be a joke and demanded their annulment. Those workers who left the PL, PSO, and PPO had concluded that they were not only at the margins of politics but also at the margins of most popular struggles, which were increasingly taking place in the streets and workplace. The political participation of workers would not come from a "real vote," and much less a defense of elected leaders, but from their organization in the workplace and, for many workers, from the leverage such organizations could wield vis-à-vis political authorities. The gradual shift to workplace organization after mid-1912, coupled with the challenges to the legal order brought about by peasant and military rebellions and eventually the Huerta coup in February 1913, ended a cycle of participation in electoral politics that had begun with the promise of electoral freedom in 1909.[32] Before addressing the specific labor policies of Madero and the Twenty-sixth Congress, it is necessary to look at the pattern of workplace organization that emerged in the shadow of elections.

From Mutualist to Resistance Societies

In spite of the continued emphasis on political organization in the first year after the fall of Díaz, the working people of Mexico City also took seriously the restoration of their rights to associate freely as individuals, guaranteed by the 1857 constitution and invoked by Madero in his 1910 presidential campaign. During the year following May 1911, mutual aid societies in Mexico City multiplied, flourished, and expanded their membership and activities, accelerating an organizational trend that dated from the previous decade. At the same time, the organizational efforts of workers came to challenge both mutualist forms of organization and the legal limits of liberal doctrine on the collective organization and demands of workers. The new wave of mutualist organizations thus provided an important stepping stone to the formation of new, combative, as well as pragmatic worker organizations.

Some work-based organizations formed immediately in the days and weeks before and after the fall of Díaz, particularly among craftworkers who had a long history of previous organization. Many of these new societies broke with the recent past, and rather than incorporate a variety of workers from different sectors in the same organization, they attempted to consolidate workers from a single sector into a single organization. At the same time, these new organizations initially relied on a certain corporate or "trade" consciousness rooted in colonial and nineteenth-century guilds. Many referred collectively to their membership as the "gremio" of a particular profession, and though apparently no formal distinction was made between small shop owners, masters, and journeymen, some continued to deny "voice and vote" to affiliated apprentices. By 1912, unified mutualist societies numbering between five hundred and fifteen hundred members had been organized in the capital among printers, stonecutters, boilermakers, restaurant workers, office workers, federal employees, and shop employees, in addition to a number of smaller new mutualist societies.[33]

The initial consciousness among these workers was rooted in an increasing articulation of the idea that modern industries had created unfair monopolies in traditional crafts, factories, and sweatshops. Even the mutualist newspaper El Obrero Mexicano, organ of the Mutualist and Moralizing Society, in November 1911 commented positively on a strike of two hundred women garment workers and acknowledged that not alcohol but "monopolies are the greatest enemies of our class, the means of exploitation to bleed the worker and take away his energies." Similarly, monopoly was often associated with foreign entrepreneurs and foreign firms, an identification unmistakable in the call by stonecutters to form a union in September 1911:

It is sad and shameful that Mexican workers serve as a stepping stone so that foreigners can climb up and treat us worse than caciques or foremen. Catalan, Italian, and French contractors receive the best jobs, as if we couldn't undertake them, supposing that they are better and diligent and have greater necessities, that they know how to eat, dress and wear better shoes than the Mexican, who is satisfied with tortilla and chile, wears sandals and wraps a sash around his waist instead of a belt . . . No *compañeros*, we must rise up and reclaim the justice that in the name of our families we need to demand.[34]

The resentment of the presence of foreigners at all levels of industry was common, whether among skilled craftworkers who competed with large foreign companies or among workers in those companies who were subject to the orders of foreigners. For example, the "Cuitlahuac" Political Club to Instruct Workers (Club Político Instructivo de Obreros "Cuitlahuac") was founded by a variety of workers in June 1911 and listed among its diverse goals that of "procuring by whatever methods are within our grasp that in factories, workshops, etc., the owners, directors, and maestros be Mexicans."[35]

Such methods often involved requesting government interventions on behalf of workers and thus pushed the limits of the liberalism of the Madero regime. A mutualist organization of owners of small carpenter shops combined an invitation to President Madero to be the club's honorary president with a request that "those who undertake all the carpentry and cabinetry jobs for public offices be Mexican." A somewhat different appeal to the government that echoed the sense of an unjust assault upon national craft production was that of the Great National League of Tailors (Gran Liga Nacional de Sastres), which demanded in early 1912 that tariffs be raised on imports of foreign goods. Government actions such as the gradual Mexicanization of ownership and management of the railroads, initiated under Porfirio Díaz and continued under Madero, were popular among railroad workers and urban workers alike.[36]

The organization of mutual aid societies was encouraged by the newly formed Labor Department, an acknowledgment both of the importance of the "labor question" and of the government's willingness to move cautiously toward intervention. The Labor Department was set up at the initiative and under the guidance of Madero and embodied the goals of his administration. These goals were to assure industrial peace by avoiding or settling conflicts between workers and employers, to protect women and children in the workplace, and to discourage militant and independent organization among workers. Arbitration by the Labor Department required the agreement of workers and employers but even then was not binding. The Labor Department largely attempted to formalize the patronage and mediating roles of public officials under Porfirio Díaz. The executive proposal sent to Congress acknowledged the need for the positive "intervention of the State in the situation and future of the working classes" and even for "official interference in the questions raised between capital and labor, though without intervening in a decisive way." As such, it was an important step in the development of the postrevolutionary government labor policy; but it had limited legal and moral authority to force employers to accept workers' organizations or to impose solutions to labor conflicts and was regarded with suspicion by many of the more skilled and organized workers in the city.[37]

In late 1912 the Labor Department supported the Great Workers League, perhaps the same organization that had formed in the spring of 1910, in an attempt to create a "Great Confederation of Labor" (Gran Confederación del Trabajo) under the leadership of such key Porfirian labor intermediaries as Angel Montalvo and Carlos Peralta. But by then the initiative for unifying workers' organizations had passed to groups such as the Casa del Obrero Mundial, and the organization divided over the issue of government intervention. In spite of its failure to capture the initiative among the city's working people, the remnant of the Great Workers League continued to meet within the offices of the Labor Department through 1915.[38]

The most significant government intervention in the organization of workers occurred in the aftermath of the massive and national textile strikes of 1911–12, discussed at greater length in the next chapter. In the context of the July 1912 textile convention, the Labor Department created a permanent Central Committee of Workers based in Mexico City that represented textile workers nationally before the government, though not directly before employers. The purview of the Central Committee of Workers was restricted by its dependence on the Labor Department for funds, office space, and the narrow definition of its responsibilities. Nonetheless, the convention and its structures were the most far-reaching labor innovations of the Madero government. The textile convention and the Central Committee of Workers had two consequences in terms of the participation of textile workers in the labor movement in Mexico City: the first was to provide textile workers with an incipient national structure, and the second was an early orientation of textile workers toward seeking government intervention. Both consequences would initially distance this key industrial sector from patterns of organization and mobilization elsewhere in the city.

Elsewhere in the capital, craftworkers set the pace and tone of organization. Many of the newly organized societies first responded to the challenges of the changing industrial structure and foreign influence by turning to cooperatives. In the rush to form new organizations, projects for cooperatives of credit, production, and consumption intended to bypass monopolies and contractors were common, particularly among skilled craftworkers but even among industrial and unskilled workers. On the symbolic date of 20 November 1911, one year after Francisco Madero's call for the overthrow of Porfirio Diaz, the Great National League of Tailors announced the formation of a cooperative workshop that would allow tailors an alternative to the system controlled by the large clothing stores and their middlemen. The project faltered for lack of administrative experience and lack of access to sufficient capital. Similarly, the stonecutters found that the only way to bypass big contractors was to appeal directly to the government for a share of state projects.[39]

Workers' organizations verbally attacked the control of a handful of banks ("those Frenchmen of the Bank of London and Mexico . . . who do more for foreigners than for Mexicans") and sought to "Mexicanize" and democratize credit, but mutual credit projects were almost always unsuccessful. In early 1911, the Railroad Workers' Alliance (Alianza de los Ferrocarrileros), which represented one of the most proletarianized occupations in the country, announced its intention to establish a savings bank for "railroad workers, so that they can slowly put together sufficient capital to become small owners." But these projects stood little chance of survival, given the limited capital available to workers, the burden of inflation and changing currencies, and the concentrated ownership of production and credit. The Labor Department encouraged such cooperative efforts by workers verbally if not materially, even when in doubt of their success; citing European examples, the director acknowledged to the minister of development that, while such efforts had rarely proved successful, cooperatives were a more positive channel for workers' organizations than the "tyranny" of "unions of resistance."[40]

The appeal of such projects was strong among skilled trade workers in small or medium-sized workplaces but was less obvious among skilled and unskilled workers in large factory settings. A variety of other attempts to create cooperative foundries, print shops, farms, and worker housing never got off the ground, failed quickly, or turned to appeals for government grants or contracts as the only chance of survival, as occurred with attempts by the stonecutters and garment workers.[41] These new organizations, particularly those of craftworkers, briefly teetered between the goals and ideology of mutualism, that of small producer organizations concerned with issues of security as well as cultural and moral improvement, and those of workers who sought to assert themselves within the structure of modern industry.

An important transitional organization in the shift from mutualist societies to unions was the Confederation of Graphic Arts (Confederación de las Artes Graficas), founded on 21 May 1911, days before Díaz resigned. The confederation was to a large extent the realization of the project of the same group of printers who in 1910 had published the newspaper *Evolución* and supported Madero's presidential campaign. In spite of its name, the confederation was a single organization that sought to bring together all workers within the printing industry "with mutualist goals and for the moral and intellectual progress of the profession." Within two months the confederation attracted over 500 members and a year later had over 750 associates from a variety of professions within the printing industry, including apprentices and women. Among them were printers like Rafael Quintero, who was steeped in popular liberal traditions and had supported Madero's first presidential campaign. Working-class leaders like Quintero were influenced by the anarchist and utopian socialist ideas brought by southern European immigrants such as the Spaniard Amadeo Ferrés, founder and first presiding officer of the confederation.[42]

Almost immediately the confederation distanced itself from concerns of mutual aid and security and proclaimed itself to be a society "in the spirit of resistance in the workplace" and created a "resistance fund."[43] But while increasingly taking on the forms of a union, the group remained conservative in their professed anarchist ideals. While liberally quoting the radical writers of European revolutionary movements in their meetings and publications, Ferrés and the cadre of educated printers closest to him saw the role of the organization and its members as that of proselytizing and regenerating the mass of unenlightened workers, to be done primarily through the organizing of cultural events and the publication of their newspaper, El Tipógrafo Mexicano. Not only were two thousand copies of their biweekly printed, but many of its articles were reprinted in both mainstream and working-class newspapers. In reality, their everyday project was one of education and self-help, in which the printers held a privileged position and responsibility to bring enlightenment to their fellow workers. One such project, never fulfilled, was the planned creation of a Rationalist School based on the ideas of the recently martyred Catalan teacher Francisco Ferrer Guardia. Another project eventually implemented was a cooperative print shop to provide work for unemployed affiliates.

At least according to the anarchist rhetoric of the group's leadership, capitalism and political authority were eventually to be defeated by promoting "union and fraternity" among workers, through the creation by workers of their own, alternative forms of organization and through the eventual and inevitable instrument of the general strike. In the meantime, from the columns of the confederation newspaper, leaders either rejected strikes—echoing in slightly different terms the advice of former Governor Landa y Escandón that "in all strikes it is the worker that is hurt rather than capital, since he never has a penny saved and can't stand the aversions of adversity"—or at best urged workers to use the strike carefully "so that the blow given by it is mortal, without cutting the fingers of those who manage it." When spontaneous conflicts broke out, usually in some of the city's larger shops (such as in the newspaper *La Prensa*), the confederation reluctantly offered moral support and money from their resistance funds while admonishing strikers to "stay within the order of law."[44]

An inherent tension emerged in the confederation between the more conservative leadership led by Ferrés, which felt that confrontations with employers should be avoided until some distant future when workers had achieved stronger organizations and greater enlightenment, and those led by Rafael Quintero, who advocated more direct action and confrontation with employers. If people like Ferrés brought radical and anarchist ideas from Europe, it was people like Quintero who would Mexicanize and apply them selectively to the changing industrial and political situation of Mexico. The differences also paralleled divisions within the membership: some worked in and even owned small artisan shops, where antagonisms between owners and employees were muted. Others worked in the large print shops and publishing companies in the capital, such as the foreign-owned American Book Company, government print shops, and the principal newspapers of the capital, including *El Imparcial* and *Nueva Era*. Quintero, who was employed in the large shops of the government's *Diario Oficial*, would eventually lead this group out of the confederation and into the Casa del Obrero Mundial.[45]

After the creation of the Confederation of Graphic Arts , the term "resistance society" was commonly taken up among new worker organizations, such as those of the stonecutters, tailors, and boilermakers, while many older organizations changed their names and much of their corporate language accordingly.[46] As with the printers, this shift may have reflected the rise to prominence within these organizations of workers from large rather than small shops and the reorientation that came from increasing association among workers within the city and from different trade and skill levels.

Solidarity among workers' associations occurred to some extent nationally, among workers of the same trade in other cities, and especially locally, among different groups of workers within Mexico City. For example, the Confederation of the Graphic Arts corresponded with printer associations in many provincial cities and even sent one hundred pesos to support printers on strike in Torreón. But more significantly, it established close ties with other groups of workers within the city, offering newly organized groups such as the stonecutters meeting space within its building and even a section of its newspaper. At different times during the confederation's three-year existence, at least four other workers' organizations that registered with the Labor Department listed the same address. Such solidarity helped to move many workers' organizations in Mexico City from a "gremialist" identification to one based more on class.

In the flurry of organization in the first year of Maderista rule, this shift to a working-class identification was also obvious in the language of these new organizations. For example, the Mexican Union of Stonecutters (Unión de Canteros Mexicanos) announced its formation in September 1911 with a denunciation of the role of foreign monopolies within the trade. By May 1912, in a speech at the first anniversary of the founding of the Confederation of Graphic Arts, the stonecutters' secretary general, Severino Rodríguez Villafuerte, attacked property relations, rather than just corruption and foreign monopoly, and appealed to all workers instead of just those of a particular trade. In flowery rhetoric, Rodríguez Villafuerte urged workers to "throw far away the heavy burden of the monstrous granite block that weighs on the shoulders of the producing class; cut the iron tentacles of the enormous bourgeois octopus that sucks from us day after day, hour after hour, minute after minute, the integral product of our energies." The passage suggests an increasing radicalization of the language of at least the leadership of these new organizations of skilled crafts, one that differed dramatically from the language of mutualism and served as a catalyst to organize more workers from different sectors and in ways that approximated the form of modern unions. At the same time, the speech acknowledged the limited consciousness and participation of the vast majority of workers. Rodríguez Villafuerte blamed not only the "bourgeois octopus" but also "those slaves of their own moral misery, those wretched who are satisfied with receiving, in exchange for their enormous effort and long hours of exhausting days, a miserable crumb of bread that the master despotically and insolently throws them."[47]

The leadership and cultural orientation for much of worker organization and the definitive move away from mutualism soon passed to the anarchist-inspired Casa del Obrero (House of the Worker), which soon took the organizing momentum away from the Confederation of Graphic Arts. In September 1912, the Casa del Obrero grew out of an attempt by the cultural group Luz and the Mexican Union of Stonecutters to form the Rationalist School that the printers had proposed but not consolidated. When the project's principal mover, Colombian teacher Juan Francisco Moncaleano, was expelled from the country by the Madero government for his organizational activities, the locale rented for the school was converted instead into the Casa del Obrero, a "Center of Doctrinaire Dissemination of Advanced Ideas." The term "mundial" would be added to the Casa del Obrero name the following year.

Founding and early members were made up of two groups. The most important was a variety of skilled craftworkers and their mutualist or resistance societies, including the stonecutters, tailors, coach drivers, and the workers of the textile factory La Linera. These groups were led by, among others, the tailor Luis Méndez and the mechanic and metalworker Jacinto Huitrón, both of whom had passed briefly through the Socialist Workers Party. A number of Spanish immigrants were important organizers and frequent speakers at Casa del Obrero Mundial cultural events, such as Eloy Armenta and José Colado of the shop and restaurant employees' unions, but immigrants were neither as numerous nor as important in the leadership of the Casa del Obrero Mundial as its critics at the time and some later historians have claimed.

The second group was a handful of middle-class radicals and intellectuals, including the journalist Rafael Pérez Taylor, Antonio Díaz Soto y Gama, and the congressional deputies Heriberto Jara and Serapio Rendón, many of whom had briefly passed through the PLM of the Flores Magón brothers as well as the more moderate PL. While lacking any clear union base, these self-identified freethinkers were readily incorporated and central to public activities and cultural events of the Casa del Obrero Mundial and in many cases played important roles in organizing specific groups of workers. Their significant intellectual influence was reinforced by the financial difficulties of the component unions (with the exceptions of the relatively wealthy printers' and electricians' unions), which often made it necessary for middle-class members such as Díaz Soto y Gama or sympathetic members of Congress, such as Jesús Urueta and Heriberto Jara, to help sustain the Casa del Obrero Mundial with personal funds. At the same time, the considerable influence of these intellectuals depended very much on their daily participation in the workings of the Casa del Obrero Mundial. Even an intellectual of the stature of Díaz Soto y Gama maintained little influence in the Casa del Obrero Mundial after he joined the Zapatistas in Morelos in early 1914. Similarly, in spite of the respect many Casa members felt for the Flores Magón brothers, their insurrectionary urgings from Los Angeles or from U.S. jails to "take the land, the machinery, the modes of transportation and even the houses" were greatly resented by the working-class leadership of the Casa del Obrero Mundial and had little effect on decisions within the organization and its component unions.[48]

The Casa del Obrero Mundial as a whole had a dual role. The first was as a cultural organization, publishing newspapers aimed at workers, instituting night classes to develop vocational skills and self-improvement, organizing plays and poetry readings, and offering general exhortations to sobriety and discipline in work and family life. "Enlightenment is the most important factor of socialism," Rafael Pérez Taylor insisted in the first months of the Casa's existence, noting the nation's 78 percent illiteracy rate. Drawing in part on Mexican working-class traditions, the efforts of the Confederation of Graphic Arts, and the program of Catalan educator Ferrer Guardia, founders of the Casa del Obrero Mundial sought to educate workers in ways that identified working-class traditions and interests as unique and central to the organization of society. The texts they chose were primarily the writings of radical European thinkers, particularly anarchists, and the histories of other working-class movements or historical moments, such as the 1870 Paris Commune.

Government officials and the pro-Madero *Nueva Era* warned of the "dangerous and dissolving ideas" propagated within the Casa and on

occasion jailed or exiled its leaders. But an employee of the Labor Department acknowledged that, while anarchist doctrine was indeed terrible, it would be tolerable if "all those workers who professed it were as
inoffensive as the Mexicans adept to that doctrine, who settle for such
thoughts as signs: 'cerebral dynamite' written on blackboards hung at
the entrance of the Casa del Obrero Mundial."[49] Indeed, while aspects of
anarcho-syndicalist doctrine, such as the advocacy of direct action and
the rejection of politics, were common currency in the newspapers,
speeches, and statutes of the Casa del Obrero Mundial, the diversity of
participants and ideas among the Casa membership, and the previous
and eventual political positions of many self-proclaimed anarchists,
suggests that anarchism was at best a prominent component among a
variety of orienting ideologies that included popular liberalism and even
social democracy (the latter through the affiliated Socialist Workers
Party). Rather than a set of firmly held abstract principles, anarchism
became Mexicanized to fit national traditions and contexts.

As such, the main contribution of anarchist ideas to organizations
like the Casa was to provide a vocabulary for articulating class differences and an imperative for independent organization, free of many of
the constraints of mutualism. Anarchism also provided a timely explanation for the limits of Maderista democracy. This ideological openness
was inherent in the various attempts of the Casa to create a Rationalist
School in which "all doctrines that are in agreement with nature and
reason will be taught without restriction."[50]

Many Casa leaders invoked anarchist doctrine in denouncing the "tri-
ple octopus" of "the clergy, capital, and the government," but an absolute adherence to anarchist beliefs would have further separated the "intellectual workers" from their rank and file, for whom religion and
nationalism remained powerful elements of the social order. Even
within the ranks of the Casa intellectuals, Díaz Soto y Gama preached a
Christian Communism that probably appealed to the rank and file more
than did denunciations of church and religious belief. Rather than issuing outright attacks on religion and government, the statutes of the constituent organizations of the Casa usually followed late-nineteenth-cen-
tury working-class traditions in rejecting the inclusion of religion and

politics as legitimate concerns, since these matters could "champion passions that can destroy the organization of workers." "In the bosom of the syndicate," wrote the tailor Luis Méndez, "there is room for all the oppressed, all the unfortunate, no matter what religion they profess."⁵¹ This meant that in everyday practice, at least in its first two years, both professions of faith and overt political alliances were largely avoided, as were virulent attacks on organized religion or political factions.

At the same time that the Casa del Obrero Mundial offered working people "cerebral dynamite" for their minds, it also appealed to their pragmatic desire to improve their skills. For example, in June 1913 they offered classes in cloth cutting, line drawing and calligraphy, clay modeling, geometry, grammar, bookbinding, geography, mechanics, physics, and the French and English languages. Even their newspapers—Lucha, La Tribuna, Emancipación Obrera, and Ariete—combined anarchist proclamations with excerpts from a variety of classics from European literature, such as Victor Hugo, and notices of strikes and union meetings along with practical reflections and announcements about the everyday activities of workers.⁵²

While emphasizing self-improvement, the Casa challenged much of the moralizing discourse of middle-class reformers and government officials. For example, the educational project of the Casa challenged the dominant, middle-class discourse that women were to be schooled separately and primarily in the economy of household management and the moral education of children. The Casa insisted on the equality of the sexes in all spheres of society and advocated a "scientific and rational" curriculum that would not differentiate between men and women in content or separate men and women in different classrooms. Three women were among the initial members of the group Luz, and women participated fully in the educational and cultural activities of the Casa del Obrero Mundial. In Casa meetings, teacher Paula Osorio pushed members to read books that would scientifically prove the equality of both sexes, and she and other women played a prominent role by teaching classes for adults and children within the Casa. While the Casa rarely incorporated women into positions of leadership, and was at first slow to organize sectors where women predominated, from its conception women were fully incorporated into the educational project of the Casa as both students and as teachers.[53]

Similarly, Casa propagandists urged sobriety but refused to blame alcohol and other vices for the conditions of working people. Typical was printer Federico de la Colina, who wrote from the pages of *Emancipación Obrera* that "alcoholic stimulants are yet another vehicle of relaxation for the working classes—they represent a vital factor, since the momentary exaltation that they produce picks up and strengthens the organism, which their miserly nutrition doesn't sufficiently sustain." The solution for improving the conditions of working people was not to eliminate vice, he went on, but rather was that "proletarians should make of each occupation [*gremio*] a powerful and solid union that demands and conquers the right to the life we all deserve."[54]

This organizational imperative was the second role the Casa played, as a catalyst for the formation of unions and eventually the implementation of direct action, generally through strikes. Within months of its founding, the Casa del Obrero Mundial moved away from its almost exclusive emphasis on education and moral regeneration to more directly criticize the terms of labor and the political sources of inequality, to declare a syndicalist orientation, and to provide a loose confederating structure for the various new workers' organizations in the city.[55] Through both roles, education and organization, the Casa del Obrero Mundial was fundamental in nursing the transition from mutualist societies to unions, while maintaining links across work and community.

The transition from mutualism to resistance was aided by the material conditions brought on by the military fighting of the revolution. The multiple currencies and disruption of the economy brought by each successive occupation of Mexico City during the period 1913–16 spurred an inflationary cycle that decimated the funds held by mutual aid societies for the compensation of workers in cases of unemployment, sickness, and death. Mutualist funds became worthless just as members lost their jobs or faced sickness or death from the hunger and disease that frequented the city after 1914. For example, the value of the accumulated funds of the Mutualist and Moralizing Society, endowed generously by Governor Landa y Escandón in 1911, dropped by more than half in 1916.

These conditions encouraged a shift in strategy for many organizations toward more open confrontation with employers (even though strike funds were decimated as well) or direct demands on the government. The venerable Mutualist Society of Commercial Employees (Sociedad Mutualista de Empleados de Comercio) lost 135 members in a single quarter in 1915 to sickness and unemployment, was forced to move to a smaller place, and tried to sell its furniture to replenish funds. By 1916, the organization finally abandoned much of its mutualist language, if not its name, and began for the first time to talk of "defending ourselves from the bosses."[56]

While some of the most powerful new unions achieved a de facto recognition from employers who were forced to negotiate and some union leaders rejected any type of government interference, including legislation, most unions pushed authorities to establish legal identity for their new organizations. This demand was increasingly echoed even by remaining mutualist societies, which, even if unwilling to make direct demands of employers, increasingly saw the need for specific laws to protect their accumulated funds from inflation and to facilitate the stability of their organizations.[57]

Within two years after its founding, many of the principal workers' groups in the city had joined the Casa del Obrero Mundial (teachers, carpenters, shoemakers, printers, bricklayers, boilermakers, painters, textile workers, streetcar workers, and so forth), whose leadership increasingly attempted to bring women and less skilled workers into its ranks (cigarette workers, seamstresses, telephone operators).[58] This process of incorporation of less skilled workers, clear by September 1914, would culminate in late 1915 and early 1916.

The terms of resistance were continually debated within workers' organizations and the Casa del Obrero Mundial. Workers within a particular sector might organize in a number of ways: retreating toward mutualism, organizing industrial unions, or forming elite trade unions that protected the strategic position of the most skilled workers. All three types of organizations coexisted to some extent within the Casa del Obrero Mundial, in spite of the radical leanings of the leadership and the clear organizational shift toward unions. For example, the Union of the Manufacturing Arts (Sindicato del Arte Fabril y Similares) of textile workers reorganized in September 1914, allowing half of the weekly dues of twenty centavos to go for "the class struggle" and the other half for a mutual aid fund ("taking into account that some comrades cannot forget the old patterns of 'mutualism'"). Similarly, the Union of Rental Carriage Drivers (Sindicato de Conductores de Carruajes de Alquiler) assigned 75 percent of dues to a strike fund and administrative costs and 25 percent to mutual aid. Many newly formed unions continued to allow the participation of owners of small shops, though in that of the carpenters, owners were excluded from administrative positions. The prelude of the statutes of the Union of Rental Carriage Drivers in 1916 suggests the multiple functions and coexistence of mutualist and syndicalist goals: "The Union is for the male and female worker a second family, being an institution that procures them relief and consolation in bad times and a shelter in disasters; it is also a provider of jobs and a support so that justice is done them; it is the spokesman for their demands and their ruler in dealings with employers and public powers; it is also an instrument of technical education and moral elevation for the professional and rationalist teaching that it imparts to members."[59]

Given divergent goals within these organizations, sometimes heated debate occurred between groups of workers in the same industry or across sectors. Two years after the founding of the Confederation of Graphic Arts, a Printers' Union (Sindicato de Tipógrafos) was formed in September 1913 when Rafael Quintero, aided by Antonio Díaz Soto y Gama, Rafael Pérez Taylor, and Luis Méndez, led the bulk of the printers out of the confederation and into the Casa del Obrero Mundial. The newly formed Printers' Union denounced mutualism as "a trick and opportunity for the bourgeois to . . . exploit the working class," while another venerable mutualist organization of printers, dating from the previous century, the Francisco de León Mutualist Society, condemned the "dissolving and anarchic ideas" of the new union. After the bitter split, the conservative minority of the confederation veered again toward mutualism and cooperativism before finally disappearing in 1915, by which time the founder, Ferrés, had returned to his native Spain.[60]

Apparent splits occurred among other crafts. In mid-1913 there were two rival Unions of Stonecutters, one housed in the headquarters of the Confederation of Graphic Arts on Academia Street, the other in the Casa del Obrero Mundial on Estanco de Hombres Street. Similarly, the National League of Tailors remained at the Confederation location, while a Union of Tailors (Sindicato de Sastres) met at the Casa. These and other affiliations suggest that both the Confederation and the Casa coexisted as poles of organization in the city, splitting openly in September 1913 over the defection of many printers to the Casa. But the Casa clearly dominated organizational efforts by the end of that year. By late 1914, virtually all new organizations and many older ones were based physically at the Casa or at least had close ties with the Casa.

Restaurant workers were briefly represented in the Casa del Obrero Mundial by both a mutualist-cooperative society, one of its earliest affiliates, and a *sindicato*. The latter was formed within the Casa del Obrero Mundial in October 1914 after long discussion and "with some difficulties." The difficulties continued and seemed to be more personal than ideological. Members of the older and larger group insisted that, in spite of the name, they actually functioned as a union. The uneasy coexistence of these two groups within the Casa proved short-lived: soon after Eloy Armenta was expelled from the Casa del Obrero Mundial in January 1915 for accepting a position in the Labor Department, he led the recently formed union out as well.[61]

In the months after the Casa del Obrero Mundial celebrated the first May Day in Mexico in 1913, the majority of the workers' groups affiliated with the Casa del Obrero Mundial took on the name and many of the functions of syndicalist unions, commonly invoking "the class struggle and direct action." Thus unions existed in form and practice years before a legal framework for them was established. The following year, on 1 May 1914, the Casa del Obrero Mundial attempted to create a more centralized structure with formalized statutes for the city's unions, the General Workers Confederation of Mexico (Confederación General Obrera), just weeks before military dictator Huerta used force to close down the Casa del Obrero Mundial.[62] Not until January 1916 would the consolidation of a regional federation be possible.

In the first years of the revolution, while mutualist societies did not disappear, they clearly became marginal or at best subordinate to the patterns of mobilization in the city, as events of the revolution made them increasingly anachronistic. Records of the Labor Department indicate that membership in mutual aid societies dropped considerably from 1913 on. The drop was particularly dramatic in the case of former Governor Landa y Escandón's Mutualist and Moralizing Society; over three thousand members abandoned the organization during 1911–12. By 1918 it had barely two hundred members.[63] Similarly, the formation of *sindicatos* coincided with a deep crisis among the Catholic mutualist societies in the capital. Jesuit Alfredo Méndez Medina responded preemptively in 1913 by forming the first Catholic *sindicato* among bricklayers in the capital, declaring that the Catholic "*círculos* would die as they had everywhere, not because the *sindicatos* killed them, but because they lack life." But such efforts met immediate resistance from within the church, and workers' organizations backed by the Catholic Church seem also to have lost considerable support, at least among Mexico City workers during the decade of the revolution, and would not make a significant comeback anywhere until after 1917.[64]

By contrast, the trend toward organizing unions and including unskilled workers became clearly dominant after Huerta's defeat in August 1914 and a new group of sympathetic revolutionary military leaders from the Constitutionalist army held power in Mexico City. In a period of a few months, the ranks of existing Casa unions swelled, and dozens of new craft and factory workers organized and initiated strikes. By the time of the Casa-Constitutionalist Pact in February 1915, the Casa claimed a membership of fifty-two thousand within the Federal District and included at least twenty-three affiliated unions and federations.[65] Undoubtedly the numbers were exaggerated or hid tremendous variations in attendance and the payment of dues. But ultimately, the novelty of these organizations was not simply their number or size but also their ability to move beyond the defensive goals of mutualism to actively confront employers with their demands.

The perceived and real differences between the old and new forms of organization were summarized succinctly by workers of the jointly owned Mexico Tramways Company and the Mexican Light and Power Company, who organized their union in December 1914. Their manifesto denounced previous efforts to form a mutual aid society and asked a series of rhetorical questions:

> Can a mutualist society ask a powerful enterprise to raise the daily wage of millions of employees and workers, as our Federation has? When a powerful enterprise decides to lay off half of those who serve it just because, can a mutualist society confront it and demand that it return those positions? Can a mutualist society that promises gymnasiums and libraries also promise to defend the workers from the tricks and machinations of the capitalist? And finally, can a mutualist society formed by only a few of the best paid, who for the same reason have no idea of the sufferings of those who earn little, have the force of a Federation that includes all the personnel?[66]

Workers and the Limits of Political Reform

"Politics is the venom that slowly annihilates our life," observed Jacinto Huitrón. "In spite of their promises," wrote Díaz Soto y Gama, "politicians would never save the working class," whose salvation would only come through unions and the direct action of the strike and boycott.[67] Both remarks, published in 1913 in the Casa newspapers *Lucha* and *El Sindicalista*, were typical of the Casa leadership in its first year of existence. Formally, the Casa del Obrero Mundial rejected all involvement in politics, be it voting strategies, the launching of working-class political parties and candidates, petitions to political leaders, or even formal criticism of political groups and leaders.

Such a public position of political neutrality in these new organizations represented a shift away from the political aspirations and participation that had characterized the initiation of workers in the revolution in 1910 and 1911 and that had indeed been a deep-rooted part of popular liberalism through much of the previous century. Many key Casa leaders had previously taken active parts in political organizations and campaigns: the printer Rafael Quintero had organized workers on behalf of

Madero in 1910, and the mechanic Jacinto Huitrón had backed Madero
in 1910 and been a member of the Socialist Workers Party, which embraced electoral democracy.[68] The rejection of electoral politics and political alliances by late 1912 was the result of the perceived failures of
Maderista democracy to address workers' needs, the growing influence
of anarchist ideas, and, after the military coup of February 1913, the
farce of electoral democracy under General Huerta.

Besides rejecting electoral strategies, many Casa-affiliated unions in
the early years consistently rejected any attempts by the Maderista
government, particularly its recently created Labor Department, to intervene in workplace conflicts, even on behalf of workers. This position
was relatively easy to maintain by the skilled craftworkers of the Casa,
who enjoyed a privileged position within the labor market, but became
harder to sustain over time. As the Casa rapidly expanded its membership and incorporated less skilled workers and women in it ranks, its
leadership felt the tension between devotion to principles of political
neutrality that would almost certainly keep them distant from the struggles of the majority of workers and the search for political alliances that,
while giving them leverage against employers and prestige among the
mass of workers, meant straying from political neutrality and relinquishing some of the autonomy of their organizations.

For many working people, the prospect of forming new organizations and the defense of class interests remained inextricably linked to
their view of their political role as workers in the nation. For example,
when taxi-coach drivers announced the formation of their association in
February 1912, they not only celebrated the evident "unification of the
proletariat" to defend itself against exploitation and oppression but also
pointed out that such organization is "a communal good and a beautiful
hope for the Patria, because the day that she needs the support and defense of her good sons, she won't look for them isolated, one by one, to
reunify them with difficulty around the flag, but rather will find them organized and within reach, disciplined, strong, and ready to offer their
interest and life in defense of the liberty and the integrity of the Territory."[69] Such statements may have been used to publicly justify the new,
class-based organizations, but they also reflect the continued appeal of

popular liberalism and the periodic willingness of workers to form their own militias if requested by reluctant officials.

At the same time that the Casa publicly maintained a position of political neutrality and pursued its organizational strategies primarily in the workplace, they welcomed sympathetic middle-class deputies from Congress into their ranks. In his memoir, Casa member Luis Araiza lists seven deputies among the early members of the Casa, including Serapio Rendón and Heriberto Jara, key members of the pro-Madero Bloque Renovador. The prominence of these men in the Twenty-sixth Congress, and the reliance of the Casa on financial contributions from both intellectuals and deputies, made its position of political neutrality difficult, though not impossible. One chronicler of the period, Francisco Ramírez Plancarte, suggested that the Casa was created by the Maderista deputies as a way to fill up the galleries of the congress and counter the reactionary crowds mobilized by the Catholic Party. Although the radical deputies participated freely in the activities of the Casa and occasionally became involved in strikes, they neither created it nor dominated its activities.[70] The main strategy of the Casa through most of 1913 and 1914, during which time it came to dominate the workers' movement in Mexico City, was to organize workers in the workplace and in the working-class community rather than in elections and in the political arena.

A primary reason for the general rejection of political strategies by late 1912, at least among most workers affiliated with the Casa, was the generally tepid attitude of the Madero government toward labor reforms that in any way might contradict traditional liberal positions. As a result, the Madero government as a whole proved unable to adequately address the needs of workers. Besieged by challenges from former revolutionary allies (Orozco, Zapata, and Vázquez Gómez) as well as privileged elements of the Porfirian order (the church, the army, wealthy landowners, científicos), Madero and his cabinet proved slow to propose significant social legislation on behalf of workers. The Twenty-sixth Congress, during the few months it was in session under Madero, followed the lead on Madero's somewhat directionless labor policy rather than initiating its own proposals.

Congress itself was divided between its bare and fluctuating Maderista majority and a substantial and outspoken minority of deputies who either were staunch independents, identified with the Porfirian regime, or were affiliated with the new and outspoken Catholic Party. The Maderista group in Congress was itself divided: a conservative majority was most concerned with supporting their beleaguered president in his cautious path of compromise with Porfirian elements and limited and gradual reform, while a small but outspoken radical faction, at least in the last weeks before the Huerta coup, pushed for more dramatic reforms to fulfill the promises of the revolution that had toppled Díaz.[71] The diversity of opinions and factional divisions within Congress, both fairly dramatic departures from most of the Porfirian era and signs of an incipient democratic process, in the short term hindered any effective elaboration of social reform. And the short term was all Madero and the Twenty-sixth Congress would have.

Madero's labor program consisted primarily of the creation of the Labor Department, which was in turn charged with elaborating a federal labor code. At the time of the Huerta coup, the Labor Department had generated little besides a series of internal documents proposing very modest reforms, mostly related to the working conditions of women and children. In the meantime, his government was forced to respond to strikes that constituted direct threats to the economic and social order, primarily the December 1911 textile strikes that broke out soon after Madero took up office. That national conflict led to the only legal initiative of the Madero government related to urban workers, the textile tax bill that became known as the "Ley Obrero." Madero responded to the strikes by convening industrialists in January 1912, followed in July by a national textile convention to which both workers and industrialists sent representatives. Textile workers played a secondary role in the negotiations, never actually facing industrialists directly or generating their own proposal for negotiation. Nonetheless, they made some significant gains in the agreement, such as the confirmation of a ten-hour workday, limitations on the much hated system of fines, and a complex system of minimum wages that attempted to make salaries more uniform nationally. The biggest bureaucratic shortcoming of the agreement, besides its failure to acknowledge the right of workers to organize, was that the observance of its terms by industrialists was completely voluntary. In sum, the textile convention, and the labor regulation that resulted, was a preliminary but important precedent to later patterns of state intervention between workers and industrialists. While it moved well beyond previous interventions by the Porfirian state, its goals and methods were modest by European standards and distant from those enshrined in the 1917 constitution.

Madero's brother Gustavo and Minister of Development Rafael Hernández orchestrated the textile convention, while the Labor Department handled the nuts and bolts of organization. At the time of the textile strikes and convention, Congress was still controlled by deputies elected under Porfirio Díaz and played no role in the entire process. A few minor labor proposals were discussed but not passed by the lame-duck Porfirian (Twenty-fifth) Congress.[72]

The newly installed Twenty-sixth Congress became involved months later, as the voluntary observance of industrialists proved a problem. After a second flurry of strikes by textile workers furious with the failure of industrialists to implement the agreements, a Committee of Industrialists asked President Madero to universally reduce taxes on textile production from 5 to 4 percent, as a reward for observing the convention wage rates. Madero revised their proposal, raising the tax to 8 percent but offering a rebate of 4 percent to those industrialists who observed the convention agreement. Such a fiscal change required the approval of Congress for what was, in essence, a tax reduction, demanded by industrialists in return for compliance with the convention agreement. So what became known within the Congress as the "Ley Obrero" was really a tax bill and also a congressional endorsement of the regulations of the national wage and work conditions as negotiated by the Madero administration at the textile convention.

The tax bill gave the deputies a sustained opportunity to debate the so-called worker question, with discussion continuing sporadically from the first reading of the bill on 25 September 1912 to its final passage on 12 December 1912. In spite of its limited and indirect benefits, there was significant support for the bill among textile workers, who felt that there were net gains from the convention agreement and that the tax rebate would assure observance by industrialists. While the Casa apparently rejected the provisions and structures of the textile convention, workers from 114 textile factories sent a petition appealing to the deputies for approval of the bill. In addition, it is clear from the records of the debate—full of remarks directed to the public and frequent shouts—that the galleries of the Chamber of Deputies were filled with workers. At the same time, no mention was made in the debates or in newspaper accounts of the presence of the Casa del Obrero Mundial, which had been founded in the weeks before the bill was introduced.[73]

Given the modest aims of the tax bill and the public presence of workers in the galleries, few deputies were willing to oppose it, even if they objected to certain aspects of the convention agreement. The general drift of the debate was support for the tax measure and textile convention and vague promises of future legislation to benefit workers. Although everyone who spoke in the debate declared his interest in improving the condition of workers, deputies attacked or supported aspects of the textile convention agreement, even though the Congress had only been asked to decide on the tax increase and rebate. Moreover, deputies mapped out in the debate their views for future laws to regulate labor-industrial relations and their views of the workers they hoped to help.[74]

The limited opposition to the tax bill and the textile convention was led by Carlos Zetina, the Liberal Party candidate and shoe factory owner who had appealed to workers in Tacubaya for their support in the June elections. Zetina argued that, by pushing industrialists to set wages, the government violated the laws of the free market. One consequence, he claimed, was that higher wage levels would cause hardship to industrialists, particularly the small firms that could not afford to pay wages. Poor consumers, Zetina and other deputies claimed, would be forced to pay higher prices for the basic textiles most factories produced, thus undermining the very groups that the deputies hoped to help. Worst of all, Zetina predicted, the textile convention would be just the beginning—inevitably workers in other sectors would follow suit and make similar demands. On a different level, Zetina argued from his own factory experience (where "I have, like sons, some 700 workers") that workers were morally not ready to have their wages raised all at once: "what does a man do who earns four *reales* (forty centavos) and the next day earns twelve? In what does he employ those twelve *reales* if he doesn't have necessities?" His answer, which workers in the audience anticipated with angry shouts, was "stop working, go to the *pulquería* to spend them."[75]

The majority, led by the Bloque Renovador deputies, expressed their support for the bill and made general demands that "everything possible be done to assist the laborer." The defense of the bill was led by Deputy Heriberto Jara, who sat on the joint commission introducing the bill and would play a similar role a few years later in the elaboration of Article 123 at the constitutional convention of Querétaro. Jara rose repeatedly to answer every criticism of the bill, insisting that regulating wages was indeed in the purview of the government, and he welcomed workers from other sectors who might come and demand the same rights. Jara invoked the "*fantasma*" of the labor conflicts of Río Blanco and Cananea, warning that otherwise "those miserable workers, remembering that they are men, will stand up straight, rise up and reclaim what is theirs, and they will tie us up and hang those of us who haven't been able to do anything for them."[76]

Strong support for the bill came from two of the factions most bitterly opposed to each other in Congress, the Renovadores and the Catholics. Certainly much of the debate was over whether the Catholic Party or the Progressive and Liberal Parties were more inclined to help workers. Key Catholic Party deputy Francisco Elguero denounced various socialist tendencies in Europe and Mexico and invoked the *Rerum Novarum* of Pope Leo XIII with its call for a family wage. Deputies from the Catholic Party claimed to have been the first to address the social question in Mexico and pointed to the substantial labor laws passed by the legislature of the state of Jalisco, which was controlled by the Catholic Party. Deputy Jesus Macías, who defended the bill, elaborated on the labor theory of value to justify Mexico's eventual move toward socialism. Even so, Macías shared with Zetina a certain disdain for Mexican workers; the current measure was a small step toward socialism, he explained, but real socialism would have to wait until "the worker has become enlightened, when the worker has an intelligence more full of truth, when he has withdrawn from all vices . . . in a word, when we have the Belgian worker."[77]

The bill was finally passed by a wide margin and signed by Madero on 12 December 1912. Remarkably, during two months of debate, hardly a single concrete proposal for labor legislation was proposed or elaborated, even though various deputies mentioned projects that were common demands among workers in all sectors. The most concrete proposal was an amendment to the textile tax bill proposed during the debate by the deputies Heriberto Jara, Jesús Urueta, and José Lozano, all from the joint commission that introduced the original bill. Their proposed amendment would have allowed the government to return the 4 percent tax rebate directly to workers instead of to owners in those factories where the terms of the textile convention were not followed—but after the original bill was passed, the amendment was maneuvered back into commission on a technical question, from where it would never emerge.

Other proposals were mere speculation. On introducing the tax bill, the commission had promised that in the future the government would bring to workers "other various dispositions that tend to protect them in a direct and efficient way, finally assuring them against accidents, finally regulating work, procuring them comfort and health in the workplace; finally guaranteeing them full liberty for the formation and functioning of associations and unions of workers; finally favoring and protecting associations of learning and recreation; the formation of cooperative and consuming societies, and in a single word, all that elevates the moral, physical, and economic level of the worker." In the context of the debate, various deputies echoed these future projects, with minimum detail. Most common were references to the need for cooperatives, savings accounts, and industrial schools. Only one, Catholic deputy Salvador Moreno Arriaga, acknowledged one of the key demands among labor organizations throughout the country, the need to give mutual aid societies and unions formal legal status (*personalidad jurídica*) that would allow their organizations to acquire property, to appear before authorities as organizations, and most important, to negotiate collective work contracts directly with employers. Veracruz deputy Miguel Hernández

Jáuregui asked why the Renovadores had not simply presented a project to form a Ministry of Labor or a law to regulate the hours of work, to legalize strikes, to protect women, and to compensate workers who suffered accidents—in short, "why don't we proceed to the creation and formation of a Labor Law?"[78]

But none of the individual or global proposals made during the debate got to the point of a formal proposal in the few remaining weeks of Madero's government. By the time of the Huerta coup in February 1913, neither the Madero cabinet nor the Congress had generated promised reforms to protect workers, with the modest exception of the textile convention and the related tax bill.

Under the government of Huerta, the Labor Department continued to elaborate proposals: In late May 1913, perhaps in response to the first May Day mobilization and a Casa petition for an eight-hour day, the Labor Department presented to the Congress a constitutional reform that would simply empower Congress to issue industrial, mining, and commercial laws that would be obligatory throughout the Republic, but the law was still pending discussion in October 1913 when the Congress itself was dissolved by Huerta. Conservative and Catholic deputies presented initiatives in April 1913 that would require Sunday rest and in May that would allow legal identity to "professional unions," but these bills similarly died in commission.

Toward the end of the debate on the textile tax bill in December 1912, Luis Cabrera, the Progressive Constitutional Party deputy who presided over the debate, complained to the chamber that entirely too much time was being spent discussing labor issues rather than more pressing matters such as agrarian reform—a valid point, except that the prolonged debate on labor issues that arose in the context of the "Ley Obrero" produced little more than the tax bill, a measure that conservative deputy Querido Moheno referred to as "the hat thrown to the bear to delay his blow."[79] In sum, Madero and the short-lived Twenty-sixth Congress had an unimpressive record of labor reform.

While the particular failure to enact significant labor reforms can hardly account for the final collapse of the Madero government, it is perhaps suggestive of the broader reluctance of the Madero government to

incorporate workers and popular sectors beyond elections. For example, throughout 1912, as Madero's government came under siege from a
series of rebel and army revolts, various groups of workers in Mexico
City, including fifteen hundred streetcar workers, offered to form local
militias that could work for the "defense of the fatherland and for the
consolidation of our interests." Similarly, a popular militia was briefly
organized by City Hall to defend the city against the potential attack of
rebels in the spring of 1912 and mobilized considerable groups of workers from the city's factories and working-class neighborhoods. Yet as regional revolts spun out of control in the last months of the Madero
government, both conservative anti-Maderista elites and pro-Madero re-
formists backed away from the militias because, according to historian
Rodríguez Kuri, "the success of the militia project would have implied
incorporating new actors in the political scenario of the city." A similar
attitude characterized the final crisis of Madero's regime during the
Decena Trágica of February 1913. During those "twelve tragic days,"
while Madero's key federal general, Huerta, orchestrated a false battle
with rebel federal troops holed up in the Ciudadela in the heart of District Six, a group of fifteen hundred volunteers from the popular classes
offered to defend Madero during the siege of the Ciudadela. On the eve
of Huerta's coup and his own assassination, Madero again rejected such
popular participation, perhaps afraid of the consequences of arming the
urban masses.[80] By the time Huerta dissolved Congress in October 1913,
workers for the most part had abandoned voting booths and the galleries of the Federal Congress and had taken their struggles back to the
factories, shops, and streets.

★ ★ ★

On 4 March 1913, ten days after Madero's assassination, a group of textile workers from the La Carolina factory abandoned work and marched
publicly to where they believed Madero's body had been buried. Such an
act of defiance by workers, one of very few that took place in the city now
dominated by the old Porfirian army, made sense. Madero had been genuinely popular among broad sectors of Mexico City's working people,
and the mobilization of working people had been initiated in political

terms first by Madero's electoral challenge to Porfirio Díaz in 1910 and then by a series of elections in the first years of the revolution. But their possibilities for political expression, so manifest in 1910, proved over time to be limited and frustrating. In the absence of strong working-class organizations in the workplace, projects for political parties of workers proved limited in appeal or else were subordinated to the very different goals of middle-class sectors and political elites. Urban workers or candidates that tried to represent them failed to make gains through the electoral process and in turn were unable to wrest significant reforms from their new president or Congress. A modest exception was the textile convention, in which unprecedented government intervention was precipitated by massive strikes. The gains of the textile convention may help explain the public mourning for Madero and the implicit anti-Huerta political protest of the textile workers of La Carolina. By contrast, the Casa del Obrero Mundial remained silent during the Decena Trágica and the weeks after the coup.[81]

For the most part, Madero and his political allies failed to make democratic institutions work for urban workers in Mexico City or to cement a cross-class alliance that incorporated workers and that might have created a more viable government. Excluded from real participation in the new government, working people turned their efforts to transforming and strengthening their own organizations in the workplace and their communities. With a national background of heightened polarization, strategic and numerically significant groups of workers in Mexico City became radicalized after the congressional elections of 1912, incorporating the language of class into their speeches and publications and moving from traditions of mutualism to more sustained organization in formal unions and cultural and organizational groups such as the Casa del Obrero Mundial. The political participation of workers would not come from a "real vote" and much less a defense of elected leaders but rather from their organization in the workplace and the leverage such organizations could wield vis-à-vis employers and political authorities.

The predominance of foreigners in the new industrial system heightened the sense of injustices among workers and accelerated notions of class solidarity; at the same time, it also reinforced their nationalism and disposed them toward alliances with revolutionary leaders willing to curb the worst abuses of industry. European radical ideologies, including anarchism, mixed with the nationalism and popular liberalism of workers and provided an important catalyst to organizational efforts.

These new organizations incorporated an unprecedented number of working people in Mexico City and helped to bring together workers who had historically been separated by skill, gender, and cultural traditions. This organizational transformation set the stage for more direct confrontation with employers and, eventually and inevitably, a reckoning with the leaders of the revolution who rose to challenge Huerta.

5 | DIRECT ACTION AND A CITYWIDE WORKING-CLASS MOVEMENT

Just weeks after crowds of poor and working people had filled the streets of downtown Mexico City to push for the resignation of Díaz, and on the eve of an unprecedented wave of working-class organization, Carlos González Peña reflected on the change in elite perceptions of the popular classes in the magazine El Mundo Ilustrado: "We didn't believe in the existence of the pueblo, we—the youth born in an era of democratic pessimism, in ignorance of that which the multitudes were capable— didn't know the pueblo ourselves. The pueblo itself didn't seem conscious of its own existence: the worker didn't see beyond the dark workshop."[1] The revolution accelerated the consciousness of working people, who asserted themselves within and beyond the workshop in unprecedented ways. It also forced middle-class intellectuals, professionals, and military leaders to move beyond their traditional concerns with the moral reform of the popular classes and attempt at various moments to embrace their demands and control their new organizations.

New levels and ways of organization among workers emerged not simply from changes in the structures of production and the dissemination of ideas but, even more importantly, from a process of continual interaction between workers, employers, and government and military officials. This chapter follows the process by which newly created workers' organizations confronted employers and made greater demands on government officials and the military leaders of the revolution. Many workers almost immediately turned to the political authorities they had helped to elect in order to achieve the demands that they saw as simple justice. Political citizenship thus implied for many that collective rights be sanctioned and enforced by government. Other workers, especially the skilled craftworkers of the Casa del Obrero Mundial, strove to implement the anarcho-syndicalist imperative of "direct action," which they defined as "the resolution of conflicts that arise between workers and bosses with the exclusion of intermediaries," using the tools of the strike, boycott, sabotage, and ultimately the general strike. Many of these tools had long been part of the "repertoires of contention" of working people. But the rise of new ideas, interests, opportunities, and organization during the revolution allowed for the full expression and expansion of the mechanisms by which working people confronted employers and authorities.[2]

Complete autonomy from the government proved difficult enough for workers in skilled and strategic sectors of the economy, but it was almost impossible for the vast majority of those who worked in unskilled and casual labor. Ultimately, Casa-affiliated organizations could not avoid dealing with political authorities.

Workplace conflicts and strikes were not the only collective experiences that shaped the identity and consciousness of working people. They also drew meanings from a variety of changing public symbols and rituals that were a part of and apart from strikes. Individually and collectively they incorporated new language and symbols to help them make sense of their situation. Working people asserted themselves more directly in the workplace at the same time as they began to manifest their presence in public spaces and demonstrations, thereby helping to consolidate a citywide working-class community.

Demands and Direct Action

Conflict within factory and shop walls often preceded the creation of formal worker organizations oriented toward making collective demands of employers. Mexico City workers responded to the impositions of industrial discipline, market-determined wages, and management control of work and leisure time in a variety of ways that are as universal as the process of industrialization itself yet are distinctive to their cultures and conditions. Individually they resisted and asserted themselves within the industrial order by stealing, staying away from work to celebrate religious holidays, regularly observing "San Lunes," being absent frequently or simply quitting periodically to rest, return to agricultural or artisanal production, or find waged work elsewhere. Such behavior could also be expressed collectively, as when over half the workers at the San Idelfonso textile factory abandoned work after lunch in June 1912 to observe Corpus Christi.

Other responses to the pace of industrial work and discipline were often collective and occasionally violent. When factory owners tried to change wages and work routines or impose greater discipline, workers or their commissions regularly petitioned bosses or political authorities. Because of limitations imposed on organization and mobilization in the Porfiriato, workers had an incentive to keep demands modest, while the desire of factory owners to give some substance to their claims of paternalism could lead them on occasion to grant some of the petitioned demands. But when oral or written petitions proved ineffective, workers often turned to work slowdowns, walkouts, strikes, destruction of machinery and the occasional riot in shops and factories, or demonstrations in public spaces that addressed public authorities. Complaints by industrialists over such behavior were commonplace throughout the Porfiriato and well beyond.[3]

Spontaneous and defensive actions by workers continued after the outbreak of the revolution. But after 1911, workers moved more quickly from petitions to open protests and from defensive to assertive actions, even in the absence of formal organizations. And after the fall of Díaz, bosses could not always count on the complicity of authorities to put down conflicts. Overt resistance by workers increased significantly and paralleled the social effervescence of the revolution itself. Lasting achievements for workers in these conflicts, ones that permanently changed the terms of work, usually depended not on the solidarity of the moment but on the ability of workers to maintain a level of organization during and between conflicts. With the threat of government repression diminished after the fall of Díaz, and with the formation of new types of workers' organizations with goals distinct from mutualism, workers sought to change the terms of their participation in the workplace as well as in society at large. This change soon involved putting into practice the direct action—with varying degrees of intervention from government authorities—that had initially been a deferred method of the new and cautious resistance societies.

The skilled craftworkers who constituted the first resistance societies and the leadership of the Casa del Obrero Mundial often aspired to participate in management decisions and retain a degree of control over production and hiring decisions. Such demands for workers' control within the workplace were strongest in industries that maintained aspects of traditional craft organization in spite of changes in ownership, technology, and work organization and also among the most skilled workers in factories, railroads and streetcars, and the electrical company. But the most common demands among semiskilled and unskilled workers, who were the vast majority of workers and soon became the majority of the Casa, concerned work conditions, hours and wages, and an end to mistreatment and arbitrary firings by managers.

Certainly basic issues of wages and hours were the most frequent demands made by workers.[4] Given the pattern of declining real wages in the late Porfiriato and the periods of hyperinflation during the revolution, the demand for higher wages was a constant in the strikes of the decade. In addition, as part of an increasingly dynamic urban and national labor market, workers in some sectors frequently asked for minimum and uniform wages among shops and factories in the same sector as well as between foreign and Mexican workers. Workers repeatedly complained about discounts taken from their wages to pay for company-sponsored benefits or to pay for specific tasks such as the weighing of materials. Even more strenuously, they protested fines for misbehavior, tardiness, or damage to machines and materials, fines that according to one group of textile workers "have grown so large, that they almost leave us without pay." Many workers insisted that just as important as the cost of fines was the fact that fines were "immoral," since, as one group of electrical workers insisted, "only judges have the right to impose fines."[5]

The reduction of hours and Sundays off were also frequent demands, suggesting that, although workers resisted many of the impositions of "time-discipline," such as fixed schedules, they later came to accept some of the terms and engage employers over them. In demanding a ten-hour day, for example, the seamstresses in La María stocking factory insisted, "as you know Señor, in work, the time doesn't work—the hands do, which is why we all aspire to leave at least by 6:30." The eight-hour day became a central demand among craftworkers, one posed as much in terms of the use of leisure as of productive time. The Mexican Union of Stonecutters explained to the workers and employers of Mexico City in 1913 that the leisure gained from a shorter workday would not be dedicated to vice but rather to "peaceful and well-earned rest" and "to cultivate relations with comrades, to habituate ourselves to fecund and moralizing association, to frequent our humble libraries, and in a word, so that we, the sons of work, can be as capable of thinking and feeling as the rest of humanity integrated by Sybarites and idlers." Sundays off would become the central banner of shop workers in the downtown area throughout 1912 and 1913. Frequently workers also demanded the regulation of the hours of women and children, even though such regulations often meant hardship for single women and struggling families by further limiting the areas of work deemed legitimate for them. Demands over hours were almost inevitably linked to wage demands, since a reduction in work hours could mean a reduction in income. These basic bread-and-butter issues were commonly expressed in terms of workers' rights: their most basic right to earn a living but also their right to participate fairly in the profits of employers or, more generally, to participate through better wages in the progress of the nation.[6]

Almost as common as wage demands were appeals for an end to arbitrary abuse by bosses and managers, often of foreign origin, or the related demand for respect. Mistreatment provided a catalyst for many strikes, particularly among the most poorly paid and among women workers. For example, textile workers in La Carolina threatened to go on strike in March 1912 after one of the floor managers shot at one of his workers. "Is this good treatment?" workers wrote rhetorically to the Labor Department, answering that throughout the factory "the worker is treated as a slave rather than as a person."[7]

Conflicts often involved very different and changing concepts of honorable behavior. For example, since colonial times, many workers had "appropriated" factory materials for elaboration at home or for sale elsewhere, often with at least the acquiescence of bosses. Such traditional practices were seen by workers as part of their right to earn a decent living, in this case by taking a part of the fruits of their own labor rather than stealing the property of the factory owner. But with the implementation of new workplace organization and discipline, bosses came to view such theft as a crime. Workers in turn saw attempts by managers to stop theft as moral insults. For example, in the factory Miraflores, workers walked out en masse after spies were planted to prevent theft, and workers in La Carolina did the same when body searches were imposed. One U.S. critic of the vices of Mexican labor indirectly acknowledged the moral logic to theft when he pointed out that workers "stole a sum about equal to their wages." The issue of mistreatment or slights of honor could be the catalyst to justify a strike, followed by a series of demands related to wages and hours, as was the case with the shooting in La Carolina.[8]

Contention frequently emerged over changes in work conditions or routines that could affect the pay workers received. For example, textile workers often complained about the quality of the materials used in production, since the thread produced from inferior cotton often broke, requiring them to stop their machines and ultimately reducing the pay of those paid by piece rates. A power outage that forced workers to go home without pay, or to work beyond the usual shift, could lead to a riot or, more common after 1911, a walkout or a strike. In the city's largest textile factory, La Carolina, night workers rioted and destroyed machinery when an internal power outage made extra hours necessary to earn their usual daily wage.

Other changes were perceived more as threats to established procedures and prerogatives, violations of tacitly agreed norms and traditions. Days before the La Carolina riot just mentioned, over five hundred workers went on strike when management demanded that workers clean the machines on a day that was "contrary to custom." Textile workers walked out of the factory La Hormiga after heavier spools were put on spinning machines and the extra weight was subtracted when their output was weighed. Workers often expressed various demands over work routines, especially during the fluctuating economic conditions of the revolution, in simple terms: things "should be returned to the way they were before," indicating an insistence that economic relations were also social ones, subject to the values of workers and at times to the oversight of public officials.[9]

Material demands were almost always linked to other demands that workers also expressed in terms of rights. The question of hiring and qualifications for workers was a central one, especially for craftworkers who attempted to preserve or recover traditional artisanal controls. For example, cigar rollers in the Puebla factory La Balsa went on strike in 1908 when the administration refused to promote two apprentices who had been tested and qualified as *operarios* by the League of Tobacco Rollers. When the administration ceded to the league, the newspaper El *Ahuizotito* exalted that "the iron hand of the League of Tobacco Rollers . . . reconquered the triumph that seemed lost . . . making itself respected by the tyranny of the bosses." While guildlike controls over categories of skill were rare in Mexico City, such lost rights were not forgotten. With support of the Confederation of Graphic Arts, printers in a government print shop protested in 1914 the hiring of incompetent workers for skilled positions simply because they were related to the director. Similarly, striking railway mechanics in 1912 insisted on a series of standardized requisites for hiring. Railway workers and textile workers often demanded that foreign managers be fired and replaced by Mexicans. After Constitutionalist generals intervened in the Mexico Tramways Company in 1914, streetcar workers implemented a hiring tribunal that approved or rejected job applicants proposed by management, and newly organized workers of the Mexican Light and Power Company in 1915 immediately tried to make membership in their union a requirement for employment. Such a role both harked back to guild privileges and anticipated some of the post-1917 prerogatives of state-supported unions.[10]

Even more widespread than attempts to control hiring were workers' protests and strikes over firings they perceived as unjust, including firings that bosses justified because of absences or tardiness, periodic overproduction or lack of materials, or the organizational activities of workers. Indeed, given the overabundance of cheap labor in Mexico

City, job security and protection from arbitrary layoffs were central concerns of workers and were perceived as rights. Striking railway mechanics in 1912 included among demands the reduction of hours rather than staff if work became scarce.[11] When women workers of the woolen factory La Linera were fired, reportedly for "sympathizing with our ideals of union," their coworkers appealed to the Labor Department to intervene on behalf of these "weak beings from whom the crumb of bread has been taken." Indeed, these workers went on to express their right to work in constitutional terms: "we are from the great family of the disinherited; yes [disinherited] from riches, but not from guarantees that we are granted by our Constitution, which has cost great streams of blood since its promulgation up to the present days." In the context of a permanent labor surplus made worse by the material conditions of the revolution, the insistence on the right to work itself became fundamental and was the central demand for a variety of petitions and marches of both men and women (see fig. 13).[12]

Finally, workers insisted even more vigorously after 1911 on the recognition of their organizations by both employers and the government. While employers had accepted and even subsidized mutual aid societies that had focused on issues of security and sociability, they refused to acknowledge or negotiate with the new resistance societies and unions as their demands and methods came to resemble collective bargaining. Although the constitution only guaranteed the right of individuals to associate, workers insisted that among their rights as citizens was that of organizing as workers; for example, streetcar workers in 1912 complained that the manager of the company, in refusing to recognize their organization, had violated "a right that the Constitution concedes in Article 9," a violation that was "doubly sensitive since he is a foreigner, and as such, has fewer rights than any other to not recognize our constitutional guarantees."[13]

As workers' organizations battled for recognition by employers, they soon drew the obvious conclusion that such recognition of the forms and functions of new organizations had to come first from the government. For example, in February 1913, when the German-born owner of the clothing store Cuidad de Hamburgo fired an employee for organizing a demand for Sundays off on behalf of the Mutualist Society of Free Employees (Sociedad Mutualista de Empleados Libres), the society organized a massive demonstration with other working-class organizations and the Casa del Obrero Mundial that demanded both Sundays off and a "Law of Associations." In the face of employer intransigence, most unions and the remaining mutual aid societies pushed authorities to establish the legal status of unions, which would give stability to their organizations and allow them to press demands within the workplace and in the legal system. Such a demand for the formal recognition of unions by the state, rather than just by employers, was in theory problematic for anarchists in and outside of the Casa del Obrero Mundial. Yet the importance of this demand to most workers meant that the Casa often, as in the "Ciudad de Hamburgo" strike and soon after in petitions to Congress, ended up supporting constituent unions' demands for formal recognition from the government.[14]

In other words, the new mass constituency of the Casa after May 1913 required a shift in strategy by the craft-based leaders to accommodate the needs and demands of the semiskilled and unskilled. Demands over the legal status of unions, wages, job security, and work conditions, particularly the eight-hour day, were more universal in the Mexico City economy, given the nature of work, than the specific concerns of craftworkers over control of production and hiring and helped unify a citywide union movement.[15] Pressing for such universal demands allowed the Casa to incorporate much of the city's working class in strikes, demonstrations, and appeals to authorities for protective legislation or military decrees.

Other unifying demands were those that extended beyond work to consumption issues of food, rent, and provision of basic services. This was a relatively natural link, given mutualist and anarchist traditions, but it was also a response to the increasing concentration of production and commerce in the capital.[16] Moreover, the military conflicts throughout Mexico brought drastic changes in the material conditions of the city and in turn helped radicalize worker demands and methods. During the worst years of fighting, the increasing importance of consumption issues helped to straddle the division between skilled and unskilled, male and female workers, and unions and popular classes.

The demands outlined here indicate a considerable degree of continuity between the prerevolutionary and revolutionary periods. Similarly, the range of methods by which workers pursued their demands did not differ hugely from previous patterns. Rather than an attack on property or the capitalist system, their increasing militancy was aimed at ameliorating the worst abuses of the capitalist system, asserting greater control over aspects of the work process, and claiming citizenship rights in and out of the workplace to which they felt entitled by their role in Mexican development. The demand for justice was inherent in many of the most basic bread-and-butter issues, and it associated economic life with moral values. During the revolution even the most radical workers and the organizations they led never tried to carry out the immediate seizure of the means of production, except on a few occasions when it involved a foreign company, and even then only when the instrument of intervention was the state or revolutionary generals.[17] What is different from the prerevolutionary period is the unprecedented scale on which working people asserted their longstanding demands. Working people collectively challenged bosses more quickly, more directly, and more often. Their collective actions demonstrated links to organized workers in the same and other sectors and extended more broadly to the working-class community as a whole. The following narrative examples suggest both the scale of actions and the directions taken by newly organized workers as they asserted themselves in the workplace and in the urban community.

1911–12: Tramways and Textiles

One of the first real tests of workers' rights in Mexico City after the fall of Díaz was the streetcar workers' strike of July 1911, during the provisional government of Francisco León de la Barra. Streetcar workers had gone on strike repeatedly, though without success, in the previous decade (1899, 1900, 1901, 1903, 1906, 1907), with strikes often ending in police repression. In 1905, they formed a mutualist society that launched strikes in 1906 and 1907, but this organization seems to have disappeared by 1911 in the face of company hostility. Barely six weeks after the fall of Díaz, in the middle of the rainy season when streetcars were even more important to the articulation of the city, over one thousand streetcar workers made a series of "respectful and prudent" demands to the Anglo-Canadian Mexico Tramways Company that incorporated longstanding concerns: that they receive a wage increase; that workers be allowed to buy their uniforms wherever they wished, rather than at the overpriced store chosen by the company; that they only be charged for damages to streetcars in the case of justified cause; that firings be only for justified causes; and that the company establish norms of compensation for workers incapacitated on the job. Related demands that came up in the course of the strike were the right to form a mutual aid society and a return to the previous system of weekly rather than biweekly pay, which the company had imposed to promote greater regularity in the work force. After three days, the company responded by rejecting all demands, firing one hundred workers who had organized the petition, appealing to the British ambassador to intercede with the Mexican government, and hiring local replacement workers and bringing in streetcar workers from Veracruz and Guadalajara. On 3 July, three days after sending their petition, over two thousand workers went on strike, virtually shutting down the city's transportation system.[18]

In spite of the considerable inconvenience caused by the strike, the general public response within the city was immediate and sympathetic. Indeed, perhaps because of the nature of the streetcar system, the strike and its defense were very much an affair of the streets, and one that overflowed to include broad sectors of the popular classes, particularly from working-class neighborhoods around the Indianilla repair shops in the south of District Four. As the strike began at noon, crowds of workers, family members, and neighbors surrounded streetcars operating near the Indianilla shops and in the Zócalo, throwing stones, shouting "Viva Madero!" and forcing the strikebreakers to flee (see fig. 14). Crowds commandeered several streetcars and set at least one of them on fire, reflecting a deep public hostility toward the streetcar company. Demonstrations also had an element of festivity, hierarchies were inverted, and patterns of deference toward managers and respect for company property were reversed. One manager fired into a crowd, wounding a child in the arm, before hiding in the Indianilla shops. In response, the outraged crowd began to riot, throwing stones at the streetcar facilities as their numbers grew to as many as twelve thousand people. The crowd dispersed only when police arrested and removed the manager.

In what would become a common ritual, the next day thousands of workers and sympathizers gathered for a demonstration at the monument to Juárez in central Alameda Park. Many recently formed worker organizations, such as the railway workers' Union of Machinists, the Union of Stonecutters, and the Great National League of Tailors, showed solidarity by providing funds to the strikers, joining in demonstrations, and sending messages of support from across the country. Many streetcar workers brought in by the company from Veracruz and Guadalajara refused to work once they understood the situation, instead asking the assembly of striking streetcar workers to provide funds for their return home.

Middle-class reformers, concerned about the role of foreign capital in the economy, announced their support for the strikers. Newspapers such as El Demócrata, Diario del Hogar, and El Radical all initially covered the strike sympathetically, the first starting a collection for the strikers.

In the euphoria of such widespread support, hundreds of streetcar workers assembled repeatedly to consider their strategy in the Cine Club, off of the posh Cinco de Mayo Street. Operating in an organizational vacuum, that is, with no previous organization and a refusal by the company administration to negotiate directly with workers, the strikers looked for intermediaries. The secretary of the interior told the strike committee that the federal government would not intervene to end the strike and assured them that "we are no longer in the epoch in which a strike can be answered with gunfire, as in Rio Blanco." Members of several emerging political groups hoping to gather working-class support, including Reyistas, offered their services. While streetcar workers rejected what they perceived as political maneuvers, they followed previous norms and turned to municipal authorities for mediation, in this case the new governor of the Federal District, Alberto García Granados. The governor would later report that any energetic intervention by the police in the early days of the strike would have been dangerous, given "popular effervescence" and that "public opinion unanimously supported the strikers."[19] Indeed, the newly proclaimed tolerance toward strikes created a dilemma for the government between resorting to old forms of repression or creating new forms of intervention that were contrary to past laissez-faire labor policies. This dilemma was particularly acute when the strike occurred in a sector that was fundamental to the functioning of the urban economy.

On the second day, the strike committee accepted behind closed doors a deal negotiated by the governor and a group of lawyers close to the interim president, Francisco León de la Barra, a settlement that allowed for a slight pay raise and guaranteed that strikers could return unpunished to their jobs. But when the deal was presented to the entire assembly of striking workers, the majority rejected both the deal and its own strike committee and voted instead to remain on strike until all their demands were fulfilled. The division among the strikers gave the governor the room he needed to maneuver vis-à-vis public opinion, since those who rejected the agreement were now said to be acting illegally. When on 5 July the militant but dwindling majority gathered in front of the Indianilla shops to block the entry of those who had given up on the strike, the mounted police charged the crowd with sabers drawn, wounding several women and children and arresting over one hundred people. The next day, amid continuing confrontation, a group of the strikers appealed with little result to presidential candidate Madero, and police guarding the company entrance and escorting streetcars effectively put an end to the strike. A final attempt by striking workers to cut the electrical cables that powered the streetcars proved futile. The new government, concluded the newspaper El Radical, had proven itself "gently tyrannical." Another lesson, according to the same newspaper, and one echoed by other groups such as railroad workers, was that workers needed greater organizational unity and financial resources before resorting to the strike. In spite of the wide support and apparent militancy of the 1911 strike, the streetcar workers would not succeed in creating a permanent organization or in wresting real concessions from the company until 1914.[20]

Like streetcar workers, textile workers of Mexico City were among the earliest in asserting their demands—even in the absence of formal organizations. Their conflicts with employers and their demands to the government helped define the labor movement in the first years of the revolution. The assertiveness of textile workers was related to a variety of structural and conjunctural factors. Textiles constituted the largest factory sector in the country, and workers were aware—through job mobility and informal communication networks—of conditions and organizational initiatives in other factories in their regions and throughout the country. Working conditions included twelve- to fourteen-hour workdays, and wages often varied considerably from factory to factory and region to region. Finally, textile workers had high expectations for change that were rooted in the frustrations and violence of the 1906–7 textile conflicts and in their enthusiastic support for Francisco Madero in 1910 and 1911.

Textile conflicts and strikes broke out almost immediately and continued sporadically during the summer and fall of 1911 in Orizaba, Nogales, Puebla, Tlaxcala, Atlixco, and the Federal District, demonstrating the general discontent in that sector. By November, immediately following the inauguration of Madero, conflicts intensified, suggesting that workers closely associated newly recovered political rights with a restoration of their rights as workers. On 22 December 1911, fifteen textile factories in Puebla went on strike, and other textile workers in Puebla, the Federal District, and Orizaba had plans to strike on 7 January, a date that would commemorate the anniversary of the Rio Blanco massacre of 1907. But events in Mexico City, where strikes in key sectors were harder for federal authorities to ignore, pushed forward the start of what would become a general nationwide strike in the sector. On 26 December 1911, workers in the San Antonio Abad textile factory in the heart of Mexico City's industrial district went on strike when the manager changed the size of the pinions in the looms, an adjustment that reduced the weight of the cloth produced and thus lowered the final payment workers received by about five centavos a day. The change of pinion sparked a strike that soon spread across the city and then the nation. The workers of San Antonio Abad immediately sent commissions to other factories in the city. The workers of the La Carolina factory seconded the movement, abandoning their jobs and stoning the factory building, as did workers of La Hormiga in the nearby town of San Angel. They were joined by a commission of seamstresses from the garment shop La Sinaloense, where a strike had begun weeks before.

An editorial in *Nueva Era* urged workers to show their patriotism in the current difficult circumstances by giving up for the moment their right to strike. Similarly, the director of the recently formed Labor Department, Antonio Ramos Pedrueza, wrote a national circular to textile workers, insisting that "It is patriotic to avoid conflicts and I hope that understanding that, the Señores Workers will know how to conduct themselves patriotically and with all prudence." But the words and actions of textile workers suggest that they made a different connection between their workplace demands and the new political context. The next day, over two thousand textile workers marched to the monument to Juárez in Alameda Park and on to the National Palace in the Zócalo to insist on an audience with the president. When President Madero finally received them, textile workers demanded that "salaries be raised, work hours reduced, and last, that the *caciquismo* predominant in all factories of this type be eliminated." Other demands included the elimination of fines and the official recognition by management of the leadership of workers' associations. One speaker insisted that since "they the workers had elevated Señor Madero to the presidency, it was only just that he support the petition they were making." By pressuring the government to act, textile workers contradicted the claim Madero had made in his 1910 campaign speeches that workers wanted neither "increases in wages nor decreases in working hours [to] depend upon the government."[21]

Lázaro Pérez, a twenty-six-year-old strike leader from the factory La Carolina—where months before workers had gone on strike when denied permission to greet the candidate Madero at the train station—claimed that the industrialist treated workers like "slaves." He explained that "we won't permit under a democratic government, like the actual one, that they do to us what was done under the dictatorship." Another of their manifestos presented the strike in nationalist terms, denouncing the despotism and abuse industrialists imposed on the "Raza Mexicana," which workers would not permit, "especially since those who abuse most are foreigners and haven't the slightest consideration for the Worker."[22]

Further street demonstrations over the next weeks by the strikers brought considerable public support and encouraged workers in most of the textile mills in the Federal District to join. By 9 January 1912, over nine thousand Federal District textile workers had walked off the job, as had forty thousand textile workers nationwide, primarily in the states of Orizaba, Puebla, and Jalisco. Newspaper accounts suggest a level of co-ordination and organization at the factory, regional, and national levels that had not been seen since the formation of the Gran Círculo de Obreros Libres in 1906. Workers in Mexico City factories named com-missions to communicate with other factories and named others to or-ganize demonstrations and approach the president. In various dem-onstrations of four thousand to five thousand people in Mexico City, demonstrators carried banners for various clubs and factory commis-sions that supported the workers' demands and suggested an extensive if preliminary level of organization at the base. Finally, by 9 January Fed-eral District workers named a regional strike committee, headed by Lá-zaro Pérez, which possibly included one woman, Piedad Colín. The committee became national in stature when Lázaro Pérez invited work-ers from Hidalgo, Puebla, and Veracruz to send their own commissions to a convention of workers in Mexico City, which many did by 18 January.

In these efforts they were at first helped by such middle-class inter-mediaries as inveterate organizer and Liberal Party member Lázaro Gu-tiérrez de Lara and engineer Ezequiel Pérez of the Popular Workers Party. Gutiérrez de Lara seems to have been quickly marginalized, per-haps because of his often outright opposition to the Madero govern-ment. But so too was the Maderista Ezequiel Pérez, who was eventually dismissed by the strike committee for trying to negotiate a solution to the strike in which textile workers would abandon factory work to form rural guards and agrarian colonies, an idea that appealed to a small mi-nority of factory workers.[23] By late January, under the leadership of worker Lázaro Pérez, textile workers had taken the initiative on their own to create a tentative national structure and had sustained their strike for almost a month, forcing both the government and industrialists to respond to their demands.

Textile industrialists quickly formed a committee of their own to deal with the strike, relying largely on the structures of the powerful Mexican Industrial Center (Centro Industrial Mexicano), which had formed in 1907 in response to labor conflicts. Their spokesperson publicly insisted that "if they reduced the hours of workers, the workers themselves would be hurt . . . since the less time workers spend in the factory, the more they would employ in drinking and other excesses." As to raising wages, he replied that any increase would make the factories unprofitable; to dramatize the point, the committee of industrialists offered to sell their factories to the government, which could then grant the raises that workers demanded. While they refused to meet directly with strikers, they agreed to a meeting with key government officials, including the president's brother Gustavo and the ministers of treasury and development.[24]

After thirty days and with more than forty thousand textile workers throughout the country on strike, officials coaxed a temporary and nonbinding agreement from textile industrialists. Workers were offered a provisional reduction of the workday to ten hours, and those paid piece rates or already working ten hours or less were offered a tentative pay increase of 10 percent, pending a definitive arrangement to be worked out in the coming months. This temporarily put an end to the nationwide strike but did not keep textile workers in individual factories from continually striking in the months that followed to push for formal fulfillment of their demands. For example, four days after the workers' committee called an end to the strike, the workers of the woolen factory La Linera went on strike when the manager insisted that they work ten and a half hours daily instead of the ten hours agreed on by most industrialists. During the five months between the January agreement and a definitive accord in July, over fifty textile strikes occurred throughout the country.[25]

In response to continued unrest, the Madero government and its newly organized Labor Department eventually scheduled the promised convention of textile workers and industrialists for July 1912 in Mexico City, to be held immediately after the congressional elections. Even as the convention met, striking workers in the states of Puebla and Vera-cruz had brought the textile industry there to a close to protest the long delay. Textile industrialists prepared for the convention by forming the powerful Mexican National Manufacturing Confederation (Confedera-ción Fabril Nacional Mexicana), which grouped together the largest owners of textile factories in the country.

Delegates to the workers' committee were selected from each factory using criteria handed down from the Labor Department, criteria that in practice excluded women and by procedure excluded potential "agita-tors," including many of the key figures in the January strikes. Worker delegates arrived divided and denied any external organization of their own or even the possibility of negotiating directly with the industrialists' committee. The group of workers from Puebla walked out, suspecting that they would have a limited role, and left the permanent Central Com-mittee of Workers under the control of Juan A. Olivares, a moderate with close ties to the Labor Department, who quickly managed to displace the remnants of the leaders from the January convention of textile workers. As a result, workers were for the most part marginalized in the negotia-tions and depended on government officials (Gustavo Madero, Minister of Development Rafael Hernández, and the director of the Labor Depart-ment, Antonio Ramos Pedrueza) to present their demands and hammer out an agreement with textile industrialists.[26]

The material benefits and organizational results of the final textile convention agreement were mixed. Important gains made by workers in the final textile labor regulation were the confirmation of a maximum ten-hour workday, an end to the much hated system of fines for absence and misconduct (though not for damages or faulty work), the prohibi-tion of verbal or physical abuse of workers by supervisors, and the elim-ination of the infamous *tiendas de raya* (company stores), which were more important in company towns like Rio Blanco than in Mexico City. All these provisions satisfied important worker demands that had been pending since well before the 1906–7 strikes.

Industrialists proved more willing to reduce hours than to fulfill wage demands. Workers demanded an increase in wages of 50 percent and uniform wage rates throughout the industry. But industrialists insisted that any negotiated wage increase would be an unconscionable interference with market mechanisms and that uniform wage scales would make little sense, given regional differences in labor markets and the cost of living as well as factory variations in technology. Instead, the labor regulation provided for a complex system of minimum wages designed to accommodate different types of salaried work and piecework. For most textile workers in factories where the labor regulation was implemented, the minimum meant a modest increase of on average 10 percent, to 1.25 pesos daily. Still, a minority of workers already making that level saw no increase at all, and some workers even complained that employers had used the new minimums to reduce their wages. As a result, the leisure gained was probably more significant than the wage increases. Regulations of the hours of women workers ultimately served to reduce their numbers in textile factories, as Luis Cabrera had warned in congressional debate over related tax measures. Since the entire agreement was voluntary, the primary incentive for textile owners to accept it was the hope of industrial peace and, eventually, the government tax reform that favored those industrialists who complied and punished those who refused.[27]

At the same time, industrialists rejected a series of demands that the workers' committee had made, such as the formation of worker representatives with a "voice and vote" in the organization of the factory, particularly in the naming of foremen (maestros) and the firing of workers, and the compensation of a month's salary to workers who were laid off. In direct contrast to these demands and the public discourse of textile workers, a key spokesman for the industrialists, Tomás Reyes Retana, insisted that "the concessions made at this convention should be seen as acts of deference by the manufacturers, not as the recognition of rights." Instead, the final labor regulation confirmed a series of controls over worker behavior in the workplace and in company housing, such as restricting the movement and nonwork activities of workers within the factory and requiring employees to work the entire week in order to be paid. The regulation specified fifteen sanctioned holidays a year in the hopes of ending the multiple religious feasts and "San Lunes" that workers often observed at will.[28]

Industrialists refused to include any explicit recognition of the right of workers to organize unions; on the contrary, wording in the agreement prevented any discussion of workers' complaints during work hours or the taking up of collections or subscriptions inside the factory and preserved the right of owners to dismiss any worker for "disobedience, insubordination or lack of respect to superiors," all provisions that were later used to dismiss workers who tried to organize unions or strikes.[29] The national Central Committee of Workers, which was to remain in Mexico City and monitor the implementation of the regulation, in theory represented all the nation's textile workers but had no formal parallel structures at the regional or factory levels.

Years later Antonio de Zamacona, the director of the Labor Department in 1915, commented that the labor regulation had done nothing practical for the working class—the text was deliberately vague in some places, he complained, with complicated mathematical calculations for wages in others, "so that each factory applies it as they wish to understand it." The results, he went on, were insignificant wage increases and an accumulation of complaints by workers. One former labor inspector later identified the dependence of the Central Committee on the Labor Department for funds and headquarters as an example of the inherent organizational weakness and "idiosyncrasy" of textile workers in this period. But the official creation and control of the Central Committee suggests even more the determination of the government to impose limits and control the unprecedented organization of textile workers during the first half of 1912.[30]

For several years after the 1912 labor regulation, textile factory owners in Mexico City and elsewhere continued to refuse to recognize any worker organization other than mutual aid societies, and workers who attempted to organize or join unions continually met with dismissal and blacklisting. Even so, workers in many textile factories sustained informal commissions—probably linked to the "*mesas directivas*" that had been formed during the strike and continued in preparation for the July convention—to present demands to bosses and to appeal to the national Central Committee and the Labor Department. The very precedent of the textile convention and the existence of the permanent Central Committee of textile workers resident in the capital forced owners to accept a degree of representation that workers continually managed to expand.[31]

In spite of limitations, the precedent of the textile labor regulation gave added legitimacy to the struggles of textile workers and provided an organizational incentive to workers in other sectors. If textile workers had limited participation in drafting the textile labor regulation, the actual occurrence of the convention and the terms of the regulation reduced some traditional mechanisms for control and provided a basis for contesting those that remained. One Puebla factory owner complained soon after the textile convention that, since workers' successful strikes had forced owners to negotiate, "workers no longer accept either observations or punishments of any kind . . . To throw out a worker for whatever powerful reason, even drunkenness . . . is an absurd attempt, since they will all walk out." In the years following 1912 and up until the next textile convention of 1925, textile workers repeatedly challenged the actions of employers by invoking the 1912 regulation in strikes. In the year between January 1912 and January 1913, over one hundred strikes occurred in the textile mills of the country. In the face of high inflation between 1914 and 1916, workers continually used gold equivalents of the 1912 tariffs as a standard by which to make their wage demands. At the same time, material demands necessarily extended to issues of control in the workplace, since textile workers insisted on participating in any decision that might affect the 1912 minimum wage rates, such as the quality of raw materials and machinery, the size of thread spools, or the number of machines they tended. With this knowledge they elaborated a careful critique of industrialists' complaints about the inferiority and inefficiency of Mexican workers and showed a considerable mastery of the technical aspects of their work.[32]

Formed after the textile convention, the Casa del Obrero Mundial took a critical attitude toward the Central Committee and its dependence on the Labor Department that reflects a general tension between the craft-based and industrial workers as well as between the particular leadership that emerged from the textile convention and the Casa. Rafael Pérez Jiménez of the Central Committee wrote a letter to the Casa newspaper, *Emancipación Obrera*, expressing his disappointment that on arriving in Mexico City to assume his position, he had approached the Casa to "exchange ideas and instruct myself on socialism, but I only found enemies that constantly challenge me to a battle in which before-hand I acknowledge defeat since I can't count on the elevated instruc-tion required." Casa members responded to Pérez Jiménez by dismiss-ing the textile convention, insisting that "all the regulations that are called favorable to the worker, as good as they might be, will never be more than decorative figures." Though the conflict was ostensibly over ideas and strategies, more immediately it was a battle for influence over textile workers. Casa leaders especially criticized Central Committee members who tried to influence workers in textile factories that had workers affiliated with the Casa, such as those of the Mexico City woolen factory La Linera.[33]

But with the fall of Huerta, the Casa strategy and influence among textile workers in the Federal District changed. By October 1914, the Union of Textile Workers of the Federal District affiliated with the Casa del Obrero Mundial had taken control of the Central Committee from Juan Olivares and more moderate workers. Casa control of the Central Committee required a certain approximation to the Labor Department, where the Central Committee was housed, while forcing textile indus-trialists in the Federal District into a de facto recognition of the Casa. But outside of the Federal District, the influence of the Casa among textile workers remained limited and, at times during 1915, highly conflictive.[34]

Although the textile convention was voluntary and unenforceable, the 1911–12 strikes and the resulting agreement had truly national signifi-cance: textile workers had taken their own message of justice and partic-ipation to the streets to make demands for long overdue reform of work conditions, often in explicitly political terms. The forcefulness of their organization and longstanding demands and the deep-rooted intran-sigence of industrialists forced the Madero government to abandon its earlier reluctance to intervene in issues of hours and wages and to push an agreement on both capital and labor that exceeded the cautious and personal intervention of Porfirio Díaz in the 1906–7 textile conflict and the limited program of Madero in both his presidential campaigns. The

textile strikes and convention were a preliminary but important precedent for later patterns of institutionalized state intervention between
workers and industrialists and almost immediately had repercussions
elsewhere: workers in other sectors frequently referred to the 1911–12
textile strike as a precedent for organizing strikes and invoked the textile
convention standards in demanding wage increases and reductions in
hours; industrialists in other sectors used the textile *reglamento* as a
model to regulate the behavior of workers; and the stonecutters' union,
restaurant workers, and the owners of hat factories in Mexico City all
asked the Labor Department to convoke similar conventions for their
sectors.[35] Worker actions and government response provided a valuable
if somewhat contradictory lesson to workers in other sectors: unity
among workers could sometimes force employers to negotiate, or at
least force government officials to intervene on workers' behalf to bring
employers to the bargaining table; but at the same time, state intervention could transform the forms and nature of working-class unity.

1912–14: "To Conspire against Order"

The ideas, material conditions, and political shifts of the revolution helped move workers from defensive responses to changes in conditions or
policies toward more assertive and ambitious actions that expressed
their longstanding demands. By the fall of 1912, soon after the congressional elections and the formation of the Casa del Obrero Mundial, the
paralysis of Madero's modest social program and the increasingly open
opposition of forces of the right and left exhausted the patience that
many workers and their new organizations had exhibited in pressing
long-deferred demands. The "direct action" explained and advocated by
the Casa del Obrero Mundial, and put into practice even earlier by such
groups as the streetcar workers and textile workers, gained increasing
general appeal among working people who had mostly mobilized
around general projects of political support, cultural improvement, or
the strengthening of organization among particular trades.

Deteriorating economic conditions in the capital provided both a
limit and a catalyst toward action, particularly from mid-1914 through
1916. As war raged across the country, violence rarely touched Mexico

City directly, with the exceptions of the Decena Trágica, the "tragic twelve days" in which Porifirian military factions ended Madero's government and life, and periodic sacking by Zapatistas of factory towns in the southern half of the Federal District bordering Morelos. But the disruption of the railroad system caused by revolutionary armies and bureaucracies cut off Mexico City from its markets for manufactured goods such as textiles and cigarettes and from supplies of food and raw materials, especially the cotton needed to maintain the textile mills. As production dropped, so too did employment levels. The specter of unemployment and an army of potential replacement workers provided a clear disincentive to strikes. At the same time, work stoppages and layoffs, and the abandonment of all money standards except paper in 1914, tended to radicalize workers' actions, even as high unemployment and excess production curtailed their chances of success. The rapid decline of real wages and employment opportunities pushed workers beyond cautious concerns with education and the forms of organization into direct confrontation with employers and eventually into conflicts and alliances with the new revolutionary authorities. In the process, their organizations were transformed.

While textile workers of the Federal District organized within their factories and broadly within the textile sector, they proved secondary to attempts to form broad links across different groups of workers within the city, at least through 1916. Skilled craftworkers and workers in the strategic service sector were far more pivotal in creating broad-based worker organizations and supporting the popular mobilizations that burst on the local and national scene in these years, and the craft-based workers of the Casa del Obrero Mundial were the key organization tying this movement together. According to one account, the Casa del Obrero Mundial participated in more than seventy strikes in its first year of existence.[36]

Under the military dictatorship of Huerta (February 1913 to August 1914), organized workers in Mexico City proceeded with relative caution, seeking to gradually test the limits of official countenance of their activities. To the extent that these organizations avoided political statements or positions, they were given considerable scope in their cultural activities and even in their conflicts with employers. Moreover, Huerta's strong denunciations of U.S. intervention in Veracruz in April 1914 helped to divert much of workers' antagonism toward his regime. But the last desperate months of Huerta's rule brought repression, heavy forced recruitment of factory workers into the army, and finally the closing down of the Casa del Obrero Mundial by police in late May 1914. Various leaders of the Casa del Obrero Mundial fled, several to Morelos to join the Zapatistas and a few north to join the Constitutionalists. Many of the Casa del Obrero Mundial's constituent unions went briefly underground.[37]

When the Constitutionalist armies of the north defeated Huerta and marched into Mexico City in August, the Casa del Obrero Mundial immediately reopened as one of the most coherent organizations in the city. With the Casa del Obrero Mundial taking the lead, workers began a vastly accelerated cycle of organizational and strike activities that would continue uninterrupted for two years. The following examples, primarily from the fall of 1914 while the city was for the most part under the control of Constitutionalist forces, suggest the nature of workers' demands, actions, and alliances in this period.

The crucial educational and organizational roles of printers, first within the Confederation of Graphic Arts and then within the Casa del Obrero Mundial, have already been discussed. Similarly, the far more numerous tailors played an important role within the extensive garment industry. Tailors made a rapid transition from mutualism to syndicalism and soon after entered into an alliance with lesser-paid seamstresses. Three years after their failed attempt to create a cooperative, and buoyed by the fall of Huerta and the reopening of the Casa del Obrero Mundial, the Tailors' Union (Sindicato de Sastres), which split from the Great National League of Tailors, challenged the system of contractors directly. In September 1914, they struck against the fifty-seven principal clothing shops of the city. Their demands were concerned as much with reasserting control over their craft as with increasing the pay they received for their work. The most important demands were recognition of their union, uniform payments for sewing particular articles of clothing, and union participation in the classification of categories of shops, intermediaries, and tailors, with union-issued identification cards required for employment. This last point, guaranteeing a degree of control over production, was typical of the demands of skilled craftworkers.

The inspector of the Labor Department reported that the more than five hundred striking tailors were determined to stone the major clothing stores if they did not negotiate and went on to describe how the tailors gathered "to preach sedition and opposition to the work of the Revolution, lack of respect for the law as well as government; even if it is true that they have the legitimate right to assembly, they don't have the right to conspire against order." The strike leaders, he explained, opposed any intervention by the Labor Department, since they were absolutely convinced that they would triumph. Indeed, as in the case of textile workers, the Casa and the Labor Department were increasingly in competition for influence over broad sectors of working people. Even so, the Casa and its constituent unions often were forced to turn to the Labor Department or government officials for help. For example, the tailors, while determining the terms and rhythm of the strike, were obliged to request and accept from the Labor Department access to a place large enough for them to meet with shop owners. By contrast, when leather tanners went on strike in the same month, their union leader rejected the overtures of Casa leader Eloy Armenta, insisting that they had an obligation to the Labor Department.[38]

The fluidity and heterogeneity of production within the clothing industry is suggested by some of the key protagonists. The radical tailor Luis Méndez, whose small shop was categorized by the tailors' union as "second class," was a key member of the Casa and was also on the strike committee of the union in charge of regulating his shop, among others. The head of the junta of bosses, Manuel Crespo, whose shop was classified as "first class," insisted that he too "belonged to the humble class" and had also struggled hard to get where he was. Within a week, the majority of stores had indeed agreed, in the absence of government intervention, to all of the tailors' demands, though it is unclear from the various accounts if any of the big department stores included in the first classification, such as El Palacio de Hierro, had agreed to the union's terms.[39]

Unions of skilled workers often backed strikes initiated by other skilled workers, suggesting an increasing identity of class among these groups. Solidarity most frequently came in the form of declarations of support or donations to help maintain striking workers and their families. But on occasion these unions, often in unrelated sectors, chose to back a particular strike by walking off their own jobs, even in the absence of a clear federated structure between workers' organizations, as in the case of carriage drivers in the streetcar strike discussed later. Solidarity strikes proved particularly effective when they involved the more strategic or high-profile unions within the city, as occurred in the teachers' strike during the spring of 1914, when the printers, streetcar workers, and bakery workers supported the teachers by shutting down many of the city's newspapers, modes of transport, and bakeries.[40]

Newly formed unions of skilled and strategic workers, such as streetcar and electrical workers, extended their tradition of strikes and with each strike became more aware of the considerable political power of their control over the city's electricity and transport.[41] The streetcar workers' strike of October 1914 announced the definitive entry of what would prove to be one of the most militant unions on the city stage for the next decade. Resentments dated back at least as far as the bloody repression of their July 1911 strike and later conflicts related to their demand for the recognition of their union. In the face of the deteriorating urban economy and the increasing difficulty of remitting profits earned in paper currency abroad, the Anglo-Canadian Mexico Tramways Company began dramatically cutting staff, replacing master mechanics with their assistants, neglecting the repairs of streetcars, and finally cutting wages by 20 to 30 percent in divisions such as the repair shops. As working conditions deteriorated, workers became more vocal in their complaints of poor treatment, often denouncing the "slave-driving" foreign foremen and the company's "tendency to humiliate Mexicans" in their appeals to newspapers and the Labor Department.[42]

Disgruntled streetcar workers organized around two groups: those who worked the streetcars organized a union of inspectors, motorists, and drivers, which affiliated with the Casa del Obrero Mundial; those who worked inside the repair shops organized around the Central Me-

chanics' Union (Unión Central de Mecánicos), which initially formed
close ties with the Labor Department. On 7 October 1914 the first group
met in the headquarters of the Casa del Obrero Mundial and voted to go
on strike the next day. The second group met almost simultaneously in
the offices of the Labor Department to present their complaints to a labor inspector and an official representing the governor. Both officials
urged a "pacific solution" to worker complaints, but when the assembly
of mechanics allowed a commission from the Casa to speak (the labor
inspector later complained), the Casa commission insisted before the
assembly that the Labor Department "had never done anything in favor
of the worker, and so those attending should move to the Casa del
Obrero Mundial where they had always worked without the assistance of
the Department, and without that of the Government of the District."
Inspired by the commission, the mechanics voted to join the motorists
and conductors on strike the next day and to hold all future meetings
with them in the Casa del Obrero Mundial, thus forming the Federation
of Employees and Workers of the Mexico Tramways Company (Federación de Empleados y Obreros de la Compañía de Tranvías de México).[43]

The next day, mechanics walked out of the Indianilla shops of the
streetcar company at 7 A.M., as the federation delivered a list of demands to the manager of the company, C. B. Graves, and gave him four
hours to respond before the motorists and conductors would shut down
the streetcars. At noon, when Graves insisted he needed to first consult
the board of directors in London, motorists returned the streetcars to
the shops, removing the detachable handles of the controllers of the
streetcars to guarantee that strikebreakers would not take them out.
When two days later over six hundred drivers of rental coaches joined
the streetcar workers strike in solidarity, transport in the city came to a
virtual halt, leaving middle-class clerks, managers, and bureaucrats who
lived in the suburbs to walk, hitchhike, or bicycle to their jobs in the
center.

The long list of streetcar workers' demands to the company included
recognition of their union, an end to fines, an end to layoffs, the dismissal of a few abusive and foreign foremen, an eight-hour day, compensation for accidents, and a raise in wages. After two days, company

manager Graves announced that the London board had cabled instructions to suspend operations, given that the financial circumstances of the company and the country would not allow them to meet the workers' demands.[44]

Though striking streetcar workers had chosen to embrace the Casa and reject the intervention of the Labor Department, they almost immediately found themselves negotiating with the governor, just as they had in 1911. But the circumstances of 1914 were quite different from those of the 1911 strike. Before joining the Constitutionalist army, Gov. Heriberto Jara had himself been an early member of the Casa and an outspoken progressive in Madero's Twenty-sixth Congress. Jara repeatedly told strikers he sympathized with their movement, and, in marked contrast to the streetcar strike of 1911, the police even stopped a group of motorists who attempted to break the strike by putting the streetcars in service. Even the city council formally expressed their sympathy with the strikers and sent a memorial to the secretary of communications, denouncing the "trust" that had exploited clients as well as workers and proposing that a variety of violations of previous contracts be used to expropriate the company. Instead of blaming workers for threatening public order, as an earlier governor had done in the 1911 streetcar workers' strike, Governor Jara lamented instead that "public tranquillity was exposed to the caprice of a powerful corporation," in this case a foreign company. Jara's old Casa colleagues, such as Rafael Pérez Taylor, moved freely between the strike headquarters in the Casa and the governor's office and even met with Constitutional First Chief Carranza to discuss the fate of the streetcar company.[45]

When the Mexico Tramways Company refused to make any concessions to workers, Carranza, citing "public utility," ordered that the company be temporarily intervened and run by a Constitutionalist official while a commission was set up to study the feasibility of a wage increase and other demands. This did not satisfy all streetcar workers, some of whom felt they had simply exchanged one exploiter for another without any clear gains. Though the Casa now cautioned prudence, the streetcar workers threatened to strike again if wages were not increased. But fifteen days later, Governor Jara extended the intervention indefinitely and declared a provisional wage increase of 25 percent. Conflicts between streetcar workers and the appointed director continued over the next months, but having established a close relationship with a handful of key Constitutionalist generals, the newly formed Federation of Employees and Workers of the Mexico Tramways Company kept turning to military authorities to gain leverage in their demands. One such victory was the requirement that all employees of the company belong to the union, which in essence gave the union recognition and control over hiring.[46] These concessions to streetcar workers would pay dividends for the Constitutionalist generals months later, when members of the streetcar union constituted the largest group within the Red Battalions.

Of perhaps greater significance was the organization of electrical workers. Since the same Anglo-Canadian company owned both the Mexico Tramways Company and the Mexican Light and Power Company, electrical workers initially joined a federation of workers from both companies that was dominated by streetcar workers. But by December 1914, the electrical workers decided to form a union of their own, the Mexican Union of Electricians (Sindicato Mexicano de Electricistas). The Union of Electricians opened its ranks not only to electrical workers of the Light and Power Company but also to electricians employed elsewhere in the Federal District as well as nonelectricians employed in related companies, such as the city's two telephone companies. Even so, its primary membership was workers from the Light and Power Company. The Union of Electricians immediately tested its strength two weeks later, when the director of the Mexican Light and Power Company fired a member of the Union of Electricians for attempting to organize his coworkers. When the management refused to negotiate the dismissal with the union's committee, the Union of Electricians threatened to strike. The director met with the committee, a de facto recognition of sorts, and the worker was reinstated.[47]

The Union of Electricians soon affiliated with the Casa del Obrero Mundial and, already at a time of considerable turmoil, immediately affected the balance of power within the Casa and the citywide union movement. The newest affiliates shared with the craft leadership of the Casa del Obrero Mundial a certain pride in and confidence about their skills and leverage with employers; but the financial solidity of their union and the extension of their influence over the functioning of the entire city gave them a claim to leadership. Indeed, a year earlier, Rafael Pérez Taylor had predicted that if the electricians managed to organize, "a well-organized strike of the electricians means nothing less than a general shutdown" for the entire city. Such power produced tensions vis-à-vis other unions. For example, in a meeting organized by the Union of Textile Workers on 7 January 1915 to commemorate the massacre of Río Blanco textile workers, the Union of Electricians delegate, Ernesto Velasco, commented that the electricians had a special calling among workers to be "the most important," to which the printer Rafael Quintero, secretary general of the Casa del Obrero Mundial, importuned that the "assembly not distinguish superiorities." Velasco defended himself by referring to "the material importance that [the Union of Electricians] necessarily has, given the importance of electricity to any civilized nation."[48] This rivalry for leadership of the labor movement, in which the electricians' claim was strategic and the printers' was cultural, would blow up two months later over the Casa del Obrero–Constitutionalist Pact.

Ties That Bind: Alliances across Skill and Gender Lines

Craftworkers and those skilled workers who serviced the modern infrastructure of the city wielded considerable material and organizational resources to carry out their strikes, to attract or reject the attention of government authorities, and to win recognition for their organizations and wage concessions from individual employers. Rather than simply protecting their advantage vis-à-vis less skilled workers and veering toward a conservative trade unionism, the dominant trend in Mexico City by 1913 among the most dynamic and numerous groups affiliated with the Casa del Obrero Mundial was to bring less skilled workers and women into their cultural and organizational activities and to support them in strikes. This strategy became crucial if they were to make collective action against the city's biggest employers effective and to make the term "working class" relevant to the diverse groups of working people in the city. Unskilled and nonstrategic workers were not only a clear majority of the working people of Mexico City, but by the fall of 1914, they were a majority of those who participated in the marches, meetings, and unions supported by the Casa.

A fairly successful alliance occurred with "respectable" clerks and waiters in downtown businesses, whose cultural background and incomes were similar to those of craftworkers. When restaurant workers of the Café Inglés in the heart of the downtown went on strike for a fixed wage (rather than working just for tips), their jobs were immediately filled from the abundant ranks of the unemployed. The Casa del Obrero Mundial responded by mobilizing a variation of the boycott. Workers from various unions, dressed in their rudest clothing, ordered cups of tea and occupied all the seats in the restaurant all night long, preventing wealthy clientele from receiving service and strikebreakers from receiving tips. The employer eventually ceded to the strikers' demands. A similar boycott was undertaken in February 1913 by the Casa del Obrero Mundial and the two thousand affiliates of the Mutualist Society of Free Employees against the clothing store Ciudad de Hamburgo off the Zócalo, after the German owner fired a worker for his attempts at organization. The Casa del Obrero Mundial supported a series of storefront demonstrations in support of the demands of sales clerks for Sundays off, showing, in the words of one Casa leader, "that the middle class also knows how to threaten its tyrants (see fig. 15)." This very public campaign included awards of prominent green stars to downtown shops that agreed to close their stores on Sundays, on the assumption that consumers would favor stores sympathetic to labor over recalcitrant ones. These consumer strategies helped to emphasize the important link between production and consumption issues to both workers and the public at large, though their ultimate success is not clear from the sources.[49]

Far more significant in terms of building a citywide movement were attempts by skilled and organized workers affiliated with the Casa to incorporate unskilled workers and their demands. The most successful attempts at such a plan occurred within the same sector or workplace. For example, the Printers' Union from its origins encouraged the incorporation of those people, mostly women, who were employed by print shops in the tasks of folding, packing, and binding. Similarly, the Union of

Electricians incorporated nonelectrical workers in companies dealing in electricity, in particular female telephone operators, and defended them in their strikes. Many unions collected dues as a percentage of earnings, rather than a fixed amount, to allow those with minimal wages to join. Of course incorporating unskilled workers into labor organizations led by skilled workers did not necessarily mean that those leaders would look out for the interests of the unskilled in their negotiations with employers. But various unions, including those of the electricians and commercial employees, often demanded a higher percentage of wage increase for workers with the lowest wages during their strikes throughout 1915 and 1916.[50]

Certainly one of the greatest challenges Casa unions faced was the incorporation of and support for women workers. The majority of women in turn-of-the-century urban Mexico were invariably seen by men and often saw themselves as wives and mothers first, in spite of the reality that most working-class women worked in and out of the home. The role of women was represented in middle-class discourse as centering above all on the home and community, the defense of which involved rights and obligations specific to women.

Women workers in general were less likely than men to strike or join unions, a perspective shared by bosses, husbands, fathers, and women workers alike. Esther Torres recalled her initial attempts to organize her fellow seamstresses, who replied that if "the boss finds out that we go to the union, he could fire us, or retaliate, or give us the worst work." These women insisted that organizing was a risk and a luxury that only women with working husbands could afford. Torres's own widowed mother repeated disapprovingly a fairly common refrain: unions were "a male thing" (cosas de hombres). The profound uneasiness that many working-class husbands and fathers felt over the necessity that their women work may have also made them reluctant to encourage women to organize. Instead, women workers were far more likely than men to turn to the Labor Department with their complaints, where their appeals were often anonymous and their tone at times abject, as in the following complaint about hours: "The women workers of the Stocking Factory that is on Calzada del Niño Perdido beg you attentively, if possible, to deign to attend our entreaty, since we, weak and silly [tontas] women implore your powerful aid for everything."[51]

The structures of work reinforced this pattern. In Mexico City, where women constituted over 35 percent of the paid work force and in many industries worked much longer hours than men did, women usually moved in and out of the work force and through a series of different occupations depending on their age, their civil status, and the availability of work for their spouses and relatives. That women in Mexico City at the turn of the century were almost by definition unskilled workers, and therefore had little leverage by which to make their demands, explains in part their limited participation in labor organizations and conflicts. Another explanation, explored in chapter 7, is that women in general were more likely to initiate collective action when it clearly involved their mandate to defend home and community, such as the mobilizations related to food riots or rent or general strikes, rather than strikes over work conditions.

Male-dominated labor organizations and the Labor Department expressed concern for the conditions under which women worked in factories and shops. The Labor Department included a section devoted to women workers that sought, through gathering information and applying pressure, to assure hygienic work conditions, limit hours, and eliminate women's night work. Labor unions and government officials occasionally collaborated in supporting regulations to exclude women from working in certain positions or at certain times, as in the textile convention's prohibition against women working the night shift or the successful attempt of the Waiters' Union in 1912 to keep the best downtown restaurants from hiring women as strikebreakers.

Where the work force was mixed, though invariably segregated by task, as in textile factories, women often seconded men in strikes. As wives and family members, they frequently supported men in their strikes and organizational activities, showing solidarity through their presence at meetings, demonstrations, and picket lines, as they had in the 1911 streetcar workers' strike. Their participation suggests that conflicts were not simply between employers and workers but between employers and the broader working-class community. At the same time, the burden of making ends meet at home during a strike often fell to wives, who may have been less willing than men to sustain lengthy strikes, as suggested by the play *Un gesto*, written by Casa member Rafael Pérez Taylor and performed in June 1916. And when women workers did organize and strike, it was not unusual, even where they were a majority, for men in or outside the workplace to assume leadership.[52]

Nonetheless, on occasion and often with little previous formal organization, women defended their position in the workplace through very bitter strikes. One of the earliest and most highly publicized strikes under the Madero government involved two hundred seamstresses of La Sinaloense, who in December 1911 struck to protest a reduction of piece rates. Encouraged by PLM veteran Lázaro Gutiérrez de Lara, the seamstresses marched to confront Madero in the National Palace with cries of "If the president doesn't pay attention, *vamos a la revolución!*" Weeks later during the national wave of textile strikes, the seamstresses of La Sinaloense joined textile workers in their marches. Their employer, Ricardo Otero, was a Porfirian deputy in Congress who held a contract for uniforms from the secretary of war. A month into the long and bitter strike, Otero tried to contract out uniforms to women working out of their homes at even lower rates. The striking seamstresses responded by guarding the sweatshop premises around the clock, locking the manager in the building when he tried to remove a quantity of cloth, and denouncing Otero publicly in government buildings. In spite of their tenacity, after a month of vigilance most strikers had given up and sought work elsewhere. The intensity of this strike was unusual; its failure—symptomatic of the weak position of unskilled women workers in the labor market—was not.[53]

When strikes occurred among women workers, the immediate catalyst was frequently abuse rather than wages or hours and often involved the mistreatment of one or several women workers by a disrespectful boss or foremen. During the first years of the revolution, letters from women workers appeared constantly in the newspapers or were sent to the Labor Department, complaining of lewd or abusive conduct by managers. Typical is the letter that appeared in the newspaper *El Radical* on 13 July 1911, in which the women workers of the clothing factory La Nacional complained that the foreign owner, "not taking into account our sex, uses with all of us a treatment and vocabulary so crude and arrogant, appropriate only to individuals of the lowest quality." These statements testify not only to the abuse itself but also to the perception that such mistreatment should be made known to the community at large, by appealing either to male workers, public authorities, or progressive newspapers, whose idealization of the purity of women, and of their own masculinity, often made them quicker to defend any perceived dishonor of women workers than to defend the wages and working conditions women faced. The demand for respect from owners or supervisors could be linked to demands for better wages or hours, but the question of respect was often both the initial demand and the last one to be surrendered.

The phrase "not taking into account our sex" suggests that the demand for respect, common enough among all workers, was of particular importance to women. Abuse and disrespect toward women were magnified by perceptions of the physical and sexual vulnerability of working women and were made symbolically more serious when women were under the control of supervisors who were not only male and of a different class but also often foreign-born. Stories were common in middle-class novels and the working-class press of working women who were sexually dishonored by male supervisors in shops and offices and left to prostitution.[54]

Affronts to the honor of women workers could also erupt directly into strikes or precipitate unionization. For example, in September 1914, the seamstresses of Le Trousseau requested a raise in the most respectful, if not servile, tones. The Spanish owner replied that, since Mexicans eat only tortillas, chile, and pulque, his wages were sufficient to satisfy their needs. Given the dual role of these women, who as working mothers often both figuratively and literally put food on the table, the insult resonated deeply. They immediately initiated a strike, followed by the organization of a union. A photograph from the period captures this sense of violation: a group of striking women holds up a banner that reads, "We're on strike because when we demanded a raise—they insulted us, directing us to the road of prostitution."[55] (See fig. 16.) These women turned the traditional fear that work experiences would lead to their moral downfall on its head: it was the lack of work, or badly paid work, that would lead women to moral downfall and prostitution.

Casa leaders in particular recognized the importance of incorporating women workers into their organizations. As noted, women participated fully in the educational and cultural activities of the Casa del Obrero Mundial. By late 1914, the Casa had considerable success incorporating women into its ranks as workers—particularly among textile workers, the majority of whom were men, garment workers, the miserably paid and overworked women of the masa mills, and the large tobacco factories such as Buen Tono, where women workers predominated. Just weeks after their victory over the fashion shops of downtown Mexico, the Tailors' Union, which included only a few women, backed the efforts of lower-paid seamstresses working out of their homes to form a union of their own.[56]

In the same month, a strike broke out in the workshop of the city's biggest department store, El Palacio de Hierro, when the foreign-born administrator physically struck a seamstress working in the shirt department. The entire section of women workers walked out, demanding, in addition to the dismissal of the administrator, an end to piecework and a raise in wages. The link between demands for respect and economic demands was apparently reinforced by the presence of male workers in the workplace. The Tailors' Union and the Casa del Obrero Mundial quickly moved to support the strikers, rejecting outright any mediation by the Labor Department. According to a Labor Department inspector, the women leaders were much more willing to stick to the issue of respect and accept arbitration from the Labor Department than their male allies from the Tailors' Union and the Casa del Obrero Mundial, who he felt had taken over the leadership of the strike—a now familiar scenario. With demands for raises and dismissals of abusive managers across all departments and with widespread solidarity outside, the strikers managed to close down the store for over a week.

The French owner of El Palacio de Hierro, Justino Tron, insisted his wages were better than those paid in other stores and refused any negotiation with the strikers as long as the Casa del Obrero Mundial was involved. With few resources on which to survive besides the modest support from the Tailors' Union and other Casa unions, strikers were soon hard-pressed to continue. Unlike with strikes in strategic sectors such as textiles and streetcars, government authorities like Governor Jara felt no need to intervene beyond the limited means available to the Labor Department. After two weeks, the strikers finally appealed to the Labor Department to intervene; when Tron still refused to negotiate, they dropped all their demands except the question of honor, demanding only the dismissal of the administrator who had struck a seamstress and finally a simple public apology. After Tron repeatedly rejected this minimal request and denied the Labor Department a mandate to negotiate, two-thirds of the workers returned unconditionally to their jobs. Two months later, Tron had completely turned the tables on the strikers; a group of former El Palacio de Hierro seamstresses complained bitterly to the newspaper Mundo Libre that, in order for them to return to work, Tron had insisted that they write a letter pleading for absolution for their strike.

In spite of widespread solidarity, the position of the seamstresses was inherently weak, since they were striking against a wealthy employer in a nonstrategic industry in an economy reeling from civil war. Even with the support and previous successes of the Casa del Obrero Mundial behind unskilled or nonstrategic workers, direct action without the mediation of government officials could prove disastrous for them. The Union of Home Seamstresses (Sindicato de Costureras a Domicilio), sponsored by the Casa, had greater success petitioning the government to contract directly with the union for military uniforms, thus bypassing contractors.[57]

The Casa's piecemeal actions on behalf of unskilled workers, while important to extending its influence, could not win such common workers' demands as uniform hours and wages. The Casa del Obrero Mundial needed to win broader concessions for less strategic and unskilled workers as well as those who saw themselves as middle class. To organize the mass of workers, wrote Casa member Federico de la Colina in October 1914, "we must adapt our methods of action to the confusion of their moral and material state, winning them over by the incentive of benefits, which is what most attracts them."[58] The eight-hour workday and a six-day workweek had, of course, been formative demands for all European and U.S. labor movements and eventually were won universally in those countries only through political pressure for government laws and regulation. Likewise in Mexico City, the uniform hours, wages, and job security at the heart of most workers' demands could only be won through intervention by government authorities, as had been the case for the ten-hour day won by most textile workers in 1912.

Symbols and Rituals of Mobilization

Parallel to the shift to unions and rise in confrontations with employers was a transformation in working-class political culture. Popular identification with the patriotic symbols of traditional nineteenth-century liberalism (the struggles and heroes of independence, the liberal Reform, and the wars against foreign interventions), as discussed, had been fundamental to the organization of mutualism and political mobilizations of workers and popular classes during the late Porfiriato. The 1910 revolution at least initially added new national heroes to the nineteenth-century liberal pantheon, such as the triumphant and then martyred Madero, who was closely identified with the ideals and heroes of the nineteenth century. Leaders of early radical worker organizations such as the Confederation of Graphic Arts, in spite of its Spanish founder and anarchist inspiration, were rooted in these national symbols and the idea of the patria. At no time did this discourse of popular liberalism disappear, though, as with the old organizational models, it coexisted, mixed, and occasionally conflicted with other traditions.

At the same time, popular liberalism took on stronger class dispositions, already palpable in the late Porfiriato, as workers drew more upon working-class heroes and the events and struggles of the revolution. Almost immediately workers gave their political clubs or resistance societies such names as "Aquiles Serdán," after the Puebla shoemaker killed in Madero's revolt, or "Martyrs of Río Blanco," after those workers executed in the 1907 labor conflict. Workers commemorated these names and events first within their organizations and eventually in the streets of the city in ways that memorialized recent worker struggles and martyrs against exploitation and tyranny or that concretely symbolized the centrality of workers and their organizations in the push to transform Mexican society.[59] The antagonism that many urban workers felt toward the role of foreign capital and foreign managers was closely linked to this working-class nationalism. While working-class nationalism proved a powerful instrument of class organization, it also overlapped with the symbols and ideology of middle-class revolutionaries and ultimately encouraged integration into a reformed, more inclusive political system.

After 1912 the growing influence of European and U.S. radicalism and their heroes, thinkers, and battles helped develop strong, even militant, class dispositions among some workers. This trend is clearest in the Casa del Obrero Mundial, where the cultured craftworkers at the heart of the organization, best represented by leaders like the mechanic Jacinto Huitrón and the printer Rafael Quintero, imbibed the writings of anarchist thinkers such as Kropotkin and Bakunin, sang "the International," pondered worker participation in such rebellions as the Paris Commune, and commemorated the martyrdom of the Chicago anarchists and the educator Ferrer Guardia in Barcelona. The transformation can be seen clearly in such figures as the printer Rafael Quintero. As the editor of *Evolución* in 1911, Quintero rallied workers behind Madero's candidacy, and his writings were filled with references to the historical struggles of the Mexican people. The shift of his restless intellect to a European iconography can be seen first on the pages of El *Tipógrafo Mexicano* of the Confederation of Printers during 1912 and more definitively in the Casa del Obrero Mundial's *Ariete* in 1915. Quintero's imagery and references characterize the general tone of many of the speeches given and articles written within the newspapers of radical organizations. Of course, the commemoration of national heroes such as Morelos and Hidalgo and the teaching of a patriotic, nationalist version of Mexican history were never completely abandoned by Casa leaders, but throughout 1913 and 1914, as they attempted to sustain an apolitical position, the centrality of these national historical symbols was minimized in favor of internationalist symbols that diminished the importance of the *patria*. The term "*mundial*" was added to Casa del Obrero's name in the spring of 1913 to reflect this international orientation.

Such a cultural idiom provided a sense of an international community for workers and a strong imperative for organization and direct mass mobilization. But the discourses of internationalism and nationalism could also come into conflict, both as positions taken by different individuals and as expressed through the pronouncements and actions of groups. Many illiterate workers certainly must have struggled to understand the abstract speeches and international references of Quintero or Díaz Soto y Gama or the strident, erudite poetry of the printer Rosendo Salazar.[60] Similarly, one can imagine the negative reaction of some workers to such decisions as that of the Casa del Obrero Mundial to reject the Mexican flag for the anarchist-inspired, red-and-black flag in their demonstrations or to occasionally use the motto "Without Fatherland" ("Sin Patria") on Casa stationary. Those in the Casa leadership who pursued an internationalist class discourse helped differentiate themselves from the nationalist and liberal discourse of middle-class revolutionaries but risked alienating much of their constituency and left themselves open to accusations by authorities (Maderistas, Huertistas, and Constitutionalists alike) that they were little more than foreign agitators.

If such symbols divided as much as they united, other forms of sociability among working people helped to consolidate what increasingly became a citywide working-class movement. The newly formed resistance societies and unions organized workers not only in the workplace but also in the streets, neighborhoods, and public places where working people lived and worked. The Confederation of Graphic Arts was located on Academia Street, between the tenement district immediately east of the Zócalo and the neighborhoods farther east. For the first year after its foundation, its offices served as the meeting place for the organizations of plumbers, stonecutters, chauffeurs, and other groups, as well as a community cultural center. Other unions transformed cafes, taverns, or even the patios of tenement houses into their meeting places.[61]

The role of the Casa del Obrero Mundial as a focus of working-class community was explicit in its name. In the four years of its existence, it solidified and gave consciousness to the diverse and fragmented "other Mexico" of Porfirian creation as a community of working people. The

Casa del Obrero Mundial newspapers (*Lucha, El Sindicalista, Emancipación Obrera, La Revolución Social*), for all their florid prose and sometimes confused radical rhetoric, provided a voice to workers, reporting on their struggles, featuring poems and short stories about the struggles of work and poverty, and announcing upcoming events. On a typical evening the Casa del Obrero Mundial headquarters might hold classes for workers on grammar, math, sewing, or sociology; house the meeting of a member union; or host a "casino" or dance. Sundays, like Catholic masses, brought the entire working-class community together for lectures, speeches, and cultural activities. Its first locations near Tepito Plaza (first on Matamoros Street and later on Estanco Street) were in the heart of the popular neighborhoods; with each change of location the Casa del Obrero Mundial moved closer to the center of the city, paralleling its increasing prominence in the city.

Of course the very occupation of the city by troops partially inverted the prerevolutionary hierarchy of space, as officers of the Constitutionalist army occupied the homes of the Porfirian elite or as the peasant armies of Zapata camped out in the Zócalo and took breakfast at the luxurious Palace of Tiles (Casa de Azulejos), which had housed the exclusive Jockey Club. Sympathetic generals from the Constitutionalist faction gave the Casa del Obrero Mundial a series of downtown buildings for their headquarters, including the eighteenth-century Church of Santa Brígida—which a 1910 guidebook identified as the "most elegant church in the capital where the most distinguished families are married"—in the heart of the downtown district on San Juan de Letrán Street (today Eje Cárdenas). The Casa's physical trajectory within the city culminated in the fall of 1915 with their brief residence in the Palace of Tiles. This new foothold in the heart of the financial district—as their newspaper *Ariete* put it, in the "sumptuous mansion of the privileged" transformed into a "temple of instruction and work"—must have symbolized for many poor and working people a retaking of the downtown and convinced wealthy residents who remained in Mexico City that the world had indeed turned upside down.[62]

Many of the public demonstrations of workers after the start of the revolution were conscious attempts to reassert their presence in the exclusive downtown areas. In contrast to exclusionary decrees and the controlled parades of national unity imposed and choreographed by Porfirian officials, workers' meetings and marches affirmed a different view of their presence in the public plazas and principal streets of the city and, by extension, of their place in the spatial and social order. The monument to President Juárez in Alameda Park, built in 1909, became the regular starting or ending point for any popular march. From there, marches of working people usually headed down the exclusive San Francisco Street to the huge gathering space of the Zócalo, which was dominated physically and symbolically by the Cathedral, the National Palace, the Ayuntamiento building, and the key department stores; this path became a standard rite by which workers made public their protest against a particular employer, presented demands to authorities, or venerated past struggles. For example, the 7 January 1915 commemoration of the Río Blanco massacre led by the Casa-affiliated Federation of Textile Workers (Federación de Obreros de Hilados, Tejidos y Similares) organized a reported fifteen to twenty thousands participants, who began at the monument to Juárez, marched down the posh San Francisco Street, and continued on to the National Palace.

Mass demonstrations in the streets of the city were as much a form of debate about differing visions of society as those that did (or could not) take place in workplaces, newspapers, and the Congress. The first public observance of May Day in Mexico in 1913 was just such a debate. Factions of the Mexican working class had attempted since 1891 to join international workers in commemorating the martyrdom of the Chicago anarchists. In that year, the Catholic Church had set the tone for the official attitude by referring to the "fearful date of the first of May, when agitations of the great mass of workers are still manifested in different nations."[63]

On 1 May 1910, the Anti-Reelection rally held by workers for Madero along with the inauguration of the printers' newspaper *Evolución* had functioned within the limits of the political moment as a disguised observance. On the same symbolic date in 1910, a national convention of railroad workers was held in the capital. The following year, in the final weeks of the Madero revolt, Landa y Escandón's Mutualist and Moralizing Society petitioned Díaz to declare 30 April a labor holiday, a date that deliberately distinguished Mexican workers from their European counterparts. In 1912 under Madero's presidency, the Great National League of Tailors and the Great Workers League petitioned Congress unsuccessfully to decree 1 May a labor holiday. Instead, only the tiny Socialist Workers Party commemorated May Day in the pages of their newspaper El Socialista and within the confines of their meeting place.[64] By contrast, workers in 1913 took to the plazas and streets and galvanized the working-class community around them.

That the first May Day occurred in 1913 during the military government of General Huerta, rather than under the civilian government of Madero, reflects not only the consolidating effect of the Casa del Obrero Mundial's formation eight months earlier but also the oppositional aspect of the procession itself, which was the first massive public demonstration in Mexico City since the brutal murder of Madero two months earlier, and in many ways presented an indirect challenge to Huerta's authority.

The initiative came from the Casa del Obrero Mundial, but various currents and groups competed within the organization of the 1913 May Day. At least one historian has offered the occurrence of the first May Day as evidence of Huerta's reformist labor tendencies; but the Casa organized May Day in spite of the Huerta government. When the governor of the Federal District warned that the event should remain indoors, the committee in charge of the event chose to proceed anyway. The decision to move ahead and march in the streets in spite of these warnings was due in part to support from members of the Socialist Workers Party within the Casa del Obrero Mundial and from opposition deputies in Congress, particularly Heriberto Jara and Serápio Rendón, who welcomed the event as an embarrassment to Huerta. El Imparcial repeated the same admonition the Porfirian government had given in the past: "Why commemorate in Mexico a date that has no relation with the life of our workers? To choose it, it seems that Mexicans attempt to stir up the same European turbulence."

When it became clear that the Casa del Obrero Mundial was determined to take its march to the streets, authorities and the official press attempted to publicly interpret the event in as harmless or neutral a light as possible. At best, authorities sought to present May Day as a celebration of work, and at the last minute a rival "festival" was organized by officials in the neighboring town of Tacubaya by a "Committee of Independent Clubs." In Tacubaya, around two thousand workers feted the Huertista generals Felix Díaz and Manuel Mondragón, as those stalwarts of the Porfirian regime distributed clothes to families of workers.[65]

By contrast, the Casa organizers saw the first May Day in much the same terms as most of their European counterparts had in 1890, as above all a protest against the terms of work and past repression of the workers' movement, symbolized by the execution of anarchists in the United States after the Chicago Haymarket riots.[66] The Casa del Obrero Mundial called all workers to abandon work on May Day, rallying in the Zócalo early in the morning. On that day, work in the city practically stopped, in what for some anarchists may have appeared as a type of rehearsal for the eventual general strike by which they hoped to transform society. Whether employers obliged their workers with the day off is not clear; according to one newspaper, much of commerce shut its doors not as a concession to workers but out of fear of disturbances. Historian Miguel Rodríguez argues that attendance was bolstered by the coincidence of 1 May with a religious holiday, Ascension Thursday.[67] At any rate, all accounts suggest a huge turnout.

According to different estimates, between twenty and twenty-five thousand workers gathered behind red and black flags and a huge banner declaring, "The Casa del Obrero Mundial Demands the Eight-Hour Day and Sundays Off." Another banner declared, "Neither Hatreds Over Race nor Divisions Over Creeds." Others carried banners for their constituent unions and mutual aid societies. The crowd of men and women marched defiantly past the National Palace and through the principal downtown streets, mixing celebration with protest as they chanted for an eight-hour day. The crowd paused at the monument to Juárez on the southern edge of Alameda Park for a series of speeches by Casa members and opposition deputy Isidro Fabela. Antonio Díaz Soto y Gama compared the French and Mexican Revolutions and praised the teachings of Jesus Christ, while the tailor Epigmenio H. Ocampo and Jacinto Huitrón invoked the class struggle, commemorated the Chicago martyrs, and lashed out at the clergy. At midday workers marched to the Chamber of Deputies, in the heart of the city on Cinco de Mayo Street, and submitted a project to legalize the eight-hour day, grant legal personality to unions, and compensate workers for accidents, which was warmly received by a handful of deputies of the opposition Bloque Renovador. Finally, they stopped at a park dedicated to Jesús García, the "hero of Nacozari." In the evening, a dance in the Tívoli del Eliseo and a literary-musical event in the Xicoténcatl Theater culminated a day of protest with celebration.

The first May Day demonstration also served as a celebration of working-class unity. Among the marchers were most of the key workers' groups in the capital: textile workers, shop employees, restaurant workers, carpenters, tailors, railroad workers, and shoemakers, among others. Both resistance societies and a wide array of mutualist societies, including the Mutualist and Moralizing Society, marched side by side along with affiliates of the Socialist Workers Party and the Great Workers League (see fig. 17).

Of course debate occurred within working-class organizations over the meaning of the May Day events. Some anarchists, particularly those within the Confederation of Graphic Arts (which had not yet split or affiliated with the Casa del Obrero Mundial), felt the political aspect of the march—both its implicit challenge to Huerta and its coordination with opposition congressmen—would compromise principles of nonparticipation in politics and bring an unnecessary risk of repression. But if the march compromised the declared neutrality of the Casa del Obrero Mundial, the political demands for labor reforms guaranteed broad participation among Mexico City workers, and the success of the march accelerated the formation of unions and their affiliation with the Casa del Obrero Mundial.[68]

In fact, repression soon became a reality three weeks later when Casa members associated with the Socialist Workers Party organized a series of public meetings, the last coinciding with the 25 May anniversary of the resignation of Porfirio Díaz. Antonio Díaz Soto y Gama set the tone in his speech by directly attacking the military regime and was followed by the opposition deputies Hilario Carrillo and Serápio Rendón. The governor responded by arresting fifteen Casa members, including Jacinto Huitrón and Luis Méndez, and deporting five foreigners associated with the Casa, including Spaniards José Colado and Eloy Armenta, who would soon find their way back into the country.[69] Somewhat chastened, the Casa remained cautious in the next months, avoiding any actions that could be seen as political and apparently promoting cultural and organizational activities over conflicts with employers.

By contrast to the first May Day celebration in 1913, the following year would be a disappointment for its organizers. Since the previous year, federal troops had lost key battles to Constitutionalist forces in the north, and Huerta had cracked down hard on his internal opposition: open critics of Huerta such as Deputy Serápio Rendón and teacher and labor activist Nestor Munroy had been assassinated, the Twenty-sixth Congress, elected under Madero, had been closed down and replaced by one to Huerta's liking, and various Casa members had been jailed and exiled. Working people in general suffered from the decline in production and commerce, and, perhaps worse, Huerta's predatory draft made them fearful of gathering in any circumstances outside of work, be it in bars or at union meetings.

But repression alone is insufficient to explain the failure of the Casa's convocation for 1 May 1914. More important was the 21 April landing of U.S. troops in Veracruz, which created an intense anti-Americanism that was particularly strong in Mexico City, where anti-American riots briefly filled the streets and groups of students and workers offered to form battalions to battle the "gringo pigs." As had Díaz and Madero before him, Huerta rejected the formation of worker battalions. Even so, some groups of workers, such as the Union of Railroad Brakemen, led by Casa member Rafael Pérez Taylor, formed armed brigades that left to fight the Americans. Some of those who volunteered for the army to fight in Veracruz were surprised to find themselves on trains heading north to face Constitutionalist troops. In this context, the leaders of the Casa del Obrero Mundial, who apparently remained silent over the U.S. occupation, were unable to convoke a gathering anywhere near the scale of the previous year. Perhaps to compensate, the Casa chose May Day to declare the formation of the short-lived General Workers Confederation of Mexico (Confederación General Obrera de México). As one disappointed Casa member lamented two weeks later, "in view of the circumstances of their beloved *patria*, [workers] abstained from all manifestations that were not patriotic."[70]

As part of the crackdown, Huerta moved to close the Casa on 27 May 1914, a date that coincided with a teachers' strike that had been seconded by printers, streetcar workers, and bakers. Some members went into hiding in Mexico City; others joined Zapata in Morelos or the Constitutionalists in the north. Ten weeks later, when Constitutionalist general Alvaro Obregón marched into Mexico City, the Casa reopened almost immediately and began anew the debate on the role of working people in Mexico City and, eventually, in the revolution itself.

Collective rituals can be as important to forging unity as other types of struggles. The first May Day became a fundamental conquest in the collective memory of participants as well as later generations of workers.[71] The struggle that began in 1913 between workers and the postrevolutionary state to appropriate and reclaim the meaning of May Day (as well as the streets and plazas of the city) has continued ever since.

* * *

After 1911, organized and unorganized workers confronted employers and made demands on government officials in ways that reflected long-held aspirations yet were unparalleled in their assertiveness and unprecedented in scale. Radicalization was a response to new ideas, conditions, opportunities, and organization. Ideologies such as anarchism gave working-class leaders a vocabulary of class organization and struggle, even while nationalism and a class-infused popular liberalism remained central to the self-conception of most workers and their justifications of their actions to bosses, authorities, and the broader public. As a result, their increasing militancy was aimed not at overthrowing capitalism but rather at addressing the worst abuses of industry (particularly when foreign owned or managed), asserting greater control over aspects of the work process, and guaranteeing just wages and work conditions. Their collective actions in and out of the workplace invoked not only class-based demands but also citizenship rights to which they felt entitled by their role in Mexican development and in the revolution, as suggested by the appeal of striking textile workers to the president whom they had helped to elect.

The first significant labor conflicts in Mexico City after the fall of Díaz were the strikes of streetcar and textile workers in 1911, which occurred in the absence of strong organizations. Together these strikes confirmed the possibility of continued repression of labor conflicts as well as the possibility of unprecedented government intervention on workers' behalf. Starting in 1912, strikes multiplied among newly organized craftworkers and to a lesser extent among unskilled workers. By the fall of 1914, labor conflicts extended to almost every sector in the city, including those where women were a majority.

The skilled workers who formed the core of the Casa del Obrero Mundial faced a series of related dilemmas that were rooted in the gap between skilled and unskilled workers and were resolved by the forces and events of the revolution. The first was whether to focus exclusively on educating workers or to support strikes that might improve the material conditions of workers; they chose over time to support strikes and challenge traditional relations with employers. The second was whether to exclusively build strong trade unions among the crafts or to seek the organization of all urban workers; they chose to increasingly incorporate unskilled and women workers. The final dilemma was whether to abstain from politics or to pursue political alliances and government intervention that would allow them to deliver benefits to the newly organized working class.

Working people pursued their own image of community in a variety of public activities and demonstrations, none more extraordinary than the 1913 May Day protest and celebration. At the same time, the May Day activities forced working-class leaders who had come to reject politics into a political position challenging General Huerta and advocating government intervention in favor of better working conditions. Tensions emerged between devotion to principles that would almost certainly keep them distant from the struggles of the majority of workers or to political alliances that, while giving them leverage against employers and prestige among the mass of workers, by definition meant straying from anarchist principles and relinquishing some of the autonomy of their organizations. As the country became more polarized between 1913 and 1915, a public stance of political neutrality toward revolutionary factions became more difficult for working-class organizations to sustain. The outcome of this dilemma is the subject of the next chapter.

FIG. 10. Federal District governor Guillermo de Landa y Escandón presides over a special "oath to the flag for workers of the capital" at the Column of Independence during the centenary celebration, 30 September 1910. Courtesy of Conaculta-INAH-SINAFO-Fototeca del INAH.

FIG. 11. Federal District governor Guillermo de Landa y Escandón at a dinner with women workers, beneath a portrait of Porfirio Díaz. Courtesy of Conaculta-INAH-SINAFO-Fototeca del INAH.

FIG. 12. March of working- and middle-class people in the city center in support of presidential candidate Francisco Madero in 1910. Courtesy of Conaculta-INAH-SINAFO-Fototeca del INAH.

FIG. 13. Demonstration of women demanding work, 1912 or 1913. Workers often protested arbitrary layoffs and insisted on the right to work. Courtesy of Conaculta-INAH-SINAFO-Fototeca del INAH.

FIG. 14. The streetcar workers' strike of July 1911 brought public transportation to a stop and elicited broad community support against the Anglo-Canadian streetcar company. Courtesy of Conaculta-INAH-SINAFO-Fototeca del INAH.

FIG. 15. Demonstration by shop employees demanding Sundays off, circa 1913. The nature of such demands led union leaders to turn to government officials for the regulation of work hours and conditions. Courtesy of Conaculta-INAH-SINAFO-Fototeca del INAH.

FIG. 16. Women protesters insisted that not work itself, but rather badly paid work, would lead women to their moral downfall. Their banner reads, "We're on strike because when we demanded a raise— they insulted us, directing us to the road of prostitution." Courtesy of Conaculta-INAH-SINAFO-Fototeca del INAH.

FIG. 17. The first public demonstration of May Day in 1913 brought together recently formed unions and traditional mutualist societies, including the Philharmonic Mutualist Society shown here. Courtesy of Conaculta-INAH-SINAFO-Fototeca del INAH.

PART THREE

Working People in the Revolution

URBAN POPULAR CLASSES
AND REVOLUTIONARY POLITICS

The Revolution is the Revolution. LUIS CABRERA

The Revolution cannot triumph over the Revolution.
HIGINIO C. GARCÍA, 7 July 1915

We were in the time of the revolution, miss, and in the time
of the revolution, one wants to just live, nothing more, right?
ESTHER TORRES, interview, February 1975

In mid-July 1914, with the union movement in Mexico City dispersed by Huerta or operating underground, Casa del Obrero Mundial
administrator Jacinto Huitrón and treasurer Luis Méndez wrote a letter
to the organizers of the International Anarchist Congress in London.
"The Mexican commotion," they explained, "is a revolution that has
much to do with economics, but it is not the social revolution that we are
waiting for, which will not yet happen, as much as we might want it and
as necessary and just as it might be." Although their own organization
was clearly anarchist, they explained, the motivation for the national
movement of Carranza "has much to do with politics, since the people
have been . . . cruelly exploited by all the privileged of the world who
come to exploit the poor Mexican proletariat." By contrast, they insisted, Zapata was a true revolutionary but one who confessed his ignorance of "all that about socialism and anarchism." Because of the lack of
consciousness of the masses, the Casa del Obrero Mundial had little role
in the revolution. "The revolution that we preach needs much preparation," they reasoned. "What are we going to do here where eighty percent are illiterate? If Europe, which is better educated and enlightened,
has not been able to bring about the Social Revolution, how are we, who

can barely read, going to bring it about?"[1] The letter, written in a moment of despair, reflects doubt not only about the national events of the revolution but also about the capacity of Mexican urban workers to initiate a social revolution.

One month later Constitutionalist troops defeated Huerta, and Gen. Alvaro Obregón took control of Mexico City on 15 August 1914, allowing the Casa del Obrero Mundial to reopen and initiating a new era of relations between workers and revolutionary authorities. The backdrop of this new relation was the increase of tensions within the victorious Constitutionalist troops, which exploded in October in the midst of the Convention of Aguascalientes called to establish the new order. A majority of the northern troops, loyal to Francisco Villa, allied with delegates representing Emiliano Zapata's Army of the South to gain control over the Convention and declared themselves the sovereign power in Mexico. Venustiano Carranza rejected the Convention and retreated to Veracruz with key generals such as Alvaro Obregón, evacuating Mexico City throughout the month of November. The fate of the revolution would depend to a large extent on the ability of each of these factions to consolidate a social base for their armies, offer a national project to a divided nation, and achieve victory on the battlefield.

The Convention government, or more precisely the troops of Emiliano Zapata and Pancho Villa, would control Mexico City almost continuously from 24 November 1914 until mid-July 1915, with the exception of six weeks beginning in late January 1915. During those six weeks, the Constitutionalist troops of Obregón forged their alliance with the core of the Casa del Obrero Mundial, consummated in a formal pact in which the Casa endorsed the Constitutionalist cause and agreed to form armed "Red Battalions" of workers to defend the Constitutionalist cause. The following month, Casa administrator Huitrón departed with five thousand to seven thousand Red Battalions to join the Constitutionalists in Veracruz, and treasurer Méndez remained in Mexico City as a delegate to the parliament of the Convention, each perhaps convinced that the "social revolution," or the first step toward it, would not be in the hands of workers alone.

The February 1915 alliance of the Casa del Obrero Mundial with Constitutionalist forces had and continues to have great significance. In the official history, the alliance is symbolic of the postrevolutionary state's commitment to the working class. But for many revisionist historians, the pact is the first of a series of dependent alliances of workers with the state. For example, Adolfo Gilly calls the pact "the birth certificate of the union 'charros,'" using the term for cowboy that emerged in the 1940s to refer to labor bosses corrupted by government financial and political manipulation. For Gilly and others who have used essentialist class categories for the contending factions, the Red Battalions pitted the working class—manipulated by bourgeois or petty bourgeois Constitutionalists—against the peasant armies of Villa and Zapata.[2]

This chapter examines the relations of the victorious and contending revolutionary military factions with the poor and working people of Mexico City during the year after the defeat of Huerta, which coincided with the greatest military and social conflicts of the revolution. Revolutionary generals of the Convention and Constitutionalists battled each other and to varying degrees sought control of Mexico City and the support of its newly organized working people. The first section traces the convergence between a portion of the Mexico City labor movement (led by the Casa del Obrero Mundial) and the Constitutionalist generals most willing to make concessions to organized workers. This convergence was the product neither of one-sided manipulation by Constitutionalist generals nor of "false consciousness" on the part of workers. Working people responded to the dire circumstances and overt sympathies from Constitutionalist generals by asserting themselves in the workplace and vis-à-vis political authorities in unprecedented ways. Indeed, for many workers, the Red Battalions legitimized their participation as workers in social struggles during and after the revolution, as they tried to impose specific conditions on employers and politicians that were linked to many of the central aspirations of workers. Moreover, the formation of the Red Battalions constituted an assertion by workers as citizens in historic national events that tapped into a rich vein of popular liberalism. Their role as protagonists within and outside of the alliance can be seen in the military and organizational activities of the Red Battalions outside of Mexico City, as well as in the continued patterns of mobilization that took place in Mexico City under Convention control in the absence of the Casa del Obrero Mundial.

Resistance and Accommodation

Under Madero and the relatively hostile government of Huerta, the unions of the Casa had minimized both political activity and appeals to government officials in work conflicts. But when the Casa reopened in August 1914 and resumed activities that had been halted by Huerta, the political climate was markedly distinct from any the Casa had known since its formation during Madero's presidency. Constitutionalist generals desperately needed a social base to support them in their battle to consolidate local and national power against the Convention forces and so sought support, among other groups, from urban workers in general and their most organized representative in particular, the Casa del Obrero Mundial.

After the fall of Huerta, the Constitutionalists broke with the remnants of Porfirian institutions by destroying the federal army, attacking the Catholic Church, and promising agrarian reforms that threatened the landed elite. For the first time since 1910, the declarations of national leaders over social policy began to reflect the degree of social mobilization that had marked the nation. In rural regions, Constitutionalist generals pronounced a series of decrees to establish minimum wages for peons, abolish debts and *tiendas de raya*, regulate production, and at times even condone the confiscation and distribution of land. These decrees often went well beyond the wishes of First Chief Carranza, who had been an important Porfirian politician and owned a large estate in Coahuila. Yet the sweeping promises of reform culminated in Carranza's own announcements of decrees in December 1914 and January 1915—proclaimed from a position of retrenchment in Veracruz—that significantly expanded the minimal social goals of his 1913 Plan of Guadalupe. As declared and even enacted in many regions, these policies were first of all an official response to the popular agrarianism unleashed by the revolution. Second, they reflected the rise to power of a new generation of mostly northern "proconsular" leaders, men epitomized by the Sonorans Salvador Alvarado, Adolfo de la Huerta, and Alvaro Obregón, who were willing to go beyond the previous liberal limitation on state action to intervene in the economy and mediate conflicts between social classes. Finally, and just as important, reform decrees were attempts to counter popular support for rural plebeian leaders Zapata and Villa, at a time when their combined forces dominated much of the country.[3]

In spite of the primarily rural dynamic of the revolution, Constitutionalist agrarian policies had urban counterparts that reflected similar criteria: they were often implemented by the same military leaders, who responded to unprecedented urban mobilization and the need to incorporate new social groups in the upcoming conflict for national power. Labor reforms aimed specifically at urban workers were decreed where urban workers were concentrated and most active, particularly in Veracruz, Puebla, Tampico, Mexico state, and the Federal District. In Puebla, Gen. Pablo González decreed an eight-hour day and a minimum wage in early September 1914. Soon after, Puebla governor Francisco Coss ordered that all Spanish managers be fired from factories and haciendas, a decree that was quickly overturned by Carranza, who in turn fired Coss. In Veracruz, Gen. Cándido Aguilar imposed a nine-hour day and obligatory Sunday rest for all workers. Carranza's January law included a promise of "a complete labor legislation" that would regulate work, minimum salaries, and work conditions, though no mention was made of the right to organize or strike.[4] Labor decrees by Constitutionalist generals were mostly wartime measures, public commitments to future reform designed to win over working-class support. They were a logical and significant progression from the voluntary standards engineered by the Madero government in the 1912 textile convention and were the best area for the Constitutionalists to make common cause with workers without endangering private property or control over fiscal policy. Of course, many employers would not take these and subsequent measures seriously for years.

If Carranza's key general, Alvaro Obregón, was still largely unknown to Mexico City workers, many of his key subordinates were not. Former deputy Heriberto Jara, who had participated fully in Casa activities under Madero and had helped to organize the celebration of the first May Day in 1913 under Huerta, now returned as a Constitutionalist general and soon was appointed governor of the Federal District. Ex-PLM member and Casa supporter Antonio Villareal also returned as a general. Eloy Armenta and José Colado, two Spanish-born Casa members deported by Huerta, had returned to Mexico to organize Constitutionalist support among workers and now returned to Mexico City. Colado was soon employed in the same Labor Department that the Casa had vehemently denounced, and by December, Armenta joined him as an inspector. According to the Casa's first chronicler, Rosendo Salazar, "old comrades" showed up in uniform to applaud the efforts of the reopened Casa and to participate in its celebrations. Even without such personal ties, Casa members could not help but be sympathetic to the Constitutionalists, who had defeated the military dictator who had jailed their leaders and ultimately closed their organization.

In late September, Governor Jara issued an extensive decree aimed at the city's most marginal workers. The prelude to the decree minimized previous patterns of organization in the city and emphasized the redemptive role of the Constitutionalists; the decree went on to mandate a nine-hour day in the Federal District and Sundays off, partially fulfilling the Casa del Obrero Mundial's earlier May Day demands. In addition, Jara ordered shops selling basic necessities to stay open a minimum number of hours and, like Madero before him, required *pulquerías* to close at noon on workdays and an hour later on Sundays and holidays. The decree even extended to domestic servants and provided for severe punishments for those employers and merchants who violated it. Notable absences in the decree were any attempt to regulate wages and any guarantee of the rights of workers to organize or strike. Many workers objected to the measures, since in the absence of minimum wages or legally recognized unions, fewer hours also meant less take-home pay. Others used the decrees to justify their demands and initiate strikes.[5] Within five weeks of the decree, the Constitutionalist forces began evacuating the city, making the decree a dead letter for employees and a suggestive memory for workers.

Efforts were also made to strengthen the role of the Labor Department, which would be crucial to the effective implementation of Constitutionalist reform decree. In early October, the new head of the Labor Department circulated an order to the Casa del Obrero Mundial and to the secretary of development that required all labor organizations to register with the Labor Department within thirty days. More significantly, it required both parties in any labor conflict to "exhaust all possible resources" before declaring a strike and even then to wait at least five days to initiate the strike.[6] The order does not seem to have been implemented but is notable for anticipating some of the more interventionist labor provisions of the 1917 constitution. In spite of such attempts, which coincided with the employment of former Casa members as inspectors, the Labor Department during Constitutionalist control of the city was largely marginalized from multiple labor conflicts due to two factors: first, the large numbers of skilled and unskilled workers who began organizing after the fall of Huerta turned increasingly to the Casa del Obrero Mundial rather than to the Labor Department for support in their labor conflicts, leading to much more direct confrontations with employers, as in the previously described strikes of tailors and El Palacio de Hierro workers. Even individual and unorganized workers, the previous constituency of the Labor Department, began showing up at the Casa del Obrero Mundial to settle differences with employers. Second, when workers did turn to officials for help in their conflicts with employers during the Constitutionalist occupation, including those in unions affiliated with the Casa, they often turned for support directly to the source of power, Constitutionalist generals, as in the October streetcar strike.

The ties between Casa members and Constitutionalist generals became closer in late September when Casa leaders negotiated with First Chief Carranza to replace their tiny rented offices on Leandro del Valle. As the Constitutionalist generals occupied the houses of the Porfirian elite in Colonia Juárez, Casa leaders asked for the use of the Hotel Sáenz, facing the Alameda. Obregón offered them instead the former Santa Brígida convent in the heart of the city as its new headquarters. The symbolism of turning an upper-class church building over to an organization of workers must have been irresistible for Constitutionalist officers and Casa leaders alike. The new building solved the Casa del Obrero Mundial's ongoing problem of space at a time when its membership burgeoned and eliminated one of their key financial burdens. The change in attitude of the city's temporary rulers encouraged not only the disposition of workers to confront employers but also the attitude of workers and their organizations toward collaboration with the military authorities.

That political authorities would seek a rapprochement with urban workers, or that workers would seek and accept their support, was hardly new; before the revolution Presidents Lerdo de Tejada and Díaz, and Governor Landa y Escandón had all established close ties with labor organizations, particularly in moments of crisis, and Madero and even Huerta had cultivated working-class organizations such as the Great Workers League. Even the offer of public and church buildings, or at least of official spaces for worker activities, was not without precedent.[7] But there were significant differences in the fall of 1914.

One dramatic difference was that the principal authorities in the city by October 1914 were military rather than civilian. The shift was not immediate but rather paralleled increasing tensions between Carranza and Villa. In August Carranza revived elements of the civilian city council elected under Madero in 1912 and moved to restore its pre-1903 powers; he appointed the civilian Alfredo Robles Domínguez, who had been the key Maderista in the city in 1911, as governor of the Federal District. But by September, the limits that military leaders imposed on the city council had become obvious, and Gov. Robles Domínguez had resigned and been replaced by Heriberto Jara, one of Carranza's closest generals. A similar shift of power from civilians to generals occurred in the October convention as it moved from Mexico City to Aguascalientes. The military leaders in control of Mexico City were more concerned with actions than legal procedures and were willing to intervene forcefully in labor conflicts in the areas they controlled—often in favor of workers. These concessions reflected both their distinct views of what the role of the state toward labor should be and their need for the support of urban workers in the upcoming struggle for power. Díaz had been alternately paternalistic and repressive with workers but rarely moved to force owners to give concessions to workers. Madero and his Labor Department attempted to avoid labor conflicts by facilitating negotiation between workers and employers, but even the most important labor reform of his administration, the textile convention agreement, remained voluntary on the part of textile factory owners. By contrast, Constitutionalist generals were willing to regulate by decree the minimum conditions of work and, if necessary—in industrial sectors crucial to the urban, national, or war economies—to temporarily take over the operation of a business or even turn its administration over to workers.

Workers in any strategic sector always had to consider the reaction of government and police authorities, whether it be to repress or to intervene in favor of workers, so the distinct possibility of favorable intervention was understandably attractive. Members of the Casa del Obrero Mundial also distinguished between turning to revolutionary generals for support in labor conflicts, which they did often in the fall of 1914, and their continued rejection of the interventions of the Labor Department.[8] Even though Constitutionalist generals ultimately saw the price of such intervention as loyalty and subordination, workers under the Casa leadership were able to shape the outcome of labor conflicts that involved Constitutionalist officials and impose many of their own conditions. The streetcar workers' strike that broke out in October 1914, discussed in the previous chapter, is a good case in point. The workers' strike committee and its supporters in the Casa del Obrero Mundial remained in constant touch with Governor Jara and even met with First Chief Carranza, agreeing on the basic rules that strikers and police would observe and eventually coming to terms over the public intervention of the company and later wage increases and other concessions.

The leadership of the Casa del Obrero Mundial was faced with unprecedented support from military leaders at the same time that they felt increasing pressure for immediate reforms from its recently expanded membership, which now included workers from skilled and strategic sectors such as streetcar and electrical workers as well as less skilled workers such as seamstresses. Whether or not membership reached touted levels of fifty-two thousand, the meetings and activities of the

Casa clearly approached mass proportions in the fall of 1914.[9] From its own position of perceived strength, the Casa del Obrero Mundial shifted its strategy of distance from authorities to one more in line with that of many of its constituent unions and their new mass public.

Their appeals to the Constitutionalists became more ambitious and assertive, pressing the new would-be rulers of Mexico to enact long-standing demands for the regulation of work and expanding the scope of their demands to areas of consumption and a variety of public policies. On 2 October 1914, as the first session of the convention met in Mexico City, the Casa del Obrero Mundial presented a series of ambitious labor proposals to First Chief Carranza, Governor Jara, and the city council president. The tone of the petition suggested complicity with Constitutionalist leaders: further reforms were needed because the difficult material situation and high unemployment could "allow the enemies of the revolution the opportunity to whisper in the ear of the working masses that the current Government is incapable of improving the economic conditions in which we find ourselves." Specific work proposals included the eight-hour day, a minimum wage of 1.50 pesos, and the elimination of piecework and the putting-out system in the garment trade. In the sphere of consumption, the Casa del Obrero Mundial called for a mix of regulations and participation by workers to force prices of basic goods down to their 1912 levels and to drop rents by one-third, while tripling the tax on empty rooms. Finally, they proposed that the Casa del Obrero Mundial enforce housing sanitation regulations, replacing contractors with their own teams of inspectors and construction workers to implement such improvements as the construction of bathrooms and toilets in tenement houses.[10]

Two days later the Casa organized a "March of Labor" to support its petitions. Starting from three of the four cardinal points of the city (near Tlatelolco, San Lázaro, and the Belem prison), marchers articulated the periphery of neighborhoods where poor and working people lived before concentrating, three thousand strong, in front of the new Casa headquarters in the heart of the city. From there they marched down the principal downtown streets to the National Palace, carrying a banner with the figure of independence leader Miguel Hidalgo, and presented a

new petition to First Chief Carranza that repeated and expanded on earlier demands. Among the new demands were that capitalists be required
to create work, that pawnshops—which profited from workers' poverty—be closed down, and above all that the printing of paper money be
eliminated. The Casa del Obrero Mundial reasoned that, instead of
printing money, the Constitutionalists should finance the revolutionary
armies through a special contribution imposed on property owners and
an extraordinary tax on all exports from the country. In mid-November,
barely a week before the last Constitutionalist troops left the city, the
Casa threatened a general strike if Governor Jara did not concede legal
recognition to unions.[11]

Such initiatives questioned the core of Carranza's fiscal policy and
business ties and suggested the potential for future conflict with Constitutionalist authorities. At the same time, the exigencies of war, the radicalization of a sector of the Constitutionalist forces led by Obregón, and
the need to counterbalance any potential urban popular base of Villa and
Zapata would soon force Obregón and other generals toward dramatic
wartime gestures that seemed less remote from the goals of the Casa del
Obrero Mundial.

In spite of the shared sympathies and approximation of the Constitutionalists and the Casa del Obrero Mundial in the months of August
through November 1914, their flirtation would not be decisive. By early
November, the split among delegates at the Convention of Aguascalientes was definitive, and Carranza and Obregón abandoned Mexico
City, issuing manifestos urging capitalinos to enlist and follow their re-
treat to the more defensible Veracruz. Some students and textile workers
apparently accepted Obregón's invitation, but the Casa leadership, in
spite of their collaboration with Constitutionalists over their new headquarters and key strikes, still prided themselves in their neutrality in
what they still perceived largely as a political struggle. Moreover, at the
time, a Carranza victory was by no means obvious. According to Salazar,
Casa leaders "didn't dare to communicate [the Constitutionalist invita-
tion] to the constituent unions." Instead they awaited the advance of the
Convention forces led by Zapata and Villa with expectant neutrality.[12]

The Casa-Constitutionalist Pact

Ten weeks after the Casa leadership rejected Obregón's initial invitation to join the Constitutionalists, and after two more evacuations and occupations of the city, a group of sixty-seven Casa del Obrero Mundial leaders made the decision to take up arms to defend the Constitutionalist movement and soon brought a significant portion of the Casa behind their decision.

How did such a shift take place? The signing of the pact can only be understood in terms of the particular context of Mexico City in the midst of a civil war and a national revolution, the relations of the Casa unions with both Constitutionalist and Convention authorities during the previous six months of alternation in power in the capital, and the immediate and historic aspirations of many of the working people of Mexico City.

Certainly a crucial factor underlying relations between workers and the revolutionary factions was the material conditions of the city. Starting in the last months of the Huerta government, conditions in Mexico City steadily deteriorated, worsening with every subsequent abandonment and takeover of the city, and became particularly acute after Obregón abandoned the city to Convention forces in November 1914. Nor would the general situation in the city improve during the six weeks in which Obregón held the city in early 1915, as the Zapatistas continued to harass Obregón's supply lines from Veracruz, attack the southernmost areas of the Federal District, and cut off the main water supply to the city, the Xochimilco aqueduct.

This deterioration was in many ways an inevitable consequence of war. Both factions commandeered railway systems, horses, and mules to move troops and military supplies in territory they controlled and attempted to disrupt the lines of communication in enemy territory. Such disruptions in the national transportation system, along with occasional expropriations of haciendas and the recruitment of rural workers, in effect broke the regional and national markets that had emerged in the Porfiriato and on which Mexico City depended more than most cities. Mexico City was cut off from its principal supplies of food as well as manufacturing inputs, though the *type* of shortages often depended on which faction controlled the city. For example, depending on who held the Federal District, cotton was alternately imported through the port of Veracruz under Constitutionalist control or brought in from the northern Laguna region under Villista control. In either case, textile factories in the Federal District were forced to close down intermittently for lack of supplies, and many workers were periodically laid off or had their hours severely reduced.[13]

Each faction initiated its occupation of the city by declaring the paper currency of the previous faction to be illegal. Shopkeepers inevitably responded by closing down their shops until they could be coerced or cajoled into opening again and accepting the new currency. The value of each new paper currency depended in turn on the amount of paper printed, the supplies of basic necessities available, and the speculation that occurred in food and paper currencies among the public, merchants, and currency "coyotes." Often the value of paper currency fluctuated with the fate of each faction in distant battlefields—thus the value of Convention currency in Mexico City peaked around 9 December, when Zapatista forces took Puebla, and plummeted on 5 January, when the Zapatistas were forced to evacuate Puebla. At the same time, the Constitutionalist "*coloraditos*" recuperated their value and began to circulate in the city in spite of Convention prohibitions. In these circumstances, the real value of wages went up and down like a roller coaster, though the general trend was down.[14]

These conditions were further exacerbated by the attitude of each faction toward the city. Carranza, Obregón, and other northern Constitutionalists made abundantly clear their hostility toward a capital city that they as northerners had always felt had infringed on their regional autonomy. Obregón condemned Porfirian elites in the capital for their support of the usurpation of Huerta, reproached Maderista politicians for their prolonged acquiescence to Huerta, and in public acts shamed the city's residents for remaining neutral throughout the national conflict. Similarly, Zapata and many of his generals shared the distrust of country people for a city they perceived as the center of corruption and privilege, though this was expressed more as indifference and suspicion

toward the city rather than the virulent hostility of the Constitutionalists. Antipathy toward the political, economic, and cultural metropolis
was shared by all factions in 1914, as was the problem of whether or how
to incorporate its population into the revolution.

Moreover, Mexico City was not deemed vital to winning the country
but only to ruling it. It was difficult to defend and was not crucial to the
military strategies of either faction. Soon after his brief return to the city
in January 1915, Obregón announced to the metropolitan press: "I don't
concede any importance to the city of Mexico from the military point of
view. It doesn't constitute a strategic position, it isn't a railroad center,
and it isn't a place where the troops can find elements of food or war
that they need. On the contrary, to protect Mexico City, we would have to
divert a numerous force that is needed in other areas, where greater
gains would be made. That is why for us, to hold this City or not, is all
the same." Similarly, when Convention president González Garza
pleaded with Villa weeks earlier for reinforcements from Mexico City,
Villa responded that, for all he cared, "the capital might go to ruin."[15]
The combination of hostility and neglect toward Mexico City as a whole
would only make material conditions worse.

The most immediate response of working people to such conditions
was to defend what they saw as their fundamental right to work. They
responded to layoffs and drastic reductions in the days and hours they
worked by striking, by organizing marches, and by making a series of
proposals to employers and officials to create work, such as mandating
public works or improvements to tenements. The Printers' Union even
considered a "solidarity" rule by which employed printers would allow
the unemployed to work in their place a couple of days a week. Poor and
working people also protested the price and availability of food and fuel
and in the worst months of the crisis often turned to rioting, a topic discussed more fully in the next chapter. Of course striking in the midst of
such a crisis was an inherently difficult proposition: striking electrical
workers might succeed in reversing layoffs and reductions in hours,
since for political reasons the company could not simply be allowed to
close down; by contrast, striking textile workers were more likely to face
a lockout.[16]

The economic crisis facilitated the recruitment of urban workers in the different factions of the revolution. Workers had a vested interest in continued industrial production, and their greatest participation in the revolution coincided with the period of greatest economic disruption. In mining areas like Chihuahua, workers shared an interest in the continued operations of foreign-owned mines, and violence against the mining companies, or recruitment in the ranks of the revolutionaries, was most likely to occur when the mines were closed down. So too did hunger and unemployment in Mexico City contribute to what critics of Obregón at the time referred to as "conscription by hunger."[17] But economic conditions, while an important factor, are insufficient to explain the decision of organized workers to take up arms, and on the scale of the Red Battalions. Nor do they explain why the Casa ultimately favored one faction over another.

One explanation for the alliance with the Constitutionalists offered by various historians is the cultural gulf between city and countryside: the cultural and material interests of urban workers were closer to those of the urban middle class than to those of peasants, and the Casa identified more with the middle-class Constitutionalists than with the peasant Zapatistas.[18] These differences have validity but can be overdrawn. Country people joined the armies of both factions, and Obregón's Yaqui Indians' march into the city in August 1914 caused reactions of wonder among the population similar to the entrance of the campesinos of Morelos three months later. Similarly, middle-class revolutionaries also joined the armies of Villa and even Zapata, though the popular-plebeian leadership of the Convention forces was distinct from that of the Constitutionalists, and the middle-class generals and advisors in the Convention army were subordinate to its plebeian leadership. How these cultural and social differences influenced the decision of Casa workers is another matter.

The break between countryside and city was far from absolute, if only because over half of the population in 1910 were migrants, many of them from rural areas. According to most accounts, huge crowds of the popular classes warmly welcomed the Zapatistas into the city. One eyewitness observed that "the poor people of Mexico, those of the 'pulque-ridden' neighborhoods, those who were most suffering the rigors of hunger and the contingencies of the battle . . . shared with them [the Zapatista soldiers] what little they had." Urban workers and popular classes were as likely to be familiar with and sympathetic to the peasants of the south as they were with northern soldiers and officers, particularly the Sonorans, who with their gringo ranger uniforms and insults over the capital's neutrality were considered arrogant and condescending in the penny press and *pasquines* (lampoons) of the day.[19]

Of course, as noted, a significant gap existed between the skilled and lettered craftworkers who dominated the Casa and the unskilled and casual laborers who were just starting to organize, some of them in association with the Casa. Indeed, the strongest evidence for the cultural disdain of urban workers for the Zapatistas is from the Casa leaders themselves, who later penned vivid descriptions of humble and superstitious Zapatistas marching into Mexico City behind the banner of the Virgin of Guadalupe and begging for food. But these denunciations of the Zapatistas must be taken with some caution. Many prominent Casa members expressed admiration for the Zapatistas (far more than for the Villistas), as suggested by Huitrón's letter to the International Anarchist Congress. By the time Huerta closed down the Casa in May 1914, several key Casa members had fled to Morelos and joined the Zapatistas, such as Antonio Díaz Soto y Gama and Luis Méndez. Other members and specific unions formed close relations with the Zapatistas during their control of the city, relations that in some cases led to formal affiliations that endured after the signing of the pact, as with the Union of Electricians and Rafael Pérez Taylor. If these Zapatista sympathies, ties, and affiliations were limited compared to those resulting from the pact, they at least suggest that a rejection of the Zapatistas by Casa leaders was not inevitable or unanimous and that familiarity did not automatically breed contempt.

The different religious attitudes of the Casa and the Zapatistas have also been noted by historians as emblematic of the gulf between city and *campo* and a factor in the Casa's decision to join the Constitutionalists. Religious belief remained a central value for the Zapatistas and thus contrasted with the rabid anticlericalism of many Constitutionalist leaders. But among the Zapatistas there was no conflict between their religious devotion on the one hand and opposition to the institutions and representatives of the church hierarchy on the other. In the Plan de Ayala, Zapata invoked the Reform's confiscation of church lands as a precedent for village confiscations of land taken by haciendas, and the agrarian program of the Convention government called for punishing the high clergy for supporting Huerta. In May 1915, a Convention dominated by Zapatistas voted overwhelmingly to eliminate the church presence in education. The Zapatistas did not perpetrate any of the spectacular attacks on the clergy and church property that characterized Obregón's second occupation, but neither did they accept money from the church, a frequent Constitutionalist accusation made against them. And Pancho Villa, while generally more tolerant of religious belief than Constitutionalist leaders, was as quick to denounce and harass clergymen as Obregón had been in Mexico City, at least in northern states under his control.[20]

As noted earlier, the religious views among Casa intellectuals ranged from rabid anticlericalism to a vague Christian socialism but differed from those of the vast majority of poor and working people for whom religion remained an important cultural orientation. In spite of the anticlericalism of anarchist ideology and of many of the Casa leaders, the individual unions of the Casa del Obrero Mundial for the most part avoided or showed restraint in religious matters, which, like political affiliations, were inherently divisive issues.

Indeed, the visceral reactions of Casa leaders to the Zapatistas date for the most part *after* the pact was signed and the Red Battalions were formed. Similarly, the virulent and public anticlericalism in the articles and acts of the Casa del Obrero Mundial emerged in the weeks around the time of the alliance, largely in conjunction with Obregón's own spectacular acts of anticlericalism. The anticlerical invectives against the Zapatistas in the propaganda organs of the Red Battalions, such as *Revolución Social*, were the efforts of prolific individuals like Juan Tudó and Rosendo Salazar, who were determined to defend their decision to ally with the Constitutionalist leaders. Jacobin generals like Alvaro Obregón manipulated inherent tensions between Casa leaders and the clergy by confiscating church buildings and giving them to workers' organizations, even when Casa members had made demands for other types of property. Similarly, Obregón publicly painted Zapata as "at first a convinced and sincere revolutionary . . . [who] later was transformed, by his clerical ideas, into a conservative." After the demobilization of the Red Battalions, the Casa once again returned to a position of relative religious tolerance with their return to Mexico City in the fall of 1915.[21]

Like the material conditions of the city in early 1915, the cultural gap between workers and peasants seems inadequate in itself to explain the Casa's participation in the revolution on the side of the Constitutionalists. The importance of these two factors—the cultural affinities of Casa members with the Constitutionalists and their cultural disaffections with the forces of the Convention—to the formation of an alliance depended primarily on how they transferred into specific policies and actions taken by the contending factions toward urban workers in general and the Casa del Obrero Mundial in particular.

"Tierra y Libertad" in the City of Palaces

Zapatista forces entered Mexico City from the southern towns of the Federal District on 24 November 1914 to the warm acclaim of the popular classes, a welcome that was repeated days later for Villista troops from the north. Respectable classes were in turn relieved that troops led by the "Attila" of the south refrained from violence or the confiscation of property and instead ordered the return of all houses that had been confiscated by Constitutionalist generals. Zapata himself entered the city quietly, avoiding the National Palace, where all previous conquerors had arrived, and lodging instead at a cheap hotel by the San Lázaro railroad station on the eastern edge of town. As dramatic as the meeting of countryside and city was, the disorientation and discomfort was greater for the peasant guerrillas than it was for the local population—as suggested by the armed attack of Zapatista soldiers on a fire engine that surprised them on the streets of Mexico City.[22]

The uneasy photographic session of Villa and Zapata seated in the chairs of political authority in the National Palace would come to symbolize a revolution where "the underdogs" (los de abajo) could end up on top, briefly in control of the nation's capital. In retrospect, the uneasiness of Villa and Zapata in Mexico City suggests how fragile their control of the city would be. The Convention government had little success at either running the city they occupied (much less the nation) or winning the lasting allegiance of the city's poor and working people, who soon felt considerable frustration at the Convention's ineffectiveness. The Convention suffered two principal divisions that in turn undermined its will to govern both nationally and in Mexico's largest city. First, the strength of the Convention military forces (and of the Zapatistas in particular) was precisely in their close ties to their geographical bases (Villa in the north and center of the country and Zapata barely beyond the limits of Morelos) and in their concern with rural issues. Military cooperation between the two factions soon proved impossible. Rather than pursue the retreating Constitutionalist army and corner them in Veracruz, in December Villa and most of his troops retreated north to Torreón to protect supply lines and to be close to their strongest base of support. Zapata quickly occupied Puebla but proved unwilling to move farther beyond Morelos or even to hold Puebla for very long. The failure of Villa and Zapata to create a single, national military structure gave Carranza and Obregón time to consolidate their position and initiate an offensive against Villa in the north.

Second, in the midst of war, an approximation to democratic forms of governance within the Convention (a nicety that the "Constitutionalist" forces of Carranza astutely avoided) proved extremely difficult and even counterproductive. Coordination between the military and political branches of the Convention, and between the political cadres of the two factions within the Convention parliament—where the Zapatista and the Villista blocks bickered over control of cabinet positions and the executive—proved as difficult as coordination between the two armies. The Convention was the supreme body of the government and dominated a weak president, but real power as well as the reality of or potential for revolutionary transformation lay with the distinct armies of the north and south. The group of middle-class figures around Convention president Eulalio Gutiérrez and his successors was unable to either control or represent the social base of the Convention forces, much less the urban popular classes of Mexico City. When President Gutiérrez abandoned Mexico City and the Convention in early January 1915, eventually to make his peace with Carranza, the legitimacy of the Convention government plummeted along with the Villista currency. The powers of his successor, Roque González Garza, were restricted even further by the Convention assembly, whose parliamentary ramblings made the government increasingly irrelevant to the fate of the national military conflict or the daily lives of those who lived under its rule.[23]

A series of military decrees and parliamentary laws aimed at alleviating the conditions of the urban popular classes had limited effect. A decree by Gen. Eufemio Zapata that required pawnshops in Mexico City to return all goods pawned for less than five pesos to their owners won the initial sympathy of the popular classes. But owners of pawnshops responded by closing down, depriving the poor of their only source of credit, and so Convention president Gutiérrez virtually nullified the decree. The Zapatistas briefly introduced badly coined but high quality silver, which provided a degree of relief to the functioning of commerce. But soon abundant paper money printed by the Convention drove the metal currency out of circulation. Price controls were imposed on basic products, a policy that Villa had implemented successfully as governor of Chihuahua in 1913. But there he had been able to draw on supplies of cheap meat from the haciendas that his generals controlled. In Mexico City, by contrast, prices were impossible to control without also assuring an adequate supply of food, something that the Convention government and military forces were unable or unwilling to do. Finally, the Convention forces made no apparent effort to recruit soldiers from among the city's unemployed, an effort that would have provided some relief to the poor and might have helped to consolidate a popular base for the government. At one point, the Conventionist military commander of the city explicitly prohibited the recruitment of residents, since "that way you obtained recruits by convenience and not sympathizers of libertarian ideas."[24] The absence of recruitment efforts contrasted markedly with Villa's practice in Chihuahua, differed from the brutal forced conscription under Huerta, and, above all, contrasted with the earlier and later attempts by the Constitutionalists to recruit both the unemployed and organized sectors of the urban population.

On entering the city in November, the Zapatistas left the organization of the city's police force in the hands of ex–federal soldiers who had been disbanded by Carranza months before. The Zapatistas and the Convention government confirmed Carranza's reinstallation of the Maderista city council and the restoration of its pre-1903 functions and revenues; but rather than giving the city council a clear delineation of functions, the government of the Federal District, under Gen. Manual Chao, increasingly turned jurisdiction for problems it could not or would not handle, such as the food situation and strikes, over to the city council. If these problems confounded the Convention generals, who had a monopoly on force and controlled access to transportation and food supplies, they were insurmountable for the fledgling city council.[25]

One of the biggest conflicts between military and civilian authorities was over questions of public order. If the Zapatistas proved for the most part well behaved, Villista soldiers, in what Friedrich Katz calls the "Terror of Mexico City," scandalized *gente decente* and squandered support among popular sectors through their high-profile revelries in bars and cabarets, assassinations, and kidnappings. Villa ordered or allowed the execution not only of members of the upper class and partisans of the Huerta regime but also of Zapatista civilian and military leaders allied to the Convention.[26] The Convention presidents and the city council continually and ineffectively tried to censure and fine soldiers as well as proprietors of bars and theaters for public scandals and disorders. Villa himself caused a minor diplomatic scandal when he jailed the French owner of the Hotel Palacio for hiding a pretty cashier he had propositioned. In contrast with his earlier "social banditry" and bouts of urban populism in Chihuahua, Villa's activities in Mexico City in 1915 seemed closer to plain banditry.[27]

In the first weeks of their occupation of Mexico City, the Conventionists, particularly the Zapatistas, established relatively cordial contacts with workers' organizations, and Zapata himself quickly confirmed the Casa del Obrero Mundial's occupation of the former convent Santa Brígida. Good relations were due in no small part to the participation in the Convention Congress of prominent former members of the Casa del Obrero Mundial such as Antonio Díaz Soto y Gama, Luis Méndez, and

Rafael Pérez Taylor, who had fled to Morelos to join the Zapatistas during the worst period of Huerta repression. Other current Casa del Obrero Mundial members and the Union of Electricians also maintained close contacts with the Zapatista soldiers, who were respectful visitors at union meetings.[28]

In spite of the adverse economic conditions in the city and evident tensions within the working-class movement, discussed later, in these weeks of Convention control, the city's labor movement reached its greatest expansion to date, most notably with the formation of the Union of Electricians in December and the incorporation of Federal District textile workers within the Casa. The Casa repeated their efforts of the previous year, cut short by Huerta, to formalize their loose organizational structure through the creation of a Confederation of Workers of the Federal District (Confederación de Sindicatos del Distrito Federal), under the leadership of printer Rafael Quintero. On 7 January 1915, with the support of the new confederation, the Federation of Textile Workers organized a huge public march of twenty thousand to commemorate the assassinations of textile workers in Rio Blanco eight years before. Press accounts mention the participation of all of the key unions in the city—including those of the newly prominent streetcar workers and the electrical workers—but mention no mutual aid societies, suggesting the definitive shift toward unions among the principal working-class sectors of the city. Speakers included the ever present Díaz Soto y Gama, though this time "in representation of the *campesinos* of the South," and a commission of officers from the Zapatista army.[29]

In November, the Convention government turned the direction of the Labor Department temporarily over to Casa member José Colado, who had first been named inspector under Carranza. The Casa responded by expelling Colado and Eloy Armenta for accepting political positions. But that a key Casa intellectual and organizer would be named to head the Labor Department suggests a brief radicalization of the legal goals of that department. Indeed, one of the first actions of the Convention Labor Department, responding to earlier Casa demands, was to call for a convention of workers for 15 January 1915 to consider the formal recognition of the legal status of unions. Still, Colado, as head of the de-

partment, abandoned some of his previous radical rhetoric and assumed much of the department's institutional language, referring in
public statements to the need to make "the interests of Capital and Labor harmonious." In January, the far more conservative Antonio Zamacona replaced Colado, and the convention of workers was postponed indefinitely. Zamacona would complain months later that the Labor
Department, due to the intervention of military authorities, now played
a marginal role in labor conflicts. Several months later the moribund
Convention government would pass a series of progressive labor reforms, discussed later, that for the first time in Mexican history explicitly
guaranteed workers the right to organize and strike. But in the meantime, the immediate actions of generals of each faction would prove
more important than what one former Casa member later referred to as
the "abracadabra radicalism" of the Convention legislature.[30]

One of the first labor conflicts the Convention faced was, predictably,
over the streetcar company. On occupying the city, the Zapatistas, pressured by British and U.S. diplomats, ordered company management
restored without insisting first on any guarantees for labor. Restored
general director C. B. Graves immediately eliminated union gains, including the 25 percent raise that Constitutionalist governor Jara had decreed, and streetcar workers immediately threatened a strike, prompting the Convention government to intervene again in the company. The
streetcar workers spent the next month in tense negotiations with the
new government intervener, Tomás Ramos, who granted the union control over hiring decisions but refused to raise wages according to the union's demands. Throughout January, the union appealed to the Convention president to replace the intervener, but on the eve of Obregón's
retaking of the city, González Garza had not responded, thus creating
considerable resentment among streetcar workers toward the Convention government.[31]

The relative hesitancy and ambiguity of Convention authorities toward labor conflicts—particularly when compared to Constitutionalist
policies in the months before and after the first Convention occupation
of the city—is perhaps best exemplified by the strike against the Telephone and Telegraph Company, which began on 19 January 1915 under

Convention control of Mexico City and was resolved during the following six-week Constitutionalist occupation. Striking telephone workers, many of whom were women, were backed by the Union of Electricians, streetcar workers, and to a lesser extent the Casa del Obrero Mundial. They demanded an increase in wages, an eight-hour day, compensation for sickness, and the firing of an abusive manager. Although divisions among telephone workers prevented them from making a formal demand of union recognition, any settlement negotiated with the Union of Electricians would mean a de facto recognition of the union by the foreign-owned telephone company.

The Convention government refused to either repress the telephone workers or impose a settlement. The first three weeks of the strike were a virtual standoff, as a minority of nonstriking workers in the company were able to sustain operations of the company and union affiliates were fired. The electricians supported the telephone workers by contributing a portion of their salaries to their maintenance, while Casa del Obrero Mundial members undertook a type of sabotage by applying for and accepting positions as strikebreakers but not showing up for work. When the Convention government withdrew and General Obregón's troops retook possession of the city on 28 January, the strike was at a crucial juncture. The Union of Electricians had to decide whether to call a general strike in support of the telephone workers, a move that, in the midst of high unemployment and the martial law of military occupation, was very risky.[32] By contrast to the hesitancy of Convention authorities, Obregón would move quickly to settle the strike.

The two months of Convention occupation of the city, from 24 November 1914 to 28 January 1915, were less than decisive in forging close ties with the city's poor and working people. Neither Zapata nor Villa proved particularly concerned with the affairs of urban workers or the well-being of the population of Mexico City. Good intentions, hesitant actions in labor conflicts, and delayed proposals for labor legislation—eventually passed by the Convention in the spring of 1915—proved insufficient to the needs of urban workers in times of crisis. As evacuation of the city became inevitable, no attempt was made by the Convention government or either of its armed components to mobilize workers or other sectors of the urban population as armed supporters.

In disarray over the defection of the president and the approach of Obregón's troops to Mexico City, the Convention retreated to Cuernavaca, Morelos, in late January. There one of its first acts was to approve as a "legitimate act of war" the cutting off of Mexico City's water supply, which depended on the water pumps in the town of Xochimilco, which bordered Morelos. The situation in the city they had abandoned became more desperate as the population depended on a sprinkling of artesian wells. One irony of the Convention's actions and inactions toward the urban population is that they would coincide with the dramatic reorganization of rural society in Morelos, during which land and political power were redistributed to peasant communities. For much of 1915 these villages, with the blessing of the Convention government, would finally, for a while, carry out their own revolution and live unto themselves.[33]

Ultimately, the same factors that gave strength to Zapatismo and Villismo at the local levels proved liabilities in the national contention for power as well as in their relations with urban workers: close ties to their region of origin, the primacy of local and rural concerns over national and urban ones, and an indifference or hostility to national government and the capital city. The "parochialism" of both forces within the Convention contrasted sharply with the national perspective of Constitutionalist leaders.[34]

"To the Terrain of the Practical"

In contrast to the increasing divisions within the Convention between civilians and the military, and between Villista and Zapatista forces, Carranza and the Constitutionalists used the two months after the breakup of the Convention of Aguascalientes to consolidate their military forces with generals, recruits, and arms (including those abandoned by the U.S. Marines in Veracruz) and to refine their political and social project as articulated in Carranza's additions to the Plan of Guadalupe. This consolidation was reflected in their second occupation of Mexico City. By contrast to the ineffectiveness of the Convention government, Obregón reentered Mexico City on 30 January 1915 with a decisiveness that both offended and impressed, ruling by decree rather than the divided attempts at parliamentary democracy of the Convention.

This time, Obregón reoccupied Mexico City with no intention of holding it, given the cost of defending and feeding its population. In late January, Obregón telegrammed Carranza that he could not defend Mexico City and later made clear that he hoped to control the city only long enough to assure Constitutionalist control over supply lines from Veracruz through Pachuca, receive ammunition, and then push on to confront Villa's forces directly in the cities of the Bajío to the north.[35] Secondary goals during his stay were to recruit human and material resources to continue his military campaign, and in this task, Obregón acted resolutely and strategically on the city stage, disrupting the traditional order with the assurance of one who did not expect to be around the city for very long. Constitutionalists were no more effective in these months than the Convention government had been at stabilizing the material conditions in the city, which instead continued to deteriorate. But Obregón skillfully used the crisis situation to mount dramatic, populist gestures that helped to incorporate one of the most organized sectors of the city's population to the Constitutionalist cause.

Obregón arrived with the colorful Gerardo Murillo in tow, who had quickly become an important interlocutor with urban popular sectors. Murillo was an artist who had taken the name Dr. Atl (from the indigenous Nahuatl word for "water") and who later became a mentor for the younger painters who would constitute the muralist movement of the 1920s. Atl sat out the first part of the revolution in Paris, painting, meeting leftist intellectuals and politicians, and trying to set up a utopian community for artists. A few days before the fall of Huerta, he stepped off a boat in Veracruz spouting the language of social revolution, claiming he had just consulted with Pres. Woodrow Wilson about the revolution, and seeking an interview with Carranza. With remarkable facility he got close to Carranza and, more important, to the group of progressive generals under Obregón's leadership who were pushing the first chief to declare support for social reforms. During Carranza's first occupation of Mexico City, Atl was named director of the School of Fine Arts, organized a Union of Revolutionary Artists, and gave at least one talk on the war in Europe to the Casa del Obrero Mundial.[36]

Intense, austere, and charismatic, Dr. Atl impressed the leaders of the Casa del Obrero Mundial as a prophet of social change and appeared to have the complete trust of and authority from Carranza. Casa member Rosendo Salazar, awed in particular by Atl's "internationalist" experiences in Europe, described him as "a thin little man with brilliant eyes . . . that look with profundity on the multiple Mexican landscape, inside and out; a dark beard the color of sapphire . . . not just any revolutionary, but rather of those that believe that the world belongs to the poor."[37] The presence of Atl among the Constitutionalists may have seemed the passionate guarantee of social change, the counterpart to the virile, vengeful, and manipulative Obregón.

The Constitutionalist reoccupation of the city began on the wrong foot. On orders from Carranza, Obregón declared that all paper currency not of Constitutionalist issue was illegal, a decree that brought commerce to a standstill and resulted in a series of public protest marches. During the first two weeks of February, large crowds of women holding worthless Villista money in their hands marched to Obregón's headquarters and then on to the monument to Juárez, demanding that Convention currencies be accepted and that the water supply, restricted throughout early February to one hour a day, be restored. Groups of women "agitators" circulating among the city's markets tried to organize a demonstration against the economic situation, attempts that the Constitutionalists ultimately prohibited and repressed.

Obregón's response to the crisis was astute. He organized a high-profile Revolutionary Committee for the Relief of the Poor, headed by engineer Alberto Pani and Dr. Atl, who were given broad leeway to distribute a total of five hundred thousand newly printed Constitutionalist pesos to the poorer classes at relief stations.[38] Esther Torres, unemployed at the time and not yet affiliated with the Casa, later described her own experience of Constitutionalist relief:

> At the time that Carranza was here, we all had money . . . we would go to the factory and say, "Good Morning, Sir . . ."
>
> "There is no raw material, come back in eight days."
>
> . . . and a coworker said: "Let's go girls, they are giving away money in Guatemala [Street], in the northern part of the National Palace."
>
> . . . And we went, and it was true . . . we saw all types of bills, of all denominations, and we got in line and my sister who was very delicate said, "No, what an embarrassment, unemployed and they give me money, no, no."[39]

According to one estimate at the time, 85 percent of the ten thousand people who accepted relief were women, suggesting that the embarrassment Esther's sister felt at accepting money was felt even more acutely by men. Men were supposed to work to provide for their families and might therefore go on strike to assure their families' survival. But asking authorities for food or money called into question their masculinity. By contrast, women could, as argued by Temma Kaplan, "appear dignified and even heroic demanding food for their children according to female consciousness and practical gender interests."[40]

The effect of such monetary relief on the popular classes was temporary but sensational, easing hostility if not fostering loyalty. The intention of the distribution was clear in a speech Dr. Atl made after the distribution: "If the inhabitants of Mexico City continue permanently neutral in the face of the social, military, and political activity of the Revolution, they will always be the victim of all parties and will suffer the consequences, every day more serious, of their inertia and lack of consciousness." Obregón wrote Carranza that the distribution of money had been a success and was worth repeating.

Rather than address the problems of excess paper currencies and scarce food supplies to the city, Obregón and the relief committee denounced merchants as the scourge of the people. Given that foreigners, particularly Spaniards, dominated much of the city's commerce, the attack on merchants soon took on a xenophobic aspect that had deep roots in the population. In mid-February, Obregón ordered all wholesale merchants of primary necessities to deliver 10 percent of their stocks to the relief committee for distribution to the needy. Many of the shop-keepers responded to what they saw as an attack on the freedom to trade by shutting down and, if they were foreign, hanging a consular seal and their native flag on their doors to assert diplomatic protection.[41] Days later, Obregón imposed a tax on all capital investments in the city, including manufacturing industries and the streetcar and electricity companies, a measure similar to the one the Casa had proposed in October. After the deadline for payment had passed, Obregón called a meeting of hundreds of businessmen and immediately had them arrested. Those merchants who still refused to pay the tax were marched each morning between Yaqui soldiers to sweep the street in front of the National Palace (see fig. 18). It is unclear how much food or taxes Obregón managed to collect from such interventions or whether the resources gathered were used by the military or distributed to the needy. The few government food depots that were actually set up in the last days of the Constitution-alist occupation were woefully understocked. But such measures were as much about public, symbolic politics as about relief.

Dr. Atl and Alberto Pani threatened to take over the numerous outlets of the Compañía Mexicana Molinera de Nixtamal, which sold masa, the ground corn used to make tortillas, a warning that briefly forced the monopoly company to lower its prices. Military authorities imposed Solomon-like justice on eighty-six ice cream vendors accused of selling contaminated ice cream to soldiers; they were rounded up and forced to eat large quantities of their own wares. The *Mexican Herald* reported that thirty-three vendors died and the rest were released as innocent.

Similar attacks were orchestrated against the church. Nowhere was the hostility of military leaders toward the institutional church ex-pressed more spectacularly during the revolution than by Obregón in Mexico City during the month of February 1915. Obregón rounded up and jailed 116 priests, a number of them foreigners, after they refused to pay a contribution of five hundred thousand pesos needed to alleviate "the precarious situation of the people of Mexico City, and in particular the laboring classes." The amount demanded corresponded to the sum of newly printed money that Dr. Atl and Alberto Pani were distributing to workers and the poor, giving the demand an apparent measure of justice that was further enhanced by the appropriation of ornate colonial church buildings in the heart of the city to workers' organizations. Obregón would later insist that forty-nine members of the clergy were certified to have venereal disease.[42]

Foreign diplomatic responses to the interventions of Obregón eventually forced Carranza to order him to abandon the city by 19 March and proceed with his offensive against Villa. By then, he had gathered sufficient human and material resources to move on.[43] The public humiliations of the "reaction," identified by the Constitutionalists as merchants and the church, effectively identified a plausible enemy and did not escape the notice of workers within the Casa.

The policies of Obregón in Mexico City during February 1915 were designed to punish a portion of the metropolitan population and recruit another, but they were not the policies of a governor who intended to stay. While these actions had great symbolic importance, they actually made conditions worse for the popular sectors of the city, as the value of currency and thus wages dropped, as merchants responded to Constitutionalist bullying by closing down their shops, and as military priorities continued to determine the use of transportation and supplies.

But Obregón did move effectively to improve the strategic and material situation of organized labor, and in particular of the unions associated with the Casa. Constitutionalist troops arrived in the middle of the stalemate between workers affiliated with the Union of Electricians and the Telephone and Telegraph Company. Rather than call a general strike, the union instead proposed to Dr. Atl that the company be intervened. The precedent for this was the earlier Constitutionalist intervention in the streetcar company in October, which had in fact been fraught with tensions between workers and the government intervener. On 5 February Obregón acceded to a provisional intervention, though rather than appoint a government manager they turned the administration of the company over to the Union of Electricians, which named one of their own members, Luis N. Morones, to run the intervened company. The decree also allowed any workers who had refused to join the union during the strike to be fired. Dr. Atl reflected years later that with the appointment of a union administration in the telephone company, "workers were convinced that there was something beyond incendiary speeches." For many workers, this intervention seemed an endorsement of the possibility of extensive worker control of portions of the economy, and over the next two years, workers and Constitutionalists alike held up the company as a model of efficiency and worker-management relations.[44]

When the Union of Electricians met with Dr. Atl to discuss the intervention, Jacinto Huitrón, then general administrator of the Casa del Obrero Mundial, warned the Union of Electricians against any appeal to the government that might "restrict our liberty to exercise the 'direct action' that should be the norm of syndicalism." The Union of Electricians insisted that the intervention was "due to justice."

Other gestures toward the Casa occurred in rapid sequence. Constitutionalist generals had given the Casa del Obrero Mundial the former convent Santa Brígada for their headquarters in September 1914 and, upon retaking the city four months later, on 9 February granted their request for the adjoining Church of Santa Brígada and the printing press of the Catholic newspaper La Tribuna.[45]

Dr. Atl and the relief committee offered the Casa del Obrero Mundial fifteen thousand of the newly printed Constitutionalist pesos to distribute among its members and unemployed workers. On 7 February six hundred Casa members met for six hours before agreeing to accept the money, explaining that it was "not charity, but an indemnity paid them for damages suffered because of the decree . . . declaring the Villista notes worthless." Each time Obregón acted in favor of workers, it was accepted as "nothing more than justice." The money was divided among three thousand members who were out of work because of factory closures, mostly in the textile sector.[46]

The printer Rosendo Salazar reflected a few years later that, for many Casa del Obrero Mundial members, the receipt of gifts from Obregón signified "long desired demands [revindicaciones], just revenge for poor proletariats against lazy rich people." Another Casa del Obrero Mundial member supposedly put it more crudely: "Now we have a reason to fight; now we have a 'Patria' to defend: the printing press of 'La Tribuna,' the ex-convent and the Church of Santa Brígida and the Colegio Josefino. Long live the Revolution!"[47] Such gifts gave the Casa del

Obrero Mundial a degree of financial independence but inevitably created obligations toward their benefactors. In addition, they coincided with Obregón's campaign to punish and make an example of the clergy and further provoked the anticlerical tendencies within the Casa.

The interventions of Obregón and Dr. Atl—the new building, the distribution of new pesos, and union control of the telephone company—all occurred in the week before a group of Casa del Obrero Mundial leaders voted to support the Constitutionalists. Other groups of workers moved on their own, ahead of the Casa, toward an understanding with Constitutionalism. Weeks before the pact was signed and soon after two key textile factories in the Federal District closed down for lack of raw materials, a group of unemployed textile workers offered to join the Constitutionalists in exchange for job guarantees when peace was established. The day before the Casa came to their decision, Dr. Atl met with three hundred workers of the arms factory, who offered to travel to Veracruz as a unit to either take up arms or manufacture and repair arms for the Constitutionalist cause. Similarly, a group of Federal District teachers and government bureaucrats agreed to join Carranza in Veracruz, though not to take up arms. Such precedents certainly pressured the Casa to take a stand or risk losing its leadership of organized workers in the city.[48]

Internal strains and conflicts within the Casa del Obrero Mundial may have weighed heavily on their decision. In the months after the fall of Huerta, the Casa had expanded rapidly and had absorbed organizations with different backgrounds and agendas. Recent affiliates such as the Union of Electricians and a group of radical students and teachers led by Aurelio Manrique and Lorenzo Comacho Escamilla may have challenged the leadership of the group of craftworkers around Rafael Quintero and Jacinto Huitrón. In December 1914, influential members Eloy Armenta, José Colado, and Rafael Pérez Taylor were expelled "for using the name of the Casa del Obrero Mundial for a personal, political affair," presumably related to the decision of the first two to accept positions with the Labor Department and of Pérez Taylor to accept a position as a Zapatista delegate to the Convention government. The expulsion of Armenta led to the withdrawal of the Restaurant Workers' Union, which in early January 1915 publicly denounced the Casa del Obrero Mundial as controlled by six men who "command, administer, and direct." Indeed, printer Rafael Quintero had consolidated considerable personal power by maintaining his position as secretary general of the Casa del Obrero Mundial while provisionally taking on the same position in the revived Casa-affiliated federation, now called the Confederation of Federal District Unions (Confederación de Sindicatos del Distrito Federal). Also in January, plans were announced to open a rival Liga del Obrero Mundial, which may have been the project of expelled members Colado and Armenta. Although the evidence is unclear, one can speculate that, by leading the Casa del Obrero Mundial into an alliance with the Constitutionalists, its leaders sought to preempt further divisions over political affiliation or an internal split or takeover of the organization.[49]

The tensions within the Casa over collaboration with revolutionary factions inevitably exploded. A general meeting of the Casa del Obrero Mundial was called on 7 February 1915 to confirm a manifesto condemning militarism and demanding that the Convention and Constitutionalist factions alike put down their arms. The manifesto was consistent with the position they had maintained throughout the conflicts of the last three years and may have been prompted by concerns some members had over the series of Constitutionalist gifts made to the Casa. But after initial approval of the manifesto, Constitutionalist representative Dr. Atl asked to speak. Atl made a passionate speech denouncing the manifesto and claiming that the Constitutionalist movement was the incarnation of workers' aspirations for social reforms. The speech effectively sabotaged the manifesto of neutrality. One of the signers of the pact, Rosendo Salazar, would later attribute the shift to a "collective psychological phenomenon," namely the mesmerizing influence of Dr. Atl.[50] But Atl effectively brought his forceful personality and ties to Obregón to a body already torn over its proper role in the revolution.

Little is known of the circumstances of the meeting three days later in which the decision to support Carranza was made. The sixty-seven members who attended the second, closed meeting were not the constituted delegates of the constituent unions, although they included most of the key leaders of the Casa del Obrero Mundial. Notably absent were the principal leaders of the Union of Electricians and student leaders who had recently been participating in Casa events. Those invited may have been selected for their predisposition to support the Constitutionalists. Even so, various secondhand accounts attest that the discussion was long and heated before the decision was made to offer support to the Constitutionalists.[51]

The following day, an open meeting of the Casa del Obrero Mundial was called to present the decision to join the Constitutionalist cause. Over three thousand members attended, and again there was considerable disagreement. Finally on 12 February the Casa del Obrero Mundial leadership called together the elected union delegates to the Casa del Obrero Mundial and asked them to put the decision to their constituent unions. But their approval was already a formality—a Revolutionary Committee had been formed with the principal officers of the Casa del Obrero Mundial and others from the group of sixty-seven and was set to leave the next day for Veracruz to negotiate the terms of the pact with Carranza. In the face of continued debate, Quintero insisted that now "the issue is not to propose or give opinions, but rather to answer categorically if you accept [the alliance] or not." The strong-arm tactics of the committee apparently upset many of the delegates.[52]

The next day, the eight members of the Revolutionary Committee, including the printers Rafael Quintero and Rosendo Salazar and the shoemaker Celestino Gasca, left for Veracruz to negotiate (in Quintero's words) "what can be defined between the Revolution and us, what we will bring to the terrain of the practical, whether the others like it or not." In Veracruz, First Chief Carranza proved suspicious of the commission but finally allowed his acting interior minister, Rafael Zubáran Capmany—who was far more cordial to the commission—to negotiate the formalities of the pact. In a short but not particularly concise document, devoid of the usual flamboyant Casa style, the Casa promised to form Red Battalions of workers to defend areas under Constitutional control, "combat the reaction," and propagandize among workers in favor of the Constitutionalist cause. In return, Carranza confirmed his earlier resolutions to pass laws to improve the conditions of workers and attend to their demands in conflicts with bosses, promised to provide for the material needs of the Red Battalions and their families, and agreed to allow Casa members to create centers to facilitate the organization of workers throughout the country.[53]

Although a degree of manipulation or orchestration is evident in the actions of the Constitutionalists toward the Casa, and the Casa leadership toward its base, the decision to support the pact clearly resonated with an important part of the Casa membership and with working people in general, enough for at least five thousand workers to collectively and individually join the Red Battalions in the next weeks. Several distinct and perhaps contradictory factors help explain an alliance that some people at the time saw, and many historians since have seen, as a betrayal, whether of anarchist principles, the working class, or the peasantry.

Hunger and unemployment certainly played a role. As discussed earlier, in February conditions deteriorated rapidly and reached crisis proportions in the last week of February as Obregón prepared to abandon the city to its fate. The press, which frequently wrote about imminent shipments of food and fuel that never seemed to come, also ran stories of despairing mothers who attempted suicide because they could not feed their children, of soaring death rates related to food problems, of those who chopped down trees in Alameda and Chupultepec Parks for fuel, and of desperate fights over garbage. Indeed, in the initial document that the Casa leaders presented to their constituent unions, they explained the "social necessity to rise up in arms now to save the people of the Mexican Region, especially those that constitute the proletarian part, from the hunger that threatens them." In the midst of these circumstances, the Constitutionalist army promised those recruited under the terms of the pact between one and two pesos plus rations, support for families, and promises of eventual postwar employment.

But the pact was not simply "a final capitulation in the face of unemployment and hardship." Nor did the Casa simply sell out "in a pitiful manner, for a scrap of bread, tossed to them by the barbarian of Sonora, Alvaro Obregón," as former Casa member Rafael Pérez Taylor would lament months later as a delegate to the Convention.[54] The workers that first supported the pact were primarily from skilled and strategic sectors of the economy. While they suffered from deteriorating conditions, they were less hard hit than most working people by extremes of hunger, unemployment, and deteriorating wages. Of course, material incentives went beyond satisfying immediate necessities. The terms of the pact also meant a continuation of the subsidy to the Casa implicit in the various actions of Obregón and Dr. Atl in early February. Members of the Casa were promised and given not only soldiers' wages but also the resources to organize and maintain the Red Battalions themselves as military troops and as agents of working-class and Constitutionalist propaganda.[55]

Beyond "scraps of bread" and significant organizational subsidies, Casa members repeatedly emphasized in their discussions of the alliance the unprecedented actions that Constitutionalist officers in different regions and in the Federal District had taken on behalf of workers.[56] In explaining the decision of the group of sixty-seven to the open meeting of three thousand on 10 February, printer Rosendo Salazar reasoned, "we are joining Constitutionalism because it is the one that moved against the clergy and the bourgeoisie, because it is the one that has put in practice our ideals, and because it is the one that will help us in our conquest." When asked by a reporter why they supported the resolution, workers attending the meeting explained that the "Constitutionalist Revolution has demonstrated wherever it has gone lately that it is of the same principles as the unionized working class." The proof, they explained, was their "having put in the hands of the workers factories, workshops, mines, foundries, and having turned churches into schools."[57] While this list of confiscations far exceeded in number and degree the actual interventions made by the Constitutionalists in Mexico City and nationally, it suggests how effective their aggressive actions on behalf of workers had been.

For many Casa del Obrero Mundial leaders, the progressive wing of Constitutionalism appeared to put working-class needs, or at least restrictions on perceived enemies of workers (foreign-owned companies and foreign-born monopoly merchants) at the center of the revolutionary struggle. In publicly presenting the terms of the pact, the Casa del Obrero Mundial declared, "Enough of ineffective exhortations that keep us in the line of neutrality . . . we are presented with the opportunity to throw the glove at our infamous tormentors, collaborating with word and deed by the side of the Revolution, which has . . . known how to punish them."

Though the pact, like earlier Constitutionalist decrees, did not include a formal recognition of the legal personality of unions, it amounted to a unilateral recognition of the Casa del Obrero Mundial and its constituent unions by the Constitutionalists. De facto recognition and facilities to organize would enable the Casa to overcome its weakness vis-à-vis many employers and to more definitively extend its organization beyond the Federal District, which many felt was necessary to consolidate local gains.[58]

At no point in the debates over the alliance or in the official documents related directly to the pact was there a direct attack on the Convention government or the Zapatistas in particular; instead, the formal act announcing the decision of the Casa leaders explained that they had had to "decide for whichever of the bands offers the most guarantees of social transformation to the worker."[59] In the "terrain of the practical," the nod clearly went to the Constitutionalists, whose at times vigorous backing of workers in labor conflicts with powerful and intransigent employers offered possibilities of present and future victories for unions that, at least in the short term, were otherwise unthinkable. What was new, surprising, and acknowledged by the Casa was the shift from previous anarchist discourse and the recognition in such statements that social transformation could and might come from the revolutionary factions and from government itself.

Of course, the tendency to participate in national political struggles had deep roots among the Mexican working class and had been part and parcel of the first initiation of workers in the revolution in 1910 and 1911 in their short-lived support of Madero. Casa leaders like Quintero and Huitrón had after all begun their public careers as working-class leaders by supporting Madero. According to one report of the debate among the sixty-seven Casa leaders, those who opposed an alliance argued in universal and class terms that coincided with anarchist internationalism: one speaker insisted that the present conflict clearly did not have the goals of social revolution and that a political commitment to either faction would compromise the class interests of the Casa del Obrero Mundial. The opposing and triumphant position argued in historic and nationalistic terms: participation was a patriotic duty for workers, insisted one speaker, who went on to speculate that if the Casa del Obrero Mundial remained neutral, then "later the proletariat will not be able to justify its militancy in the armed struggle of the revolution and will lose the right and the glory to show off with pride that they had spilled blood and stained red the battlefields."[60]

The image of workers as past and future participants in national struggles was a powerful one. As noted, during the Porfiriato workers had developed a powerful social myth around their participation in the mid-nineteenth-century liberal struggles against conservatives and foreigners, one that provided legitimacy for their organization as workers as well as for their participation in the opposition political campaigns against Díaz. While invariably opposed to the draft, from 1911 groups of workers in Mexico City had offered to form workers' defense militias under Díaz, Madero, and even Huerta during the U.S. occupation of Veracruz. As workers in Mexico City had explained to Madero in 1912, by forming militias they could work for both the "defense of the fatherland and for the consolidation of our interests."[61] Díaz, Madero, and Huerta had all backed away from such projects, in part out of fear of the consequences of arming and mobilizing workers as workers. By contrast, for Constitutionalist generals like Obregón in 1915, the advantages of arming workers outweighed the risks.

Many workers would see the invitation to form the Red Battalions as the first real acknowledgment by revolutionary leaders of the importance of urban workers to the nation, one that suddenly put workers and the Casa del Obrero Mundial, at least symbolically, at the center of the national drama of the revolution. After the signing of the pact, the groups and individuals who formed the Red Battalions expressed a sense of pride in their participation in the revolution and invoked that participation when attempting to shape the policy of authorities toward workers and popular classes. Such an alliance did not automatically mean subordination and deference on the part of workers. How much independence the Casa members would have within the alliance, and how far they could pursue their individual, union, and class interests, remained to be determined on the organizational battlefields of the revolution.

In the last weeks of February, with the alliance consummated in the signed pact, the Casa del Obrero Mundial abandoned its task of organizing unions and confronting employers in Mexico City and began to recruit its members and workers in general into the ranks of the Red Battalions. Recruiting was facilitated by the desperate conditions in the city. With the abandonment of the city imminent, Obregón refused to divert railroad cars to bring food into the city or to seek alternatives to the random printing and targeted distribution of paper money.

Still, many workers joined enthusiastically and mobilized primarily around identities of workplace and occupation, mostly among the more skilled workers who had formed the core of the Casa. Two main groups entered en masse from the workplace directly to the barracks. The first Red Battalion consisted of about one thousand workers from the government-owned national arms factory, whose manufacturing equipment had at any rate been moved to Veracruz the month before. The second was made up of one thousand streetcar workers, who had benefited from the Constitutionalist intervention in the company four months earlier. As they had in the October strike, streetcar workers removed the controllers of the streetcars and took them to Veracruz as a way to assure their employment on their return. The other three battalions were put together by a variety of volunteers from different groups of workers, in particular textile workers, printers, stonecutters, metalworkers, painters, store employees, shoemakers, and tailors, as well as other workers from diverse backgrounds. The contingent of store employees, "a hundred or so," according to Obregón, was probably typical of the representation of these smaller groups.[62] In the final days before leaving Mexico City for Veracruz, the Casa del Obrero Mundial recruited broadly among the working class and not just among its own members. In spite of their diverse backgrounds, the new soldiers clearly identified with their status as workers and looked to the leadership of the Casa del Obrero Mundial. Estimates of the number of soldiers in the Red Battalions vary among contemporary observers and later historians from as low as two thousand to as high as ten thousand but probably ranged somewhere between five thousand to seven thousand troops. Such a mobilization was no small feat, though it was far less than the fifteen thousand the Casa had announced that it could mobilize among its claimed fifty-two thousand affiliates.

Also formed in accordance with the pact was a group of forty-two women who constituted the Sanitary Brigade "Acrata." These women, most of whom worked in the garment industry, wore uniforms made of the anarchist colors, a red blouse and a black skirt. Many more women and even children accompanied the troops, becoming, in order to survive or to keep their families together, the camp followers and *soldaderas* who accompanied all military factions of the revolution. Provisions for families had been a specific condition of the pact and almost certainly made it far easier to convince workers to leave their homes. In total, probably about ten thousand men, women, and children left under the auspices of the Red Battalions for Veracruz.[63]

The Constitutionalist invitation to workers to organize politically inevitably increased the level of agitation in the city. Under the auspices of the pact and Obregón's attack on the status quo in the city, the Casa took on even greater prominence, as they were authorized to carry weapons and began to undergo military training. In the last days before leaving for Veracruz, the Casa del Obrero Mundial formed a police corps and arrested a handful of Zapatista sympathizers who were recruiting among unions in Mexico City. A biting Zapatista manifesto that appeared in the city denounced what they insisted was not a "'Casa del Obrero Mundial' but rather a *Casa de Enganche*."[64]

As the Casa frantically organized the Red Battalions and as Obregón pursued his more spectacular retribution against businessmen and the church, the anticlericalism of the Casa surged and spread briefly to the popular classes. During the months of worst turmoil in Mexico City, *capitalinos* either rallied around the institutional church or attacked it. Obregón's measures provoked a broad reaction among different social strata within the city. The arrest of a good portion of the clergy led to a virtual closing down of most of the city's churches, as priests were either jailed or went into hiding. A series of marches were organized by the faithful to military headquarters to protest the jailing of the priests and the confiscations of church buildings. Confrontations between these groups and the Casa del Obrero Mundial, already armed and recruiting for the Red Battalions, often escalated into violence. On one occasion the two groups clashed in front of the monument to Juárez in the central Alameda, and police intervention resulted in two deaths. According to two accounts, the demonstrations in support of the clergy were mostly composed of women of the middle class, the group most clearly associated with the church hierarchy.[65]

Installed since September 1914 in their new sanctuary, the ex-convent of Santa Brígida, members of the Casa del Obrero Mundial engaged in ritual reversals of religious ceremony: they preached unionization from pulpits and replaced a bust of Ignatious Loyola, founder of the Jesuit order, with a bust of the Catalan founder of the Rationalist School, Francisco Ferrer Guardia. In preparation for the Red Battalions, they turned church parchments into military drums and religious vestments into banners.[66]

After the Casa del Obrero Mundial had rallied behind the Constitutionalist cause and was spurred on by the campaign of Obregón against the city's clergy and commerce, both groups closely tied to the Spanish community, occupations of churches went beyond inversions of rituals and symbols to the violent destruction of images, the breaking of urns, and the burning of scapulars and prayer books. Violent acts also took on elements of the burlesque and carnival, the inversions of society that were embedded in such popular traditions as *calaveras* and Judas burnings. Casa del Obrero Mundial member Ramírez Plancarte later described with horror the occupation by women and men that he witnessed in the Concepción Church in Mexico City: "they covered themselves in farcical and carnivalesque uproar in order to ridicule the practices of the church, one with a surplice, one with a cap and pluvial cape, another with a cassock . . . and while some climbed to the altar to imitate the ceremonies of the mass in the middle of ridiculous genuflections, muttering prayers mixed with dog Latin, nasally mimicking holy songs; others climbed to the pulpit and pretended to be preaching, orating, or rather vomiting tremendous blasphemies against Catholic dogmas and the institution of the Eucharist."[67]

Occasionally, "liberal" anticlericalism coincided with "popular" anticlericalism, and the scope of attacks on the church went beyond the skilled and educated craftworkers at the helm of the Casa to include broad sections of workers and the popular classes, many of whom probably maintained deep-rooted religious beliefs even as they attacked the institutions of the church. In the last days before abandoning the city, Obregón gave the Casa del Obrero Mundial for the purposes of a barracks the exclusive Colegio Josefino, which was adjacent to the Church of Santa Brígida and convent buildings they had acquired in the previous months and weeks. During the Porfiriato, the wealthiest members of the Porfirian elite were married in the Church of Santa Brígida and consigned the education of their daughters to the nuns and priests of the Colegio Josefino.

Poor and working people must have been awed by the sumptuous accommodations and possessions of the elite girls school: the variety of rich jewelry, the closets and sewing rooms full of lavish clothing, and the music, theater, and art rooms full of pianos, paintings, and decorations. As the Casa del Obrero Mundial took possession of these buildings, huge crowds came to see the extravagant building that for so long had been hidden from public view. The extent of the crowds who pressed into the new headquarters was so great that Casa del Obrero Mundial speakers often could not accommodate them inside the buildings. They set up boxes outside the former church building and held meetings, as if to recreate the sixteenth-century open-air evangelization of indigenous peoples.[68]

On the day before the last of the Red Battalions left for Veracruz—with the city suffering from scarcity and commerce virtually closed down—the Casa del Obrero Mundial administrator, Jacinto Huitrón, opened the doors of the exclusive Colegio Josefino to a multitude of waiting poor people, primarily women, and urged them to enter and take what they could use. Crowds of the poorest of the city converged on the school, removing fine colonial furniture and what bits of cloth or religious images they could find. In possession of the temples of the elite for the first time, poor people ripped apart the floors in search of the legendary buried treasure of the church. Finding nothing, they carried off floorboards and window sashes to use for firewood. The following day another crowd returned to take apart the Church of Santa Brígida, this time clashing with a crowd of "Mexicans of the higher class" who tried to stop them.[69]

These public, symbolic confrontations took place in the heart of the city, and their observance by the dominant classes was as important as the actions in themselves; indeed, Casa del Obrero Mundial members delighted not only in the spectacle of desecration but also in their perceptions that the rich and the high clergy observed, some from jail, and "trembled with rage and impotence." This was the exalted headiness of a social order turned upside down. The attacks on the churches were not simply the secular, anticlerical manifestations of *artesanos cultos* against the purveyors of "obscurantist" religion, but they involved a considerable degree of participation by traditional popular classes that expressed deep-rooted class antagonisms. Driven by dire need as well as moral outrage at abuses by the high church and their wealthy clients, the poor people of Mexico City helped to gut the symbols of privilege and deference.

On 2 March 1915 about one thousand workers bearing arms marched from the Casa del Obrero Mundial headquarters down the central avenues to the National Palace to proclaim their support for the Constitutionalist cause. Speakers invoked the French Revolution, demanding, according to one newspaper, that Mexican workers "must start a social revolution and establish guillotines in every plaza to punish all enemies of the laboring classes." Such speeches were interspersed with "¡vivas!" to Carranza, Obregón, and the "Social Revolution." Finally, a colonel representing Obregón appeared and told those assembled that "the political reforms initiated by President Benito Juárez had not yet been concluded, and that Juárez, represented in the person of General Venustiano Carranza, is in Veracruz summoning all Mexicans to support him to finish the political program of the great patriot."[70] In this marriage of convenience and ideals, the class-based demands of the Casa del Obrero Mundial and the nationalist goals of Carranza would merge. Throughout the following week, Obregón and the Red Battalions abandoned Mexico City for Veracruz.

The Casa Away from Home

When the U.S. labor organizer and socialist John Murray visited the Red Battalions in Orizaba, Veracruz, in the spring of 1915, he marveled at what he presumed to be the first major agreement between a national government and a labor organization. "It is plain," he observed, "why organized labor supported the Constitutionalist government in Mexico; food, guns in the workers' hands, opportunity to organize, to strike and raise the standard of living." Indeed, the immediate gains that resulted from the alliance of the Casa with the Constitutionalist cause seemed extraordinary from the perspective of the U.S. trade union movement or when compared to most of Latin America in the same period. Murray celebrated the unity of the workers and Constitutionalists, as did Casa newspapers, particularly *Revolución Social*, published from Orizaba.[71] Such a defense of Constitutionalism was an essential part of the pact.

But the alliance between the Casa del Obrero Mundial and Constitutionalists was very temporary in nature, as almost immediately differences emerged among and between the signers. Carranza was determined to minimize their role from the very beginning. Over the objections of Obregón and the Casa leadership, Carranza insisted on separating the six battalions, subordinating each battalion to generals who were not workers and sending them to different fronts. Such a strategy made military sense, given the inexperience of Casa members as soldiers, but even more important to Carranza, dividing up the Red Battalions diminished any possibility, however unlikely, of an autonomous military role for urban workers akin to that of the regional guerrilla movements that had been incorporated into both the Convention and Constitutionalist armies with their social base intact. In spite of the symbolic importance and public commendation of the military contribution of the Red Battalions by Constitutionalists and workers' organizations alike, their practical contribution to the military victory of the Constitutionalists over Convention forces was less than definitive. In the two most important battles, El Ebano and Celaya, soldiers of the Red Battalions comprised only 12 and 9 percent of total Constitutionalist forces. The uneasiness of Carranza with the Red Battalions as a military force became clear again in August 1915, when many of the Red Battalions were demobilized, and in January 1916, when the rest were definitively licensed.[72]

The military formation of the Red Battalions also created divisions among Casa members. Key figures such as Rafael Quintero and Jacinto Huitrón, who had been central to the organizational tasks of the Casa in Mexico City, lost influence and were demoted from the Revolutionary Committee, as more pragmatic members, such as the metalworker Samuel Yúdico and the shoemaker Celestino Gasca, emerged with greater power. Gasca quickly demonstrated his abilities as a military leader and rose to the rank of general, remaining in the army for several years after the rest of the Red Battalions were demobilized. After 1920 Gasca and Yúdico used their ties to Obregón to achieve prominence within Mexico City politics and the labor movement.[73]

Differences between Constitutionalists and Casa members arose mostly over the provision that allowed the Casa to organize workers throughout Constitutionalist territory, a task they began immediately upon arriving in Veracruz. By April they had organized twenty-two propaganda commissions with over 139 militants throughout Constitutionalist territory. Within weeks, Carranza labeled the organizational work of the Casa as "subversive" and insisted that the Red Battalions in Orizaba not be armed until they left the city because of "the spirit of indiscipline and hostility that they have shown toward the workers of Orizaba." The accusation of hostility toward local workers was not completely unfounded; Veracruz textile workers in particular resented the attempts of the Casa propagandists to impose their organizations and leadership over previously existing ones.

But the greatest tension arose over very different concepts of workers' organization held by the Casa del Obrero Mundial and Carranza. The Constitutionalist Labor Department in Veracruz tried to organize a series of "directive boards" (*mesa directivas*) within textile factories and "workers' groups" (*agrupaciones de obreros*) elsewhere as an alternative to the Casa-supported unions. A series of conflicts arose throughout 1915 over strikes and organizational initiatives in the industries, crafts, and services of the cities of Veracruz and Orizaba, with the Casa del Obrero Mundial and the Constitutionalist Labor Department consistently at odds.[74]

Marcos López Jiménez, the head of the Constitutionalist Labor Department, would lament from Veracruz in July that "up until this moment the Labor Department has almost played a role of spectator in the face of the bitter and determined struggle between Capital and Labor taking place in recent times." He went on to complain of an "invasion of functions on the part of some authorities in their eagerness, certainly very commendable, to make clear to the people the affection and goodness of the Revolution." But besides the interference of authorities (that is, military officers), López Jiménez went on to explain another factor in the Labor Department's marginalization: "The syndicalists in general, and especially the syndicalists dependent on a particular institution called the 'Casa del Obrero Mundial,' reject completely the presence of the Department, under pretext that they don't accept the intervention of any form of the State in the affairs of workers, and thus that intervention is in direct conflict with their anarchist principal of direct action."

The various tensions implicit in the organizational task of the Red Battalions are suggested by the exchange among the Labor Department director, Casa members, and tobacco workers in Orizaba in mid-April. In what would become almost a refrain, director Marcos López Jiménez sent the following message to striking tobacco workers: "Strikes were more or less justified in the time of Generals Díaz and Huerta," he said, "but now are absolutely inappropriate and inconvenient given that the Constitutionalist authorities support the working class." At an assembly of tobacco workers the next day, Jacinto Huitrón asked in response to the director's attempt to mediate the strike, "Why does the Labor Department exist?" Huitrón's answer: "For those *compañeros* that aren't organized, for those that are not united . . . but not for those of us who are; and that is why I protest the intervention of the inspectors of the Department, who seem to make politics against us." The positions of the Labor Department and Huitrón suggest significant differences over the terms of the Casa-Constitutionalist alliance. While rejecting direct government interference in labor disputes, Huitrón did endorse the project of Interior Minister Zubáran Capmany for the legal recognition of labor unions, since "when we are already recognized, then we will deal directly with the bosses and then they will be obligated to pay attention." Another Casa member insisted that "at the moment there is no government, but only the Revolution" and "if the Casa del Obrero Mundial joins the Revolution it is because it sees that it can make the people great." So why, he asked, should the Labor Department not help in labor conflicts, since "the Labor Department at this moment is part of the machinery of the Revolution"? While the tobacco workers ultimately rejected the Labor Department's mediation, one of their leaders assured the departing director "that if we are not with the Labor Department, we are not either under the tutelage of the Casa del Obrero Mundial. We tobacco workers have always been independent workers!"[75]

Progressive generals like Obregón or Adolfo de la Huerta would occasionally defend the organizational activities of the Casa against the hostility of Carranza, the Labor Department, or Constitutionalist governors. In April, Carranza's interior minister, Rafael Zubáran Capmany, responded to Casa demands and issued a lengthy "Project for Labor Contracts," bypassing the Labor Department, which for the first time acknowledged the legal personality of unions. Although the project remained only that, it circulated widely among unions and was even incorporated by some unions into their statutes.[76] Thus the terms of the pact continued to be contested by Casa members as well as by many of the workers they attempted to organize.

Living and Working under the Convention

A majority of the Casa del Obrero Mundial leadership supported the pact and joined the Red Battalions. But key figures and entire unions from within the Casa del Obrero Mundial stayed in Mexico City during the long and difficult months of the Convention's final control of the city from 10 March to 1 August 1915, as the armies of Obregón and Villa engaged in the defining battles of the central Bajío. Key unions that rejected the pact were those of electricians, teachers, and shop employees, as well as a minority faction of the streetcar workers' union. And deliberately or by default, the vast majority of those affiliated with the Casa del Obrero Mundial on some level (officially some fifty-two thousand members) and most unorganized workers did not join the Red Battalions. Some members, led by the student leader Aurelio Manrique, stayed out of fidelity to the principle of rejecting political participation and militarism, and others stayed out of affinity or open affiliation with the Zapatistas or the Convention government. For example, the Teachers' Union sponsored a demonstration in support of the Convention government in early March that reportedly mobilized some ten thousand people.[77] But most simply desired to remain and defend their jobs. Perhaps the attitude of the majority of Mexico City's poor and working people toward all military factions was best expressed by a local version of the Villista anthem "Adelita," popular at the time of the pact:

> If Carranza gets married with Zapata
> Pancho Villa with Alvaro Obregón
> Adelita and I will get married
> And so ends the Revolution.[78]

For the majority of working people, military disruptions undermined the economy, sources of work, and therefore their bargaining position vis-à-vis employers. But in spite of the departure of the Red Battalions and much of the Casa del Obrero Mundial leadership, popular mobilization and union activity continued in Mexico City during their absence. Rejection of or lack of interest in the military struggles did not mean a general apathy or passiveness among those who did not take up arms. Organizational and strike activity was widespread, with leadership falling mainly in the hands of the Union of Electricians and to a lesser degree the Union of Commercial Employees. The headquarters of the first, the former cinema Salón Star near Alameda Park, served as a meeting place for other workers' groups and the working-class community in much the same way that the Casa del Obrero Mundial had before. Many unions regrouped or were formed for the first time, including those of the tailors, streetcar workers, and restaurant workers.[79]

From his position as administrator of the telephone company and his continued role in the Union of Electricians, Luis Morones rose to prominence among metropolitan workers. In spite of his eventual role as architect of labor's cooperation with Presidents Obregón and Calles in the 1920s, his public position during this period of Convention occupation was to urge workers toward direct action and away from politics. In a speech at a large workers' assembly he condemned all unions (and by implication the Casa del Obrero Mundial) that "made politics, supporting a party because that party feeds them." Those who wished to "do" politics, he went on, have the right as citizens but should not use unions, which were exclusively "the instrument of the class struggle." At the end of June, perhaps anticipating the approaching defeat of the Convention and the return of the Casa del Obrero Mundial, the principal unions in the city met to organize in a General Confederation of Labor (Confederación General del Trabajo), naming Morones as secretary-general.

Of course the lines between class struggle and politics were never very clear, as with the Constitutionalist intervention that had put Morones in charge of the telephone company. At public meetings where Morones and union members met, they commonly shared the podium with the tailor Luis Méndez and intellectuals Antonio Díaz Soto y Gama and Rafael Pérez Taylor, all former Casa del Obrero Mundial founders and now deputies in the Convention parliament. The mixed group of union leaders and Convention deputies often referred to themselves as the Socialist Party, which through the participation of people like Luis Méndez could claim continuity with the party formed in 1911.[80] The delegates worked tirelessly to provide support to workers in their organizations, from within the Convention government, and through the metropolitan press. But the extent of their support was limited by both the reality of the Convention and their own ideas about the roles of unions and government.

After reoccupying Mexico City in March 1915, the Convention began to discuss a series of social reforms, including decrees favoring urban workers and their organizations. But the well-being of urban workers was hardly a priority for the Zapatista delegates (now a majority) concerned with taking apart the sugar haciendas and confirming legally the deep process of social transformation already under way in Morelos.

When the Convention finally began to consider labor legislation on 22 March, delegate Luis Méndez, backed by Antonio Díaz Soto y Gama, proposed a short but remarkable program (Articles 14 and 15) that guaranteed workers the absolute right to organize, complete autonomy from government, and the right to strike and to implement sabotage and boycotts. Their ally Rafael Pérez Taylor briefly contradicted his support for the bill by insisting that since unions were strong and since syndicalists like himself opposed all government, it would be ridiculous for workers in unions to expect or want government recognition.

A more serious challenge came from the opposing faction of Villistas, who proposed a series of restrictions that would allow only mutualist and "unionist" organizations but not anarchist "syndicates" and would permit strikes only "as long as in practice they do not degenerate into riots or acts of violence." The position of the Villistas was closer in intent to the labor measures eventually elaborated in the 1917 constitution, with their emphasis on regulating the form of workers' organizations and maintaining public order, but the Zapatista position eventually triumphed. The labor reforms that were finally passed in April 1915 were largely those proposed by Méndez and Díaz Soto y Gama, excluding the right to sabotage and including the elimination of tiendas de raya and payment in tokens.[81] By contrast, no mention was made of state regulation of wages, hours, or work conditions.

The remarkable libertarian character of these reforms provides an interesting contrast with the regional interventions and regulating decrees of the Constitutional factions; generals such as Alvaro Obregón and Pablo González had restricted hours, imposed wage hikes, and even intervened in companies, but they had never clearly endorsed the rights to organize and strike and on occasion moved to deny workers both rights. In different circumstances, the Convention labor reforms might have facilitated the formation of powerful and autonomous labor unions. Instead, reforms were passed by a teetering government that would soon have little pretension to being national in scope.

In fact, the labor reforms ratified the position already taken by the Convention government in Mexico City. Their general refusal in times of crisis to intervene in labor conflicts to help workers who otherwise could not sustain their organizations, much less their strikes, had cost them the support of an important segment of the metropolitan working class.

Strikes and labor conflicts continued unabated during the months of continued Convention control. The Convention maintained a small Labor Department, and the governor of the Federal District and the city council sometimes offered their mediation services or even expressed mild threats against workers who upset the public order. But in general, the success or failure of strikes did not depend on the government. And in the relative absence of government mediation, labor conflicts often achieved unusual intensity.

One of the most extensive conflicts between workers and employers was the mid-May 1915 textile strike of ten thousand Federal District workers, the largest since the 1912 strike under Madero, in which workers forced many textile industrialists to implement a minimum wage. Throughout the months of March, April, and May, telephone workers backed by the Union of Electricians waged a bitter strike against the Ericsson Telephone Company, after the Swedish manager fired almost one hundred workers who had demanded pay increases. Only when telephone workers began cutting telephone lines, and after a May Day rally brought together workers throughout the city on their behalf, did the company agree to hire back half of the employees. On 4 May the Union of Electricians briefly shut down the power in the city and forced the Mexican Light and Power Company to rehire employees who had been fired for their refusal to cut off electricity to delinquent customers. The strike was the most recent of a series of conflicts and negotiations between the electrical company and the new union and showed the extent of the electrical workers' confidence. For the first time the city "woke up without light, power, streetcars and water" because of a decision by workers. Other more minor labor conflicts took place, such as the June strike of employees of El Palacio de Hierro, which were remarkable in that they occurred in the midst of a deep commercial crisis and massive unemployment. Similarly, the Union of Commercial Employees boldly called a strike for the eight-hour day and wage increases on 8 July 1915, even as the Convention forces abandoned the city and most of the city's stores closed down.[82] In each of these conflicts workers directly took on "capital" without the hope or fear of government interference as the ultimate determinant of their success.

In general, the Convention government policy toward workers (for reasons of ideology, rural priorities, or its own disarray) was to grant their organizations all legal facilities but to rarely interfere in conflicts between capital and labor, a legal and ideological position made consistent by the weakness of the Convention and its executive. This attitude was in sharp contrast to the vigorous intervention of the Constitutionalist generals in earlier conflicts.

A pattern of mobilization among different groups of workers can also be generalized for this period of Convention control of the city: in the absence of the connecting structure provided by the Casa del Obrero Mundial and because of the Convention government's policy of limited intervention, skilled and strategic unions strengthened their organizations, while the weaker unions—with less strategic leverage and a precarious position within a depressed labor market—lost ground and even disappeared. For example, the streetcar workers, with the support of the Union of Electricians, managed to reorganize in a unified union in June 1915; by contrast, all organization among shoemakers disappeared. Finally, as conditions in Mexico City continued to deteriorate, mobilization often occurred over consumer issues around community networks of exchange and solidarity, as discussed in the following chapter.

Few historical accounts of this period pay attention to this level of mobilization—the assumption being that, in the absence of the Casa del Obrero Mundial leadership, organization among workers in Mexico City disappeared or was paralyzed.[83] The relatively free operation of unions under the Convention would inevitably result in tensions between independent unions and Constitutionalist generals when the latter finally resumed definitive control of Mexico City in August 1915.

* * *

With the defeat of Huerta by Constitutionalist forces, workers suddenly encountered military leaders willing to regulate by decree many of the insecurities of work, to force foreign and national employers to negotiate with unions, and to give workers a role in wage, hiring, and even production decisions. In spite of its declared principle of political neutrality, the Casa del Obrero Mundial and individual unions received favors and support from the Constitutionalists that helped them to consolidate their organizations. The Casa del Obrero Mundial's influence over the interventions of the generals facilitated the expansion of their membership to include the unskilled workers, who were a majority of the city's population.

After the split between the Constitutionalists and the Convention, neutrality for an organization of growing importance like the Casa del Obrero Mundial became harder to maintain. Contradictory factors drove the Casa leadership and a portion of its membership to offer armed support to Carranza: material hardship and unemployment in Mexico City, the disarray of the Convention, the contrasting vigorous interventions of Obregón on behalf of workers, and tensions within the greatly expanded organization. Whether they believed that the "social revolution" proclaimed by the Constitutionalists was close enough to that envisioned by workers' organizations, many Casa members felt that they could no longer avoid participation in a historic national struggle. The workers of the Casa who took up arms on behalf of the Constitutionalists felt they had a fundamental role to play, both as citizens serving their country and as workers who were in a position to press for greater social transformation.

If U.S. labor organizer John Murray understood why the Casa del Obrero Mundial supported the Constitutionalist government, what was less clear to him was why middle-class Mexicans like Cabrera and Obregón would support a program that called for land reform and what Murray himself perceived as "the preliminary steps . . . to a socialization of industry." He concluded that middle-class Constitutionalist leaders shared with urban workers an aversion to foreign ownership that translated into "Better government ownership than foreign ownership."[84] The convergence that led to the pact required an overlap of goals that included the Constitutionalist willingness to intervene in the affairs of national and foreign companies. Many Constitutionalist leaders did have a very different view about the role of government in social and economic affairs than did their predecessors and their rivals. In addition, they needed support among broad social sectors both in their battle against the Convention and ultimately in order to create a viable ruling coalition. But while the Casa chose adherence to the Constitutionalist cause, they immediately tried to assert themselves and impose many of their own terms in their difficult relationship with their new allies.

While the Red Battalions left for various fronts, the majority of workers and even of organized workers remained in Mexico City. Some stayed to support the Convention, and others stayed to continue organizing workers and making demands on employers, sustaining an intense cycle of labor conflicts. And many stayed simply in order to struggle to survive and retain their jobs.

7 | CONSOLIDATION AND CONFRONTATION

The neutral *capitalinos*, proselytes of the belly, don't aspire to the liberties that await our Fatherland. What they desire anxiously is that soon there be a drop in [the price of] noodles and garbanzo.

B. SUGO, El Demócrata (Veracruz), 25 August 1915

Everything's gotten expensive with this Revolution,
Milk is sold by the ounce and coal by the gram.
. . . Cockroaches are much admired in this sad Nation,
So much silver from the mines has turned into paper bills.

Broadsheet version of "La Cucaracha," 1915

Soon after taking Mexico City for the first time in August 1914, General Obregón made a speech at the site of Madero's grave in which he denounced the men of Mexico City for sitting out the revolution. To add insult to injury, he singled out of the crowd the schoolteacher María Arias Bernal, who had accompanied the Constitutionalist troops in the fight against Huerta, and declared, "Men who can carry a gun and did not, for fear of leaving their homes, have no excuse. I abandoned my children, and as I know how to admire valor, I cede my pistol to the señorita Arias, who is the only one worthy of carrying it." Obregón's intention was to question the masculinity of the men of Mexico City for failing to fight in the revolution rather than to urge women to transgress gender boundaries by becoming *soldaderas*. Even so, the image and occasional reality of the armed female soldier fighting for social justice was compelling, and the incident soon became the basis of a popular musical in metropolitan theaters, *María Pistola*.[1]

Another work of literature written during the revolution suggests what was probably a more typical but no less important role of urban women in that social turmoil. Julio Sesto's 1920 novel, *La ciudad de los palacios*—one of the most popular and least memorable novels written during the revolution—opens with a poor and hungry crowd waiting anxiously outside of a bakery in Mexico City. Soon the elegant heroine of the novel pulls up in a carriage and leads the crowd, mostly women, in an assault on the bakery. Finally, the protagonist hands the distraught Spanish baker a stack of Villista bills in payment, offers the incredulous police a chance to arrest her, and then takes off in her carriage.[2]

In Mexico City during the years of the revolution, women (though rarely the upper-class women of Sesto's novel) provided the initiative and the majority of participants for a series of mobilizations that included public denunciations of merchants with stockpiles of food, the taking over of markets and bakeries in order to administer a just exchange, and the occupation of municipal and national government buildings in order to press demands for food and services. With these actions women politically engaged organized workers and revolutionary authorities over the meaning of the revolution and in turn helped to shape broader patterns of urban mobilization.

The mobilization of poor and working people in Mexico City reached its climax in the final months of Convention rule in mid-1915 and in the following year of Constitutionalist control. This chapter examines the increasing tensions among the poor and working people in Mexico City, employers and merchants, and revolutionary leaders. These tensions accelerated the mobilization of working people across genders and skill levels and were expressed in a variety of ways, including riots and strikes, which finally climaxed in the general strike of July–August 1916.

When the mobilizations of urban workers in this period are considered, they are usually interpreted narrowly in one of two ways. In the first view, their apparent militancy is seen as primarily the product of the dire material conditions predominant throughout the period of greatest military disruption. The importance of material conditions in shaping popular urban mobilizations is undeniable but in itself is insufficient to explain the pattern and extent of mobilization. In another view, conflicts are the result of a minority of militants schooled in secular radical ideology, with limited participation by the mass of working people.[3] Both views overlook the degree of participation in these conflicts and the scope of demands.

Labor historians have often seen consumption demands as somehow less class-conscious and more primitive than those concerned primarily with issues of production. But recent studies of urban history and the literature on contemporary urban social movements allow us to reconsider the importance of consumption-oriented demands to the formation of working-class movements.[4] In Mexico City, the links between work and community, between skilled and unskilled, and between male and female workers were strengthened throughout 1915 and 1916 by the consumption orientation of many demands. Moreover, this cycle of mobilization was not the product of a limited conjuncture but rather drew on patterns of organization and protest dating back years before. Finally, the pursuit of consumption demands, because they were so widespread, involved working people in an unprecedented intervention in the political life of the city and so led to an inevitable confrontation with political authorities. For this reason, the general strikes of 1916 should be considered not only in terms of the previous years of workplace organization and conflicts but also in terms of mobilizations around consumption issues, including the riots that marked the preceding year. The pattern of mobilization among poor and working people that led up to the general strikes, and the manner in which revolutionary elites responded, can tell us much about the relations of working people and the postrevolutionary state.

Women, Riots, and the Defense of Community

Urban riots and the political participation of urban masses before the era of post-1930s populism have been largely ignored in Latin American history, in contrast to an extensive European literature. Riots were, of course, part of the traditional repertoire of collective action by urban masses, dating back to the colonial riots of 1624 and 1692 that shook Mexico City. For nineteenth-century Mexico, a few well-known riots stand out historically and historiographically, in particular the 1828 attack on the Parián market in Mexico City. In her study of the Parián riot, Silvia Arrom identifies the mix of popular support for the opposition "Yorkino" elites and the antagonism of artisans toward free trade and

Spanish merchants that shaped that episode of popular violence. In 1883, crowds attacked various markets and vandalized the National Palace when merchants refused to accept new small coins made of nickel. The same year, a similar riot converged on the Chamber of Deputies to protest the proposed government recognition of the debt owed to England. Both 1883 riots, like that of Parián, coincided with a presidential succession crisis, and crowds cheered opposition politicians who had opposed the coining of nickel and recognition of the foreign debt. Lesser riots occurred during the Porfiriato, as suggested by the repeated use by the penny press of a Posada engraving of women with empty baskets in the air attacking a shop (see fig. 19).[5] And, of course, as shown in the previous chapters, industrial workers often resorted to violent community confrontations when they felt they had been wronged, the best-known example being the 1907 riots known as the Rio Blanco strike, which began with an attack on the company store.

Riots in the period of the revolution are often ignored or seen exclusively as the product of dire material conditions. In contrast to most historians of the revolution, Alan Knight recognizes the significance of urban riots during the revolution and notes that "the urban masses made their presence felt principally through riots and the threat of riots," particularly those led by artisans in the declining manufacturing cities of the Bajío.[6] By contrast, the craftworkers of Mexico City, where the decline of artisans was partly offset by the rise of new, skilled professions, were more inclined toward "modern" forms of association such as the political clubs, mutual aid societies, and unions that multiplied after 1910. Still, riots and the fear of popular violence would play an important role in shaping events in the city, one that belies the relegation of riots to "premodern" relics of the past.

The single most important riots in Mexico City were those that accelerated the resignation of Díaz on 23–25 May 1911, discussed in chapter 3. Like the riots of 1828 and 1883, the May 1911 riots were heterogeneous in their social base and possibly linked to dissident political elites who, like their Yorkino counterparts, were quick to condemn the violence once it exceeded acceptable limits. Similar riots in the same year deposed or attempted to depose municipal officials in the Federal District and throughout much of the country. As shown in chapter 5, riots were also part of the "repertoires of contention" of workers as they responded to changes in the terms of work and were even a part of formal strike actions.

As in the case of worker-employer relations, the overthrow of traditional authorities and the periodic occupation of the city by soldiers brought new attitudes of equality and defiance among common people that transformed everyday public encounters between members of different social groups and between members of popular classes and authorities. The collective assertiveness of urban crowds was obvious from the first months of the revolution. For example, in December 1911, a crowd set fire to a pawnshop after the owner struck a customer who had accused him of charging excessive interest rates. Collective acts of violence could be isolated and random, singling out wealthy residents or authorities and presenting small challenges to the social order—a form of rebellious street culture. For example, in March 1915 a petty thief was caught in the Zócalo in the act of picking the pocket of a wealthy pedestrian. When police tried to arrest him, a crowd descended and forced the suspect's release, continuing their rough treatment of the officers until nearby soldiers began to fire in the air.[7]

But far more serious challenges to the social order were the series of consumer riots that rocked the city and thrust poor residents, mostly women, into newspaper headlines and face to face with revolutionary leaders. Consumer riots in Mexico City began as early as 1911 and continued well through mid-1916, though they were concentrated particularly from May through August 1915, reflecting not only dire material conditions but also the absence of stable political authority and the weakening of the formal associational life of unions among the most unskilled, informal, and unemployed sectors in the absence of the Casa.[8]

Contrary to the impressions of economic and political elites and diplomatic observers, these violent attacks on economic targets were not simply irrational expressions of violence or crude responses to the economic stimuli of hunger and poverty. Of course, material conditions were the immediate context and trigger for riots. The scarcity and high unemployment that characterized Mexico City during the weeks in which the Red Battalions were formed in February and early March 1915 did not improve during the extended Convention occupation in the spring of 1915 and worsened considerably in the last weeks before the definitive occupation of the city by the Constitutionalists in August 1915. In addition, refugees from the embattled countryside streamed into an already desperate city.

The situation for poor and working people was worsened by the fact that virtually every revolutionary faction financed war and government by printing its own currency, without backing by any bank or gold guarantee. As each faction alternately occupied the city, they nullified the previous paper currency, repeatedly causing all commerce to temporarily shut down. Since metallic coins had long since disappeared, the only constant currency recognized by both factions during much of this period was the cardboard tokens issued as change by the streetcar company.[9]

Many merchants and currency "coyotes" conducted a brisk speculative trade in basic foods and in the paper money of both factions, or they simply shut down stores and sat on supplies when conditions were not favorable to commerce. Military authorities of both factions publicly blamed conditions of extreme scarcity of food and fuel entirely on merchants. At the same time, official denouncements of merchants or "coyotes" were in part a cover for the political or personal priorities of military leaders, who overall proved themselves to have little concern for the inhabitants of Mexico City in the midst of civil war. Popular wisdom reflected veiled hostilities; broadsheets and songs lampooned particularly the Constitutionalists, who were often referred to as "Con-sus-uñas-listas" ("With nails ready to dig in") for their propensity to grab everything of value for their military campaign each time before evacuating the city. For example, in March, departing Constitutionalists stripped two of the main hospitals of all medicines, instruments, and sheets. While Convention forces seem to have been less systematic in their theft, Zapatista and Villista soldiers were also notorious for diverting to military use or even personal profit any supplies that were brought into the city.[10] So poor and working people came to distrust all revolutionary authorities as either corrupt or incompetent in their management of food supplies and paper money.

Legitimizing notions for riots also came from longstanding community resentments over the concentration of commerce in Mexico City that had occurred during the last half of the Porfiriato. Scarcity and unemployment exacerbated perceptions of the injustice of the urban economy, which poor and working people saw as controlled by monopolies that profited from moments of crises through speculation and hoarding. The fact that a very high percentage of small merchants and virtually all of the large merchants were foreign, particularly Spanish— and were quick to hang the foreign flags and diplomatic seals on their closed stores—only increased popular hostility to what was seen as a monopoly not simply of capital but of *gachupines* (Spaniards) against Mexicans. Workers and the urban poor harbored greatest hostility toward owners or sellers of two basic products, the ground corn masa, used to make tortillas, and bread. As discussed in chapter 2, masa was largely controlled by the Spanish-owned Compañía Mexicana Molinera de Nixtamal, which owned 100 of 130 total corn mills in the city. Similarly, most of the thirty-five bakeries throughout the city were either owned by the Spaniards Braulio Iriarte and Arrache y Cordova and the Mexican Pedro Laguna or depended on these three millers for access to flour. In turn, so too did the hundreds of bread distribution outlets and street bread vendors throughout the city. In December 1914, small bakers joined together with bread vendors and bakery workers to demand that Convention president Eulalio Gutiérrez intervene against the "terrible monopoly of the potentate Ibero and a few Iberianized Mexicans" who controlled the price and supply of flour. The resulting rise in bread prices, they complained, led to rising conflicts between consumers and bread distributors. Poor families were also resentful of pawnshops, always crucial to surviving between paydays, which now might pawn objects at one price in one currency and redeem them at another price in another currency.[11]

The statements and dramatic actions of Constitutionalist and Convention authorities against merchants reinforced popular perceptions. On the eve of the March 1915 departure of Constitutionalist troops from the city that he would neither feed nor defend, Obregón invoked the right of crowds to popular justice, a "sacred right . . . in peoples' hands." "At the first attempt at riot," he insisted, "I will leave the city at the head of my troops in order that they may not fire a single shot against the hungry multitude, as the merchants did not accept the invitation which was made to them to assist the people and prevent violence."[12] In the days and months that followed, crowds often utilized this "sacred right" to organize food riots and other actions against merchants and eventually against political authorities.

Patterns of consumer riots are discernible from the newspaper, consular, and police reports, though the rioters themselves apparently left no written record. While price levels and availability of goods certainly played a role in determining when riots occurred, other factors served as catalysts and shaped actions. For example, several riots were triggered by changes in the military occupation of the city, when stores often shut down because of concerns over public order and shifting currencies. Similarly, the declaration by military leaders of the illegality of one currency over another invariably provoked protests and often triggered riots. Riots frequently followed unsuccessful appeals to government officials to resolve ongoing problems of scarcity. On repeated occasions, crowds moved from market to market with their empty baskets, looking for food before approaching government officials, including police, the governor, the president, and the Convention (see fig. 20). When appeals or even explicit threats to officials failed, crowds often returned to commercial areas and initiated riots. Riots also occurred when shopkeepers refused to observe official decrees regulating commerce. For example, during the first weeks of Convention rule in 1914, crowds repeatedly attacked and sacked pawnshops that refused to obey the regulations imposed on them by revolutionary generals. More immediately, tense confrontations turned into riots after shopkeepers insulted, threatened, or made fun of women demanding food at lower prices.[13]

Though a few descriptions of crowds refer simply to *"gente del pueblo,"* most leave no doubt that the vast majority of those participating in riots were women, generally from the popular classes. The primary participation of women reflects their central role as consumers in working-class families as well as the ties forged daily among women in popular communities through their gender-specific chores such as shopping and washing. For women, the consumer riot became, as Temma Kaplan argues, part of the "consistent defense of their right to feed and protect their communities."[14] For men to participate in consumer riots was problematic, since riots were so closely linked to the task of shopping and often were preceded by "unmanly" appeals and supplications to officials and merchants. In addition, officials could accuse any men present at a riot of taking advantage of the situation to steal, while women's demands for food were harder to dismiss as mere theft.

Government authorities and newspapers throughout the months of scarcity referred often to "agitators" who urged otherwise "passive" crowds to riot and even noted on occasion specific women who "harangued" their followers. One newspaper made much of fifteen-year-old Carmen Macías, "of good appearance and well dressed," who reportedly led a crowd of poorer women against shops in the wealthy District Eight. The incident may have inspired the opening scene of Sesto's novel.[15] But crowds seem to have been for the most part leaderless. By definition, the women who participated in food riots were anonymous, a part of and representing the broader working-class community with their actions.

The most common targets of consumer riots were small merchants who sold basic necessities. In spite of the concentration of control over food supplies in the city, riots most often occurred in coal dispensaries, small food stores, and bakeries in working-class neighborhoods, where working people routinely acquired credit and purchased their food and fuel. In these neighborhoods, commerce was still premised on personal relations between buyer and seller, and refusing to sell food stocks or charging high prices could be seen as a violation of community standards.[16]

Other targets of crowds were less tied to routine community transactions and were more notable for the scale of accumulated supplies or their symbolic importance. Crowds often attacked the major markets of the city, particularly La Merced and San Juan, and occasionally targeted the major grain mills of the city. Groups of women also stopped carriages and cars in the streets and confiscated their cargos of food, took possession of train wagons of corn at railroad stations, and entered and sacked prisons. On at least one occasion, crowds attacked the posh commercial stores in the heart of the city center (see fig. 21).[17]

Women pursued common rituals in their negotiations with merchants and officials and in their attacks on stores. Invariably armed with empty baskets and sacks, women first pressured merchants, bakers, and individual hoarders to distribute their goods at a just price, occasionally dragging along a policeman to supervise the exchange. Such conduct, one sympathetic journalist noted, "raises very high the prestige of the groups that have been circulating in the streets demanding corn and food." In many cases, merchants obliged them by selling cheaply or even distributing food freely. Refusal to sell at what the crowd considered a just price often led to forced distribution or violent sacking, though even then rioters sometimes insisted on taking only what they needed. If shopkeepers resorted to insults or violence, crowds responded by throwing stones, removing goods from the store, or setting the storefront on fire. In various cases, irate shopkeepers fired into crowds, on at least two occasions killing women.[18]

Although localized and isolated riots occurred throughout these months, on several occasions they occurred almost simultaneously throughout the city, spread along neighborhood networks of information and by the crowds themselves. On 15 May large-scale food riots began in the Lagunilla market northeast of the Zócalo before spreading throughout the eastern part of the city. On 25 June a large crowd of women attacked the San Cosme marketplace and a bakery by the Buenavista train station on the west side of the city. Hours later they regrouped, their numbers increased, and moved east through the heart of the city to the San Juan market and on to the city's largest market, La Merced, east of the Zócalo. When the police finally arrived, the crowd dispersed to the working-class neighborhoods in the south of the city. Meanwhile, similar attacks on supplies of food occurred in train stations and the principal markets in all eight districts of the city and continued the next day, along with attacks on the municipal prison Belém.[19]

The immediate reaction of police and military authorities varied.

Obregón's endorsement of food riots before abandoning the city could not help but be seen by some as an official endorsement by the revolution of the justice of rioting in the face of scarcity and hoarding, one that at least some members of the Convention also endorsed. On at least one occasion, Zapatista soldiers helped a crowd assault a store in District Two of the city. The perpetration of violence against women by shopkeepers sometimes forced authorities to intervene. Constitutionalist soldiers shot a shopkeeper who had fired into a crowd surrounding his store, and the proprietor and employee of another store, appropriately called "Las Cumbres de Maltrata," were jailed and possibly tried after they shot into a crowd and killed a woman.

But police and soldiers were ultimately committed to repressing riots, even if it meant moving against women. On several occasions, Convention soldiers used fire hoses or fired bullets into the air to disperse crowds. During the first day of the riots that began on 25 June, over two hundred people were arrested, mostly women. In breaking up a riot on 15 July in La Merced, Constitutionalist troops fired into a crowd and wounded several women. Occasionally police or military authorities became targets of crowds when they refused to help negotiate a fair exchange, tried to break up a crowd, or made arrests of participants. When police detained various women involved in a riot in La Merced market, the crowd followed police back to jail and demanded and obtained the women's release.[20]

Food riots represented a gender-specific defense of the working-class community; while men struggled with their employers over the terms and remuneration of employment, supported political candidates in elections, or joined the different military factions of the revolution as soldiers or as part of the Red Battalions, women asserted themselves first in defense of their community, often taking over markets and streets to demand a just exchange value for the product of their husbands' or their own work. But the flurry of food riots that shook Mexico City in the spring and summer of 1915 were more than a simple defense of women's private, domestic sphere. Through their actions and protests over food, women intruded into the public and political life of the city and pursued their demands outside of the male-dominated arenas of electoral politics, unions, and military participation, where they had traditionally been marginalized or denied full citizenship.

Throughout this period, women organized a series of protest marches that almost inevitably occurred when the new occupiers of the city canceled the previous faction's currency, as when Obregón first reoccupied the city in January 1915. Official responses usually targeted women, as with Obregón's distribution of newly printed Carrancista money.

In mid-May, crowds of women daily approached the offices of the governor and the president before finally, on 19 May, taking over a session of the Convention Congress. Women descended with their empty baskets from the galleries to the seats of delegates and demanded that something be done to alleviate the food situation. The debate that followed only reflected the paralysis of that body and the Convention executive, with different factions alternately blaming the current crisis in the food supply on Carranza, the speculation of merchants, corrupt Zapatista soldiers, or the ineffectual Villista-backed president. Finally, the delegates took up a personal collection for the women occupying the hall, only to be met with cries of "We don't want money, we want corn!" Two days later, crowds of women returned to the Convention Congress, demanding that they not be deceived and shouting "We want to eat. We want to live." Only when deputies abandoned the hall and turned out the lights did the crowds finally disperse.[21]

In response, the Convention passed a series of measures, ordering the executive to spend up to five hundred thousand pesos on food to be sold at cost, authorizing the city council to fix prices, forbidding soldiers from selling food, fining hoarders, and authorizing police to shoot anyone caught stealing food. In the last week of May, thousands of women formed lines in front of the Palace of Mines to purchase subsidized corn. But none of these measures proved effective at solving the city's ongoing problems of food and currency, and by mid-June, the Subsistence Commission of the Convention proposed a return to free trade, a measure that pushed prices back up and helped initiate another round of food riots.[22]

Using examples from twentieth-century Spain, Pamela Radcliff argues that "the power of the female consumer riot lay, not in its contestation of male authority, but in its questioning of that authority's ability to live up to its own self-image." Similarly, by appealing to authorities, occupying the Convention Congress, and ultimately resorting to consumer riots, poor women in Mexico City did not challenge patriarchal male dominance but instead questioned the legitimacy of political authorities whose self-image as men mandated that they resolve the food crisis.[23] This self-image was not simply that of paternalistic officials but also that of revolutionaries. Rioters and the working-class community that defended them challenged authorities over the very meaning of a revolution supposedly based on the implementation of social justice. For example, after a cycle of riots in late June, a group of neighbors from the Colonia Santa Julia sent a long appeal to the Convention, explaining that on the day before, merchants had refused the request of a crowd of women to sell them food to feed their children and instead "made fun of their sorrow"; when the women responded by seizing the deposits of grain and taking only "what is necessary for the sustenance of their children," they were attacked and shot at by Villista soldiers. The next day the soldiers entered various tenements by force and removed food the women had taken the day before. "After this," the *vecinos* concluded, "it is worth asking: The Revolution, the grandiose revolution, brought about in favor of the humble people, has triumphed, or are we still in the times of tyranny, when the unprotected were assassinated with impunity?"[24]

The debate over the significance of the riots was echoed in the Convention, the metropolitan newspapers, and among the organized working class. In spite of the prominence of women in food riots, it is notable that the journalists, deputies, union leaders, and diplomats who recounted and reflected on the riots were invariably men, and their comments reflect their own gendered views of the origins and significance of women's actions. Editorials spoke of reactionary "hordes" and random anarchy. Prominent members of the Villista faction of the Convention insisted that private property be respected and denounced the women who had perpetrated the food riots as " antirevolutionary." Was the Convention government to prove itself as reckless as General Obregón, asked one delegate, by threatening merchants and giving free reign to the mob?

While women who rioted invoked their role as mothers to justify their actions, conservative delegates questioned the origins and morals of these women. Some newspapers made much of the rags that rioters wore, equating their dress with lumpen origins rather than the hardships of the moment. The rioters, delegate Angel Castellanos claimed, were not "the people" who the revolution represented but were rather *mujerzuelas* (loose women) and *populacho* (rabble) who had never defended their own rights or those of their liberators.[25]

With the term "*mujerzuela*," conservative delegates painted women rioters as the opposite of *señoras decentes*: they were idle, public, and promiscuous. As with prostitutes, their behavior stemmed not from poverty but from their environment and their own moral decadence. Women who acted publicly and aggressively transgressed traditional gender boundaries, were seen as out of control, and ultimately were presented as a threat to the revolution, just as prostitutes had been a threat to Porfirian progress. In the zarzuela *A saquear tocan* (A call to riot), which hit the metropolitan stage soon after the food riots, the principal protagonists were portrayed as domestic servants, a group of women that was often closely linked to prostitution in the imagination and occupational reality of the day. Of course domestic servants and prostitutes probably did join other women in the riots, especially given that prostitution seems to have swelled dramatically as food shortages drove desperate women to exchange sex for food, often catering to the armies that periodically occupied the city. But the identification of rioters with these stigmatized professions served to question the legitimacy of the riots themselves.[26]

Another group of intellectuals and Convention delegates defended the actions of the rioters, primarily the group within the Zapatista faction most identified with the labor movement. Some sympathetic journalists referred to the events as a "just popular movement," with the women being legitimate representatives of "the people."[27] Delegate Luis Méndez insisted that shopkeepers who fired on poor hungry women deserved the death penalty and along with two other delegates adopted the petition of the Santa Julia neighbors as his own. Many sympathizers accepted the categorization of rioters as fallen women but drew upon a parallel image of women as victims of an unjust social order. Delegate Rafael Pérez Taylor defended rioters and prostitutes, asking, "How many *mujerzuelas* have been seduced or stolen because of hunger?" In the pages of *El Renovador*, former Casa member Octavio Jahn defended the rioters and pointed out the hypocrisy of those who condemned prostitutes, "the saddest victims of the present social order," while "we all sell, rent, prostitute our arms, our brains, our energy, our intelligence to the highest bidder." Defending rioters and invoking the use of the guillotine against monopolists during the French Revolution, Pérez Taylor called for the confiscation and distribution among the population of any basic foods withheld from the market.[28]

While primarily pursuing a strategy of raising wages, organized workers endorsed the actions of women rioters as legitimate in themselves. In early June, perhaps prompted by the recent takeover of the Convention Congress by unorganized women, union leaders held a meeting to demand that the government confiscate food holdings. Speakers urged the population, in the absence of government action, to take their own measures and called for a hunger march for the following week. But after a meeting with the Convention president, organizers called off the march, declaring that they now believed "enough was being done" to resolve the food crisis. Only after the most intense cycle of food riots in late June did organized workers again take the initiative or, rather, follow the initiative of rioting women. The Union of Commercial Employees and the Union of Electricians sponsored a public meeting that filled the Teatro Colón to discuss problems of hunger and to defend the rioters. In the face of misery and government inaction, one speaker declared, riots were an acceptable example of direct action and a sign of what could be resolved through collective action—even if riots would not by themselves solve the food problem.[29]

In spite of such endorsements, the links between workers' organizations and consumer riots remained indirect. Although some newspapers claimed that "agitators" had organized the riots, there is no evidence to suggest that radical Convention delegates or union leaders somehow manipulated or organized women rioters. Riots and confiscations remained a part of the political culture of the streets, with no direct ties to unions or political groups. In fact, women rioters may have deliberately avoided participation in formal unions or politics at this point to avoid endangering their appeal—rooted as it was in their identity as women—for the resolution of food problems to merchants and political authorities. Still, consumer riots did force unions to consider broader community problems in the months that followed and pushed them to incorporate more women in their ranks.[30]

In July, the pace of popular unrest increased. As Constitutionalist troops approached the capital, many merchants again shut their stores rather than accept Convention money that they knew would soon be worthless. In the days that followed, local authorities of the Convention government undertook little forceful action against shopkeepers or to guarantee shipments of food; instead, on 5 July the minister of the interior ordered that all those who begged or were publicly idle in the streets be rounded up and given forced "asylum" in the municipal prison. Before the end of the week, in the disorder that took place as the Convention forces again abandoned the city, crowds freed the prisoners held in Belém prison, seized food supplies, and burned the prison archives.[31]

In the three weeks of military skirmishes in the Federal District that followed, neither Zapatista nor Constitutionalist forces controlled the city very long or very completely. Food riots continued sporadically throughout the month of July, but police reports indicate that they were most intense around the days when control of the city changed hands and the consequent change in the official currency was imposed. Constitutionalist general Pablo González took the city on 9 July and initiated a new round of consumer riots a few days later when he outlawed all Convention currencies. On 17 July the Constitutionalists abandoned Mexico City again to the Zapatistas, before returning for good on 2 August.[32]

Consumer riots eased after the Constitutionalists definitively controlled Mexico City, though residents were not spared persistent problems of currency devaluation and food supply, in spite of greatly diminished fighting throughout the nation. Instead, protest shifted from riots to more formal channels led by a reunited and expanded labor movement. In the mobilizations that continued and culminated in the general strike a year later, women—whether on the margins of workers' organizations or participating fully within their ranks—provided an important link between the demands of the working-class community and labor unions. Indeed, women's participation guaranteed the continued orientation of collective action around consumer issues.

Toward the General Strike

By the summer of 1915, Constitutionalist forces were the dominant faction, if not yet the undisputed masters of Mexico. With the major military battles against Villa won, First Chief Carranza began to favor business interests over those of peasants and workers and to distance himself even further from his reluctant alliance with the Casa del Obrero Mundial. The attitudes and interventions of Constitutionalist leaders in labor conflicts in Mexico City and the rest of the country would be a far cry from those of the previous fall and winter. At the same time, workers in Mexico City began a year of unprecedented mobilization, culminating in the general strike of July–August 1916. This cycle was characterized, on the one hand, by increasing unity among working people and, on the other, by conflict among working people, employers, and Constitutionalist officials.

Real consolidation among Mexico City workers came after the first Red Battalions were demobilized and returned to their homes in August 1915, six months after their departure. Realizing that the risks of allowing the Casa members to continue as armed and uniformed labor organizers were greater than the benefits of their continued military service, Carranza dismissed them with two months' pay. By February 1916, the remaining Red Battalions were demobilized, though a few Casa members who had risen within the army ranks, such as Celestino Gasca, remained in the army for several years more.[33]

Demobilization of the Casa del Obrero Mundial came as the Constitutionalist forces maintained most troops and even stepped up recruiting efforts in Mexico City for what was hoped to be a final assault on the remaining Villista and Zapatista forces.[34] Since his defeat at the battle of Celaya in April 1915, Villa had been on the run in northern Mexico, with his troops dwindling rapidly into a guerrilla army that could not directly confront Constitutionalist forces or hold major cities but could make strategic attacks and put into question at home and abroad the Constitutionalists' control of the nation. After July, Zapatistas controlled only the state of Morelos and would soon hold only its mountains, forests, and the allegiance of its people against the periodic scorched-earth invasions sent by Carranza.

At the same time, tensions grew between First Chief Carranza and the key generals on whom his military dominance depended. Alvaro Obregón and his cohorts from Sonora had gained popularity both through military victories and through dramatic reforms in regions they controlled. On a policy level, Carranza had been far more reluctant than Obregón to alienate traditional business elites and landowners, and as military hostilities declined, he began to push for a shift toward civilian government and the return of the confiscated properties of both Porfirian elites and foreign companies. On a personal and political level, Carranza grew jealous of Obregón's influence among different social sectors, within the army, and especially among the very capable generals from his native Sonora, namely, Plutarco Elías Calles, Adolfo de la Huerta, and Benjamín Hill. By late 1915, many military figures had begun the transition from conducting military campaigns to accumulating wealth and power in preparation for the upcoming political struggles over the shape and leadership of the postrevolutionary order.

In spite of the sudden and chilly demobilization of the Red Battalions, armed participation in the revolution gave returning workers a heightened pride in their participation in national struggles, as many Casa leaders had predicted at the time of the signing of the pact. Their pride in turn informed and justified their frenetic organizational activities in the following months. Just as Porfirian workers for decades had invoked their participation in the struggle against the French intervention, so too would workers use their military participation and sacrifice to justify their organizational efforts. Many workers continued to wear their military insignia at work and in union meetings. The Casa weekly *Ariete* commemorated the recent fall of "Red" soldiers on the battlefield of Tonila, Jalisco, comparing their efforts to those of the Niños Héroes, who had defended Chapultepec Castle in 1848 against U.S. troops, and celebrating "this new and glorious page that is written with the blood of workers." These workers were the heroes who should be noticed, the article went on, by "those that still don't recognize the [legal] personality of the 'Casa del Obrero,' as if it hadn't conquered it [legal recognition] sufficiently with the blood of its martyrs!" In the same journal a returning streetcar worker insisted, "It is urgent, *compañeros*, that that blood [spilled], like a vivifying seed, gives fruit." Even two years later a group of printers would sanctify the formation of their new union by referring to "those of us who have drunk the blood that was spilled yesterday by the national heart." Over time, the historical memory of workers' sacrifice in the military campaigns of the revolution would only grow. Esther Torres's sister Ignacia, who eventually married a veteran of the Red Battalions, would remember years later: "we won, because ten thousand working men went and I believe two or three hundred came back . . . the majority died in combat." Of course, most working people in Mexico City had not fought with the Constitutionalists, and a few still begrudged the Casa its participation in a political struggle, but the symbolic significance of workers' fighting for the victorious "revolution" took on significance far beyond the specific individuals who fought in the Red Battalions.[35]

The Constitutionalists could not completely ignore the promises that had been made to workers. On 30 August Carranza's key supporter, Gen. Pablo González, issued a labor decree for the Federal District confirming the eight-hour day and Sundays off and requiring that any worker fired for reasons other than bad conduct or incompetence be compensated with three months' salary. The provisional governor of Veracruz, Heriberto Jara, went further, declaring for the first time the legal recognition of unions in that state. A month later, Sonoran general Adolfo de la Huerta gave the Casa del Obrero Mundial the Palace of Tiles, formerly the elite Jockey Club, to serve as its headquarters in the heart of the downtown (see fig. 22). An editorial in the official newspaper El Demócrata explained that the dramatic gesture of putting workers in the "Alcazár of the Aristocracy" symbolized the commitment of the new authorities to workers. But such support had its price. In return, the editorial continued, workers needed to reject violence and agitators and make no inappropriate demands, "to elevate themselves without harm to the interests of others." A handful of union leaders who had risen to prominence in the Red Battalions, such as former general-secretary Samuel Yúdico, were offered government jobs; but in spite of guarantees made explicit in the February pact, most of the rank and file of the Red Battalions were not returned to their jobs or offered alternatives. For example, 120 streetcar workers who had constituted the bulk of the second Red Battalion continued for months after their discharge to petition the company, still under public administration, and the government for the return of their jobs.[36]

Other Constitutionalist measures were aimed at the conditions of the city's poor, in a city whose people, complained Gen. Pablo González, "were very hostile to us." During the last desperate weeks of Convention control, the U.S. Red Cross set up various soup kitchens in Mexico City to feed the poor and began to report the city's dire conditions and hunger-related death rates in the United States. After the Constitutionalists resumed control of the city, the dramatic reports continued to circulate in the U.S. press, and Carranza, feeling personally attacked, eventually forced the Red Cross to leave. In the absence of the Red Cross efforts, General González was obliged to provide food and asylum to the poorest and set up "Constitutionalist workshops" for unemployed men and women. By the end of September, and at Obregón's suggestion, Carranza ordered that the public soup kitchens be closed down and that those receiving charity be offered facilities to travel to the northern Laguna region to pick cotton.[37]

In the first meetings that the Casa del Obrero Mundial held after returning to Mexico City, women constituted the majority of the public, and questions of consumption continued to dominate discussions for the next months. The Casa del Obrero Mundial was for the most part reconciled with those workers and their organizations that had remained in Mexico City, including the difficult reconciliation between those streetcar workers who had stayed and those who had left. A partial reconciliation between the Casa del Obrero Mundial and the Union of Electricians came in early December 1915, though the electricians refused to abandon their own headquarters in the Salón Star for the sumptuous Palace of Tiles of the Casa. At the same time, the balance of power among the different unions shifted toward the Union of Electricians and the Union of Commercial Employees, an acknowledgment of the strategic importance of the first and the role of both as centers of worker organization during the Casa del Obrero Mundial's absence. Workers in sectors in which unions had disappeared, divided, or closed down because of economic crisis or the formation of the Red Battalions—such as streetcar workers, printers, carpenters, shoemakers, hat makers, chauffeurs, molders, carpenters, and bakery workers—soon formed new unions or combined with previously existing groups, while unions were formed for the first time among workers in sectors in which employment was more precarious, including barbers, beer makers, factory seamstresses, cigarette makers, and corset makers as well as a variety of workers based in particular factories, such as the shoe factory of industrialist Carlos Zetina. Reconciliation also occurred with those members who had overtly supported the Convention, such as Octavio Jahn and Luis Méndez.[38]

It was in this period of consolidation in the fall of 1915 when union organization reached people like Esther Torres. While women concerned with issues of consumption had dominated the first open meetings of the Casa in August, by November, the initiative among women extended to the organization of unions in sectors dominated by women workers, on a far greater scale than any of the previous cycles of organization in the city. Again, the link between consumer and workplace concerns was evident in the trajectory of Esther Torres, who had struggled through the toughest years of the revolution, working as a seamstress at a variety of sweatshops between prolonged periods of unemployment. Hunger and unemployment first brought her to the Casa, where she received work distributing food in outlets organized by the Casa and municipal authorities. Having watched other working people organize and join the Red Battalions over the years, she finally got permission from her mother to attend one of the Casa meetings in November 1915. There, she recalled years later, she listened to Rafael Quintero explain "what kind of thing a union was." The next week she brought a group of seamstresses to the Casa, where with the help of Jacinto Huitrón they organized a union of seamstresses that grew within a month to three hundred members.[39]

At a meeting in mid-November, over three hundred women workers answered a call to come to the Casa to organize their sectors, and over the next weeks unions were organized among women who worked in the manufacture of hats, corsets, cigarettes, bottle caps, beer, perfume, cardboard boxes, biscuits, candy, and flour. Probably typical in size was the Union of Hat Makers (Sindicato de Obreras del Ramo de Bonetería), which organized on 17 November with 150 members. In spite of the role of men in facilitating these organizations, women constituted the executive committees of most of the new unions. Of course, the leadership of the Casa continued to be all male, but women were fully involved in its activities, though often in ways that emphasized their role as women, including educational projects such as the Rationalist School, inaugurated in October, and the organization of social events. Of course, the participation of women in the *tertulias* (social gatherings) of song and dance on occasion provided a cover for organizational activities frowned upon by authorities, and when Carranza jailed the strike committee of the Union of Commercial Employees in February 1916, the head of the Union of Hat Makers, Manuela Barrionuevo, like the biblical Judith, allowed a prison guard to kiss her while her Casa companions sneaked in to see their colleagues.[40]

The honeymoon between unions and Constitutionalist generals upon their return to Mexico City was brief. Within a week of the definitive Constitutionalist occupation, the Union of Electricians went on strike for a wage increase, leaving the city without electricity for fourteen hours. Gen. Pablo González immediately brought the parties together and forced a settlement by offering to pay the first month of the raise. Two weeks later, the Casa del Obrero Mundial supported the strike and boycott organized by the United Societies of Restaurant Employees (Socidades Unidas de Dependientes de Restaurant) when employers refused to accept the demand that only unionized workers be hired. Soon after, the Casa announced plans to form a national confederation.[41]

A series of Casa-backed strikes followed in the fall of 1915. Over three thousand bakery workers went on strike in mid-November, including "a large quantity of women." When the large bakery owners refused to negotiate, the Bakers' Union (Sindicato de Obreros y Obreras del Ramo de Panadería) set up a system of cooperative bakeries. Another important citywide strike was that of the Printers' Union, which won wage demands and widespread union recognition. Striking textile workers won wage increases and formal recognition of their union in the same month, and women bonnet workers struck for a wage increase, an eight-hour day, recognition of their union, and an end to fines, receiving support from the powerful unions of electricians and commercial employees. The flurry of strikes gave notice to Constitutionalist authorities that the moderation demanded of workers would not necessarily be forthcoming.[42]

The growing tensions between the Casa del Obrero Mundial and the Constitutionalist provisional government are suggested by the existence of, and reports from, a Carrancista agent spying within the Casa del Obrero Mundial, who during the November bakery workers' strike reported that "the Casa del Obrero Mundial already has in its history many provocations of strikes, and if in some of them they were justified, in the majority, their only purpose was to obstruct the goals proposed by our government." Likewise, the report continued, the Union of Electricians, which had threatened a solidarity strike with bakers, constituted "enemies of our government." The evil, he concluded ominously, "must be cut off at the root, to avoid later examples."[43]

The reconciliation of the Union of Electricians with the Casa made possible the revitalization of a formal, citywide federation in January 1916 that solidified the organizational ties among different groups of workers, the Federation of Workers' Unions of the Federal District (Federación de Sindicatos Obreros del Distrito Federal). The new federation remained closely tied to the Casa del Obrero Mundial, shared its headquarters, and invoked its principle of "the class struggle" and the stated eventual goal of "the socialization of the means of production"; but it also went beyond the loose encompassing structure and cultural focus of the Casa del Obrero Mundial, and its structure and leadership acknowledged the influence of the more independent-minded unions that had not joined the Red Battalions. The secretary-general was Luis Morones of the Union of Electricians, and the key administrative office, secretary of the interior, went to Federico Rocha, head of the Union of Commercial Employees. The statutes of the federation provided for a democratic framework of decision making and financial accountability for the new unions, procedures for partial and general strikes, and the usual rejection of all alliances with "governments, parties and personalities." Of course, democratic process and the commitment to political neutrality had been ignored by unions in the past, but the still lingering tensions among different labor unions over the Casa-Constitutionalist Pact and the increasing conflicts with the provisional government of Carranza reinforced both tenets.[44]

The federation joined together organizations from virtually every sector, from restaurant workers to highly skilled craftworkers, and deliberately sought to include women workers. Six months later, the federation claimed a membership of ninety thousand, representing the largest and most unified labor organization in the nation up to that date. The Casa del Obrero Mundial and the federation together went far toward building a citywide class perspective on issues of both work and consumption. In March, the federation tried to extend its influence nationally, sponsoring a convention of around one hundred unions in Veracruz, in which a Labor Confederation of the Mexican Region (Confederación de Trabajo de la Región Mexicana) was formed.[45]

Organizational bonds were tested and consolidated by the continued dire situation in the capital. Although the Constitutionalists controlled the vast majority of the country and virtually all of the railroad system by September 1915, scarcity and hunger remained serious problems in Mexico City. Agricultural production had plummeted during the period of worst fighting. A report commissioned by Carranza noted in the fall of 1915 that the amount of corn and wheat production reaching urban markets was less than 10 percent of the levels of 1910. In rural areas, producers turned inward and produced for their own domestic consumption, but since urban areas depended on distant agricultural regions, consumption levels dropped dramatically.[46]

In such a situation of scarcity, many large landowners, merchants, and millers profited enormously by cornering limited supplies of foods. Speculation was facilitated by the concentration of ownership and distribution networks in the city, a tendency that seems to have increased during the years of the revolution. As mentioned, the milling of flour and baking of bread was controlled, directly or indirectly, by three firms, the largest being the Compañía Manufacturera de Harina, and masa for corn tortillas was almost exclusively in the hands of the Compañía Mexicana Molinera de Nixtamal.[47]

Constitutionalist officers were quick to condemn these merchants publicly and to impose relatively ineffective price controls. Somewhat more effective were the thirty to forty public food stores set up throughout the city to distribute basic foods more cheaply. But military officers used their control of port cities, agricultural regions, the train stations of Mexico City, and the city council to further raise the price of food through deals and extortion. Gen. Pablo González, a miller by trade, sporadically controlled military operations in the Federal District and Morelos throughout late 1915 and 1916 and made a considerable fortune through his control of the grain trade, among other interests.[48]

When the Constitutionalists definitively retook Mexico City in August 1915, their paper peso had a value of seven U.S. cents, compared to the 1910 peso value of fifty U.S. cents. By May 1916, its value had dropped to two U.S. cents. Even after outlawing Convention money, multiple types of paper money were recognized as enforced legal currency, and the printing of new, unbacked currencies was an invitation to speculate, something soldier and shop owner alike were ready to do. Between January and April 1916, the price of a kilogram of rice rose from 1.76 to 2.27 pesos, corn from 1.13 to 1.97 pesos, and black beans from 1.88 to 2.67 pesos.[49]

In the winter and spring of 1916, the federation backed a series of successful strikes—the most notable against the textile factories, the streetcar company (still under government management), and the principal department stores—to force employers to raise wages and grant other demands. But any wage gains proved short-lived as long as the provisional government failed to guarantee regular shipments of food and to create a stable currency.

In spite of the seriousness of material conditions, it would be mistaken to see working-class mobilization in this period, at least in Mexico City, as essentially defensive or reactive.[50] Material hardship, scarcity, and inflation were fundamental motivations to strikes, public protests, and riots. But as often as unions struck for higher wages, they put forth longstanding demands such as recognition of unions, control over arbitrary treatment, and authority over firings and hirings and defended the public participation they had achieved. Even in the worst months of hunger, May through July 1915, two of the three principal strikes in the city were over arbitrary firings (in the electrical company) and union recognition (the El Palacio de Hierro store) as opposed to wages (textile factories), and throughout the following year, workers repeatedly and aggressively pursued longstanding demands along with (and at times without) wage demands.[51]

In addition to the variety of nonwage demands, the tactics of organized labor in this period also belies a defensive and materialist explanation of labor militancy. Organizational tactics demonstrated both great autonomy from the provisional government and confidence and solidarity as a class. As mentioned, in response to the intransigence of the large bakeries to the November 1915 strike, the Casa-affiliated Bakers' Union set up alternative bakeries and over forty distribution points in the poorer areas of the city, using hospital and prison ovens and wheat sold to them by city council authorities. Their endeavor provided work to the unemployed as street vendors sold bread stamped with the letters C.O.M. This production of bread filled an urgent need that neither the fledgling local government nor monopoly business was able to fulfill and in turn empowered the union by linking them to the poorer neighborhoods they served. The Casa del Obrero Mundial bakeries survived efforts by the big bakeries to control all of the ovens in the city as well as a crisis in April with the city council, when the Casa del Obrero Mundial attempted to organize a strike among municipal employees. Similar attempts to create cooperatives were made after the January tailors' strike. Other efforts in the public sphere included the formation by the Casa del Obrero Mundial of "sanitary police" to help control the typhus epidemic that swept Mexico City throughout much of 1916.[52]

The magnitude of problems of currency and food supply was great, but organizational responses were also rooted in workers' understanding of the revolution on two levels. First, as mentioned, workers in general felt entitled to receive benefits from a revolution in which they had formally participated as workers, both as individuals and symbolically as a class. Second, workers engaged employers and authorities over the meaning of a revolution that supposedly had been fought to bring about social justice. In the pronouncements of the federation and the pages of the official press, a battle took place for the moral high ground of the revolution. Union propagandists rejected the unified conception of "the Revolution" accepted rhetorically by the Casa del Obrero Mundial during the military campaign, instead using the term to refer to a process independent from Constitutionalist leaders. In their newspaper *Ariete*, the Casa del Obrero Mundial began to reprint with minimal commentary the more outrageous comments of Constitutionalist officials, such as a police commissioner's remark that "the revolution was made to sustain the principle of AUTHORITY" or the more menacing comment of the finance subsecretary that "since the revolution was made for the exclusive benefit of the working classes, the Law of the 25 of January 1862 [applying the death penalty against treason] will be applied to all workers who reclaim their rights." Even *Acción Mundial*, edited by Carranza's labor broker, Dr. Atl, began to criticize not only merchants but also the provisional government's monetary policy. The Casa and the federation began to insist that they were making their demands and organizing strikes on behalf of not only workers but also the "humble class," which, among other concerns, suffered most from the devaluation of paper currency.[53]

International events provided a rationale for increasing government repression of workers' organization. Villa, now reduced to leading a band of guerrillas, crossed the U.S. border on 9 March 1916 to attack the town of Columbus, New Mexico, killing seventeen people before retreating into the mountains of Chihuahua. A week later a punitive expedition of six thousand men headed by U.S. Army General Pershing entered Mexican territory in hapless pursuit and remained in Chihuahua for the next ten months while negotiations for withdrawal dragged on.

The Pershing expedition helped to revive Villa's popularity and undermine Carranza's credibility in Mexico. Throughout 1916, the provisional
government of Carranza used the presence of foreign troops on Mexican
soil to demand unity and repress dissent.

Carranza and his closest allies began to make unsubtle warnings to
organized workers. Gen. Pablo González proved unable to influence or
control labor in Mexico City and began to resort to repression. In January 1916, González issued a statement referring to the leaders of the
Casa del Obrero Mundial as "professional agitators, in general neither
workers nor Mexicans." The revolution, he continued, "even though it
affects workers in a very important way, must also protect other classes"
and could not sanction "proletarian tyranny." Just who these other
classes in need of protection were seemed apparent when, two weeks
later, following a strike of sixteen hundred shop employees to demand
partial wage payment in gold, General González threw the Casa del
Obrero Mundial and federation out of their three- month-old headquarters in the former Jockey Club and returned the building to its original owners, effectively ending, along with the simultaneous demobilization of the last Red Battalions, any subsidy to the Casa. In addition, the
Casa del Obrero Mundial newspaper *Ariete* was confiscated and closed
down, and key leaders of the Union of Commercial Employees, the Casa
del Obrero Mundial, and the federation (including Jacinto Huitrón and
Federico Rocha) were arrested in Mexico City and imprisoned for three
months in Querétaro.[54]

In the same month of March, the governor of the Federal District,
Gen. César López de Lara, decreed that his office must first approve any
union meeting dealing with political affairs. The May Day march of
1916, organized by the Casa and the federation, was marred when shots
were fired from a passing car full of soldiers, wounding two workers.
The same month, Carranza's provisional government began negotiating
the return of the two foreign-owned companies it controlled in Mexico
City, the streetcar company and the Mexican Telephone and Telegraph
Company, the latter still being run by the Union of Electricians. These
actions gave notice to workers that they could not necessarily count on
the backing of authorities in their struggles with employers and forced

the Casa del Obrero Mundial and the federation to rely more on their component unions (especially the electricians) for resources and meeting space. Banished from their highly symbolic headquarters in the heart of the downtown and increasingly at odds with the new masters of the city, their determination to remain central to the affairs of the city and the nation would require ever greater shows of strength.[55]

In May the Constitutionalist forces imposed yet another paper currency, the so-called *infalsificable*, which was by stages to replace all other Constitutionalist emissions. Secretary of Finance Luis Cabrera announced that a gold fund would be created to guarantee the new peso at twenty gold centavos (about ten U.S. cents). While this was meant to inspire confidence, the partial backing seemed a public acknowledgment that no money could be taken at face value. In fact, the provisional government could not even muster this level of confidence or gold reserves, and the new peso immediately fell below 20 centavos in value.

In the face of multiple currencies and constant devaluations, the wage increases that workers won in successive strikes proved futile. Such problems were, of course, national in scope; in mid-May national railroad workers went on strike to demand that wages be paid according to a metallic standard. General Obregón, now minister of war in the provisional government, responded with threats to incorporate workers on state-controlled railroads into the army, thereby bringing the strike to an unsuccessful close.[56]

In spite of the fate of the railroad workers, the federation issued a demand on 19 May to all employers in the Federal District that wages, like most prices, be pegged to a gold standard and paid according to the wage levels effective in the last week of 1914. After three days without a response, the federation initiated a general strike on 22 May, made effective by the participation of the electricians, telephone workers, and streetcar workers and supported by workers of the principal factories and shops in the city. For the third time in a year, the electrical workers turned off the lights in the city. On the morning of the strike, thousands of men, women, and children rallied around the Salón Star to show their support.[57]

The government response was less brutal than it had been during the

February strike of shop employees, in part because Carranza had transferred his key general, Pablo González, from Mexico City to Morelos,
where his talent for graft and repression was unleashed against the Zapatistas. In his stead, Carranza empowered the military commander of
the plaza, General Benjamin Hill, a close ally of Obregón, to take whatever measures necessary against the "obstructionist labor of commerce,
banks and unions." Hill moved quickly to confront the strike committee
and to call for an immediate resumption of public services, posting
troops near work centers throughout the city and threatening in particular the workers of the streetcar company, which was still run by a
government representative. Government intervention, the very act that
had rallied streetcar workers to the Constitutionalist cause eighteen
months earlier, now proved for streetcar and railroad workers a severe
constraint on union action. At the same time, in exchange for a return to
work, General Hill ordered a joint meeting of representatives of workers
and the major industrialists and merchants in the city for the following
day.[58] The meeting itself was unprecedented. Ten delegates of the federation and ten delegates of the principal employers of the Federal District met face to face on the stage of the downtown Teatro Arbeu, with
Hill mediating. The rest of the theater overflowed with thousands of
workers and employers. The delegates for the federation included four
members from the Printers' Union, including the secretary-general of
the Casa del Obrero Mundial, José Barragán Hernández, and two
members from the Union of Electricians—the secretary-general Ernesto
Velasco and Luis Morones, who headed the federation itself. The opposing commission included industrialists from the textile, tobacco, met-
als, printing, baking, and other industries.[59]

The industrialists dismissed the federation's demands and countered
with a proposal that present wage levels be paid entirely in the new
government issue of *infalsificable* bills rather than previous issues. The
committee of workers questioned whether the new currency would hold
its value, but the generals representing Carranza responded that the new
peso depended on "the confidence in the Government, which had given
a value to the new bills and would at all costs make [its value] respected."[60]

The workers' committee requested an hour break to consult with their constituent unions, but General Hill insisted that as representatives of the federation they were entitled to make a binding decision. Morones called for a secret ballot that resulted in a five to five split among workers. General Hill, "in his capacity as President [of the meeting], gave his own determining vote [*de calidad*] as arbiter, deciding in favor of the proposal of the industrialists." Additional provisions over the next days included the obligatory acceptance by merchants of all old and new legal currencies and the ruling that no worker who had participated in the strike could be fired for a period of three months.[61] The determination of Morones and the other representatives to abide by democratic procedure is notable, as is the determination of Hill to defend the government's monetary policy and forcefully arbitrate conflicts between labor and capital. The meeting anticipated the shape and balance of power in the Arbitration Juntas eventually set up by postrevolutionary governments.

The May agreement simply postponed a reckoning. Hill apparently enforced the prohibition against firing workers who had participated in the strike, but pressures mounted for workers to defend the deteriorating value of their wages. In June, the refusal of merchants to accept soon-to-be-expired "Veracruz" currency sparked a series of riots. Finance Secretary Cabrera admitted to U.S. officials that army officers were among the worst speculators in the exchange of old for new currencies. Meanwhile, popular pressure had pushed Federal District governor López de Lara to impose a freeze on rents. A week after the riots, the federation took on popular demands when it called for a march of union members and "the people of the metropolis" to protest the hoarding of goods by merchants and their refusal to accept the *infalsificables* at face value. Almost five thousand marched on 11 June from the Salón Star to markets throughout the city before returning to the monument to Juárez in the Alameda.[62]

The rejuvenated labor movement in Mexico City had far greater success linking issues of work and consumption in the first half of 1916 than during the previous riot-filled summer under Convention control, and as a result many of the city's poorest workers swelled the ranks of the federation's unions and supported their public events. But the entrance of these unskilled masses created continuous pressures from below for results that, although ostensibly directed toward employers and merchants, could only be implemented at the level of government policy. The loud condemnations the Casa del Obrero Mundial and the federation made of merchants and employers were in fact echoed and encouraged by government officials, who blamed merchants and currency speculators alone for the loss in value of its currency, but workers could not for very long avoid challenging government policy.

During the months of June and July the new *infalsificable* peso lost more than half its value, putting into question the "confidence in the government" that Carranza's generals had insisted would maintain the value of the new currency. The deterioration of the *infalsificable* coincided with a series of other local government policies that, by assuming a return to institutional normalcy in spite of dire material conditions, could only seem a deliberate rebuff to workers and popular classes. In July, the city's Commission to Regulate Commerce, which had been set up in April, was abolished. This action in essence gave merchants free reign to set prices in gold equivalents and collect from the public according to the fluctuating value of devalued paper currencies. A final 31 July 1916 deadline for spending or trading Constitutionalist currencies issued previous to the *infalsificable* bills created a frenzied cycle of devaluation, followed by spending and debt paying by consumers and delays and refusals by merchants, landlords, and creditors to accept payment in expiring currencies. In addition, Carranza announced in mid-July that any local conflicts related to work or commerce would no longer be handled by the military commander of the plaza, Benjamin Hill, but would instead be referred to the Labor Department, a measure that shifted local authority from a close military ally of Obregón to civilians who, though loyal to Carranza, had much less real power. In effect, much of the urban social policy of the government became subordinate to its fiscal needs and monetary policy and was influenced by emerging military rivalries.[63]

For the Casa del Obrero Mundial and federation leadership, this confirmed suspicions that the provisional government favored the interests of employers and merchants over those of workers, using money as their instrument; for many of their recently organized members, the fluctuations of food supplies, prices, and currency seemed a moral betrayal by authorities who were already of questionable legitimacy.[64]

Beginning 21 July the federation made a series of public petitions—ostensibly to employers but inevitably to the military authorities. Their primary demand was basically the same as it had been in May, to be paid wages according to a gold standard at 1914 wage levels. The federation insisted to General Hill that "various bosses have suggested to some of our *compañeros* that we ask for the payment of salaries specifically in hard currency [*metálico*], with the goal that the paper emitted by the Revolution be withdrawn." Their demand for payment in gold equivalents instead of gold coin, they argued, reflected their rejection of employers' insinuations and their desire to avoid doing "serious damage to the Constitutionalist Government." In addition they demanded a wage increase of 50 percent to compensate for inflation, implementation of the eight-hour day, a minimum wage the equivalent of one peso in gold, protection against firings for strike activity, and three months of severance pay in case of firings. Finally, the federation insisted that all workplaces be required to remain open for normal work weeks unless workers agreed to reduced hours. In the following days the three pro-government papers (*El Pueblo*, *El Demócrata*, and *Acción Mundial*) lashed out at workers for "not seeing beyond their own interests," which the federation and industrialists alike interpreted as "an extra-official declaration that the government supported capital and denied the rights of workers in the petitions presented."[65]

Two representatives of the strike committee met with General Hill on 24 July and at his suggestion wrote a petition to be passed on directly to Carranza. In it they repeated their demands, this time directly to the government, pointing out that a gold standard had been imposed by decree in the state of Sonora by Gen. Plutarco Elías Calles. They explained that while they were well disposed to settle their demands peacefully, they hoped that the first chief would act soon, "since in spite of the good disposition that animates this Commission, neither we, nor the Committee of the Federation think we have the power or sufficient influence to prevent the breakout of a strike movement originating in hunger, that is already felt in the homes of the majority of our *compañeros*."[66] Thus the committee put ultimate responsibility for any strike or other conflict that might occur on the government, which needed to act on their demands before any type of social explosion was initiated by the masses of the working poor, who might act in spite of their leadership. Only government authorities could impose a gold standard for the payment of wages, but to do so in Mexico City would effectively put an end to Carranza's monetary and fiscal policies throughout the nation, forcing him to find sounder ways to finance his army and administration.

The contradictions of these policies were particularly obvious to shop employees, who were paid according to the face value of devalued currencies but who worked in stores where prices were charged in gold or its equivalent in the devalued paper. On 27 July the Union of Commercial Employees began a unilateral strike against thirty-four principal commercial establishments. Store employees, they explained, in receiving pay in paper and yet charging customers in gold, had become unwilling accomplices of the merchants, and to do so "is to damage our beloved Patria; is to continue robbing the people; is to rob ourselves." The union dressed their strike in a defense of the government, which they explained was itself subject to the abuses of commerce. Therefore, they reasoned, "If our obligation as good citizens and honest men is to aid our Government in these moments of trial that it is going through; if our duty is to help our brothers and all of society against the abuses of its protected; let us do our duty, let us unite, and all together let us help the Government, since to help the government is to help ourselves."[67]

The shop employees' strike proved inadequate to force Carranza to respond to the federation petitions. The official silence compelled the federation to resort directly to the general strike, organizing secretly without the explicit warnings and deadlines given on previous occasions. Their decision, made urgent by popular pressure, made clear the final break of the organized labor movement of Mexico City with the Constitutionalists, as the federation directly confronted the provisional government over its monetary policy.[68]

Careful to avoid any preemptive move against them by military officials, the strike committee met secretly to set a date for the general strike on the night of 30 July, under cover of a dance held in the tenement building of Angela Inclán, a hat maker and member of the committee who lived in the eastern Colonia Barragán by the penitentiary. The decision was made to call the strike the next morning, which coincided with the final day in which older Constitutionalist emissions would be legal. The crucial agreement of the head of the Union of Electricians, Ernesto Velasco, was secured.[69]

At four o'clock on the morning of 31 July, the electrical workers' union cut off power, effectively closing down all production, transport, and commerce. This time workers of all public utilities and of the majority of factories and shops in the city backed them. By midmorning, thousands of working people had gathered in and outside of the Salón Star and overflowed onto nearby Alameda Park, shouting "¡Viva la Huelga!" and celebrating their unity and ability to bring the city to a stop.[70]

Few strike leaders seriously believed that, with the general strike, they were about to seize power and turn it over to workers' syndicates as imagined in the anarchist utopia. But by its very nature, the general strike was a challenge to political authorities. It both expressed the demand of workers for control over their labor and asserted the broader rights of the community of working people to act on the revolution's promises of social justice and to participate fully in the life of the city. One of the significant aspects of this mobilization was its ability to link very different sectors of the city's working population. The makeup of the primary strike committee in many ways was a microcosm of the working class of Mexico City. Its ten members, two of them women, represented the unions of seamstresses (Esther Torres), hat makers, textile workers, electricians, carpenters, waiters, printers, and shop employees, among others. The only numerically significant group of workers missing was domestic servants. According to one estimate, some eighty-two thousand workers participated in the strike, though some may have been strikers by default, since many businesses were forced to close because of the electrical blackout.[71]

The limited participation of the key Casa del Obrero Mundial leaders in the organization of the general strike is significant. The contemporary press and later chronicles suggested that the general strike of July–August 1916 was the product of a handful of anarchist agitators or else the manipulations of opportunist leaders such as Luis Morones. Both explanations are improbable. With the exception of Secretary-General José Barragán Hernández, many of the principal Casa leaders in the city were in jail or out of the city at the time of the strike. The secretary-general of the federation, Luis Morones, was either on his way back from meeting with Samuel Gompers and the American Federation of Labor in Washington DC to urge against U.S. intervention in Mexico or had just returned. Contrary to claims made by his biographer in the 1920s, Morones was not jailed during the strike.[72]

The decision to proceed with the strike, even more so than that of May, was the result of popular pressures expressed through the representative channels of the federation. The general strike was guaranteed broad support among working people by addressing the issue of currency as it affected wages and commerce, by addressing demands to all employers, and ultimately by making the government responsible for its failed monetary policy. If any groups of workers weighed particularly heavily in the organization and implementation of the strike, they were the electricians and streetcar workers, since their participation assured that the strike would shut down the city, and the shop employees, who had taken the first strike initiative a few days earlier. But members of the strike committee later insisted before government officials that the decision to carry out the strike (though not the specific date) was carefully ratified not only by the administrative council of the federation but also by representatives of each of its unions.[73]

The military forces occupying Mexico City wasted little time in responding. Through the auspices of Dr. Atl, Carranza invited the strike committee to negotiate. Instead of discussing their demands, as had occurred with General Hill in May, Carranza immediately court-martialed them, invoking a 1862 law issued by Benito Juárez during the French intervention that imposed martial law and prescribed the death penalty for treason. Martial law was extended throughout the city. In a show of force, troops marched through the major working-class areas of the city as an officer read and posted a series of profoundly antilabor decrees issued by the first chief. The decrees further denied workers the streets, meeting halls, or the right to strike and threatened the death penalty against anyone who disturbed the public peace. Various workers and union leaders were rounded up and jailed, including several electricians who soon revealed the hiding place of Ernesto Velasco. The federation conceded defeat three days later, when Velasco revealed the code necessary to reconnect power lines. With electricity and streetcar service restored, the strike committee and Velasco jailed, and other working-class leaders still being rounded up by police, the popular enthusiasm that had supported the strike dwindled and then collapsed. Even in the face of threats and overt repression, many workers stayed away from work over the next two weeks. When army soldiers were "volunteered" to fill their spots in the major factories of the capital, owners used the opportunity to fire organized workers who came trickling back to demand their jobs.[74]

The Casa del Obrero Mundial was dissolved by a combination of direct force and armed persuasion. While a military court deliberated, Minister of War Alvaro Obregón convinced the Casa del Obrero Mundial leadership to suspend all functions, and the federation was reduced for the next weeks and months to solidarity with the prisoners.

The first court-martial took place on 8 August, when order had been largely restored in a Federal District still under martial law. In a courtroom overflowing with "the working-class element," the government prosecutor insisted that the Juárez Law against treason be applied to the entire strike committee. With U.S. troops in northern Mexico, he claimed, the strike had cut off electricity to an armaments factory in the city—even though three hours later production there had resumed using in-plant generators. Each prisoner denied before the war council that they had intended to obstruct the work of the government, and two made much of their own or their children's service in the Red Battalions. Another explained, "my intention in supporting the strike movement was only to obtain an increase in salary and protest against the abuses of the bosses."[75]

The general strike had clearly been a political challenge and assertion by workers, though not in the sense Carranza claimed—that of a treasonable attempt to bring down the government. The court found the strike committee innocent of the charge of rebellion and instead invoked the 1872 Federal District antistrike decree, finding them guilty of the lesser and distinctly Porfirian crime of "having used moral force implied in a strike to modify salaries of workers." Even such a reduced charge ignored the established gains of labor conflicts and organizations in the previous six years. In addition, two members of the committee were found guilty of the crime of insulting the first chief in comic verses they had composed while in jail.[76]

But even this sentence was not a harsh enough example for Carranza, who upon review rejected the decision, jailed the judge, and convened a new military trial for 26 August. The responsibility of the strikers, argued the president of the second war council, derived from their legal obligation to advise the government that they were going to declare a work stoppage. The council adjourned at midnight and at six o'clock the next morning handed down a death sentence to Velasco on charges of rebellion, releasing the rest of the strike committee. Even this proved unsatisfactory to Carranza, who a few days later had two members of the strike committee and two members of the Casa del Obrero Mundial picked up and jailed for five more months. Velasco's sentence was soon commuted to life imprisonment, and finally in February 1918 he was set free.[77]

The response of Carranza and the Constitutionalist government to the July–August general strike was to legitimize repression by invoking its role in protecting the nation against outsiders. In the weeks that followed, repeated accusations came from official circles that "the enemies of Mexico and the Revolution," reactionary forces at home and abroad, had misled workers. The strikers, Carranza claimed, had "responded to the instigations of North American labor unions," the same claims Porfirio Díaz had made during the Cananea and Rio Blanco conflicts. For good measure, an English-born electrical worker, Luis Harris, and the director of the Anglo-Canadian Light and Power Company, Graham Fulton, were arrested and accused of instigating the strike. (The brief arrest of Fulton was probably justified by the company's public displeasure in the previous weeks over being singled out by authorities and forced to accept payments in Constitutionalist currencies at face value.) The actions and nationalist, anti-imperialist rhetoric of the revolutionary elite in response to the general strike suggested an unlikely collaboration between the two declared enemies of the revolution, foreign-inspired radical agitators and "reactionary" foreign capital. Postrevolutionary governments would repeatedly use nationalism and anti-imperialism to demand unity from working people who might otherwise define their class or community interests differently.[78]

The official newspaper, El Pueblo, directed by Dr. Atl, echoed the official view. Drawing on images from the Casa del Obrero Mundial's recent military past, strike demands for a gold standard, and even the battle cry of the U.S. Populist movement, an editorial lamented that "in every worker, given his present attitude, a soldier has risen WITH HIS RIFLE OF GOLD at the service of CAPITALISM, with the aim of annihilating the MORAL credit of the Government, nullifying its representation in paper money." Moreover, the newspaper asked, what right had workers to make such demands when the majority of those in this "passive city" had never fought in the revolution? The general strike was not really a strike but rather an "eminently anti-revolutionary" and poorly disguised "POLITICAL STRIKE."[79]

Such accusations resonated among many workers who felt a profound uneasiness toward the role of foreigners and foreign capital in the urban economy. In the months leading up to both general strikes, the federation and individual unions had emphasized the foreign origins of employers and merchants in their public denunciations of abuses and had justified their own actions in terms of their fulfillment of patriotic duty. In the weeks after the strike, many groups of workers again insisted on their patriotism as they pursued longstanding demands yet went to great lengths to disassociate themselves from the general strike and its organizers. For example, two weeks after the general strike, workers from the La Carolina textile factory wrote the governor of the Federal District, requesting permission to meet in spite of martial law to study industrywide wage rates. They began by denouncing the Casa del Obrero Mundial, which had almost "swept" them up in acts that were a "black stain of betrayal of the Patria," and ended by insisting on their desire to meet with workers of other textile factories so that "united we can work like good citizens."[80]

Also revealing was Carranza's attitude toward women strikers. He suggested that the women on the strike committee were "overly influenced by the agitators" and ordered them released. Thus in his single act of generosity in relation to these events, Carranza denied women any political agency in the general strike and, by extension, in the mobilizations that had convulsed the city over the previous eighteen months. As if to insist on her own role and that of women in general in the political life of the city, Esther Torres, head of the seamstresses' union, responded, "Sir, we women have the same representation and same responsibility in the strike as our comrades." Carranza answered by jailing and court-martialing them all. Meanwhile, the official press referred to the eight men on the committee as "strikers" (*huelgistas*), whereas the two women on trial, when mentioned at all, were simply "*mujeres complicadas.*"[81] The media's use of the term "*mujeres complicadas*" suggested both that women were "implicated" in the strike without the capacity to be equally responsible for it and that, by their very participation in such a public, political action, these women were "complicated," that is, unruly and problematic, if not quite the *mujerzuelas* who had taken to the streets in the previous summer's consumer riots.

The working people of Mexico City lost the general strike and temporarily lost their organizational integrity; but at least they won some of their concrete demands. As the city resumed a degree of normalcy on 4 August, the government announced a one-month extension on the validity of the old Constitutionalist paper currencies that were to have expired on the day of the general strike. Within three months of the strike, the *infalsificable* peso had dropped from its initial value of ten U.S. cents to a value of less than one U.S. cent. The cycle of food riots, demonstrations, and general strikes in the previous year forced the fledgling government of Carranza to eventually back down from its untenable monetary policies. On the day of elections for the Constitutional Congress in October 1916, Carranza ordered that wages be paid entirely in gold equivalents, in effect abandoning the *infalsificable* and restoring a gold standard.[82] Princeton economist Edwin Kemmerer, Latin America's "money doctor" in the 1910s and 1920s, saw Mexico's restoration of a gold standard in 1916 as the result of the "individual and collective systematic opposition to the paper money, a veritable case of boycott of everybody against everybody." But from his prison cell, electrician Ernesto Velasco saw things differently. He sent First Chief Venustiano Carranza a telegram of congratulations for fulfilling the central demand of the general strike.[83]

* * *

The general strikes of May and July–August 1916 brought to a climax a cycle of popular urban mobilization during the revolution that began with the political mobilization of urban workers in the presidential campaigns of 1909. That cycle was accelerated and shaped by the riots that marked Mexico City through the spring and summer of 1915 and by the consolidation of the union movement after Constitutionalist forces definitively took the city in August 1915.

Citizenship for working people during the revolution was for the most part gendered. While men struggled with their employers over the terms and remuneration of employment, or with political leaders over participation in elections or in the armed revolution, women asserted their citizenship first in defense of their community, often taking over markets, streets, and the halls of government to demand the availability of food and a just exchange value for the product of their husbands' or their own work. But in the process, they moved beyond the private, domestic sphere and asserted themselves as public political actors, challenging merchants, police, and political authorities over the very meaning of a revolution that claimed to be about social justice. This public participation would in turn push organized male workers to incorporate more women into the union movement and to address the consumption issues that remained central to women and the working-class movement as a whole.

Urged on by shortages, commercial speculation in currency and food, and the revolution's promises of social justice, the pattern of working-class organization during the year leading up to the general strikes is notable for its combativeness, the growing unity among workers across differences in skill and gender and around issues of work and consumption, and the increasing independence from and sharpening antagonism with the Constitutionalist leaders of the revolution. Such combativeness was not simply the product of the dire needs of the moment, but rather it drew upon longstanding demands and patterns of organization developed over the previous six years. While the July–August general strike ended in repression, it was part of a series of popular mobilizations that did force Carranza to back down from his failed monetary policies.

In spite of the severe repression of the strike and the labor movement, the poor and working people who had been mobilized in Mexico City during the revolution could be neither ignored nor completely controlled. They had emerged definitively on the municipal and national stages in the years since 1910 and in the postrevolutionary period would seize opportunities to shape and occasionally challenge the structures of work, consumption, and political participation that emerged after 1916.

FIG. 18. During his occupation of the city in February 1915, Obregón publicly humiliated merchants who refused to pay a special tax by making them sweep the streets of the city center. Courtesy of Conaculta-INAH-SINAFO-Fototeca del INAH.

FIG. 19. During the Porfiriato and the revolution, José Guadalupe Posada and his editor regularly used this image of women confronting a shopkeeper to depict consumer shortages and riots. Courtesy of the Harry Ransom Humanities Research Center, the University of Texas at Austin.

FIG. 20. Throughout much of 1915, crowds of women with empty baskets moved between markets and shops in search of food, periodically provoking riots. Courtesy of Conaculta-INAH-SINAFO-Fototeca del INAH.

FIG. 21. Consumer riots even extended to the posh commercial stores in the heart of the city center. Courtesy of Conaculta-INAH-SINAFO-Fototeca del INAH

FIG. 22. In October 1915 the Casa del Obrero Mundial received the Palace of Tiles, formerly the elite Jockey Club, to serve as its headquarters in the heart of the city center. Courtesy of Conaculta-INAH-SINAFO-Fototeca del INAH.

FIG. 23. Printers joined other protestors in May 1919 in denouncing the government's repression of union leaders and failure to pay teachers' salaries. Courtesy of Conaculta-INAH-SINAFO-Fototeca del INAH.

FIG. 24. Members of the Renters' Union of the Federal District during a demonstration at the monument to Juárez in Alameda Park, 1922. Courtesy of Conaculta-INAH-SINAFO-Fototeca del INAH.

FIG. 25. Women rent strikers were the vast majority of those who mobilized on a daily basis to prevent evictions. Their signs in this photograph read, "We're on strike and have not paid rent since May First." Courtesy of Conaculta-INAH-SINAFO-Fototeca del INAH.

8 | THE AFTERMATH OF REVOLUTION

In June 1917 a few former members of the Casa del Obrero Mundial launched another workers' paper, Luz, on a sullen note: "Don't believe that our ardor for the struggle has fallen; what has been diminished is our confidence in the virility of the proletarian phalanxes, in the consciousness of the majority that makes up our class. Events are very eloquent and there are things that are difficult to forget." In the months after the general strike of August 1916, blame and despair reverberated among working-class leaders in Mexico City as repression against their organizations continued and the Juárez Law remained in force. The Casa del Obrero Mundial of Mexico City would never again exist as an independent organization, and the Federation of Workers' Unions of the Federal District remained dormant through the rest of 1916, primarily organizing to press for the release from prison of Ernesto Velasco, the electrician who had borne the brunt of Carranza's wrath over the general strike.[1]

Martial law in the capital made organized working-class participation in elections for the Constitutional Congress, let alone any opposition to Carranza's candidates, impossible. In a further sign of his hostility toward the people of Mexico City, a week after the strike Carranza indefinitely suspended upcoming municipal elections in Mexico City, anticipating a plan he revealed months later in his draft constitution that called for the elimination of the hard-earned municipal autonomy in the capital. To assure further control of potentially unruly popular classes, Carranza decreed an end to bullfights, and the military officers serving as municipal authorities closed down most pulquerías and many dance halls near the downtown area. The frequent arrests made in this period for such crimes as "insolence" and "threats against the governor" suggest both popular defiance and a pronounced insecurity among the city's new masters.[2]

In spite of the bleak days that followed the general strike, the hostility and intransigence of Carranza toward worker organizations and the city of Mexico were not sustainable in the aftermath of the revolution, as gradual economic recovery and political divisions among different generals strengthened the position of incipient labor unions. Other sectors within the military, particularly those close to the Sonoran generals led by Obregón, were far more conciliatory toward labor and much more willing to intervene on labor's behalf, as long as they could determine many of the terms. A fledgling government that proclaimed its revolutionary legitimacy simply could not afford to resort repeatedly to the level of repression used against workers in August 1916.

A few months after the general strike, even as Mexico City remained under martial law, delegates to the constituent congress met in Querétaro, charged with writing a new constitution. Not a single delegate was from the former Casa del Obrero Mundial or the Federation of Workers' Unions of the Federal District, which had been by far the largest labor organizations in the country and had formed the most important contingent of armed workers in the revolution. With a handful of exceptions, such as the Guanajuato miner and union leader Nicolás Cano, workers were not a significant presence in the congress. Labor reforms, barely mentioned in Carranza's draft constitution, were instead pushed by radical generals like Heriberto Jara and by delegates from the state of Yucatán.[3]

The key social charter of the constitution aimed at workers' rights, Article 123, guaranteed the right to organize unions and strikes, finally fulfilling the key demand of labor organizations for legal identity (*personalidad jurídica*) that had been pending since the implementation of a liberal legal order at mid–nineteenth century that favored individual over collective rights. Other provisions established minimal work conditions and went far to restrict employer abuses of workers, providing for an eight-hour day, minimum wages and overtime pay, occupational health and safety, and arbitration boards made up of representatives of employers, workers, and the state. At the same time that the constitution assured a tutelary state role toward labor, its wording and the institutional mechanisms it provided for were cautious warnings to workers against any activities that might threaten public order or challenge the social equilibrium to be carefully administered by the postrevolutionary government. In fact, delegates made frequent references to the general strike of 1916 as they debated and approved Article 123.[4]

Many of the new constitutional labor provisions depended on the initiative of individual states for implementation, at least until the eventual formulation of a federal labor code in 1931.[5] Even so, in Mexico City, where the labor movement had been strong and where political power was so proximate, the guarantees for labor provided in the constitution had an immediate effect. In the aftermath of the Constitutional Congress, the working people of Mexico City began again to organize into unions and assert themselves in the workplace and the public arena, coming up against the hostility of bosses and the growing determination of the new government to mediate the social contradictions between classes.

Even the legal initiation of the new order reflected the inherent tension between the social mobilization of poor and working people and the expansion of government authority over labor. After Carranza handily won the April presidential elections, he chose the symbolic date of 1 May 1917 to inaugurate his own presidency as well as the new constitution. Workers turned out in the streets of Mexico City with genuine enthusiasm to celebrate the new labor charter and the end of military rule. But in spite of Carranza's orchestration of May Day to legitimize his new government, many workers chose to observe the day, as they first had in 1913, as one of protest. The reduced elements of the Federation of Workers' Unions of the Federal District used the return of legal order to organize an alternative demonstration of twenty thousand at the monument to Juárez to demand the release of Velasco from prison. On the same day, a commission of Federal District workers threatened to strike on 2 May if the government did not raise wages, "given that the new constitution legally supported their right to discuss the minimum wage." Over six thousand textile workers from sixteen factories in the Federal District simultaneously invoked their new constitutional rights by starting a two-week strike for higher wages, beginning, as they had under Madero, the first widespread collective test of industrial peace in the new regime. Within days, over forty thousand textile workers were on strike across the nation, insisting on their right to a collective contract as well as to a raise of 75 percent over wages set by the 1912 textile convention.[6]

During Carranza's presidential term, industrialists, encouraged by his conservative policies, tried to undermine the gains workers had made since 1910. Yet workers repeatedly invoked the need to fulfill the new constitution as the central justification for a wave of strikes and other initiatives. For example, on 1 May 1919 thousands of workers marched in Mexico City to protest the government's arrest and military conscription of the leader of a railroad shop workers' strike, forcing Carranza to eventually release the leader and grant the demands of the railroad shop workers. In the same month, the mostly female teachers in the capital went on strike to protest unpaid salaries, seconded by printers, streetcar workers, taxi drivers, bakers, newspaper workers, and the Federation of Workers' Unions of the Federal District (see fig. 23). The strike was finally resolved with a combination of repression and concessions. Threats of and actual solidarity strikes by other unions and the federation were frequent in these years and through the early twenties. In his annual presidential address in 1919, Carranza acknowledged the degree of labor conflict throughout the nation, noting that in the previous months the government had officially recognized some seventy strikes and eighty-five work stoppages, affecting 26,500 workers.[7]

The restoration of constitutional order brought a return to political experimentation among workers similar to that which occurred in 1911–12 after the fall of Díaz. Among the proliferation of political parties that proclaimed their identification with workers, two were significant for their cadres of experienced organizers, programs, and relative independence from the emerging military caudillos of the revolution. In February 1917, a group of "socialists, anarchists, and syndicalists" led by Luis Morones, the relative purist of 1915, announced the formation of the Socialist Workers Party. In their manifesto they explained that their new strategy of "multiple action"—defined as the expansion of the class struggle to politics—was derived from the lessons of the past year, particularly the failure of the general strike. Significantly absent from their manifesto was any reference to an eventual socialist transformation of society or a government of workers. The new party ran candidates for most of the congressional seats in the capital, with highest hopes for Jacinto Huitrón in the heavily working-class District One and for Luis Morones and José Barragán Hernández in other districts. But none were successful, and the party dissolved soon after.[8]

In the following year of 1918, another Socialist Party—the remnant of Paul Zierold's Socialist Workers Party, with virtually the same social democratic program it had introduced in 1911—fielded congressional candidates in Mexico City, including the lawyer Adolfo Santibañez, the miner Nicolás Cano, and two former Casa del Obrero Mundial leaders, Enrique Arce and Timoteo García. In the same elections Luis N. Morones and Ernesto Velasco, the latter recently freed from jail, ran under the banner of the short-lived United Independent Worker and Student Center. In contrast to the electoral experiments of 1911 and 1912, the events of the revolution had produced a cadre of candidates formed in the labor movement, and the new constitution had put labor issues clearly on the national agenda. But similar to 1911–12, working-class political endeavors emerged in the absence of strong citywide or national labor organizations, this time due largely to the repression of 1916. Working-class leaders who aspired to political participation as representatives of workers soon found that no mass political party could succeed in electoral politics without working closely with local and national military chiefs.

After the dissolution of the Casa del Obrero Mundial, the working people of Mexico City began again to rebuild the union movement. With the legal right to organize, unions multiplied, and membership eventually greatly exceeded the levels of 1916. In this effort they would have to negotiate the growing determination of the new government to mediate the social conflicts between classes. By 1918 the lessons and strategies of the next decade for diverse sectors of the urban working class began to emerge. On May Day in 1918 a workers' congress sponsored by the governor of Coahuila began in Saltillo and soon founded a new national labor federation, the Regional Confederation of Mexican Workers (Confederación Regional Obrera Mexicana, or CROM). Luis Morones and a handful of his colleagues wrested control from both the radical delegates (from Mexico City, Tampico, and Veracruz) and the docile unions that Carranza favored to lead the organization.[9]

Competing factions within the revolutionary elite, reflected in the growing tension between President Carranza and Alvaro Obregón, furthered the influence of unions that embraced political strategies. Carranza and CROM leaders remained wary of each other, but the latter were quick to embrace the upstart presidential campaign of Alvaro Obregón, who opposed Carranza's handpicked civilian successor. In 1919, Morones brought the fledgling weight of the CROM behind the creation of the Mexican Labor Party (Partido Laborista Mexicano), formed primarily to support the presidential candidacy of Alvaro Obregón. Their political participation was made urgent, the manifesto of the Labor Party declared, by the "systematic violation of the sacred principles that incarnate the revolution . . . for which they [workers] spilled blood." Labor Party statutes minimized reference to the class struggle but were genuinely nationalist in their insistence on the importance of workers as political actors, on the need for limits on the role of foreign capital, and on the possibilities for the state-supported development of national industry.[10]

As tensions turned to crisis in the presidential campaign, strikes in support of Obregón broke out in Mexico City, Sonora, and elsewhere. When Obregón and Sonoran leaders sprang their Agua Prieta revolt against Carranza in April 1920, the CROM and the Labor Party fully supported the rebellion, and union leadership and rank and file in Mexico City were active in orchestrating strikes, denouncing Carranza, and openly supporting Obregón.[11] When Obregón assumed the presidency after the September elections, the CROM leadership was in a privileged position to incorporate the majority of unions in the Federal District and to assert itself in the workplace as well as in municipal and national politics.

The alliance of the dominant faction of the national labor movement with Gen. Alvaro Obregón, from initial support for his candidacy to his successful rebellion and election, was certainly a heady moment, one that paralleled workers' support for Madero in the elections of 1910 and 1911 yet placed organized labor in a far more prominent role. By lending support to Alvaro Obregón and the Sonorans in their struggle for national power, Morones, the CROM, and the CROM-affiliated Labor Party emerged as powerful players in the construction of mass politics, imposing their organizations and regulations in the workplace and their candidates in local and national politics. For most of the period from 1920 to 1928, the Labor Party dominated municipal politics, controlling either the governorship of the Federal District, held for several years by former shoemaker and Red Battalion stalwart Celestino Gasca, or the Mexico City city council. Since the governor was responsible for administering the arbitration boards made up of worker and employer representatives, as well as for selecting the board's "neutral" state representative, the CROM wielded tremendous power in the negotiation of labor conflicts in the Federal District. Nationally, *Laboristas* formed one of the key blocks in the Federal Congress, with 11 of 58 senators and 40 of 272 deputies in 1926.

The base of the CROM during the early 1920s was primarily in Mexico City and was made up of government employees, urban day laborers, and a variety of unskilled service workers, such as street venders, maids, and theater employees, as well as some textile and most cigarette workers. Unskilled urban workers made the transition to the ranks of the CROM with relative ease. For these workers, whose insertion into the labor market had been relatively weak, stability and regulation of the terms of employment was a fundamental concern and one of the clearest rewards of incorporation into state-sanctioned unions. Of far less importance among these same groups of workers were a few Catholic unions that reemerged in Mexico City after 1917.[12]

CROM leaders, pragmatic men such as Luis Morones, Celestino Gasca, and Samuel Yúdico, had learned from the events of the revolution that cooperation with the new rulers yielded far greater personal rewards and assured affiliated workers a real presence in the workplace and in public affairs, at least for the duration of their patron in power. Through the end of the presidential term of Plutarco Calles in 1928, the CROM and Labor

Party facilitated the new government's protective regulation of the greatest abuses of capital, represented workers' demands—while keeping those demands in check—and incorporated workers into the rituals of political participation. In spite of the personalistic and authoritarian leadership of the CROM, it offered many workers clear benefits in the workplace and helped ensure their loyalty to the new regime.

The Buen Tono cigarette factory is a good example of the pattern of CROM-supported organization in Mexico City. The Buen Tono, with its Porfirian model of authoritarian paternalism and a majority of women workers, was seen by its owners and by inspectors from the Labor Department as immune to labor unrest. During the flurry of organizing in 1914, Buen Tono workers of both sexes joined the Casa del Obrero Mundial, but not in numbers large enough to significantly diminish the tight hierarchical order of the factory. As late as 1920, the "General Regulations" posted in the factory demanded absolute obedience and forbade reading or political discussion. A labor inspector that same year reported that women workers suffered from despotic women supervisors who forced them, on threat of firing, to belong to the factory's religious organization, that they worked ten hours instead of the eight required by the new constitution, and that many became ill from tobacco dust but received inadequate health care and compensation.[13]

Changes began within the Buen Tono factory with the formation in January 1920 of a union among mechanics, who immediately requested a pay raise of 25 percent from the administration. When they were granted a mere 3 percent, the male mechanics organized a Union of Employees and Workers (Union de Empleados, Obreras and Obreros) that incorporated white-collar, skilled, and unskilled workers, including, of course, the factory's female majority. Within a month of its founding, the union led the majority of workers on strike, after the factory director granted their request for an across-the-board raise of 50 percent but refused to recognize the union and fired its secretary-general. Perhaps coincidentally, the strike anticipated by a week Obregón's Agua Prieta rebellion. In September, the month of Obregón's formal election to the presidency, the union went on strike again and won recognition, affiliating around the same time with the CROM.[14]

By the spring of 1923 the factory regime had changed dramatically, at least from the perspective of the union leadership, which commonly referred to the period before 1920 as the "antiguo regimen." "Whoever knew the situation of the workers of this factory before the period of 1920 to the present could not but marvel at the conditions that prevail in the current situation," reported the outgoing secretary-general of the union, a mechanic. By 1922, the union had managed to effectively incorporate 900 of 1,029 workers, implement the eight-hour day, replace a system of arbitrary promotions with a system based on merit, allow workers in each division to choose their own supervisors, and control hiring of new personnel. In addition to such interventions in the production process, the union had successfully pushed the administration to implement the profit-sharing clause mandated in the constitution, initiated night classes for workers, and formed a cooperative for the purchase of basic necessities, starting with a grant in 1920 from provisional president Adolfo de la Huerta.[15]

In spite of the union's considerable power, its goals were clearly reformist. The outgoing secretary-general celebrated the "concord between Capital and Labor" and noted that "we understand that there is a necessity to procure the improvement of the industry and along with it, the situation of all the elements that form it." The union leadership, dominated by skilled male workers, took pride in its efforts at rationalizing various aspects of production in cooperation with management. Indeed, in April 1923, the union reported only two conflicts for the previous eighteen months. The first was an eight-hour strike in November 1921, which successfully removed several women supervisors from the "old regime." While these *maestras* were clearly abusive to women workers and central to the old model of paternalistic boss control, they were also the key organizers of a rival Catholic union, affiliated with the Knights of Columbus, that had grown out of the earlier Catholic society. With their dismissal, the Catholic union collapsed, and the remaining white-collar workers (*empleados*) came around to the official union. The second conflict occurred among workers over the union's decision to replace women with men in various redefined positions that involved "unhealthy" exertion or night work. In addition, the union insisted on a literacy requirement for new workers. While no women were apparently fired, the gradual reduction of positions defined for women reduced the percentage of women employees from 61 percent in 1920 to 51 percent two years later.[16] Thus the workers of the Buen Tono, bastion of Porfirian paternalism, experienced considerable change and real benefits through their union, but in a reformist, top-down pattern that can be generalized for many of the sectors of unskilled labor that affiliated with the CROM.

By contrast, craftworkers, skilled service workers, and a significant portion of textile factory workers tended to initially reorganize in anarchist or independent unions in Mexico City, as did railroad workers, miners, and oil workers nationally. Prominent was the core of craftworkers of the old Casa del Obrero Mundial, the streetcar workers, electricians, textile workers, and bakers. For these workers, issues of control and participation in the workplace remained paramount. Outside the workplace, they struggled to organize autonomously from the consolidating revolutionary elite, in solidarity with other unions and occasionally around issues of consumption. Many of the same leaders and skilled sectors of the city work force organized in anarchist federations, first the short-lived Great Central Corps of Workers (Gran Cuerpo Central de Trabajadores) in 1919 and then the General Confederation of Workers (Confederación General de Trabajadores), which was formed by independent, anarchist, and communist unions that through the early twenties defiantly rejected the impositions of the CROM as well as overt alliances with the government.[17]

Perhaps no group of workers in Mexico City struggled harder to assert themselves in the workplace or in the city at large than the streetcar workers. Their militancy during the revolution and throughout the twenties was rooted in a variety of factors. Many streetcar workers were highly skilled, worked in a historically strategic sector, and had extensive strike experience, beginning within weeks of the fall of Díaz. The foreign ownership and persistent intransigence of the Anglo-Canadian streetcar company infused its labor conflicts with an ardent nationalism, leading to demands for expulsion of foreign managers and government intervention in the company. And after 1915, streetcar workers were quick to invoke their military participation in the Red Battalions.

Carranza finally returned the administration of the Mexico Tramways Company to its Anglo-Canadian owners in May 1919, some four and a half years after his initial intervention in response to the prolonged strike of streetcar workers in October 1914. The restoration of a general director representing foreign owners was a rude shock for the Federation of Employees and Workers of the Mexico Tramways Company, which had achieved considerable participation in the management of the company under government control. Moreover, the restored administration was intent on returning foreigners to key management positions throughout the company and on imposing individual contracts that disavowed the existence of the federation. Within ten days of the return of private management, the streetcar workers shut down the streetcar system throughout the city in solidarity with the teachers' strike, which, as mentioned, soon ended in repression. The general director rejected worker requests in September 1919 and January 1920 for a 50 percent raise, an infirmary, and protection from accidents and random firings, blaming demands on "the seditious and intransigent labor of a few bad employees."[18] But Carranza's fall to the Agua Prieta revolt again shifted the balance between workers and management. In May and again in September 1920, streetcar workers threatened a strike over their earlier demands, on both occasions winning a 25 percent wage increase when the newly appointed governor of the Federal District, CROM leader Celestino Gasca, pressured the company into making concessions.

Over the next three years, streetcar workers were quick to call a series of strikes that paralyzed much of the transportation in the city. Their militant actions were in part shaped by the continuing influence of anarchosyndicalism among the leadership of the federation of streetcar workers, which in turn played a central role in the formation of the General Confederation of Workers in February 1921. Streetcar workers often rejected the constitutional requirement of a ten-day warning before initiating strikes and instead invoked the need to resort to "efficient if violent methods to gain what in justice is demanded." Unions affiliated with the

General Confederation of Workers were quick to muster solidarity strikes, so that streetcar strikes, such as that of June 1922, also brought widespread walkouts in the city's textile factories and bakeries, while conflicts in those sectors frequently shut down the streetcar system.

At the same time, the strategic situation of streetcar workers had deteriorated since 1911. The streetcar system had been fundamental to urban expansion and economic development in Mexico City throughout the Porfiriato, but by the 1920s, a new system of buses with decentralized ownership had begun to gradually displace streetcars. The Mexico Tramways Company began to purchase buses and to shift resources to its sister company, the Mexican Light and Power Company, which by contrast grew rapidly in the 1920s. These trends undermined the strategic hold of streetcar workers over the company and the city as a whole and led them to react aggressively but defensively. When the federation struck, it was often over excessive reductions in hours (as in July 1921) and the laying off of workers (in June 1922 and January 1923), measures taken in part to punish workers for their union activity but also because of the company's financial straits and work rationalizations. In addition, the federation consistently demanded, without success, that the company recognize their organization as the exclusive representative of workers and institutionalize collective contracts.[19]

After the first settlements imposed on the company by Governor Gasca of the Federal District in 1920, the support of Obregón's government for the streetcar workers dwindled, due to the militancy of the federation leadership, the political context of difficult diplomatic negotiations with U.S. banks over Mexican debt and regulations of foreign capital, and antagonisms between the General Confederation of Workers and the officially supported CROM. These trends would culminate on 13 January 1923, when the federation called a strike in response to the company's decision to lay off 10 percent of workers, including many of the oldest and most politically active. After two weeks of fruitless negotiations between workers and management, including meetings with Governor Gasca and President Obregón, a group of dissident workers broke with the federation, formed the Syndicalist Union of Tramway Employers and Workers (Union Sindicalista de Empleados y Obreros de Tranvías), and quickly came to minimal terms with the company. When members of the Syndicalist Union began operating streetcars, escorted by soldiers, they clashed violently with armed workers of the federation in the heart of the city, leading to four deaths and the arrest of 150 federation members. The confrontation dealt a mortal blow to the federation and proved to be a severe setback to the General Confederation of Workers. A few days later, the new Syndicalist Union affiliated with the CROM.

After the Syndicalist Union eventually fell out with the CROM and proved too close to management, the CROM organized a new, minority union, the Alliance of Employers and Workers of the Mexican Tramway and Omnibus Company (Alianza de Empleados y Obreros de la Compañía de Omnibus y Tranvías de México) and promptly initiated a strike against the tramway company in March 1925. When newly elected president Plutarco Calles threatened to expel the foreign managers of the company for failing to recognize the new union, the company reluctantly backed down. Thus the foreign-owned Mexico Tramways Company, pressured by the Mexican government, finally recognized an exclusive union of streetcar workers, though not necessarily the union, nor in the circumstances, for which many streetcar workers had struggled.[20]

If the CROM effectively organized unskilled workers and used its political connections to impose control over recalcitrant employers and even hostile skilled workers, other strategically important groups of workers, such as those organized in the Union of Electricians locally and oil and railroad workers nationally, maintained strong traditions of independent strikes, democratic governance, and political independence throughout the 1920s.

These patterns suggest that, in the immediate postrevolutionary order, the gap between skilled and unskilled and strategic and nonstrategic workers reopened. This gap was even reflected in the locations of the different confederations within the city: in 1922 the anarchist federation was headquartered in the industrial section in the south of the city, and the CROM-affiliated Federation of Workers' Unions of the Federal District was located just north of the center, close to the seat of financial and political power.[21] Alignments along skill lines were not absolute and unchanging but were clear tendencies. Many of the leaders of the CROM, the famous Grupo Acción, were skilled, well educated, and former members of the Casa del Obrero Mundial; but significantly, Morones could not bring his old trade union, the Union of Electricians, into the federation he headed.

In addition, the separation between male and female workers reemerged in the labor movement and probably widened in the workplace. The CROM extended the ranks of its organization to include many unskilled women, such as maids, prostitutes, and other service workers. But the percentage of women in the paid labor force of Mexico City declined dramatically, from 35 percent in 1910 to a low of 17 percent in 1930. This decline was in part the result of the relative success of the union struggle for the "family wage," which allowed many married women to withdraw from the work force. At the same time, employers and unions, often in collaboration (as suggested by trends in the Buen Tono cigarette factory), used regulations meant to protect women workers—such as an end to night work for women and requirements for maternity leave and workplace nurseries—to reduce the number of women in many sectors of the work force, leaving many poor working women more marginalized than ever. For example, women employees in the textile factory San Antonio Abad dropped from 24 percent in 1918 to 14 percent in 1924. In the 1920s the pages of the Revista CROM were filled with advertisements and tips for women on housekeeping and beauty, reinforcing the government's own official celebration of motherhood and domesticity over images of women as soldaderas, rioters, or workers. Even Esther Torres, who briefly served as treasurer of the Federation of Workers' Unions of the Federal District in 1917 and played an active role in the General Confederation of Workers in the early 1920s, would marry and abandon work and activism soon after, a shift related to traditional life-cycle decisions of women as well as to the gendered patterns of work and organization that characterized the 1920s.[22]

Popular, community-based mobilization did not disappear in the 1920s in the face of the formalization of union organization and class-based political identity. Other sources of working-class mobilization, including gendered and consumption demands, continued to be important, as suggested by the events of the 1922 rent strike. The dismal housing conditions in Mexico City before 1910 only worsened in the immediate aftermath of the revolution. The cost of a single room in a tenement, the typical accommodation of much of Mexico City's working population, had more than doubled from 1914 to 1921 as a result of continued postwar inflation, a doubling of the population in Mexico City in the decade of the Mexican Revolution, and a shift of capital from investments in industry and agriculture to speculation in urban real estate, all of which increased the pressure on limited housing stock. According to the 1921 census, only 4 percent of Mexico City residents owned urban property, suggesting a high concentration of property in a city primarily of renters.[23]

Government efforts to ameliorate these conditions were limited. The Labor Department periodically issued descriptions of the deplorable crowding, disrepair, and faulty hygiene of Mexico City tenements to newspapers, identifying the names of the landlords in hopes that embarrassment would remedy conditions. During the revolution, provisional governments had flirted with the regulation of rents. The Convention government in Mexico City imposed a moratorium on any rent increases during much of 1915. In 1916 the Constitutionalist forces imposed emergency rent freezes and limits on evictions of tenants in Mexico City and forced landlords to accept the paper currency that merchants refused; but as public order and a solid currency were restored, these measures were removed, and a series of reform measures brought before Congress were defeated. As in the Porfiriato, rents and housing conditions were left to the determination of the market.[24]

Mobilization of the population around housing issues came in two forms and phases. In the first years of the revolution, workers frequently made housing demands, and the Casa del Obrero Mundial had proposed a series of controls on tenements to Constitutionalist leaders in 1914. In a flurry of organization in 1916, a reformist Renters' League was formed that, over the next years, repeatedly turned to an unsympathetic judicial system to prevent evictions while fruitlessly pushing for laws in Congress to regulate the terms of low-income rentals. Radicalization of tactics of the renters' movement came in February 1922, when the Renters' League transformed itself into a Renters' Union and moved from a legalistic approach to direct action. This shift was primarily due to the inspiration that came from the success of the renters' strike initiated in Veracruz one month earlier as well as the organizational direction that came from an extraordinary group of inspired and untiring organizers in the Communist Youth, which was affiliated with the recently formed Mexican Communist Party. The Communist Party had participated in the formation of the anarchist General Confederation of Workers one year earlier but wasted little time before falling out with them. With no real affiliated unions beyond the bakery workers and a segment of railroad workers, the Communist Party turned to the renters for its social base.[25]

Within a month the Renters' Union had eight thousand members and by early May over thirty thousand. The primary demands of the Renters' Union did not differ much from earlier reformist projects: they sought a drop in rents by 25 percent; an end to security deposits; improved hygiene, plumbing, and repairs; and the creation of overseeing committees to assure these conditions. What differed was their willingness to go beyond legal channels and their determination to force landlords to negotiate as a group, independent of state intervention.

On 1 May the Renters' Union began a rent strike, with approximately thirty thousand members throughout the Federal District refusing to pay their rent. This was backed by a network of committees at the level of each tenement, block, and city district (excluding wealthy District Eight), whose primary activities were to collectively prevent evictions by landlords. Typically as many as five thousand angry renters would turn police evictions away or reinstall someone who had recently been evicted. In coordination with a group of organized carpenters, the Renters' Union used a portion of the withheld rent to implement badly needed repairs in many of the tenements. In addition, they took possession of a series of empty buildings, including a former convent that they used as headquarters.

Participation in the renters' strike was broadly working class, as confirmed by the level of their rents: over 80 percent of those on strike paid less than twenty pesos a month in rent. Similarly, the greatest concentration of striking tenants was in the working-class tenement districts near the train stations, by the factory districts in the south, and east of the central plaza. At the same time, unions themselves were only partially integrated. While unions such as those of railroad workers and public employees supported the strike, the federations they belonged to did not. The General Confederation of Workers considered the Renters' Union to be an instrument of the Communist Party and so withdrew their support during the first month of the strike. The officialist CROM resented all rival social groups and so after a month of uncertainty formed a Union of Renters of its own.

Another characteristic of the renters' movement that further indicates ties to the broader working-class community is the role of women. The vast majority of those who attended meetings in tenements and marches in public plazas and who mobilized on a daily basis to prevent evictions were women, a pattern similar to that of the food riots and confiscations of the decade of military struggle (see fig. 25). But in spite of the apparently decentralized structure of the Renters' Union, all funds and strategic decisions were dominated by its communist leadership, only one of whom was a woman.[26]

From May to mid-June the number of rent strikers rose to over fifty thousand, and the movement remained relatively united. But property owners were soon joined into a single organization dominated by the largest landlords, who put considerable pressure on the government to enforce their property rights. President Obregón, the supreme political juggler, referred the matter to the local authority, which in this case was Gov. Celestino Gasca, a stalwart of the CROM and the Labor Party.

In close collaboration with Governor Gasca, the rival CROM Union of Renters began to negotiate separate short-term deals with landlords, while a series of purges of key leaders of the Communist Party furthered the distance between the leadership and tenant members in the Renters' Union. In the month of July, simultaneous to the repression of the movement in Veracruz, Governor Gasca began to heavily reinforce police carrying out evictions. This forced the Renters' Union into a defensive legality, as they began depositing their unpaid rents in a bank and pressing once again for a government law regulating rents. By September the renters' movement had virtually collapsed.

In the aftermath of the strike, rents and housing conditions in Mexico City remained for the most part unchanged. Government housing policy turned toward sponsoring specific housing colonies on the outskirts of the city, the first such partition completed within a year of the defeat of the rent strike. This policy allowed successive governments to target largess toward specific groups of organized or federal employees, while continuing to restrict low-income access to the high-valued properties of the city center. The demands and participation of the urban poor who lived in tenements and squatter settlements came eventually to be channeled into the popular constituent components of the official, dominant party formed in 1929 and later transformed into the Party of the Institutional Revolution (Partido Revolucionario Institucional, or PRI). With the inflation spurred by World War II, a similar wave of popular protests would force President Avila Camacho to impose a longstanding rent freeze in 1942 in the neighborhoods near the historic center of Mexico City, thus guaranteeing the urban poor a foothold near the heart of the city for another half-century.[27]

Conclusion

While the actions of urban workers and masses rarely paralleled the armed insurrection of much of the Mexican peasantry during the revolution, the working people of Mexico City helped shape the revolution and postrevolutionary society. This book shows the prominence of labor after the revolution to be the result of a continuous cycle of largely autonomous urban mobilization that began years earlier. If one climax of that cycle—the general strike—ended in repression, it was also part of a series of popular challenges that helped form the postrevolutionary consolidating project of the northern revolutionary elite and pushed organized labor to unprecedented prominence in the postrevolutionary political system.

In telling this story, I have developed several related insights. First, I have argued that an important basis for understanding the social conflicts and political outcomes of this period is the transformation of Mexico City before the revolution. The Porfirian development model strengthened the dominance of Mexico City as the political, financial, and commercial capital of the nation. One result of the city's primacy over the rest of the country was a rapid increase in the population. Another manifestation was the rise to power of a small group of national and foreign merchant-industrialists and political elites, buttressed by a growing number of professionals and government employees, who envisioned Mexico City as above all the modern capital of a modernizing nation and sought to remake it accordingly.

In addition to the growth of the city, another change was the formation of a working class. The introduction of new technologies, often by foreign companies or foreign-born entrepreneurs, allowed a handful of large and medium companies to dominate manufacturing, services, and commerce. As a result, the labor force was transformed, giving rise to a small but significant industrial proletariat, the displacement of many craftworkers, and the creation of new opportunities for skilled workers in the new modern infrastructure of the city. In spite of these changes, the demand for unskilled workers of both sexes, primarily in the service sector, continued to predominate in the labor market, thus reinforcing the historic gap between skilled and unskilled and male and female workers.

At the same time, the very space of the city was transformed, as broad new avenues, public investments, and new streetcars allowed different areas of the city to become more specialized in function and as traditional multiclass neighborhoods gave way to wealthy and middle-class suburbs on the west side of the city and working-class neighborhoods and squatter settlements on the eastern and southern periphery. Thus the transformations of both the city and its work force brought new identities of collective action that helped raise fundamental questions about the character of the Mexican Republic and undermined support for the government of Porfirio Díaz.

Second, I have shown that urban workers in Mexico City embraced the opportunities for relatively free organization that emerged in 1910. Central to this process of organization was workers' understanding of their historical experience. A significant portion of workers in Mexico City rejected Porfirian paternalism and backed the candidacy of Madero in the 1910 presidential elections, in the process drawing on a type of "popular" liberalism that invoked the historical role of workers in building the nation, through their own labor and through their participation in nineteenth-century battles against foreigners and conservatives. The struggle against the tyranny of the political system of Porfirio Díaz was equated with workers' struggles against abuse and exploitation in the workplace, both of which were often linked to the role of foreigners in Mexico.

After the fall of Díaz, the possibilities for political participation by workers under Madero's reformist democratic experiment proved slow, ineffective, and disappointing, with the limited exception of the textile convention. Excluded from real participation in the new government or significant improvements in the workplace, working people turned their efforts to the formation of a more autonomous working-class movement with a focus on workplace and community mobilization. European radical ideologies, including anarcho-syndicalism, mixed with the nationalism and popular liberalism of workers and provided an important encouragement to mass mobilization. With a national background of heightened polarization, strategic and numerically significant groups of workers in Mexico City became radicalized after the congressional elections of 1912, incorporating more than ever before the language of class into their speeches and publications and moving from traditions of mutualism to more sustained organization in formal unions and cultural groups such as the Casa del Obrero Mundial. New organizations incorporated an unparalleled number of working people in Mexico City and helped to bring together workers who had historically been separated by skill, gender, and cultural traditions.

During the revolution, workers confronted employers and made demands on government officials in ways that reflected long-held aspirations yet were unprecedented in their assertiveness and scale. Radicalization was a response to new ideas, conditions, opportunities, and organization. But the increasing militancy of workers, even though influenced by the vocabulary and methods of anarcho-syndicalism, was aimed not at overthrowing capitalism but rather at addressing the worst abuses of industry (particularly when foreign owned or managed), asserting greater control over aspects of the work process, and assuring just wages and work conditions. The collective actions of working people in and out of the workplace invoked not only class-based demands but also citizenship rights to which they felt entitled by their role in Mexican development and in the revolution.

Labor conflicts began among textile and newly organized craftworkers and by the fall of 1914 had extended to almost every sector in the city, including those in which women were a majority. Mobilization among working people during the revolution took on particular significance and momentum when it joined skilled and unskilled workers and included consumption demands that echoed those of the popular classes. In this respect, women played an important role in establishing the link between work and community.

Although the union movement incorporated women into unions and strikes, mobilization within the working-class community was, like work and domestic life, gendered. Men struggled with their employers and with political leaders over the terms of work, over participation in elections, and in the armed revolution, while women asserted their citizenship first in defense of their community, often taking over markets, tenements, streets, and the halls of government to demand the availability of food and a just exchange value for the product of their husbands' and their own work. Through these types of mobilizations, which often occurred independently and alongside the more formal mobilizations of men, women asserted themselves as public political actors and pushed organized male workers to incorporate more women into the union movement and to address the consumption issues that remained central to women, and therefore to the working-class community as a whole. This pattern is manifest in the participation of women in food riots, the general strike of July–August 1916, and the rent strike of 1922.

Finally, a key theme of the book has been the labor movement's coming to terms with the national revolution. The attitude of Mexico City workers toward government intervention varied among sectors and over time. During the Restored Republic and the Porfiriato, factory workers, denied independent organization, commonly turned to government officials to mediate their conflicts with industrialists. Craftworkers had developed both a tradition of political participation and, because of those experiences, a deep distrust of the state. From 1910 to 1912, workers looked to the political opposition and then to the Madero government to realize their demands. By contrast, the failures of the Madero government and the vacuum of political authority during the years from 1912 to 1914 facilitated independent mobilization by workers, even as worker mobilization that exceeded the limits of tolerance of military leaders risked repression.

With the defeat of Huerta, workers encountered revolutionary leaders willing to regulate by decree many of the insecurities of work and to force foreign and national employers to negotiate with unions and to give workers a role in wage, hiring, and even production decisions. In spite of its declared principle of opposition to all forms of government and of political neutrality in the struggle between the Convention and Constitutionalist factions, the Casa del Obrero Mundial and affiliated unions quietly received favors and support from the Constitutionalists that helped them to consolidate their organizations and expand their membership to include the unskilled workers, who were a majority of the city's population. The role of foreigners in the urban economy also influenced worker attitudes toward intervention in industrial conflicts by revolutionary generals and eventually the postrevolutionary state. The predominance of foreign-born entrepreneurs and managers in the city heightened the sense of injustices among workers and accelerated notions of solidarity; at the same time, solidarity moved along a nexus of class and nationalism, disposing many workers toward alliances with nationalist revolutionary generals willing to curb the worst abuses of modern industry or even willing to momentarily take over the administration of some foreign companies, such as the Mexico Tramways Company and the Telephone and Telegraph Company in Mexico City.

With the split between the Constitutionalists and the Convention, formal neutrality for the Casa del Obrero Mundial became harder to maintain. The decision of a portion of the Casa del Obrero Mundial in Mexico City to take up arms in support of Constitutionalist leaders in 1915 was the result of material hardship and unemployment in Mexico City, the disarray of the Convention government during its occupation of the city, the contrasting interventions of Obregón on behalf of the working-class community, and tensions within the greatly expanded organization. A final factor was the belief by many workers—galvanized by anarchism but raised in popular liberalism—that they had a fundamental national role to play, both as citizens serving their country and as workers pressing for greater social transformation. Thus their coming to terms with the Constitutionalists was in many ways a return to the political strategy that began in 1910 with the Madero campaign, though now in support of political leaders far more willing to act quickly and decisively on workers' behalf. Even so, the elements of the Casa who chose adherence to the Constitutionalist cause immediately tried to assert themselves and impose many of their own terms in their difficult relationship with their new allies, while those who stayed in Mexico City continued to organize workers and make demands on employers, sustaining an intense cycle of labor conflicts. The consumer riots of 1915, the revitalization of a unified union movement after the disbanding of the Red Battalions, and the general strikes of May and July–August 1916 brought this cycle of popular urban mobilization to a climax, characterized as much by open conflict between working people and the Constitutionalist leaders of the revolution as by collaboration.

Ultimately, the response of the working people of Mexico City to the revolution was organizational rather than insurrectional. The decision of some workers to take up arms in 1915 was more in the nature of an alliance than a rebellion. Similarly, the general strikes of 1916 were more an assertion by working people within the existing economic and new political order than an attempt to overthrow capitalism or existing political authorities. The pattern of mobilization, accommodation, and confrontation by which the working people of Mexico City asserted their presence as workers, members of a community, and citizens of the nation during the decade after 1910 established many of the possibilities and limits for popular urban participation in postrevolutionary Mexico.

With his repression of the general strike of July–August 1916, First Chief Carranza responded to the previous half-decade of working-class organization in Mexico City. But repression slowed, but did not end, the pattern of working-class mobilization that began with Madero's electoral campaign. Previous and ongoing mobilizations of working people forced the faction that triumphed in the revolution, particularly leaders like Obregón and Calles, to acknowledge their importance.

In the aftermath of the general strikes and the military revolution, the working people of Mexico City gained some of the collective power and protection to which they had aspired before and during the revolution. The right to organize, shorter hours, limits on arbitrary firings, and minimum wages—though applied unevenly and constantly negotiated with political bosses and employers—were real gains that gave many workers security, a sense of dignity, and greater leisure time.

If anything, the combativeness of working people increased in the early twenties, fortified by their experiences of the revolution and the promises of the constitution. The frequency of strikes in the early 1920s belies any description of the labor movement in this period as one of docile dependence, even if many of the conflicts were between workers associated with different unions or federations. Similarly, the prominence of labor leaders in the twenties in appointed and elected political positions, while not without precedent in the nineteenth century, was a dramatic change from the political exclusion of workers in the late Porfirian period and in the first years of the revolution. In spite of renewed divisions among workers and the reliance of leading unions on an authoritarian, populist state, the working people of Mexico City had established themselves as key social actors in the political and economic affairs of the nation.

Notes

INTRODUCTION

1. Frank Tannenbaum, *Peace by Revolution: Mexico after 1910* (New York: Columbia University Press, 1966).

2. John Womack Jr., "The Mexican Revolution, 1910–1920," in *The Cambridge History of Latin America*, ed. Leslie Bethall (Cambridge: Cambridge University Press, 1986), 5:79–154; Ramón Eduardo Ruiz, *The Great Rebellion: Mexico, 1905–1924* (New York: Norton, 1980).

3. Alan Knight, *The Mexican Revolution*, 2 vols. (Cambridge: Cambridge University Press, 1986); John M. Hart, *Revolutionary Mexico: The Coming and Process of the Mexican Revolution* (Berkeley: University of California Press, 1987).

4. Adolfo Gilly, *La Revolución interrumpida: México, 1910–1920* (Mexico City: Ediciones El Caballito, 1974).

5. Rosendo Salazar and José Escobedo, *Las pugnas de la gleba* (Mexico City: Editorial Avante, 1922); Luis Araiza, *Historia del movimiento obrero mexicano*, 2d ed., 4 vols. (Mexico City: Ediciones de la Casa Mundial, 1964–66, 1975); Jacinto Huitrón, *Orígenes e historia del movimiento obrero en México* (Mexico City: Editores Mexicanos Unidos, 1984); Marjorie Ruth Clark, *Organized Labor in Mexico* (Chapel Hill: University of North Carolina Press, 1934; reprint, New York: Russell and Russell, 1974); John M. Hart, *Anarchism and the Mexican Working Class, 1860–1931* (Austin: University of Texas Press, 1978, 1987).

6. Barry Carr, *El movimiento obrero y la política en México, 1910/1929* (Mexico DF: Ediciones Era, 1976); Ramón Eduardo Ruiz, *Labor and the Ambivalent Revolutionaries* (Baltimore: Johns Hopkins University Press, 1976); Rocío Guadarrama, *Los sindicatos y la política en México: La CROM* (Mexico City: Era, 1981).

7. Hobart Spalding, *Organized Labor in Latin America* (New York: Harper and Row, 1977).

8. Charles Bergquist, *Labor in Latin America: Comparative Essays on Chile, Argentina, Venezuela, and Colombia* (Stanford: Stanford University Press, 1986).

9. Emilia Viotti da Costa, "Experience versus Structures: New Tendencies in the History of Labor and the Working Class in Latin America—What Do We Gain? What Do We Lose?" *International Labor and Working-Class History* 36 (fall 1989): 3–24.

10. For Latin America, see in particular the essays in John French and Daniel James, eds., *The Gendered Worlds of Latin American Women Workers* (Durham NC: Duke University Press, 1997). For Mexico, a work of fundamental importance is Rodney Anderson, *Outcasts in Their Own Land: Mexican Industrial Workers, 1906–1911* (DeKalb: Northern Illinois University Press, 1976). More recent works in a similar vein are Bernardo García Díaz, *Un pueblo fabril del Porfiriato: Santa Rosa, Veracruz* (Mexico DF: Fondo de Cultura Económica, 1981); Alan Knight, "The Working Class and the Mexican Revolution, c. 1900–1920," *Journal of Latin American Studies* 16 (1984): 51–79; María Elena Díaz, "The Satiric Penny Press for Workers in Mexico, 1900–1910: A Case Study in the Politicisation of Popular Culture," *Journal of Latin American Studies* 22, no. 3 (1990): 497–526; Jonathan C. Brown, *Oil and Revolution in Mexico* (Berkeley: University of California Press, 1993); William French, *A Peaceful and Working People: Manners, Morals, and Class Formation in Northern Mexico* (Albuquerque: University of New Mexico Press, 1996).

11. Temma Kaplan, "Female Consciousness and Collective Action: The Case of Barcelona, 1910–1918," *Signs: Journal of Women in Culture and Society* 7, no. 31 (1982): 545–66, and *Red City, Blue Period: Social Movements in Picasso's Barcelona* (Berkeley: University of California Press, 1992); Pamela Beth Radcliff, *From Mobilization to Civil War: The Politics of Polarization in the Spanish City of Gijön, 1900–1937* (Cambridge: Cambridge University Press, 1996).

1. THE SOCIAL GEOGRAPHY

1. A. Dupin de St. Andre, *Le Mexique aujourd'hui* (Paris: E. Plon, 1884), 48; Salvador Diego Fernández, *La Ciudad de Méjico a fines del siglo XIX* (Mexico City, 1937), 5; Elizabeth Blake, *Mexico: Picturesque, Political, and Progressive* (Boston: C. T. Dillingham, 1888), 58. Translations of quotations from foreign documents and publications are my own unless otherwise specified.

2. Adolfo Dollero, *México al día: Impresiones y notas de viaje* (Mexico City: Bouret, 1911), 11; Julio Sesto, *El México de Porfirio Díaz* (Valencia: F. Sempere y Compañía, 1910), 129.

3. Alec Tweedie, *Mexico As I Saw It* (New York: Macmillan, 1901), 220; José Romero, *Guía de la Ciudad de México* (Mexico: Porrua, 1910), 211; T. Philip Terry, *Terry's Mexico* (New York: Houghton Mifflin, 1911), 232–40; Moisés González Navarro, *Historia moderna de México: El Porfiriato: La vida social* (Mexico City: El Colegio de México, 1957), 789.

4. Nevin Winter, *Mexico and Her People Today* (Boston: Page Company, 1907), 46.

5. *México Obrero*, 3 September 1909.

6. James Scobie, "The Growth of Latin American Cities, 1870–1930," in *The Cambridge History of Latin America*, ed. Leslie Bethall (Cambridge: Cambridge University Press, 1986), 4:233–66.

7. Gilbert Joseph, *Revolution from Without: Yucatán, Mexico and the United States, 1880–1924* (Durham NC: Duke University Press, 1988); Scobie, "The Growth," 245.

8. Jeffrey Needall, *A Tropical Belle Époque Elite Culture and Society in Turn-of-the-Century Rio de Janeiro* (Cambridge: Cambridge University Press, 1987), 1–51; James Scobie, *Buenos Aires: Plaza to Suburb, 1870–1910* (New York: Oxford University Press, 1974); Barbara Tenenbaum, "Streetwise History: The Paseo de la Reforma and the Porfirian State, 1876–1910," in *Rituals of Rule, Rituals of Resistance: Public Celebrations and Popular Culture in Mexico*, ed. William Beezley, Cheryl English Martin, and William French (Wilmington DE: Scholarly Resources, 1994), 127–50.

9. Jeffrey Needall, "The *Revolta Contra Vacina* of 1904: The Revolt against 'Modernization' in Belle-Époque Rio de Janeiro," *Hispanic American Historical Review* 67, no. 2 (May 1987): 233–69; Teresa Meade, "'Living Worse and Costing More': Resistance and Riot in Rio de Janeiro, 1890–1917," *Journal of Latin American Studies* 21, no. 2 (May 1989): 241–66.

10. See essays in Alejandra Moreno Toscano, ed., *Ciudad de México: Ensayo de construcción de una historia* (Mexico City: INAH, 1978); Jorge H. Jiménez Muñoz, *La traza del poder: Historia de la política y los negocios urbanos en el Distrito Federal* (Mexico City: CODEX, 1993); Tenenbaum, "Streetwise History"; Mauricio Tenorio-Trillo, "1910 Mexico City: Space and Nation in the City of the Centenario," *Journal of Latin American Studies* 28, no. 1 (February 1996): 75–104; Michael Johns, *The City of Mexico in the Age of Díaz* (Austin: University of Texas Press, 1997).

11. Andrés Lira, *Comunidades indígenas frente a la Ciudad de México* (Mexico City: Colegio de México, 1983); Fanny Calderón de la Barca, *Life in Mexico* (Berkeley: University of California Press, 1982), 101, 113.

12. Jan Bazant, *The Alienation of Church Property* (Cambridge: Cambridge University Press, 1971), 114; María Dolores Morales, "Estructura urbana y distribución de la propiedad de la Ciudad de México en 1813," in *Ciudad de México*, ed. Moreno Toscano, 72.

13. Fanny Gooch, *Face to Face with the Mexicans* (New York: Fords, Howard, and Hubert, 1887), 172; Diego Fernández, *La Ciudad*, 11.

14. Jaime Rodríguez Piña, "Las vecindades en 1811," in *Investigaciones sobre la historia de la Ciudad de Mexico*, ed. Alejandra Moreno et. al (Mexico City: INAH, 1976); Terry, *Terry's Mexico*, 348–50; Miguel Macedo, *Mi barrio* (Mexico City: Departamento del Distrito Federal, 1930), 27, 30, 49.

15. Jorge González Angulo Aguirre, *Artesanado y ciudad a finales del siglo XVIII* (Mexico City: SEP, 1983), 122; Adriana Lopez Monjardín, *Hacia la ciudad del capital: México, 1790–1870* (Mexico City: INAH, 1985), 166.

16. Gooch, *Face to Face*, 164.

17. Alejandra Moreno Toscano, "Cambios en los patrones de organización en México, 1810–1910," *Historia Mexicana* 22, no. 2 (1972): 185; Richard Boyer, "Las ciudades mexicanas: perspectivas de estudios en el siglo XIX," *Historia Mexicana* 22, no. 2 (1972): 142.

18. Terry, *Terry's Mexico*, 232.

19. Paul J. Vanderwood, *Disorder and Progress: Police and Mexican Development* (Lincoln: University of Nebraska Press, 1981), 120–24; John Womack Jr., *Zapata and the Mexican Revolution* (New York: Vintage, 1968), 16–20; Mark Wasserman, *Capitalists, Caciques, and Revolution in Chihuahua: The Native Elite and Foreign Enterprise in Chihuahua, Mexico, 1854–1911* (Chapel Hill: University of North Carolina Press, 1984).

20. Richard Boyer and Keith Davies, *Urbanization in Nineteenth Century Latin America: Statistics and Sources* (Los Angeles: UCLA, 1973), 33, 42.

21. Stephen Haber, *Industry and Underdevelopment: The Industrialization of Mexico, 1890–1940* (Stanford: Stanford University Press, 1989), 68–69; María Dolores Morales, "Francisco Somera y el primer fraccionamiento de la Ciudad de México, 1840–1889," in *Formación y desarrollo de la burguesía en México*, ed. Ciro F. S. Cardoso (Mexico City: Siglo XIX, 1987).

22. Archivo Histórico del Ex-Ayuntamiento de la Ciudad de México (AHCM), 402:727.

23. David Walker, "Porfirian Labor Politics: Working Class Organizations in Mexico City and Porfirio Diaz, 1876–1902," *Americas* 37, no. 3 (1981): 257–89; AHCM, Regidores, 3891.

24. *Mexican Herald*, September 1910, centenary edition.

25. Tenenbaum, "Streetwise History"; Tenorio-Trillo, "1910 Mexico City."

26. Manuel Vidrio, "Sistemas de transporte y expansión urbana: Los tranvías," in *Ciudad de México*, ed. Moreno Toscano, 206; Diego Fernández, *La Ciudad*, 39.

27. Terry, *Terry's Mexico*, 236; *The Mexican Year Book* (London: Mexican Year Book Pub. Co., 1908), 570; Vidrio, "Sistemas," 215.

28. Manuel Gutiérrez Nájera, *La novela del tranvía y otros cuentos* (Mexico City: Fondo de Cultura Económica, 1984), 159; Verena Radkau, *"Por la debilidad de nuestro ser": Mujeres "del pueblo" en la paz porfiriana* (Mexico City: SEP, 1989), 70.

29. José Cossio, *Del México viejo* (Mexico City, 1935), 116; Morales, "Francisco Somera," 208; Lira, *Comunidades indígenas*.

30. M. Marroquin y Rivera, *El proyecto de abastecimiento de agua para la Ciudad de México* (Mexico City: Secretaría de Fomento, 1901), map 1.

31. José Lorenzo Cossio, "Algunas noticias sobre las colonias de esta capital" *Boletín de la Sociedad Mexicana de Geografía y Estadística* 5 (1937): 12, 47; María Dolores Morales, "La expansión de la Ciudad de México en el siglo XIX: El caso de los fraccionamientos," in *Investigaciones*, ed. Moreno Toscano et al., 189.

32. Sonia Lombardo de Ruiz, "Ideas y proyectos urbanísticos de la Ciudad de México, 1788–1850," in *Ciudad de México*, ed. Moreno Toscano, 183.

33. *Mexican Herald*, September 1910, centenary edition, 105; Morales, "Francisco Somera," 217, 227.

34. María del Carmen Collado, *La burguesía mexicana: El emporio Braniff y su participación política, 1865–1920* (Mexico City: Siglo XXI, 1987), 69–73.

35. Terry, *Terry's Mexico*, 255; Cossio, "Algunas noticias," 32.

36. William Beezley, *Judas at the Jockey Club and Other Episodes of Porfirian Mexico* (Lincoln: University of Nebraska Press, 1987), chap. 1.

37. Dirección General de Estadística, *Censo general de población por entidades, 1900, Distrito Federal* (Mexico City: Dirección General de Estadística, 1901–7), 4, 93–95.

38. Diego Fernández, *La Ciudad*, 11.

39. Morales, "La expansión," 196; Dirección General de Estadística, *Censo general de la República Mexicana*, 1895 (Mexico City: Dirección General de Estadística, 1897–1899), and *Censo general de habitantes* (Mexico City: Dirección General de Estadística, 1925–28); census data reproduced in *Memoria y encuentros: La Ciudad de México y el Distrito Federal (1824–1928)*, ed. Hira de Gortari Rabiela and Regina Hernández Franyuti (Mexico City: Instituto Mora, 1988), 3:281–82.

40. Sanborn Map Company, *Insurance Maps of City of Mexico* (New York: The Company, 1905); Terry, *Terry's Mexico*, 257; Carlos Aguirre Anaya, "Jerarquía y distribución de los usos del suelo no habitacionales en la Ciudad de México a finales del siglo XIX," in *Población y estructura urbana en México, siglos XVIII y XIX*, ed. Carmen Blázquez Domínguez, Carlos Contreras Cruz, and Sonia Pérez Toledo (Veracruz: Universidad Veracruzana, 1996), 339–41.

41. Haber, *Industry and Underdevelopment*, 65–74; José Luis Ceceña, "La penetración extranjera y los grupos de poder económico en el México Porfirista," in *México en el siglo XX*, ed. Mario Contreras and Jesus Tamayo (Mexico City: UNAM, 1975).

42. Tenorio, "1910 Mexico City."

43. Cossio, *De México viejo*, 120; Morales, "Francisco Somera," 192; Jorge Angulo Aguirre and Yolanda Terán Trillo, *Planos de la Ciudad de México* (Mexico City: INAH, 1976).

44. *Mexican Herald*, September 1910, 105; Romero, *Guía*, 154; Ann Shelby Blum, "Children without Parents: Law, Charity and Social Practice, Mexico City, 1867–1940" (Ph.D. diss., University of California, Berkeley, 1998), chap. 3.

45. Romero, *Guía*, 154; Blum, "Children without Parents," chap. 3.

46. Allen Wells and Gilbert M. Joseph, "Modernizing Visions, Chilango Blueprints, and Provincial Growing Pains: Mérida at the Turn of the Century," *Mexican Studies/Estudios Mexicanos* 8, no. 2 (1992): 175.

47. Beezley, *Judas*, 12; Gonzalo De Murga, "Atisbos sociológicos," *Boletín de la Sociedad de Geografía y Estadísticas* 6 (1913): 479, 486; Angel del Campo cited in Carlos Aguirre Anaya, "Jerarquía y Distribución," 350.

48. González Navarro, *La vida social*, 85, 86: Wallace Thompson, *The People of Mexico* (New York: Harper, 1921), 254.

49. Archivo General de la Nación (AGN), Ramo Trabajo (RT), 320:11.

50. AGN, RT, 227:5.

51. AGN, RT, 320:11.

52. AGN, RT, 223:10.

53. José Antonio Rojas Loa, "Población y vivienda en la zona central de la Ciudad de México, 1970," in Investigaciones, ed. Moreno Toscano et al., 59.

54. Morales, "Francisco Somera," 218; González Navarro, La vida social, 87, 89.

55. Bureau of American Republics, Mexico (Washington DC: Government Printing Office, 1907), 64; González Navarro, La vida social, 89; Gooch, Face to Face, 191.

56. Enrique Creel et al. Concurso científico y artístico del centenario (Mexico City: Tip. de la Viuda de F. Díaz de León, 1911); González Navarro, La vida social, 85–86.

57. Dirección General de Estadística, Censo, 1900, 4; Macedo, Mi barrio, 64; AHCM, Alojamiento, 1378, 360; González Navarro, La vida social, 90; John Kenneth Turner, Barbarous Mexico (Austin: University of Texas Press, 1969), 97–98.

58. Murga, "Atisbos sociólogicos," 479, 486.

59. Beezley, Judas, 112–15, 128.

60. Miguel Macedo, La criminalidad en México (Mexico City: Secretaría de Fomento, 1897), 60; Juan Felipe Leal and Mario Huacuja Rountree, Economía y sistema de haciendas en México: La hacienda pulquera en el cambio (Mexico City: Era, 1984), 121; Nueva Era, 25 January 1912.

61. Macedo, La criminalidad, 32; Mexican Herald, 16 September 1910, 105; Macedo, La criminalidad, 6; AHCM, 2684; Mexican Herald, 16 May 1910.

62. Guía Tremulla (Mexico City, 1906), 134; Mexican Year Book, 564; Diego Fernández, La Ciudad, 5; Terry, Terry's Mexico, 259; Dollero, México al día, 17.

63. Juan Pedro Viqueira Albán, Relajados o reprimidos? Diversiones públicas y vida social en la Ciudad de México duranate el Siglo de las Luces (Mexico: Fondo de Cultura Económica, 1987); AHCM, tomo 3645, ex. 1712; Pablo Piccato Rodríguez, "Criminals in Mexico City, 1900–1931: A Cultural History" (Ph.D. diss., University of Texas, 1997), chap. 1.

64. María Dolores Morales, "Rafael Martínez de la Torre y la creación de fraccionamientos: El caso de la colonia Guerrero," in Investigaciones, ed. Moreno Toscano et al.; Murga, "Atisbos sociólogicos," 489; Moisés González Navarro, Población y sociedad en México (Mexico: UNAM, 1974), 84, 86.

65. Murga, "Atisbos sociólogicos," 484; *Mexican Herald*, 22 June 1908, 2.

66. Erica Berra Stoppa, "La expansión de la Ciudad de México y los conflictos urbanos, 1900–1930" (Ph.D. diss., El Colegio de México, 1982), 392–99; Victor Manuel Sánchez Sánchez, *Surgimiento del sindicalismo electricista* (Mexico City: UNAM, 1978), 176.

67. Antonio Ramos Pedrueza, "Reglamento para las fabricas de hilados y tejidos en la republica," 17 July 1912 (copy found in AGN, RT, 91:8); Ira Katznelson, "Working Class Formation and the State: Nineteenth-Century England in American Perspective," in *Bringing the State Back*, ed. Peter Evans, Dietrich Rueschemeyer, and Theda Skocpol (Cambridge: Cambridge University Press, 1985), 267.

68. *El Imparcial*, 9 April 1902, quoted in Morales, "La expansión," 200.

69. AHCM, Colonias, 519:22; Cossio, "Algunas noticias," 22–35; Dirección General de Estadística, *Censo, 1900*, 6.

70. Beezley, *Judas*, 27, 30.

71. Terry, *Terry's Mexico*, 257; Dollero, *México al día*, 20–25; González Navarro, *La vida social*, 88; Dirección General de Estadística, *Censo, 1900*, 4.

72. *Mexican Herald*, 22 June 1908, 2; Cossio, "Algunas noticias," 23; Terry, *Terry's Mexico*, 257; Dollero, *México al día*, 28; AGN, RT, 5:1; Gustavo Casasola, *Historia gráfica de la Revolución Mexicana*, vol. 2 (Mexico City: Trillas, 1992); Beezley, *Judas*, 115.

73. Macedo, *La criminalidad*, 6.

2. WORLDS OF WORK

1. Entrevista con la Señora Esther Torres, viuda de Morales, realizado por María Isabel Souza y Carmen Nava, los días 13 y 25 de febrero de 1975 en la Ciudad de Mexico, Archivo de la Palabra, Instituto Mora, PHO/1/145; and oral interview, in Jorge Basurto, *Vivencias femeninas de la Revolución* (Mexico: INEHRM, 1992), 52–53.

2. Huitrón, *Orígenes*, 73–84.

3. Hira de Gortari Rabiela, "¿Un modelo de urbanización? La Ciudad de México de finales del siglo XIX," *Secuencia: Revista de Ciencias Sociales* 8 (May–August 1987): 42–52; Stephen Haber, "La industrialización de México: historiografía y análisis," *Historia Mexicana* 42, no. 3 (1993): 649–88.

4. Secretaria de Industria, Comercio y Trabajo, *Monografía sobre el estado actual de la industria en México*, appendix 2 (Mexico: Talleres Gráficos de la Nación, 1929), 32; Haber, *Industry and Underdevelopment*.

5. Jonathan Brown, "Foreign and Native-born Workers in Porfirian Mexico," *American Historical Review* 98, no. 3 (June 1993): 786–818; Huitrón, *Orígenes*, 73–84.

6. John Coatsworth, *Growth against Development: The Economic Impact of Railroads in Porfirian Mexico* (DeKalb: Northern Illinois University Press, 1981), 75; García Díaz, *Un pueblo fabril*, 32–41, appendix.

7. Boyer and Davies, *Urbanization*, 33, 42; Dirección General de Estadística, *Censo, 1900*; Dirección General de Estadística, *Censo de población de los Estados Unidos Mexicanos, 1910* (Mexico City: Dirección General de Estadística, 1918–20); Luis Unikel, *Dinámica de la población de México* (Mexico City: Colegio de México, 1970), 122, 129, and table v–12.

8. Departamento de la Estadística Nacional, *Censo general de habitantes, 1921. Distrito Federal* (Mexico City: Departamento de la Estadística Nacional, 1925), table 19, 59; Dirección General de Estadística, *Censo, 1900*; Francois Xavier Guerra, *México: Del Antiguo Régimen a la Revolución*, vol. 1 (Mexico City: Fondo de Cultura Económica, 1988), 338; Gilberto Loyo, *La política demográfica de México* (Mexico: La Impresora, 1935), 214, 222, reproduced in *Memoria*, ed. Gortari Rabiela and Hernández Franyuti, 3:328.

9. Dirección General de Estadística, *Censo, 1900*; John Wibel and Jesse de la Cruz, "Mexico," in *The Urban Development of Latin America, 1750–1920*, ed. Richard Morse (Stanford: Center for Latin American Studies, Stanford University, 1971), 95; Anderson, *Outcasts*, 39.

10. Frederick Shaw, "Poverty and Politics in Mexico City, 1824–1854" (Ph.D diss., University of Florida, 1975), 51; Mary Kay Vaughan, *State, Education, and Social Class in Mexico* (DeKalb: Northern Illinois University Press, 1982), 40.

11. Departamento de la Estadística Nacional, *Censo, 1921*; Loyo, *La política demográfica*, 290.

12. Dirección General de Estadística, *Censo, 1910*.

13. Scobie, *Buenos Aires*, 260; Andrés Molina Enríquez, *Los grandes problemas nacionales* (Mexico City: Impresa Carranza, 1909), reproduced in *Memoria*, ed. Gortari Rabiela and Hernández Franyuti, 3:336.

14. Fernando Rosenzweig, "La industria," in *Historia moderna de México: El Por-*

firiato: Vida economica, ed. Daniel Cosío Villegas, vol. 7, bk. 1 (Mexico City: Hermes, 1973), 392, 397; Hira de Gortari Rabiela and Regina Hernández Franyuti, *La Ciudad de México y el Distrito Federal: Una historia compartida* (Mexico City: Instituto Mora, 1988), 93; Knight, *Mexican Revolution*, 1:133.

15. Unless otherwise noted, occupational data for this chapter are taken from the following censuses: Dirección General de Estadística, *Censo, 1895; Censo, 1900;* and *Censo, 1910.* For further elaboration of occupational changes based on national censuses, see John Lear, "Workers, *Vecinos*, and Citizens: The Revolution in Mexico City" (Ph.D. diss., University of California, Berkeley, 1993), chap. 2 tables.

16. Angel del Campo, "Caifas y Carreño," in *Cuentos del arrabal* (Mexico: SEP, n.d.), 20–21.

17. *Mexican Year Book*, 564; *Guía Tremulla*, 134.

18. Jorge Vera Estañol, *Historia del Revolución Mexicana: Origines y resultados* (Mexico: Porrua, 1967), 15–17; Pablo González, *Informe que el general de división Pablo González, rinde al C. Venustiano Carranza* (Mexico: Imp. Chárez y hno, 1915), 2.

19. Semanario de Historia Moderna, *Estadísticas económicas del Porfiriato: Fuerza de trabajo y actividad económica por sectores* (Mexico City: Colegio de México, n.d.), 170–71; Augusto Génin, *Notes sur le Mexique* (Mexico City: Imprenta Lacard, 1908–10), reproduced in *Memoria*, ed. Gortari Rabiela and Hernández Franyuti, 3:244.

20. Haber, *Industry and Underdevelopment*, 63–83, 93.

21. AGN, RT, 347:9; Génin, *Notes*, 244, and Winter, *Mexico*, 48; AHCM Estadística, Censo Comercial, 1032; Luis Nicolau D'Olwer, "Las inversiones extranjeras," in *Historia moderna de México*, ed. Cosío Villegas, 2:1125; Sesto, *El México*, 176–77.

22. Adolfo Prantl and José L. Groso, *La Ciudad de México: Novísima guía universal* (Mexico City: Librería Madrileña, 1901), quoted in Hira de Gortari Rabiela, "Los años difíciles. Una economía urbana: El caso de la Ciudad de México (1890–1910)," *Iztapalapa* 3, no. 6 (1982): 112; AGN, RT, 347:9; Leal and Huacuja Rountree, *Economía y sistema*, 122, 126.

23. Lear, "Workers, *Vecinos*, Citizens," tables 2:4–8.

24. Emiliano Busto, *Estadística de la República Mexicana*, 3 vols. (Mexico City: I. Cumplido, 1880), 3:329–30; Semanario de Historia Moderna, *Estadísticas económicas*, 107–13.

25. AGN, RT, 148:6, 279:50, 299:1.

26. *Mexican Year Book*, 526: Dollero, *México al día*, 71; advertisement in *Mexican Herald*, September 1910, centenary edition; Haber, *Industry and Underdevelopment*, 49; Semanario de Historia Moderna, *Estadísticas económicas*, 111–13.

27. Secretaria de Industria, Comercio y Trabajo, *Monografía*, 39; Verena Radkau, "*La fama*" y la vida: Una fabrica y sus obreras (Mexico: CIESAS, 1984), 28; (textiles) AGN, RT, 288:12; (tobacco) AGN, RT, 292:13, 211:17, 418:4; Entrevista con la Señora Esther Torres.

28. Emile Chaubrand, *De Barcelonnette au Mexique* (Paris: Librarie Plon, 1892), 385–89, reproduced in *Memoria*, ed. Gortari Rabiela and Hernández Franyuti, 3:245–47; AGN, RT, 288:12.

29. AGN, RT, 8:4, 55:2:7, 672:20; Radkau, "*La fama*" y la vida, 70; El Ahuizotito, 13 December 1908.

30. Mario Camarena, "Disciplina e indisciplina: Los obreros textiles del valle de México en los años veinte," *Historias* 7 (1984): 4–5; Radkau, "*La fama*" y la vida, 74; Mario Trujillo Bolío, "Operarios fabriles en el Valle de México (1864–1880): Espacio, trabajo, protesta y cultura obrera" (Ph.D. diss., Colegio de México, 1995), 111 and padron 13.

31. García Díaz, *Un pueblo fabril*, 32–41, appendix; Haber, *Industry and Underdevelopment*, 50, 58.

32. Luis Chávez Orozco, *La agonía del artesanado* (Mexico City: CEHSMO, 1977); AGN, RT, 211:25, 672:20; Rodney Anderson "Gaudalajara's Artisans and Shopkeepers," in *Five Centuries of Mexican History, Mexico*, ed. Virginia Guedea and Jaime Rodriguez O. (Mexico City: Instituto Mora, 1992), 2:286–99.

33. See Lear, "Workers, *Vecinos*, Citizens," table 2:8.

34. Sonia Pérez Toledo, *Los hijos del trabajo: Los artesanos de la Ciudad de México, 1780–1853* (Mexico City: Colegio de México, 1996); Carlos Illades, *Hacia la república del trabajo: La organización artesanal en la Ciudad de México, 1853–1876* (Mexico: Colegio de México, 1996); Frederick Shaw, "The Artisan in Mexico City," in *El trabajo y los trabajadores en la historia de México*, ed. Elsa Frost, Michael C. Meyer, and Josefina Zoraida Vazquéz (Mexico City: Colegio de México, 1979); Hart, *Anarchism*, 87.

35. Kenneth L. Sokoloff, "Was the Transition from the Artisanal Shop to the Nonmechanized Factory Associated with Gains in Efficiency?: Evidence from

the U.S. Manufacturing Censuses of 1820 and 1850," *Explorations in Economic History* 21 (1984): 351–82.

36. Haber, *Industry and Underdevelopment*, chap. 8, and John Womack Jr., "The Mexican Economy During the Revolution, 1910–1920: Historiography and Analysis," *Marxist Perspectives* 1, no. 4 (1978): 80–123.

37. Directorio Industrial, 1923, AGN, RT, 595:6; Dirección General de Estadística, *Primer censo industrial de 1930*, vol. 1 (Mexico City: Dirección General de Estadística, 1930–35), 96; manufacturing employment numbers are based on the 1895 and 1910 censuses, using the occupational categories of the Semanario de Historia Moderna, *Estadísticas económicas*, 3–4.

38. Shaw, "The Artisan in Mexico City," 400; Illades, *Hacia la república*, 40; *Boletín de la Secretaría de Fomento* (segunda época) III, Industrias nuevas y aplicada, año VII, octubre de 1903, num. 3, 40–45, reproduced in *Memoria*, ed. Gortari Rabiela and Hernández Franyuti, 3:128; Rosenzweig, "La industria," 349; AGN, RT, 290:6–7, 595:6; "Censo fabril," in *Boletín de Industria, Comercio y Trabajo*, vol. 1, no. 2, 9–11.

39. Quoted in Rosenzweig, "La industria," 322.

40. AGN, RT, 173:12, 347:10; Archivo Condumex, fondo 21, L5861:53. John Mraz, "Más allá de la decoración: Hacia una historia gráfica de las mujeres en México," *Política y Cultura*, no. 1 (fall 1992) and "'Calidad de Esclavas': Tortilleras en los molinos de nixtamal, México, Diciembre, 1919," *Historia Obrera* 24, no. 6 (March 1982); Dawn Keremitsis, "Del metate al molino," *Historia Mexicana* 33, no. 2 (1983): 285–302.

41. Cited and translated in Tony Morgan, "Proletarians, Politicos, and Patriarchs: The Use and Abuse of Cultural Customs in the Early Industrialization of Mexico City, 1880–1910," in *Rituals of Rule, Rituals of Resistance: Public Celebrations and Popular Culture in Mexico*, ed. William H Beezley, Cheryl Martin, and William French (Wilmington DE: Scholarly Resources, 1994), 154.

42. AGN, RT, 25:5, 75:3, 397:2, 291:16; Archivo Condumex, fondo 21, L5861:53.

43. Rosenzweig, "La industria," 383; Busto, *Estadística*, 1:3, 3:328–29; Antonio Peñafiel, *Anuario estadístico de la República Mexicana*, 1895 (Mexico City: Secretaría de Fomento, 1896), 395–99; AGN, RT, 290:10.

44. Pablo Miranda Quevado and Beatriz Berndt León Mariscal, "José Guadalupe Posada y las Innovaciones Técnicas en el periodismo ilustrado de la Ciu-

dad de México," in *Posada y la prensa ilustrada: signos de modernización y resistencias*, ed. Jaime Soler and Lorenzo Avila (Mexico City: Patronato de Museo Nacional de Arte, 1996), 25–37; Dirección General de Estadística, *Primer Censo, 1930*, 1:298. Censo Imprentas de 1921, AGN, RT, 289:16, 14, 139, 142; Censo Periódicos de 1921, AGN, RT, 293:15, 412:2.

45. AGN, RT, 291:6; Sesto, *El México*, 131–33.

46. Illades, *Hacia la república*, 42–45.

47. "Condiciones de vida de sastres y costureras, 1921," in *Boletín del Archivo General de la Nación*, 3d ser., vol. 1, no. 2 (1977): 21–22.

48. *Nueva Era*, 26 January 1913, reprinted in Araiza, *Historia*, 3:26.

49. Labor Conditions and Problems in the Mexico City Tramway, Light and Power Company (14 June 1918), I–2515, Interview 574, Doheny Research Foundation Records, Occidental College; AGN, RT, 772:1; *Mexican Herald*, 23 July 1910; Miguel Rodríguez, *Los tranviarios y el anarquismo en México* (Puebla: Universidad Autónoma de Puebla, 1980), 11; Brown, "Foreign and Native-born Workers," 786–818; Nonoalco shop listed in "Censo fabril," in *Boletín de Industría, Comercio y Trabajo*, vol. 1, no. 2, 9–11.

50. Juan Felipe Leal, *Del mutualismo al sindicalismo en México: 1843–1910* (Mexico City: Ediciones El Caballito, 1991), 81.

51. See Lear, "Workers, *Vecinos*, Citizens," table 2:8.

52. *El Imparcial*, 18 November 1911; Sesto, *El México*, 129, 132.

53. Dirección General de Estadística, *Censo, 1910*; Entrevista con la Señora Esther Torres.

54. Dollero, *México al día*, 71; Sesto, *El México*, 132; AGN, RT, 70:27, 472:12; classified ads, *El Imparcial*, 18 November 1911; Hira de Gortari Rabiela, "El empleo en la Ciudad de México a fines del siglo XIX. Una discusión," *Secuencia: Revista de Ciencias Sociales* 3 (1985): 37–48.

55. *Nueva Era*, 16 January 1912; AGN, RT, 294:15; "Condiciones de vida de sastres," 21; AGN, RT, 290:1; 292:7; 293:9; 320:11; 710:8; 70:10, 27; 171:40; 31:4; 96:9; Entrevista con la Señora Esther Torres, 14.

56. Silvia Arrom, *The Women of Mexico City, 1790–1857* (Stanford: Stanford University Press, 1985), 158, 165.

57. AHCM, 3645:1711, 657:794.

58. "Un Quid Pro Quo," in Gutiérrez Nájera, *La novela del tranvía*, 7–12; AHCM, 3645:1711 and 2684.

59. Luis Lara y Pardo, *La prostitución en México* (Mexico City: Viuda de C. Bouret, 1908), 19–35, 49; Julio Guerrero, *La génesis del crimen en México: estudio de psiquiatría social*, 2d ed. (Mexico City: Porrua, 1977), 120; Katherine Elaine Bliss, "Prostitution, Revolution and Social Reform in Mexico City, 1918–1940" (Ph.D. diss., University of Chicago, 1996), 71; French, *A Peaceful and Working People*, chap. 4.

60. *El Imparcial*, 18 November 1911; Radkau *"La fama" y la vida*, 67–70; Genín, *Notes*, 203.

61. Sesto, *El México*. 129–132; Dollero, *México al día*, 12; Guerrero, *La génesis*, 119.

62. Turner, *Barbarous Mexico*, 99; Thompson, *The People of Mexico*, 336; Sesto, *El México*, 131; Dollero, *México al día*, 12; Semanario de Historia Moderna, *Estadísticas económicas*, 108.

63. Sesto, *El México*, 134; AGN, RT, Censo Obrero, 288:12; Thompson, *The People of Mexico*, 342, 356–62.

64. Friedrich Katz, "Mexico: Restored Republic and Porfiriato, 1867–1910," in *Cambridge History of Latin America*, ed. Leslie Bethell (Cambridge: Cambridge University Press, 1984), 5:63–65; Anderson, *Outcasts*, 62–66; Knight, *Mexican Revolution*, 1:129–30; Semanario de Historia Moderna, *Estadísticas económicas*, 149–57.

65. Anderson, *Outcasts*, 64–65; Thompson, *The People of Mexico*, 361–68; Marie Eileen Francois, "When Pawnshops Talk: Popular Credit and Material Culture in Mexico City, 1775–1916" (Ph.D. diss., University of Arizona, 1998), 227; Lanny Thompson, "Artisan Marginals and Proletarians: The Households of the Popular Classes in Mexico City, 1876–1950," in *Five Centuries of Mexican History*, ed. Guedea and Rodriguez O., 307–24.

66. AGN, RT, 55:8, 65, 71.

67. Elena Poniatowska, *Hasta no verte, Jesús mío* (Mexico City: Era, 1969), and "Vida y Muerta de Jesusa," in *Luz y luna, las lunitas* (Mexico City: Era, 1994).

68. AGN, RT, 472:12; Isabel G. de la Solana, *El emigrado* (Mexico: S. Galas, 1924); Radkau, *"La fama" y la vida*, 65, 78, 82; Basurto, *Vivencias*, 55–56.

69. Guerrero, *La génesis*, chap. 3; AGN, RT, 25:5; Huitrón, *Orígenes*, 77, 226.

70. AGN, RT, 25:5; Basurto, *Vivencias*, 18, 54; AGN, RT, 672:20; Huitrón, *Orí-*

genes, 226; William Sewell Jr., "Social Change and the Rise of Working-Class Politics in Nineteenth-Century Marseille," *Past and Present* 65 (November 1974), 82.

3. WORKING-CLASS CULTURES

1. Genaro García, *Crónica oficial de las fiestas del primer centenario de la independencia de México* (Mexico City: Condumex, 1990), 128–32.

2. García, *Crónica oficial*, 163–64. Limantour was later accused of profiting from the creation of Balbuena Park (*La Fuerza Obrera*, 31 May 1912).

3. García, *Crónica oficial*, 212.

4. Alfredo Navarrete, *Alto a la contrarrevolución* (Mexico City: Testimonios de Atla comulco, 1971), 34–35, cited in Anderson, *Outcasts*, 280–81; Federico Gamboa, *Mi diario* (Mexico City: CNC, 1994), 5:127–28, and cited in Tenorio-Trillo, "1910 Mexico City," 78.

5. Knight, "Working Class," 51–79; Jean Meyer, "Los obreros en la Revolución Mexicana: Los 'Batallones Rojos,'" *Historia Mexicana* 21, no. 1 (1971): 1–37; García Díaz, *Un pueblo fabril*, 32–41; Brown, *Oil and Revolution*, chap. 5; French, *A Peaceful and Working People*, chap. 2.

6. French, *A Peaceful and Working People*, chap. 3.

7. Knight, "Working Class," 56; Basurto, *Vivencias*, 52.

8. Manuel Gamio, *Forjando patria* (Mexico City: Porrua, 1960), 89–92; Manuel Ceballos Ramírez, "La encíclica 'Rerum Novarum' y los trabajadores católicos en la Ciudad de México (1891–1913)," *Historia Mexicana* 33, no. 1 (1983): 26, 30.

9. Thompson, *The People of Mexico*, 179; González Navarro, *La vida social*, 460; Dollero, *México al día*, 81, 82, 89; Radkau, "La fama" y la vida, 75; Miguel Navarro Martínez, *Relatos y anecdotas de un cantor* (Mexico City: INEHRM, 1990), 105, 136.

10. *Nueva era*, 28 January 1912; Thompson, *The People of Mexico*, 345; Radkau, "La fama" y la vida, 83; Navarro Martínez, *Relatos*, 46–49; "Labor Conditions," I-2515, Interview 574; AGN, RT, 211:17.

11. AGN, RT, 6:1:1, 211:17, 20; Jean-Pierre Bastian, *Los disidentes: Sociedades protestantes y revolución en México, 1872–1911* (Mexico: El Colegio de México/FCE, 1989), 64.

12. Guerrero, *La génesis*, 127; Thompson, *The People of Mexico*, 358–60; González Navarro, *La vida social*, 94, 391; Sesto, *El México*, 196, cited in Lanny Thompson,

"La fotografía como documento histórico: La familia proletaria y la vida doméstica en la Ciudad de México, 1900–1950," *Historias* 29 (October 1992–March 1993): 110.

13. AGN, RT, 211:17, 672:20; Navarro Martínez, *Relatos*, 85.

14. Guerrero, *La génesis*, 127, cited in Pablo Piccato, "'El paso de Venus por el disco del Sol': Criminality and Alcoholism in the Late Porfiriato," *Mexican Studies/Estudios Mexicanos* 2, no. 2 (summer 1995): 203–42; see the temperance newspaper *San Lunes*, published sporadically in 1910, and *El Sol*, 28 December 1914; Radkau, "La fama" y la vida, 77–78.

15. Shaw, "The Artisan in Mexico City," 405, cited in Victoria Novelo, "Los trabajadores mexicanos en el siglo XIX: ¿Obreros o artesanos?" in *Comunidad, cultura y vida social: Ensayos sobre la formación de la clase obrera*, ed. Seminario de movimiento obrero y Revolución Mexicana (Mexico City: INAH, 1991): 21; French, *A Peaceful and Working People*, 124; Katznelson, "Working Class Formation," 268; AGN, Ramo Gobernación, 817:988:1.

16. Knight, *Mexican Revolution*, 84; French, *A Peaceful and Working People*, chap. 5; González Navarro, *La vida social*, 358; *San Lunes*, 7 February 1910; Jean-Pierre Bastian, "Metodismo y clase obrera durante el Porfiriato," *Historia Mexicana* 33, no. 1 (1983): 64–65.

17. Leal, *Del mutualismo*, 15; Manuel Ceballos Ramírez, *El catolicismo social: Un tercero en discordia, Rerum Novarum, la "cuestión social" y la movilización de los católicos mexicanos (1891–1911)* (Mexico City: Colegio de México, 1991), 109; Trujillo Bolío, "Operarios fabriles," 398.

18. Anderson, *Outcasts*, 138; Alberto Híjar, "Notas sobre cultura obrera mexicana," in *Monografías obreras*, ed. Victoria Novelo, vol. 1 (Mexico City: Cuadernos de la Casa Chata, 1987), 142.

19. Angel T. Montalvo, "El Artesano," *La Clase Media*, 1 April 1909; Sergio Espinosa Cordero, ed., *Antología poética de Fernando Celada* (Mexico City: SEP, 1977), 15–47; "En la fábrica," *El Paladín*, 5 April 1914.

20. "En la fragua," *El Obrero Mexicano*, 1 April 1910.

21. See "Despertad" and Higinio García, "Para los obreros," *Evolución*, 1 May 1910; Justo Sierra, *La Evolución política del pueblo mexicano* (Mexico City: Porrua, 1900); Novelo, "Los trabajadores mexicanos," 30.

22. Illades, *Hacia la república*, 100; Trujillo Bolío, "Operarios fabriles," chap. 5; AGN, RT, 14:12.

23. Guy P. C. Thomson, "Popular Aspects of Liberalism in Mexico, 1848–1888," *Bulletin of Latin American Research* 10, no. 3 (1991): 265–92, and Alan Knight, "El Liberalismo mexicano desde la Reforma hasta la Revolución (una interpretación)," *Historia Mexicana* 35, no. 1 (1985): 59–85; Illades, *Hacia la república*, chap. 5; Gaston García Cantú, *La idea de México: El socialismo*, vol. 2 (Mexico City: Fondo de Cultura Económica, 1991), 245–50.

24. Ramón Corral MSS 84/2, Bancroft Library, University of California, Berkeley; Ignacio Eduardo Rodriguez, "Fernando Celada," in *Biografías Sintéticas*, ed. Comité Pro-homenaje a Precursores de la Revolución, 13–16.

25. Fernando Celada, *En capilla: Monólogo dedicado a los obreros de la República Mexicana* (Mexico City: Aguilar, 1898), 9–11.

26. *La Guacamaya*, 2 August 1914; poem by Pascual Mendoza reproduced in Rosendo Salazar, *La Casa del Obrero Mundial* (Mexico City: Costa-Amic, 1962), 205.

27. "Condiciones de vida de sastres," 21–34; Díaz, "The Satiric Penny Press," 497–526; Miranda Quevado and Leon Mariscal, "José Guadalupe Posada," 25–29.

28. *El Obrero Mexicano*, 1 October 1909, quoted in Felipe Arturo Ávila Espinosa, "La Sociedad Mutualista y Moralizadora de Obreros del Distrito Federal (1909–1911)," *Historia Mexicana* 43, no. 1 (1993): 130–31; Anderson, *Outcasts*, 251.

29. Poem by Mendoza reproduced in Salazar, *La Casa*, 205; Montalvo, "El artesano"; Posada, "Tu, grande amigo de los obreros," *San Lunes*, 20 December 1909, reproduced in *Posada y la prensa ilustrada*, ed. Museo Nacional de Arte, 206; Díaz, "The Satiric Penny Press," 515.

30. *El Ahuizotito*, 13 December 1908, 1.

31. Díaz, "The Satiric Penny Press," 526; Leal, *Del mutualismo*, 86–87.

32. Illades, *Hacia la república*, 69–76.

33. Alberto Trueba Urbina, *Evolución de la huelga* (Mexico City: Ediciones Botas, 1950), 37–42; Illades, *Hacia la república*, 76–82.

34. Illades, *Hacia la república*, 82; González Navarro, *La vida social*, 352–55; Leal, *Del mutualismo*, 18–19.

35. Illades, *Hacia la república*, 129–43; *El Empleado Mutualista*, 3 March 1915; Híjar, "Notas sobre cultura obrerana mexicana," 33; Leal, *Del mutualismo*, 55.

36. Leal, *Del mutualismo*, 17; AGN, RT, 14:12, 128:25, 29, 37, 40; Illades, *Hacia la república*, 87; *La Convención Radical*, 26 October 1902; Prantl and Groso, *La Ciudad de México*, 808–10.

37. AGN, RT, 14:12, 128:25, 29, 37, 40; *El Empleado Mutualista* 6, no. 32 (October–December 1914) and 13, no. 2 (November 1916); Illades, *Hacia la república*, 87; Leal, *Del mutualismo*, 25.

38. AGN, RT, 128:26, 29; Leal, *Del mutualismo*, 29; *La Convención Radical*, 26 October 1902.

39. *El Imparcial*, 25 August 1913; Ceballos Ramírez, "La encíclica," 29; *La Convención Radical*, 26 October 1902.

40. Ceballos Ramírez, *El catolicismo social*, 109–11, 256–85, and "La encíclica."

41. Bastian, *Los disidentes*, 62–66, and anexo, table 4, 321–22.

42. Leal, *Del mutualismo*, 46–55; Illades, *Hacia la república*, 103–13.

43. AGN, RT, 22:2.

44. C. D. Lopez, *Sociedades y sindicatos* (Mexico City: Tipografía de la oficina de la Secretaría de Hacienda, 1918), 24, 48; AGN, Ramo Gobernación, 817:988:1; Prantl and Groso, *La Ciudad de México*, 809.

45. Trueba Urbina, *Evolución de la huelga*, 37–42.

46. Secretaria de Industria, Comercio, y Trabajo, *Boletín de Industria, Comercio, y Trabajo* 2, nos. 1–6 (January–June 1919), Sección Trabajo, 54.

47. Anderson, *Outcasts*, 114–15; Leal, *Del mutualismo*, 20, 158; Hart, *Anarchism*, 90–92; González Navarro, *La vida social*, 308, 348.

48. Walker, "Porfirian Labor Politics," 257–89; Arturo Obregón, "El segundo congreso obrero, 1879," *Historia Obrera* 2, no. 7 (1977): 19–25.

49. Hart, *Anarchism*, 43–59.

50. John Womack, "Luchas sindicales y liberalismo social," *Libertad y justicia en las sociedades modernas* (Mexico: Porrua, 1994), 332–36; Hart, *Anarchism*, 56–59.

51. Illades, *Hacia la república*, 145–46; Pedro Rincón Gallardo, *Discurso pronunciado por el Sr. Pedro Rincón Gallardo, Regidor primero del Ayuntamiento Constitucional de México* (Mexico City: Imprenta del Comercio, 1882), 24.

52. See elections in *El Empleado Mutualista* 12, no. 2 (March–April 1915), and 13, no. 9 (9 September 1916).

53. González Navarro, *La vida social*, 352.

54. Obregón, "El segundo congreso obrero," 24; *Obrero Mexicano* quoted in Ceballos Ramírez, *El catolicismo social*, 95; Leal, *Del mutualismo*, 57–58.

55. Leal, *Del mutualismo*, 78–79; AHCM, Regidores, 3891; *Memoria del Ayuntamiento correspondiente al primer semestre de 1903* (Mexico City: La Europea, 1903); Womack, "Luchas sindicales," 337.

56. Ceballos Ramírez, *El catolicismo social*, 169; Anderson, *Outcasts*, appendix a, 331–38; González Navarro, *La vida social*, 298–99; Rosenzweig, "La industria," 419; Leal, *Del mutualismo*, 83; Knight, *Mexican Revolution*, 1:129–31.

57. Anderson, *Outcasts*, 228–32 and chap. 4.

58. Anderson, *Outcasts*, 225 and appendix a, 331–38.

59. Ávila Espinosa, "Sociedad Mutualista," 122, 136; *El Obrero Mexicano*, 11, 17 February 1911, and 24 June 1910.

60. González Navarro, *La vida social*, 351; *El Obrero Mexicano*, 24 June 1910; Ávila Espinosa, "Sociedad Mutualista"; Casasola, *Historia gráfica*, 1:137.

61. Ávila Espinosa, "Sociedad Mutualista," 125; *El Obrero Mexicano*, 17 and 24 February 1910.

62. *El Obrero Mexicano*, 19 October 1909 and 11 February 1910, also cited in Ávila Espinosa, "Sociedad Mutualista," 131.

63. *El Obrero Mexicano*, 25 November 1910 and 31 March 1911; Anderson, *Outcasts*, 226; Leal, *Del mutualismo*, 138.

64. *El Obrero Mexicano*, 11 February, 10 June, 23 December 1910, 27 January, 2 June 1911; Ávila Espinosa, "Sociedad Mutualista," 142, 148.

65. *El Obrero Mexicano*, 7 January 1910; AGN, RT, 128:31; Ávila Espinosa, "Sociedad Mutualista," 143, 147.

66. *El Obrero Mexicano*, 11 February, 3 June, and 19 August 1910; Leal, *Del mutualismo*, 156; Ávila Espinosa, "Sociedad Mutualista," 139–40.

67. Vera Estañol, *Historia*, 41, 101; *San Lunes*, 7 February 1910.

68. *El Obrero Mexicano*, 11 February and 3 June 1910.

69. Knight, *Mexican Revolution*, 1:51–55; *México Nuevo*, 22 June 1909.

70. *México Obrero*, 1 September 1909; Charles C. Cumberland, *The Mexican Revolution: Genesis under Madero* (Austin: University of Texas Press, 1952), 38.

71. *México Obrero*, 1 September 1909; Knight, *Mexican Revolution*, 51–55; Anderson, *Outcasts*, 257; Navarrete, *Alto a la contrarrevolución*, 38.

72. *México Nuevo*, 25 July 1909; Anderson, *Outcasts*, 264; *Mexican Herald*, 9 June 1910.

73. Rodney Anderson, "Mexican Workers and the Politics of Revolution, 1906–1911," *Hispanic American Historical Review* 54, no. 1 (1974): 94–113; *México Nuevo*, 17 and 28 April 1910.

74. Madero speeches from Anderson, *Outcasts*, 261–62, and Andrea Martínez and Jorge Fernández Tomás, "Asambleísmo, 'espontaneidad,' huelga y maderismo: Una ojeada y muchas preguntas sobre las movilizaciones de 1911 en el sector textil," *Historia Obrera* 5, no. 20 (September 1982): 29.

75. *Evolución*, 1 May 1910.

76. *Evolución*, 1 May 1910.

77. *Evolución*, 8 May 1910; *Mexican Herald*, 1 and 2 May 1910; photograph in Saúl Jerónimo Romero, *La incorporación del pueblo al proceso electoral de 1910* (Mexico City: INEHRM, 1995), 31, 38; *México Nuevo*, 3 May 1910.

78. Huitrón, *Orígines*, 73–84; *Evolución*, 29 May 1910, 2.

79. Shirlene Ann Soto, *The Mexican Woman: A Study of Her Participation in the Revolution, 1910–1940* (Palo Alto CA: R & E Research, 1979), 22; Frederick C. Turner, "Los efectos de la participación femenina en la Revolución de 1910," *Historia Mexicana* 16, no. 4 (April–June 1967): 32; Ana María Hernández, *La mujer mexicana en la industria textil* (Mexico City: Tip. Moderna, 1940), 38.

80. González Navarro, *La vida social*, 284; Anderson, *Outcasts*, 264–65; Vera Estañol, *Historia*, 226; Entrevista al señor José Pacheco Vadillo realizado por María Isabel Soza y Carmen Nava, el 7 de diciembre de 1924, en la Ciudad de México, Archivo de la Palabra, Instituto Mora, PHO/1/162, 17.

81. *Evolución*, 29 May 1910; *El Obrero Mexicano*, 3 June 1910; *Mexican Herald*, 1 June 1910, 1.

82. Anderson, *Outcasts*, 245, 258; *México Nuevo*, 26 April 1909; *México Nuevo*, 8 May 1910; *México Nuevo*, 3 April 1910; González Navarro, *La vida social*, 352.

83. Anderson, *Outcasts*, 265–66; *Mexican Herald*, 27 and 28 June 1910.

84. Anderson, *Outcasts*, 286–91; Knight, *Mexican Revolution*, 1:134, 172–73,

85. James Cockcroft, *Intellectual Precursors of the Mexican Revolution*, 2d ed. (Aus-

tin: University of Texas Press, 1976), 189; Gildardo Magaña, *Emiliano Zapata y el Agrarismo en México* (Mexico City, 1934), 1:119–25.

86. *El Obrero Mexicano*, 1 July 1910.

87. Anderson, *Outcasts*, 272–74; González Navarro, *La vida social*, 351; AGN, RT, 128:31.

88. *El Obrero Mexicano*, 21 April and 5 May 1911; Ávila Espinosa, "Sociedad Mutualista," 150.

89. Georgette José Valenzuela, ed., *Ultimos meses de Porfirio Díaz en el poder, antología documental* (Mexico City: INERHM, 1985), 233–36, 245.

90. *La Guacamaya*, 7 May 1911.

91. *Juan Panadero*, 28 May 1911; Roberto Cejudo, "La Salida de México del Presidente Gral. Porfirio Díaz," in *Ultimos meses de Porfirio Díaz*, 271–73; AGN, Ramo Gobernación, 4a:910–11 (8) (2); 2 (6); Valadés is cited in Ariel Rodríguez Kuri, *La experiencia olvidada: El ayuntamiento de México: política y gobierno, 1876–1912* (Mexico: UAM/Colegio de México, 1996), 225; Casasola, *Historia gráfica*, 1:308–10.

92. Rodríguez Kuri, *La experiencia olvidada*, 226–27.

93. AGN, Ramo Gobernación, 4a:910–11 (8) (2); 2 (6); *Nueva Era*, September–October 1911; *El Obrero Mexicano*, 2 June 1911.

4. MADERISTA POLITICS

1. Letters dated 31 August 1912 and 15 September 1911, in Archivo Porfirio Díaz, Universidad Iberoamericana, Fondo Cartas, 36, 20, 009813.

2. Felix F. Palavicini, *Los diputados* (Mexico: INHERM, 1976), x; Cumberland, *Mexican Revolution*, 248–51; and the dissenting view of Francois Xavier Guerra, "Las elecciones legislativas de la Revolución mexicana, 1912," *Revista Mexicana de Sociología* 52, no. 2 (1990): 241–76.

3. Knight, *Mexican Revolution*, 1:405.

4. *Nueva Era*, 3 September 1911, 25 October 1911, 6 and 8 March 1912, 25 and 29 April 1912; Rodríguez Kuri, *La experiencia olvidada*, 272; AGN, RT, 14:12.

5. *El Radical*, 13 July 1911; *Nueva Era*, 3 September and 7 December 1911.

6. *El Radical*, 2 June 1911; Araiza, *Historia*, 3:14; AHCM, 404:755–66, Regidores, 3841; and AGN, Período Revolución, 130:48:2.

7. Vera Estañol, *Historia*, 219; *Nueva Era*, 10 August and 4, 6, and 15 September 1911.

8. *El Obrero Mexicano*, 1 September 1911; Vera Estañol, *Historia*, 216; Rodríguez Kuri, *La experiencia olvidada*, 271–74; *El Radical*, 2, 8, and 13 July 1911

9. *Nueva Era*, 28 August and 27 September 1911.

10. Reprinted in *Nueva Era*, 11 November 1911.

11. *Nueva Era*, September–October and 4, 5 December 1911.

12. Rodríguez Kuri, *La experiencia olvidada*, 53; *Nueva Era*, 2 January 1912 and 16 December 1911; *El Diario*, 4 December 1911, reproduced in, *Memoria*, ed. Gortari Rabiela and Hernández Franyuti, 1:311.

13. *Nueva Era*, 3, 4, and 6 December 1911; Cockcroft, *Intellectual Precursors*, chap. 8; Salazar and Escobedo, *Las pugnas*, 44–53.

14. *Nueva Era*, 2 January 1912; AHCM, 3645:1711–14; *La Guacamaya*, 5 and 19 January 1913; *El Pueblo*, 31 October 1914.

15. Madero speech cited in Aurelio de los Reyes, *Cine y sociedad en México, 1896–1930* (Mexico City: UNAM, 1981), 112; *El Pueblo*, 31 October 1914; *Nueva Era*, 9 and 21 January 1912; *Mexican Herald*, 19 August 1912.

16. Jorge Robles Gómez, *Huelga tranviaria y motín popular* (Toluca: Universidad Autónoma del Eutado de México, 1981), 12; de los Reyes, *Cine y sociedad*, 113–14; AHCM, 3645, ex. 1701.

17. Rodríguez Kuri, *La experiencia olvidada*, chap. 7; AHCM, 403:744, 589:46; *Nueva Era*, 8 April 1912.

18. AHCM, 404:755–66, Regidores, 3841; *México Patria*, 22 December 1913; *El Renovador*, 24 July 1915.

19. *Nueva Era*, 9 December 1911, 22 and 24 April 1912; AHCM, Elecciones de Poderes Federales, 877, ex. 80.

20. *Nueva Era*, 24 and 25 April 1912; Araiza, *Historia*, 3:12–13; Barry Carr, "Marxism and Anarchism in the Formation of the Communist Party," *Hispanic American Historical Review* 63, no. 2 (1983): 282–84; *Nueva Era*, 26 February 1912.

21. Frederick C. Turner, "La mujer en la Revolución," *Historia Mexicana* 16, no. 4 (April–June 1967): 32.

22. *Nueva Era*, 4 December 1911 and 26 February 1912; Rafael Pérez Taylor, *El socialismo en México, 1913* (Mexico City: CEHSMO, 1976), 113–15.

23. Araiza, *Historia*, 3:12–14, 38; *Mexican Herald*, 30 June 1912.

24. AHCM, Elecciones de Poderes Federales, 877, ex. 81; Vera Estañol, *Historia*, 246–47.

25. *Nueva Era*, 27 November 1911; AHCM, Partidos Políticos, 1300:23; Cockcroft, *Intellectual Precursors*, 221; *La Fuerza Obrera*, 31 May 1912; Guerra, "Las elecciones legislativas," 264.

26. Lopez, 24; *Nueva Era*, 29 March 1912; *El Ideal Democrático*, 31 May 1912; Francisco Ramírez Plancarte, *La Revolución mexicana* (Mexico City: Editorial Costa-Amic, 1952), 482.

27. *Mexican Herald*, July 7 1912; *Nueva Era*, 22 April 1912.

28. Roderic Camp, *Mexican Political Biographies* (Austin: University of Texas Press, 1991), 48, 351; Ramirez Plancarte, *La Revolución mexicana*, 48, 481; Carlos Zapata Vela, *Conversaciones con Heriberto Jara* (Mexico: Costa Amic Editores, 1992), 19.

29. Guerra, "Las elecciones legislativas," 264, 274; *Mexican Herald*, 2 and 7 July 1912; Arnold Shanklin, Mexico City, to Secretary of State, 1 July 1912, in Department of State, *Records of the Department of State Relating to the Internal Affairs of Mexico, 1910–1929*, 812.00/4408, microfilm roll 19, also cited in Knight, "Working Class," 54; *La Fuerza Obrera*, 31 May 1912.

30. Cockcroft, *Intellectual Precursors*, 202, 222.

31. *El Paladín*, 18 May 1913; *El Imparcial*, 15 and 25 May 1913.

32. *Mexican Herald*, 7 July 1912; Araiza, *Historia*, 3:14; Carr, "Marxism," 283.

33. AGN, RT, 14:12; Fernando Córdova Pérez, "El movimiento anarquista en México (1911–1921)" (B.A. thesis, Facultad de Ciencias Políticas y Sociales, Mexico City: UNAM, 1971), 19–20, 26.

34. *El Obrero Mexicano*, 24 November 1911; Huitrón, *Orígenes*, 197.

35. AGN, RT, 14:11.

36. *Nueva Era*, 25 October 1911, 27 January, 19 March 1912.

37. AGN, RT, 55:8, 96:5, 70:27.

38. Córdova Pérez, "El movimiento anarquista," 78–79; *El Imparcial*, 1 March and 13 June 1913; AGN, RT, 96:5.

39. AGN, RT, 14:11; Salazar and Escobedo, *Las pugnas*, 1:78; Córdova Pérez, "El movimiento anarquista," 29.

40. Reprinted in Huitrón, *Orígenes*, 197; *El Obrero Mexicano*, 17 February 1911; AGN, RT, 41:26.

41. *El Obrero Mexicano*, 3 November 1911; AGN, RT, 41:26,78:3; *El Radical*, 8 July 1911.

42. *Obrero Mexicano*, 2 June 1911; *El Radical*, 8 July 1911; Salazar and Escobedo, *Las pugnas*, 37–40; Córdova Pérez, "El movimiento anarquista," 18–21.

43. *El Radical*, 8 July 1911.

44. Córdova Pérez, "El movimiento anarquista," 21; *Nueva Era*, 11 November 1911; Córdova Pérez, "El movimiento anarquista," 28–30; Hart, *Anarchism*, 107–10;

45. *Nueva Era*, 15 September 1911; Huitrón, *Orígenes*, 207; AGN, RT, 70:3; Córdova Pérez, "El movimiento anarquista," 18–21.

46. *El Obrero Mexicano*, 21 May and 2 June 1911; Huitrón, *Orígenes*, 193, 198.

47. Córdova Pérez, "El movimiento anarquista," 23, 24, 29; AGN, RT, 96:7.

48. Salazar and Escobedo, *Las pugnas*, 44–53; Araiza, *Historia*, 3:48; Hart, *Anarchism*, 129, and Córdova Pérez, "El movimiento anarquista," 38–39; Armando Bartra, ed., *Regeneración*, 1900–1918 (Mexico: Ediciones Era, 1977), 310.

49. Pérez Taylor, *El socialismo*, 83; López, *Sociedades y sindicatos*, 163.

50. Córdova Pérez, "El movimiento anarquista," 131.

51. Córdova Pérez, "El movimiento anarquista," 61, 130, 131; Hart, *Anarchism*, 124; Huitrón, *Orígenes*, 252; AGN, RT, 70:27:33.

52. *El Imparcial*, 28 June 1913; *Revolución Social*, 25 July 1915.

53. Córdova Pérez, "El movimiento anarquista," 129; Huitrón, *Orígenes*, 289; Ana Ribera, "Ciencia, luz y verdad. El proyecto educativo de la Casa del Obrero Mundial," *Historias*, no. 32 (1994): 67–77.

54. Cited in Córdova Pérez, "El movimiento anarquista," 126.

55. Salazar and Escobedo, *Las pugnas*, 67–71.

56. AGN, RT, 128:28; *El Empleado Mutualista*, October–November 1914, March–April 1915, and November 1916.

57. *La Convención*, 27 March 1915; *El Empleado Mutualista*, October–December 1914; AGN, RT, 14:12 and 128:25, 29, 37, 40.

58. Salazar and Escobedo, *Las pugnas*, 40; Araiza, *Historia*, 3:17; Hart, *Anarchism*, 114–17; *Nueva Era*, 29 August 1911.

59. AGN, RT, 70:27; "Estatutos del sindicato de carpinteros de Mexico" (Mexico City: Casa del Obrero Mundial, 1915), Art. 11; Sindicato de Conductores de Carruajes de Alquiler de la Ciudad de Mexico, "Libreta de estatutos de adhesion y pagos" (Mexico City, 1916).

60. *El Imparcial*, 1, 2, and 6 September 1913; AGN, RT, 56:5; Araiza, *Historia*, 3:45; Salazar and Escobedo, *Las pugnas*, 39–40.

61. Huitrón, *Orígenes*, 193, 218; *El Demócrata*, 5 October 1914; *El Sol*, 13 January 1915.

62. Huitrón, *Orígenes*, 252.

63. AGN, RT, 14:12,128:31.

64. Ceballos Ramírez, *El catolicismo social*, 360–63; Huitrón, *Orígenes*, 289.

65. Huitrón, *Orígenes*, 253–55; see the column "Vida obrera," in *El Demócrata*, November–December 1914; *Mexican Herald*, 12 February 1915; Córdova Pérez, "El movimiento anarquista," 148.

66. Sánchez Sánchez, *Surgimiento*, 156.

67. Quoted in Córdova Pérez, "El movimiento anarquista," 68; *El Sindicalista*, 30 September 1913, reprinted in Huitrón, *Orígenes*, 241.

68. *Evolución*, 1 May 1910; Huitrón, *Orígenes*, 215

69. *Nueva Era*, 1 February 1912.

70. Araiza, *Historia*, 3:20, 48; Hart, *Anarchism*, 129; Ramírez Plancarte, *La Revolución mexicana*, 468, 517; *El Imparcial*, 11 August 1913.

71. Pablo Piccato, *Congreso y revolución* (Mexico: INEHRM, 1991), 90–92.

72. AGN, RT, 56:1; Mario Ramírez Rancaño, *Burguesía textil y política en la Revolución mexicana* (Mexico City: UNAM, 1987), 76–80; Palavicini, *Los diputados*, 567–69.

73. Ramírez Rancaño, *Burguesía textil*, 87–90; Córdova Pérez, "El movimiento anarquista," 126–28; Diego Arenas Guzmán, *Historia de la Cámara de Diputados de la XXVI Legislatura Federal*, vol. 3 (Mexico: Taller Gráfico de la Nación, 1961), 17.

74. Arenas Guzmán, *Historia*, 20, 25, 45–50, 88.

75. Arenas Guzmán, Historia, 90.

76. Arenas Guzmán, Historia, 57–58.

77. Palavicini, Los diputados, 200–202; Robert E. Quirk, The Mexican Revolution and the Catholic Church, 1910–1929 (Bloomington: Indiana University Press, 1973), 32; Arenas Guzmán, Historia, 82–83.

78. Arenas Guzmán, Historia, 20, 50–52, 95, 98–99, 181–89; Palavicini, Los diputados, 199–205.

79. AGN, RT, 56:1; Palavicini, Los diputados, 564–66; Arenas Guzmán, Historia, 105; Cumberland, Mexican Revolution, 228.

80. Nueva Era, 8 and 9 March, 4 May 1912; Rodríguez Kuri, La experiencia olvidada, 233–48; El Artesano, 18 February 1913.

81. El Independiente, 5 March 1913; Córdova Pérez, "El movimiento anarquista," 69–71.

5. DIRECT ACTION

1. Carlos González Peña quoted in de los Reyes, Cine y sociedad, 112.

2. Huitrón, Orígenes, 252; Charles Tilly, "Repertoires of Contention in America and Britain, 1750–1830," in The Dynamics of Social Movements: Resource Mobilization, Social Control, and Tactics, ed. Mayer N. Zald and John D. McCarthy (Cambridge MA: Winthrop, 1979), 131.

3. AGN, RT, 6:1:1, 8:4.

4. Moisés González Navarro, "El primer salario mínimo," Historia Mexicana 28, no. 3 (1970): 378; Martínez and Fernández Tomás, "Asambleísmo," 27.

5. José Woldenberg, Antecedentes del sindicalismo (Mexico: SEP, 1983), 103; El Paladín, 19 January 1913; AGN, RT, 32:18, 70:3:1–15, 52:1.

6. E. P. Thompson, "Time, Work-Discipline, and Industrial Capitalism," Past and Present 38 (1967): 56–97; AGN, RT, 32:24:1–6; El Paladín, 19 January 1913; Huitrón, Orígenes, 227.

7. AGN, RT, 70:14, 6:6, 52:1, 97:2.

8. El Obrero Mexicano, 17 February 1911; El Sol, 22 December 1914; Thompson, The People of Mexico, 383; Radkau, "La fama" y la vida, 71–73; Piccato Rodríguez, "Criminals in Mexico City," 236.

9. AGN Ramo Gobernación, 817:988:1; El Sol, 9 December 1914; AGN, RT, 71:4.

10. El Ahuizotito, 13 December 1908; AGN, RT, 70:3:1–15, 97:1; Woldenberg, Antecedentes, 107; Ramírez Rancaño, Burguesía textil, 146; El Sol, 26 January 1915.

11. Woldenberg, Antecedentes, 118.

12. AGN, RT, 5:15; El Pueblo, 5 October 1914.

13. AGN, RT, 5:11:1–8.

14. AGN, RT, 14:12, 128:25, 29, 37, 40; Córdova Pérez, "El movimiento anarquista," 81; El Empleado Mutualista 6, no. 32 (October–December 1914).

15. Huitrón, Orígenes, 230, and Salazar and Escobedo, Las pugnas, 63; Araiza, Historia, 3:39.

16. AGN, RT, 41:26, 78:3, 96:9.

17. Sánchez Sánchez, Surgimiento, 168–83.

18. Leal, Del mutualismo, 81, 158–59; González Navarro, La vida social, 341–42; El Radical, 8 July 1911; Robles Gómez, Huelga tranviaria, 51.

19. Robles Gómez, Huelga tranviaria, 24–25, 26, 41, 61.

20. Nueva Era, 24 November 1911; El Radical, 2, 8, 13 July 1911; Juan Felipe Leal and José Villaseñor, En la Revolución (Mexico City: Siglo XXI, 1988), 250–58.

21. Martínez and Fernández Tomás, "Asambleísmo," 29–35; Antonio Ramos Padrueza to textile worker delegates, 15 March 1912, AGN, RT, 24:1, reproduced in "Las Primeras Tarifas (Salarios) Mínimas en la Industria Textil (1912)," Boletín del Archivo General de la Nación (July–December 1984): 28; Nueva Era, 28 December 1911.

22. Nueva Era, 28 December 1911 and 2, 4, 18 January 1912; Manuel González Ramírez, Manifiestos políticos (1892–1912) (Mexico City: Fondo de Cultura Económica, 1957), 646.

23. Ramírez Rancaño, Burguesía textil, 39; Nueva Era, 28 December 1911 and 3, 4 January 1912.

24. Nueva Era, 10, 15 January 1912.

25. Nueva Era, 21, 26 January 1912; AGN, RT, 55:2; Nueva Era, 18 January 1912; Ramírez Rancaño, Burguesía textil, 41, 69; "Las Primeras Tarifas," 7–14.

26. Ramírez Rancaño, Burguesía textil, 77–84; AGN, RT, 14:25, 56:2, 86:27:1; Anderson, Outcasts, 106, 122; El Imparcial, 3 March 1913.

27. Arenas Guzmán, *Historia*, 100; AGN, RT, 211:17, 418:4, 117:24, 303:5; Ramírez Rancaño, *Burguesía textil*, 77–84.

28. González Navarro, "El primer salario mínimo," 386; Anthony L. Morgon, "Industry and Society in the Mexico City Area, 1875–1920" (Ph.D. diss., Cambridgeshire College of Arts and Technology, England, 1984), 383; "Reglamento," AGN, RT, 91:8.

29. "Reglamento," AGN, RT, 91:8.

30. López, *Sociedades y sindicatos*, 35; AGN, RT, 96:5.

31. "Las Primeras Tarifas," 34; AGN, RT, 70:6.

32. Martínez and Fernández Tomás, "Asambleísmo," 27; AGN, RT, 8:4, 37:30, 52:1, 101:24; Ramírez Rancaño, *Burguesía textil*, 114–15.

33. Córdova Pérez, "El movimiento anarquista," 126–27.

34. AGN, RT, 86:27:10–15; Bernardo García Díaz, "Orizaba 1915: Textiles, constitucionalistas y 'mundialistas.'" *Historias* 8–9 (1985): 91–109.

35. *Nueva Era*, 1 February 1912; AGN, RT, 32:24, 105:10; *El Imparcial*, 7 April 1913.

36. Carr, *El movimiento obrero*, 47.

37. Araiza, *Historia*, 3:48–49; Hart, *Anarchism*, 124–25; AGN, RT, 42:9:1, 75:15.

38. AGN, RT, 70:27, 91:8.

39. AGN, RT, 70:27.

40. *El Demócrata*, 20 and 24 September 1914; Huitrón, *Orígenes*, 246.

41. AGN, RT, 5:11, 52:1, 70:18, 91:6.

42. AGN, RT, 70:18.

43. AGN, RT, 70:18, 91:6; Huitrón, *Orígenes*, 253.

44. *Mexican Herald*, 9, 11, 12 October 1911; *El Pueblo*, 9 October 1914.

45. *El Demócrata*, 9 and 12 October 1914; *Mexican Herald*, 10 and 29 October 1914; AHCM, 1050:603.

46. AGN, RT, 59:4, 70:18; *Mexican Herald*, 14 October 1914; *Mexican Herald*, 16 October 1914; *El Sol*, 26 January 1915.

47. *El Sol*, 16 December 1914, 2 January 1915; Sánchez Sánchez, *Surgimiento*, 156–59; *La Convención*, 7, 8 January 1915.

48. Pérez Taylor, El socialismo, 78; Quintero and Velasco quoted in Sánchez Sánchez, Surgimiento, 161.

49. Córdova Pérez, "El movimiento anarquista," 80–82; Huitrón, Orígenes, 227; Salazar and Escobedo, Las pugnas, 63; El Imparcial, 19 March 1913.

50. El Pueblo, 12 October and 5 November 1914; Sánchez Sánchez, Surgimiento, 164–65, 255, 290–91; Mexican Herald, 9 July 1915.

51. Basurto, Vivencias, 57, 59; Radkau, "La fama" y la vida, 82; AGN, RT, 32:24:1–6

52. AGN, RT, 61:9; Nueva Era, 28 April 1912; El Radical, 2, 8, 13 July 1911; Rafael Pérez Taylor, Un gesto (Mexico City: Botas e Hijo, 1917), 60–71; AGN, RT, 672:20.

53. Martínez and Fernández Tomás, "Asambleísmo," 29–35; Nueva Era, 28 December 1911.

54. Nueva Era, 9, 30 December 1911, 16 January 1912; AGN, RT, 70:8, 70:10; Georgina Limones Ceniceros, "Mujer y movimiento obrero en la Revolución Mexicana, 1912–1915," in Memoria del Congreso Internacional sobre la Revolución Mexicana (Mexico City: Instituto Nacional de Estudios Históricos de la Revolución Mexicana, 1991), 179.

55. AGN, RT, 70:14, and similar incidents in AGN, RT, 70:8, 6:6, 52:1, 97:2; Fototeca del INAH, Fondo Casasola, 6350.

56. Huitrón, Orígenes, 254; El Pueblo, 10 November 1914; Córdova Pérez, "El movimiento anarquista," 37; El Demócrata, 12 October 1914.

57. AGN, RT, 70:22, 70:28, 101:23; Mexican Herald, 26 October, 1 November 1914; Limones Ceniceros, "Mujer y movimiento obrero," 175; El Demócrata, 12 October 1914.

58. Federico de la Colina quoted in Córdova Pérez, "El movimiento anarquista," 135.

59. Córdova Pérez, "El movimiento anarquista," 5; El Sol, 7 January 1915.

60. El Imparcial, 13, 16 July, 14 August 1913; Barry Carr, "The Casa del Obrero Mundial: Constitutionalism and the Pact of February 1915," in El Trabajo, ed. Frost, Meyer, and Vasquéz, 607–8.

61. Araiza, Historia 3:17, 34; AGN, RT, 96:7, 105:10; Salazar and Escobedo, Las pugnas, 1:75; Ariete, 5 December 1915.

62. Pérez Taylor, El socialismo, 117–20; Romero, Guía, 237; Areite, 31 October 1915; Araiza, Historia, 3:106; Salazar and Escobedo, Las pugnas, 1:150–51; El Demócrata, 13 November 1915.

63. La Convención, 6 January 1915; El Sol, 7 January 1915; Walker, "Porfirian Labor Politics," 268–69; Ceballos Ramírez, "La encíclica," 27.

64. Leal, Del mutualismo, 119; Miguel Rodríguez, "Chicago y los charros: Ritos y fiestas de principios de mayo en la Ciudad de México," Historia Mexicana 45, no. 2 (1995): 385; Nueva Era, 19 March 1912; Salazar and Escobedo, Las pugnas, 1:61.

65. Michael C. Meyer, Huerta: A Political Portrait (Lincoln: University of Nebraska Press, 1972), 174; El Imparcial, 27 and 29 April, 1 May 1913; Pérez Taylor, El socialismo, 114; Araiza, Historia, 3:38.

66. Salazar and Escobedo, Las pugnas, 59.

67. Córdova Pérez, "El movimiento anarquista," 83; Rodríguez, "Chicago y los charros," 388.

68. El Imparcial, 2 May 1913; Huitrón, Orígenes, 230; Salazar and Escobedo, Las pugnas, 63; Araiza, Historia, 3:39; Córdova Pérez, "El movimiento anarquista," 83.

69. El Imparcial, 25 May 1913.

70. Francisco Ramírez Plancarte, La Ciudad de México durante la Revolución Constitucionalista (Mexico City: Ediciones Botas, 1941), 50; Knight, Mexican Revolution, 2:67, 158; Javier Garciadiego, Rudos contra científicos: La Universidad Nacional durante la Revolución Mexicana (Mexico City: Colegio de México, 1996), 228–32; El Imparcial, 10 July 1913; Mexican Herald, 3 July 1915; Ramírez Plancarte, La Ciudad de México, 49–50; Enrique Arce, cited in Córdova Pérez, "El movimiento anarquista," 128.

71. Huitrón, Orígenes, 246, 252; Salazar and Escobedo, Las pugnas, 63–65, 79; Córdova Pérez, "El movimiento anarquista," 128; Araiza, Historia, 3:39.

6. URBAN POPULAR CLASSES

1. Letter reprinted in Huitrón, Orígenes, 243–46.

2. Gilly, La Revolución interrumpida, 183.

3. Joseph, Revolution from Without; Knight, Mexican Revolution, 2:240–51, 313.

4. Ramírez Rancaño, Burguesía textil, 144–50, 153, 168; Carr, El movimiento obrero, 61; La Prensa, 8 February 1915.

5. Salazar and Escobedo, *Las pugnas*, 67; AGN, RT, 71:4; *Mexican Herald*, 29 September, 6 November 1914; *El Pueblo*, 2 October 1914; *El Demócrata*, 14 October 1914.

6. AGN, RT, 59:4:39.

7. *El Demócrata*, 20, 26 September, 3 October 1914; Huitrón, *Orígenes*, 253; Illades, *Hacia la república*, 142, 149.

8. Ariel Rodríguez Kuri, "El año cero: El ayuntamiento de México y las facciones revolucionarias (agosto 1914–agosto 1915)," in *Ciudad de México: instituciones, actores sociales y conflicto político, 1774–1931*, ed. Carlos Illades and Ariel Rodríguez (Mexico City: UAM, 1996), 191–222; Knight, *Mexican Revolution*, 2:254–255; AGN, RT, 98:6; *El Sol*, 9 December 1914.

9. *Mexican Herald*, 12 February 1915.

10. *El Demócrata*, 3 October 1914; *El Pueblo*, 3 October 1914.

11. *El Pueblo*, 5 October 1914; *Mexican Herald*, 18 November 1914.

12. Salazar and Escobedo, *Las pugnas*, 1:91; *El Sol*, 20 November 1914.

13. Alejandra Moreno Toscano, "El porvenir de los recuerdos: La crisis de 1915," *Nexos* 8, no. 86 (1985): 5–7; *Mexican Herald*, 13, 21 January 1915; *El Sol*, 12 December 1914.

14. Ramírez Plancarte, *La Ciudad de México*, 289.

15. Knight, *Mexican Revolution*, 2:172–73, 309; Ramírez Plancarte, *La Ciudad de México*, 65–67, 371.

16. *El Pueblo*, 10 October 1914; *El Sol*, 12 December 1914, 21, 22 January 1915.

17. Knight, "Working Class," 51–79; French, *A Peaceful and Working People*, chap. 6; Ramírez Plancarte, *La Ciudad de México*, 367, and the British consul, Mr. Hohler, to Sir Edward Grey, 9 March 1915, in *British Documents on Foreign Affairs: Reports and Papers from the Foreign Office Confidential Print*, pt. 2, ser. D, vol. 2, *Central America and Mexico, 1914–22* (Bethesda MD: University Publications of America, 1989), 126–27.

18. Knight, "Working Class," 16, 51–79; Carr, "The Casa," and Meyer, "Los obreros," 1–37.

19. Ramírez Plancarte, *La Ciudad de México*, 10, 250–52

20. Friedrich Katz, *Pancho Villa* (México: Era, 1998), 23–25.

21. Huitrón, *Orígenes*, 252, 271; El Demócrata, 29 September 1914; Carr, "The Casa," 620–21; "Desde la Atalaya," *Ariete*, 2 January 1916.

22. Ramírez Plancarte, *La Ciudad de México*, 271–77; El Sol, 30 November 1914; Womack, *Zapata*, 219.

23. Knight, *Mexican Revolution*, 2:307.

24. *Mexican Herald*, 4, 6 December 1914; El Sol, 10, 18 December 1914; Friedrich Katz, "Villa: El gobernador revolucionario de Chihuahua," in *Ensayos Mexicanos* (Mexico City: Alianza Editorial, 1994), 344; El Radical, 26 March 1915.

25. El Sol, 25 November 1914; *Mexican Herald*, 6 January 1915; Knight, *Mexican Revolution*, 2:213.

26. Katz, *Pancho Villa*, 33–38.

27. Boletín Municipal: *Organo del Ayuntamiento de México* 1, no. 1, 30 April 1915, 1–6; Ramírez Plancarte, *La Ciudad de México*, 280–83, 290–92: Knight, *Mexican Revolution*, 2:298.

28. El Sol, 30 November 1914; Sánchez Sánchez, *Surgimiento*, 152, 164–65.

29. El Sol, 7, 26 January 1915.

30. *Mexican Herald*, 23 December 1914; El Sol, 12 January 1915; El Sol, 13 January 1915; Sánchez Sánchez, *Surgimiento*, 259; AGN, RT, 71:4, 96:5; Ramírez Plancarte, *La Ciudad de México*, 287.

31. Silliman to Secretary of State, 29 November 1914 and 2 December 1914, Department of State, *Records of the Department of State*, 812.00/13940–13957; El Sol, 30 November, 19 December 1914, 26 January 1915; *Mexican Herald*, 26 January 1915.

32. Sánchez Sánchez, *Surgimiento*, 167–70, 179–80.

33. *La convención: Debates de las sesiones de la Soberana Convención Revolucionaria* (Mexico City: Editorial Jus, 1972)3:73–76; Robert Quirk, *Mexican Revolution*, 183; Womack, *Zapata*, chap. 8.

34. Knight, *Mexican Revolution*, 2:214, 318.

35. Telegrams, Obregón to Carranza, 29 January, 15 February 1915, Archivo Juan Barragán, Biblioteca Nacional, Fondo Presidencia, Caja II, ex. 31; Rodríguez Kuri, "El Año Cero," 196.

36. Arturo Casado Navarro, *Gerardo Murillo, El Dr. Atl* (Mexico City: UNAM, 1984), 31; Linda Hall, *Alvaro Obregón: Power and Revolution in Mexico, 1911–1920*

(College Station: Texas A&M University Press, 1981), 100–101; *Mexican Herald*, 1 November 1915.

37. Rosendo Salazar, *El demagogo* (Mexico City: Costa-Amic, 1961), 45–46.

38. *Mexican Herald*, 30 January, 7, 8, 9, 10 February 1915.

39. Interview with Esther Torres Viuda de Morales, in Archivo de la Palabra, Instituto Mora, 9–23, reproduced in *Memoria*, ed. Gortari Rabiela and Hernández Franyuti, 1:618–19.

40. Temma Kaplan, "Redressing the Balance: Gendered Acts of Justice around the Mining Community of Río Tinto in 1913," in *Constructing Spanish Womanhood: Female Identity in Modern Spain*, ed. Victoria Lorée Enders and Pamela Beth Radcliff (Albany: SUNY Press, 1999), 295.

41. *La Prensa*, 10 February 1915; Telegram, Obregón to Carranza, 11 February 1915, Archivo Juan Barragán, Biblioteca Nacional, Fondo Barragán, Caja II, ex. 34; *Mexican Herald*, 19 February 1915; Ramírez Plancarte, *La Ciudad de México*, 345–63.

42. *Mexican Herald*, 3, 13, 19, 24 February 1915; Ramírez Plancarte, *La Ciudad de México*, 325–30, 369; Knight, *Mexican Revolution*, 2:207.

43. General Manager of National Trust Company, Toronto, to U.S. Secretary of State, 25 February 1915, Department of State, *Records of the Department of State*, 812.78/20; Ávila Espinosa, *El pensamiento económico, político y social de la convención de Aguascalientes* (Mexico City: INEHRM, 1991), 168.

44. *La Prensa*, 7 February 1915; Archivo Dr. Atl, Biblioteca Nacional, Caja 2, ex. 41; Sánchez Sánchez, *Surgimiento*, 168–83; Desiderio Marcos, *Acaparadores y Amoladores* (Mexico City, 1915), 22–23.

45. Sánchez Sánchez, *Surgimiento*, 182; Huitrón, *Orígenes*, 258.

46. *La Prensa*, 8, 9 February 1915; *Mexican Herald*, 9 February 1915.

47. Salazar and Escobedo, *Las pugnas*, 92.

48. *Mexican Herald*, 13, 21 January, 7 February 1915; *La Prensa*, 10 February 1915; López, *Sociedades y sindicatos*, 100.

49. Sánchez Sánchez, *Surgimiento*, 161; Carr, "The Casa," 609; AGN, RT, 96:6, 72:16, 96:5; *El Sol*, 9 January 1915; *Mexican Herald*, 9 January 1915; Huitrón, *Orígenes*, 257–58; *El Sol*, 13 January 1915.

50. Salazar and Escobedo, *Las pugnas*, 93.

51. Huitrón, *Orígenes*, 259, and Araiza, *Historia*, 3:65; Carr, "The Casa," 608–9.

52. *La Prensa*, 13 February 1915; Carr, "The Casa," 613.

53. *La Prensa*, 13 February 1915; AGN, RT, 105:20:1–5

54. *Mexican Herald*, 18, 21 February 1915; Ramírez Plancarte, *La Ciudad de México*, chaps. 14 and 15; *La Prensa*, 13 February 1915; Knight, *Mexican Revolution*, 2:317, 425; Espinosa, *El pensamiento económico*, 181.

55. The daily subsidy to the Red Battalions in Veracruz in mid-March ranged from five thousand to eleven thousand pesos (AGN, Ramo Gobernación, 99:35).

56. Huitrón, *Orígenes*, 259.

57. *La Prensa*, 12 February 1915.

58. *Revolución Social*, 1 May, 5 August 1915; Huitrón, *Orígenes*, 261; AGN, RT, 105:20.

59. Araiza, *Historia*, 3:65–67.

60. Araiza, *Historia*, 3:65–67.

61. *Nueva Era*, 8, 9 March, 4 May 1912.

62. Carr, "The Casa," 613; Huitrón, *Orígenes*, 270; Mr. Hohler to Sir Edward Grey, 9 March 1915, in *British Documents*, 127; Telegram, Obregón to Carranza, 9 March 1915, Archivo Juan Barragán, Fondo Presidencia, Caja III, ex. 2.

63. Rosendo Salazar estimated 2,000 troops (*Líderes y sindicatos* [Mexico City: T. C. Modelo, 1953], 32); the *Mexican Herald* reported 5,000 troops (2, 3 March 1915); Alan Knight estimates 5,000 troops (*Mexican Revolution*, 2:320); Luis Araiza claimed 7,000 troops (*Historia*, 3:67); John M. Hart estimates between 7,000 and 10,000 troops (*Revolutionary Mexico*, 307); Huitrón, *Orígenes*, 266, 270.

64. Salazar, *Líderes y sindicatos*, 31; *Mexican Herald*, 18 February 1915; Ramírez Plancarte, *La Ciudad de México*, 368.

65. Huitrón, *Orígenes*, 264; *Mexican Herald*, 20 February 1915; Ramírez Plancarte, *La Ciudad de México*, 331–32.

66. Salazar and Escobedo, *Las pugnas*, 93, 101, 102, 108; Huitrón, *Orígenes*, 253; John Murray, "Behind the Drums of Revolution, the Labor Movement in Mexico as Seen by an American Trade Unionist," *The Survey*, 2 December 1916, 239–40.

67. Ramírez Plancarte, *La Ciudad de México*, 325–26.

68. Salazar and Escobedo, *Las pugnas*, 101–2; Ramírez Plancarte, *La Ciudad de México*, 328–29.

69. Salazar and Escobedo, *Las pugnas*, 108; Ramírez Plancarte, *La Ciudad de México*, 369; Cardoso de Oliveira to Secretary of State, 10 March 1915, Department of State, *Records of the Department of State*, 812.00/14553 and 812.00/14553.

70. Salazar and Escobedo, *Las pugnas*, 102; *Mexican Herald*, 3 March 1915.

71. Murray, "Behind the Drums," 239–40; *Revolución Social*, 1 May 1915.

72. Telegram, Obregón to Carranza, 7 March 1915, Archivo Juan Barragán, Fondo Presidencia, Caja III, ex. 2; Salazar and Escobedo, *Las pugnas*, 88, 123; Knight, *Mexican Revolution*, 2:320.

73. *Mexican Herald*, 19 February 1915; Salazar and Escobedo, *Las pugnas*, 87, 109–12.

74. Jorge Robles, Jorge Jaber, and Jorge Fernández, "Alrededor de 1915: La COM, Los Batallones Rojos, Atl y las Huelgas," in *Memoria del Segundo Coloquio Regional de Historia Obrera* (Mexico City: CEHSMO, 1979), 454; Telegram, Carranza to Obregón, 25 March 1915, Archivo Juan Barragán, Fondo Presidencia, Caja III, ex. 5; *Boletín del Archivo General de la Nación*, 3d ser., vol. 5, no. 1 (15) (January–March 1981): 3, 26; Carr, "The Casa," 603–32; García Díaz, "Orizaba, 1915."

75. AGN, RT, 96:6:7–8; Carr, "The Casa," 627; "Acta de la sesión celebrada con obreros tabaqueros en la ciudad de Orizaba (Orizaba, Ver. Abril 17 de 1915)," reprinted in *Boletín del Archivo General de la Nación*, 3d ser., vol. 5, no. 1 (15) (January–March 1981): 39–42.

76. Telegram, Obregón to Carranza, 15 June 1915, Archivo Juan Barragán, Fondo Presidencia, Caja III, ex. 18; Rafael Zubáran Capmany, *Proyecto sobre contrato de trabajo* (Veracruz: Departamento de Trabajo, 1915); Sindicato de Conductores de Carruajes de Alquiler de la Ciudad de México, "Libreta de estatutos."

77. Salazar, *Líderes y sindicatos*, 31; *Mexican Herald*, 9, 21 February, 22 March 1915; Ruiz, *Labor*, 51.

78. Ramírez Plancarte, *La Ciudad de México*, 338.

79. *El Renovador*, 1 June 1915; *El Combate*, 26, 28 June 1915; Sánchez Sánchez, *Surgimiento*, 260–61; *El Renovador*, 27 June, 24 July 1915.

80. *El Combate,* 28 June 1915; *El Renovador,* 27 June 1915.

81. *La Convención,* 27 March 1915; Luis Fernando Amaya C., *La Soberana Convención Revolucionaria, 1914–1916* (México: Editorial Trillas, 1975), 258–67.

82. *El Radical,* 3, 4, 14 May 1915; Sánchez Sánchez, *Surgimiento,* 193–219; *La Convención,* 14, 25 May, 1 June 1914; *El Renovador,* 17 June 1915; *Mexican Herald,* 9 July 1915.

83. Sánchez Sánchez, *Surgimiento,* 260; exceptions to these accounts are Carr, *El movimiento obrero,* 71, and Womack, "Mexican Revolution" 112, 118.

84. Murray, "Behind the Drums," 239–40.

7. CONSOLIDATION AND CONFRONTATION

1. Ramírez Plancarte, *La Ciudad de México,* 65–66; the zarzuela *María Pistola* is described in Armando de María y Campos, *El Teatro de Género Chico en la Revolución Mexicana* (Mexico City: INEHRM, 1956), 160–61.

2. Julio Sesto, *La Ciudad de México de los palacios* (Mexico City: El Libro Español, 1920).

3. Knight, "Working Class," 76; Salazar and Escobedo, *Las pugnas,* 200–201.

4. For Latin America, see Teresa A. Meade, *"Civilizing" Rio: Reform and Resistance in a Brazilian City, 1889–1930* (University Park: Pennsylvania State University Press, 1997), and Diane Davis, *Urban Leviathan: Mexico City in the Twentieth Century* (Philadelphia: Temple University Press, 1994).

5. Silvia M. Arrom, "Introduction: Rethinking Urban Politics in Latin America before the Populist Era," in *Riots in the City: Popular Politics and the Urban Poor in Latin America, 1765–1910,* ed. Silvia M. Arrom and Servando Ortell (Wilmington DE: Scholarly Resources, 1996), 1; Silvia M. Arrom, "Popular Politics in Mexico City: The Parián Riot, 1828," in *Riots,* ed. Arrom and Ortell, 71–96; R. Douglas Cope, *The Limits of Racial Domination: Plebian Society in Colonial Mexico City, 1660–1720* (Madison: University of Wisconsin Press, 1994); Gortari Rabiela and Hernández Franyuti, *La Ciudad de México,* 38; Ron Tyler, ed., *Posada's Mexico* (Washington DC: Library of Congress, 1979), 257.

6. Knight, *Mexican Revolution,* 1:133, 208–18.

7. *Nueva Era,* 11 December 1911; *Mexican Herald,* 3 March 1915.

8. Telegram, Carranza to Obregón, 6 March 1915, Archivo Juan Barragán,

Fondo Presidencia, Caja III, ex. 2; Rodgers to Secretary of State, 5 June 1916, Department of State, *Records of the Department of State*, 812.515/124.

9. Ramírez Plancarte, *La Ciudad de México*, 518.

10. Ramírez Plancarte, *La Ciudad de México*, 526; on the sacking of hospitals, see Cardoso de Oliveira to Secretary of State, 6 March 1915, Department of State, *Records of the Department of State*, 812.00/14515; reports of Zapatista confiscations of food entering the capital are in AHCM, Comercio e Industria, 522:27,522:47.

11. AGN, RT, Informe Compañía Mexicana Molinera de Nixtamal, S.A., 173:12, 347:10; Archivo Condumex, fondo 21, L5861:53; AGN, RT, 71:4.

12. *Mexican Herald*, 2, 3 March 1915; British consul, Mr. Hohler to Sir Edward Grey, February 18, 1915, in *British Documents*.

13. *Mexican Herald*, 18–25 May 1915; Francois, "When Pawnshops Talk," 252–54.

14. Kaplan, "Female Consciousness," 31.

15. *Mexican Herald*, 8 February, 27 May, 26 June 1915.

16. Municipal police report, 11–18 July 1915, AHCM, 3645, ex. 1761; *El Combate*, 25 June 1915.

17. *La Convención*, 25 May 1915; *Mexican Herald*, 20, 25 June 1915; Fototeca del INAH, Fondo Casasola, 41489.

18. *Mexican Herald*, 20 June 1915; *El Combate*, 26 June 1915; *El Combate*, 25 June 1915.

19. Ramírez Plancarte, *La Ciudad de México*, 427–47; *La Convención*, 25 June 1915; *El Renovador*, 25 June 1915; *El Combate*, 25 June 1915.

20. *La Convención*, 25 June 1915; *El Renovador*, 25 June 1915; *El Combate*, 25 June 1915; *Mexican Herald*, 20, 26, 27 June, 16 July 1915; see municipal police report, 11–18 July 1915, AHCM, 3645, ex. 1761.

21. *Mexican Herald*, 20, 22 May 1915; Ramírez Plancarte, *La Ciudad de México*, 427–47.

22. Decree, AGN, Ramo Convención Revolucionaria de Aguascalientes, 1601, 7:5 f. 2 and 7:8 f. 2; *Mexican Herald*, 21–25 May 1915.

23. Pamela Beth Radcliff, "Women's Politics: Consumer Riots in Twentieth-

Century Spain," in *Constructing Spanish Womanhood*, ed. Enders and Radcliff, 306; Barbara Clark Smith, "Food Rioters and the American Revolution," *The William and Mary Quarterly* 61, no. 1 (1994): 3–38.

24. Petition, AGN, Ramo Convención Revolucionaria de Aguascalientes, 1601, 7:9 f. 104–5.

25. El Combate, 25 July 1915.

26. On the increase in prostitution during the revolution, see Ramírez Plancarte, *La Ciudad de México*, 367, and Bliss, "Prostitution," 83–86; de María y Campos, *El Teatro*, 176–78.

27. El Combate, 25 July 1915.

28. El Renovador, 26 June 1915; Petition, AGN, Ramo Convención Revolucionaria de Aguascalientes, 1601, 7:9 f. 104–5; El Renovador, 1 July 1915; La Convención, 25, 26 June 1915.

29. El Radical, 5 June 1915; Mexican Herald, 6 June 1915; El Combate, 28 June 1915.

30. Radcliff, "Women's Politics," 306–7; El Demócrata, 24 August 1915.

31. El Combate, 6 July 1915; Ramírez Plancarte, La Ciudad de México, 512–13.

32. See July 1915 police summaries in AHCM, 3645, ex. 1761.

33. José Valadés, Historia general de la Revolución Mexicana (Mexico: Ediciones Gernika, 1963–65), 5:342; Huitrón, Orígenes, 292–93.

34. Charles O'Conner papers, 9 August 1915, Manuscripts, Bancroft Library, University of California, Berkeley.

35. Archivo Dr. Atl, 6:1:5; Ariete, 15, 31 October 1915; Liga Libre de Linotipistas del D.F., 15 May 1918, AGN, RT, 13:59; interview with Ignacia Torres in Basurto, Vivencias, 43.

36. Decree, 30 August 1915, AGN, RT, 75:15; Ariete, 7 November 1915; El Demócrata, 13 November 1915, 4 August 1916; Petition of 120 streetcar workers, December 1915, AGN, Período Revolución, 161:10 (75):8.

37. Pablo González, Informe que el general de división Pablo González, rinde al C. Venustiano Carranza (Mexico: J. Chávez, 1915), 52, 54; Charles O'Conner papers, diary, 21 September, 9 October 1915; Telegram, Carranza to Obregón, 29 September 1915, Archivo Juan Barragán, Fondo Presidencia, Caja III, ex 18.

38. El Demócrata, 24 August 1915; Sánchez Sánchez, Surgimiento, 258; Ariete, 7

November, 5 December 1915; *Ariete*, 24, 31 October, 5 December 1915; Huitrón, *Orígenes*, 290–94; *Ariete*, 7 November 1916; AHCM, 3857.

39. Entrevista con la Señora Esther Torres, 22; interview with Esther Torres, in Basurto, *Vivencias*, 58; Limones Ceniceros, "Mujer y movimiento obrero," 179.

40. *Ariete*, 21 November 1915; *Ariete*, 5 December 1915; Huitrón, *Orígenes*, 292–93; on *tertulias*, see interview with Esther Torres, in Basurto, *Vivencias*, 70–71.

41. Sánchez Sánchez, *Surgimiento*, 244–48; *Ariete*, 24 October 1915; Womack, "Mexican Revolution," 167.

42. El *Demócrata*, 2 September 1915; *Revolución Social*, 7 September 1915; *Ariete*, 14, 21 November 1915, and Huitrón, *Orígenes*, 290; *Ariete*, 5 December 1915; Limones Ceniceros, "Mujer y movimiento obrero," 177.

43. Archivo Condumex, Carranza papers, 3, 4 November 1915, reproduced in "Documentos," *Historia Obrera* 5, no. 17 (September 1979): 14–16.

44. Araiza, *Historia*, 3:115–16; Sánchez Sánchez, *Surgimiento*, 258, 304–5.

45. Araiza, *Historia*, 3:112; Salazar and Escobedo, *Las pugnas*, 151, 179; Hart, *Anarchism*, 141.

46. Study by Eduardo Fuentes, in Archivo Condumex, fondo 21, L 5861, Carpeta 53, 22; for a more moderate estimate of production losses, see Womack, "Mexican Revolution," 5:86.

47. Archivo Condumex, Fuentes, 23–33; AGN, RT, 397:2, 291:16; the Compañia Mexicana Molinera de Nixtamal owned ninety-one mills listed in the 1921 industrial census; AGN, RT, 173:12.

48. Womack, "Mexican Revolution," 133, and *Zapata*, 260; AHCM, La Reguladora de Comercio, 3853, 3855, and ayuntamiento reports, AHCM, 522:24, 47.

49. Edwin W. Kemmerer, *Inflation and Revolution: Mexico's Experience of 1912–1917* (Princeton NJ: Princeton University Press, 1940), 45–46; E. Cardenas and C. Manns, "Inflation and Monetary Stabilization in Mexico during the Revolution," *Journal of Development Economics* 27 (1987): 384; AHCM, 1013, ex. 150.

50. See Knight, "Working Class," 76 n. 4.

51. El *Demócrata*, 4, 10 January 1916; El *Radical*, 4 May 1915; El *Renovador*, 17 June 1915; La *Convención*, 13 May 1915; *Ariete*, 5 December 1915.

52. AHCM, 522:65, 3844:2, 3855:30, 3857, and Huitrón, *Orígenes*, 291; El *Dem*-

ócrata, 15 November 1915; *Ariete*, 14 November 1915; AHCM, 3857, 3853:11, 3855; El Demócrata, 4 January 1916; El Demócrata, 18 December 1915.

53. *Ariete*, 5 December 1915 (capitals in original); see also the editorials in *Acción Mundial*, 5, 22, 24, 26 May 1916; Federation letter of 24 July 1916 to General Hill, Archivo Condumex, fondo 21, 7689:9953.

54. El Demócrata, 19 January 1916; El Demócrata, 2 February 1916; El Pueblo, 12 March 1916; Womack, "Mexican Revolution," 169; AGN, Ramo Gobernación, Período Revolución, 13:8; Huitrón, *Orígenes*, 293.

55. Huitrón, *Orígenes*, 294; El Demócrata, 19 January 1916; Araiza, Historia, 3:174. Sánchez Sánchez, Surgimiento, 317.

56. El Pueblo, 18, 21 May 1916.

57. *Le Courrier du Mexique*, 23 May 1916.

58. Decree, May 1916, AGN, Periodo Revolución, 75:24; El Pueblo, 23 May 1916.

59. On the officers of the Casa del Obrero Mundial, see AGN, Ramo Gobernación, Período Revolución, 76:5.

60. El Pueblo, 24 May 1916.

61. El Pueblo, 24 May 1916.

62. On Hill's support for fired workers, see interview with Esther Torres, in Basurto, *Vivencias*, 62; Rodgers to Secretary of State, 5 June 1916, Department of State, *Records of the Department of State*, 812.515/124, and 7 June 1916, 812.515/130; Jiménez Muñoz, La traza del poder, 140; El Pueblo, 11 June 1916; Sánchez Sánchez, Surgimiento, 329.

63. Kemmerer, *Inflation and Revolution*, 101; El Pueblo, 18 July 1916, 5; El Siglo, 21 July 1916; AGN, RT, 75:15.

64. Archivo Condumex, fondo 21, 76–89:9953.

65. El Pueblo, 22 July, 3 August 1916; Archivo Condumex, fondo 21, 76–89:9953; El Pueblo, 26 July 1916; Archivo Condumex, fondo 21, 90–91:10100.

66. Manifesto to General Benjamín Hill (24 July 1916), Archivo Condumex, fondo 21, 76–89:9953.

67. El Pueblo, 27 July 1916, reproduced in Sánchez Sánchez, Surgimiento, 338–39.

68. AGN, RT, 75:15; Salazar and Escobedo, *Las pugnas*, 200; Archivo Condumex, fondo 21, 76–89:9953, 90–91:10100;

69. Araiza, *Historia*, 3:140–41; Basurto, *Vivencias*, 35.

70. Salazar and Escobedo, *Las pugnas*, 202.

71. Araiza, *Historia*, 3:138–72; *El Demócrata*, 4 August 1916; *El Pueblo*, 3 August 1916; Salazar and Escobedo, *Las pugnas*, 174.

72. Rosendo Salazar, *El demagogo* (Mexico City: Costa-Amic, 1961); Araiza, *Historia*, 3:140; Harvey Levenstein, *Labor Organizations in the United States and Mexico* (Westport: Greenwood Press, 1971), 44; Huitrón, *Orígenes*, 296; Rosendo Salazar *La Casa*, 232; J. H. Retinger, *Morones of Mexico* (London: Labour Publishing, 1926), 8–9.

73. Archivo Condumex, fondo 21, 90–91:10100; Araiza, *Historia*, 3:140; Basurto, *Vivencias*, 70–71.

74. Decree in Archivo Condumex, fondo 21, 90–91:1009; Araiza, *Historia*, 3:138–72; *El Demócrata*, 4 August 1916; *El Pueblo*, 3, 4, 12 August 1916.

75. *El Pueblo*, 12 August 1916.

76. *El Pueblo*, 12 August 1916.

77. *El Pueblo*, 27 August 1916; Salazar and Escobedo, *Las pugnas*, 215, 222; Huitrón, *Orígenes*, 297; interview with Esther Torres, in Basurto, *Vivencias*, 74.

78. *El Pueblo*, 3 August 1916.

79. *El Pueblo*, 3, 6 August 1916 (capitals in original).

80. *El Pueblo*, 16 August 1916, cited in Sánchez Sánchez, *Surgimiento*, 364.

81. Araiza, *Historia*, 3:144; *El Demócrata*, 5 August 1916.

82. *El Demócrata*, 5 August 1916; Kemmerer, *Revolution and Inflation*, 104.

83. The quote is from *El Economista Mexicano*, 1 December 1916, and is repeated in Kemmerer, *Revolution and Inflation*, 114; Salazar and Escobedo, *Las pugnas*, 223.

8. THE AFTERMATH OF REVOLUTION

1. *Luz*, 13, 17 June 1917.

2. Eberhardt Victor Niemeyer, *Revolution at Querétaro*, Latin American Monograph Series, no. 33 (Austin: University of Texas Press, 1974), 33; *El Nacional*,

8 August 1916; *Diario de los debates del Congreso Constituyente, 1916–1917*, 2 vols. (Mexico, 1960), 2:397–409; Jesus Acuña, *Memoria de la Secretaria de Gobernación* (Mexico City: Imcomex, 1916, 1985), 386–87; Gortari Rabiela and Hernández Franyuti, eds., *Memoria*, 1:190; AHCM, Justicia, 2684.

3. *Diario de los debates*, 2:846–58; Knight, *Mexican Revolution*, 2:435.

4. *Diario de los debates*, 2:846–58.

5. Kevin Middlebrook, *The Paradox of Revolution: Labor, the State, and Authoritarianism in Mexico* (Baltimore: Johns Hopkins University Press, 1995), 47–49.

6. Sánchez Sánchez, *Surgimiento*, 401–5; Pablo González Casanova, *La clase obrera, en la historia de México: En el Primer Gobierno Constitutcional (1917–1920)* (Mexico City: Siglo Veintiuno, 1984), 32–33, 97–99, 130; Rodríguez, "Chicago y los charros," 389.

7. Nicolás Cárdenas García, "Trabajadores y lucha por el poder político en el gobierno de Carranza: Los orígenes de la acción múltiple (1917–1920)," *Investigación Humanística* 2, no. 2 (1986): 44; Salazar and Escobedo, *Las pugnas*, 2:46–48; AGN, RT, 147:7, 378:2, 560:8

8. Rosalinda Monzón de Reyes, "El partido socialista obrero y el partido laborista mexicano," *Historia Obrera* 7, no. 25 (1982): 2–12; Salazar and Escobedo, *Las pugnas*, 235–36.

9. AHCM, 1300:23, 872:8; Marjorie Ruth Clark, *La organización obrera en México* (Mexico City: Ediciones ERA, 1979), 56; González Casanova, *La clase obrera*, 70–78.

10. González Casanova, *La clase obrera*, 113–14.

11. González Casanova, *La clase obrera*, 113–20, 126–35; AHCM, 4003:1.

12. Middlebrook, *Paradox*, 80; José Rivera Castro, "Le syndicalisme officiel et le syndicalisme revolutionnaire au Mexique dans les années 1920," *Le Mouvement Social* 103 (1978): 31–53; de los Reyes, *Cines y sociedad*, 346; Jaime Tamayo, *La clase obrera en la historia de México: En el interinato de Adolfo de la Huerta y el Gobierno de Álvaro Obregón (1920–1924)* (Mexico: Siglo XXI, 1987), chap. 4.

13. Huitrón, *Orígenes*, 254; *El Pueblo*, 10 November 1914; AGN, RT, 211:17, 25; Morgon, "Industry and Society," 409.

14. AGN, RT, 211:25.

15. AGN, RT, 211:17, 418:4.

16. AGN, RT, 211:17, 418:4, 672:20.

17. Womack, "Mexican Revolution," 186; Guillermina Baena Paz, "La Confederación General de Trabajadores (1921–31)," *Revista Mexicana de Ciencias Políticas y Sociales* 21 (1976): 113–85.

18. AGN, Presidentes Obregón-Calles, 407-T-1; Sánchez Sánchez, *Surgimiento*, 392–97; Rodríguez, *Los tranviarios*, 156–59.

19. Rodríguez, *Los tranviarios*, 160–65, 170–87, 227–28; AGN, RT, 439:3.

20. Rodríguez, *Los tranviarios*, chaps. 10 and 11.

21. Middlebrook, *Paradox*, 80; Salazar and Escobedo, *Las pugnas*, 2:241.

22. Instituto Nacional de Estadística Geografía e Informática, *Estadísticas históricas de México*, 2 vols. (Mexico City: INEGI, 1986) 1:254; Lanny Thompson, "The Structures and Vicissitudes of Reproduction: Households in Mexico, 1876–1970," *Review* 14, no. 3 (1991): 403–6; Keremitsis, "Latin American Women Workers in Transition: Sexual Division of the Labor Force in Mexico and Colombia in the Textile Industry," *The Americas* 40, no. 4 (April 1984): 491–504, and "Del metate al molino"; AGN, RT, 117:24, 772; Sánchez Sánchez, *Surgimiento*, 431; Entrevista con la Señora Esther Torres.

23. AGN, RT, 499:4; Moisés González Navarro, *Población y sociedad en México* (Mexico: UNAM, 1974), 188; Departamento de la Estadística Nacional, *Censo*, 1921.

24. AGN, RT, 324:20, 227:5, 223:10; *El Renovador*, 9 July 1916: González Navarro, *Población*, 189.

25. AGN, RT, 41:26, 78:3; *El Demócrata*, 3 October 1914; *El Pueblo*, 3 October 1914; González Navarro, *Población*, 189–90; Berra Stoppa, "La expansión," 500; José Valadés, *Memorias de un joven rebelde* (Culiacán, Mexico: Universidad Autónoma de Sinoloa, 1986), 2:123–26; Paco Ignacio Taibo II, *Los Bolshevikis: Historia narrativa de los orígenes del comunismo en México* (Mexico City: Joaquin Mortiz, 1987), 164.

26. González Navarro, *Población*, 189–90; Taibo, *Los Bolshevikis*, 169–72; Berra Stoppa, "La expansión," 526.

27. AGN, Ramo Presidentes Obregón-Calles, 731-I-5:17, 805-c-318:3; Valadés, *Memorias*, 126; Taibo, *Los Bolshevikis*, 180–81; González Navarro, *Población*, 191, 198.

Selected Bibliography

PRINCIPAL ARCHIVES

Archivo Condumex, Carranza papers

Archivo General de la Nación (AGN): Ramo Convención Revolucionaria de Aguascalientes, Ramo Gobernación, Ramo Presidentes, Ramo Revolución, Ramo Trabajo (RT)

Archivo Histórico del Ex-Ayuntamiento de la Ciudad de México (AHCM)

Biblioteca Nacional: Archivo Dr. Atl, Archivo Juan Barragán

Fototeca del INAH, Fondo Casasola in Pachuca, Mexico

Hemeroteca Nacional, Fondo Reservado

Instituto Mora, Archivo de la Palabra

Universidad Iberoamericana, Archivo Porfirio Díaz

ARTICLES, BOOKS, AND DISSERTATIONS

Anderson, Rodney. "Mexican Workers and the Politics of Revolution, 1906–1911." *Hispanic American Historical Review* 54, no. 1 (1974): 94–113.

———. *Outcasts in Their Own Land: Mexican Industrial Workers, 1906–1911.* DeKalb: Northern Illinois University Press, 1976.

Araiza, Luis. *Historia del movimiento obrero mexicano.* 2d ed. 4 vols. Mexico City: Ediciones de la Casa Mundial, 1964–66, 1975.

Ávila Espinosa, Felipe Arturo. *El pensamiento económico, político y social de la convención de Aguascalientes.* Mexico City: INEHRM, 1991.

———. "La Sociedad Mutualista y Moralizadora de Obreros del Distrito Federal (1909–1911)." *Historia Mexicana* 42, no. 1 (1993): 117–54.

Baena Paz, Guillermina. "La Confederación General de Trabajadores (1921–31)." *Revista Mexicana de Ciencias Políticas y Sociales* 21 (1976): 113–85.

Bastian, Jean-Pierre. *Los disidentes: Sociedades protestantes y revolución en México, 1872–1911.* Mexico: El Colegio de México/FCE, 1989.

———. "Metodismo y Clase Obrera durante el Porfiriato." *Historia Mexicana* 33, no. 1 (1983): 39–71.

411

Basurto, Jorge. *Vivencias femeninas de la Revolución*. Mexico: INEHRM, 1992.

Beezley, William. *Judas at the Jockey Club and Other Episodes of Porfirian Mexico*. Lincoln: University of Nebraska Press, 1987.

Berra Stoppa, Erica. "La expansión de la Ciudad de México y los conflictos urbanos, 1900–1930." Ph.D. diss., El Colegio de México, 1982.

Bliss, Katherine Elaine. "Prostitution, Revolution and Social Reform in Mexico City, 1918–1940." Ph.D. diss., University of Chicago, 1996.

Blum, Ann Shelby. "Children without Parents: Law, Charity and Social Practice, Mexico City, 1867–1940." Ph.D. diss., University of California, Berkeley, 1998.

British Documents on Foreign Affairs: Reports and Papers from the Foreign Office Confidential Print. Pt. 2. Ser. D. Vol. 2, Central America and Mexico, 1914–22. Bethesda MD: University Publications of America, 1989.

Brown, Jonathan C. "Foreign and Native-born Workers in Porfirian Mexico." *American Historical Review* 98, no. 3 (June 1993): 786–818.

———. *Oil and Revolution in Mexico*. Berkeley: University of California Press, 1993.

Camarena, Mario. "Disciplina e indisciplina: Los obreros textiles del valle de México en los años veinte." *Historias* 7 (1984): 3–15.

Camarena, Mario, and Lief Adleson. "Historia social de los obreros industriales mexicanos, 1918–1929." *Historias* 8–9 (1985): 69–89.

Carr, Barry. "The Casa del Obrero Mundial, Constitutionalism and the Pact of February 1915." In *El trabajo y los trabajadores en la historia de México*, ed. Elsa Frost, 603–33. Mexico City: Colegio de México, 1979.

———. *El movimiento obrero y la política en México, 1910/1929*. Colección Problemas de México. Mexico DF: Ediciones Era, 1976.

Casasola, Gustavo. *Historia gráfica de la Revolución Mexicana*. 5 vols. Mexico City: Trillas, 1992.

Ceballos Ramírez, Manuel. *El catolicismo social: Un tercero en discordia, Rerum Novarum, la "cuestión social" y la movilización de los católicos mexicanos (1891–1911)*. Mexico City: Colegio de México, 1991.

———. "La encíclica 'Rerum Novarum' y los trabajadores católicos en la Ciudad de México (1891–1913)." *Historia Mexicana* 33, no. 1 (1983): 3–38.

Celada, Fernando. *En capilla: Monólogo dedicado a los obreros de la República Mexicana*. Mexico City: Aguilar, 1898.

Clark, Marjorie Ruth. *Organized Labor in Mexico*. Chapel Hill: University of North Carolina Press, 1934. Reprint, New York: Russell and Russell, 1974.

Cockcroft, James. *Intellectual Precursors of the Mexican Revolution*. 2d ed. Austin: University of Texas Press, 1976.

Córdova Pérez, Fernando. "El movimiento anarquista en México (1911–1921)."

B.A. thesis, Facultad de Ciencias Políticas y Sociales. Mexico City: UNAM, 1971.

Cumberland, Charles C. *The Mexican Revolution: Genesis under Madero*. Austin: University of Texas Press, 1952.

del Campo, Angel. *Cuentos del arrabal*. Mexico: SEP, n.d.

de los Reyes, Aurelio. *Cine y sociedad en México, 1896–1930*. Mexico City: UNAM, 1981.

Departamento de la Estadística Nacional. *Censo general de habitantes, 1921. Distrito Federal*. Mexico City: Departamento de la Estadística Nacional, 1925.

Department of State. *Records of the Department of State Relating to the Internal Affairs of Mexico, 1910–1929*. 812.00 series. Washington DC: National Archives and Record Service, 1959.

Diario de los debates del Congreso Constituyente, 1916–1917. 2 vols. Mexico, 1960.

Díaz, María Elena. "The Satiric Penny Press for Workers in Mexico, 1900–1910: A Case Study in the Politicisation of Popular Culture." *Journal of Latin American Studies* 22, no. 3 (1990): 497–526.

Dirección General de Estadística. *Censo general de la República Mexicana, 1895*. Mexico City: Dirección General de Estadística, 1897–99.

———. *Censo general de población por entidades, 1900, Distrito Federal*. Mexico City: Dirección General de Estadística, 1901–7.

———. *Censo de población de los Estados Unidos Mexicanos, 1910*. Mexico City: Dirección General de Estadística, 1918–20.

———. *Primer censo industrial de 1930*. 3 vols. Mexico City: Dirección General de Estadística, 1930–35.

Dollero, Adolfo. *México al día: Impresiones y notas de viaje*. Mexico City: Bouret, 1911.

French, John, and Daniel James, eds. *The Gendered Worlds of Latin American Women Workers*. Durham NC: Duke University Press, 1997.

French, William E. *A Peaceful and Working People: Manners, Morals, and Class Formation in Northern Mexico*. Albuquerque: University of New Mexico Press, 1996.

———. "Prostitutes and Guardian Angels: Women, Work, and the Family." *Hispanic American Historical Review* 72, no.4 (1992): 529–53.

Frost, Elsa, Michael C. Meyer, Josefina Zoraida Vazquéz, eds. *El trabajo y los trabajadores en la historia de México*. Mexico City: Colegio de México, 1979.

García, Genaro. *Crónica oficial de las fiestas del primer centenario de la independencia de México*. Mexico City: Condumex, 1990.

García Díaz, Bernardo. "Orizaba 1915: Textiles, constitucionalistas y 'mundialistas." *Historias* 8–9 (1985): 91–109.

————. *Un pueblo fabril del porfiriato: Santa Rosa, Veracruz.* Mexico DF: Fondo de Cultura Económica, 1981.

Gilly, Adolfo. *La Revolución interrumpida, México 1910–1920.* Mexico City: Ediciones El Caballito, 1974.

González Casanova, Pablo. *La clase obrera en la historia de México: En el Primer Gobierno Constitutcional (1917–1920).* Mexico City: Siglo Veintiuno, 1984.

González Navarro, Moisés. *Historia moderna de México: El Porfiriato: La vida social.* Mexico City: El Colegio de México, 1957.

Gortari Rabiela, Hira de. "El empleo en la Ciudad de México a fines del siglo XIX. Una discusión." *Secuencia: Revista de Ciencias Sociales* 3 (1985): 37–48.

Gortari Rabiela, Hira de, and Regina Hernández Franyuti, eds. *Memoria y encuentros: La Ciudad de México y el Distrito Federal (1824–1928).* 4 vols. Mexico City: Instituto Mora, 1988.

Guadarrama, Rocío. *Los sindicatos y la política en México: La CROM.* Mexico City: Era, 1981.

Guerra, Francois Xavier. "Las elecciones legislativas de la Revolución mexicana, 1912." *Revista Mexicana de Sociología* 52, no. 2 (1990): 241–76.

————. *México, del Antiguo Régimen a la Revolución.* Mexico City: Fondo de Cultura Económica, 1988.

Guerrero, Julio. *La génesis del crimen en México: Estudio de psiquiatría social.* 2d ed. Mexico City: Porrua, 1977.

Gutiérrez Nájera, Manuel. *La novela del tranvía y otros cuentos.* Mexico: Fondo de Cultura Económica, 1984.

Haber, Stephen. *Industry and Underdevelopment: The Industrialization of Mexico, 1890–1940.* Stanford: Stanford University Press, 1989.

Hall, Linda. *Alvaro Obregón: Power and Revolution in Mexico, 1911–1920.* College Station: Texas A&M University Press, 1981.

Hart, John M. *Anarchism and the Mexican Working Class, 1860–1931.* Austin: University of Texas Press, 1987.

————. *Revolutionary Mexico: The Coming and Process of the Mexican Revolution.* Berkeley: University of California Press, 1987.

Harvey, David. *Consciousness and the Urban Experience.* Baltimore: Johns Hopkins University Press, 1985.

Híjar, Alberto. "Notas sobre cultura obrera mexicana." In *Monografías obreras,* ed. Victoria Novelo. Vol. 1. Mexico City: Cuadernos de la Casa Chata, 1987.

Huitrón, Jacinto. *Orígenes e historia del movimiento obrero en México.* Mexico City: Editores Mexicanos Unidos, 1984.

Illades, Carlos. *Hacia la República del Trabajo: La organización artesanal en la Ciudad de México, 1853–1876.* Mexico: Colegio de México, 1996.

Instituto Nacional de Estadística Geografía e Informática. *Estadísticas históricas de México.* 2 vols. Mexico City: INEGI, 1986.

Jiménez Muñoz, Jorge H. *La traza del poder: Historia de la política y los negocios urbanos en el Distrito Federal.* Mexico City: CODEX, 1993.

Johns, Michael. *The City of Mexico in the Age of Díaz.* Austin: University of Texas Press, 1997.

Jones, Gareth Stedman. *Languages of Class: Studies in English Working Class History, 1832–1982.* Cambridge: Cambridge University Press, 1983.

———. *Outcast London.* New York: Pantheon Books, 1984.

Kaplan, Temma. "Female Consciousness and Collective Action: The Case of Barcelona, 1910–1918." *Signs: Journal of Women in Culture and Society* 7, no. 31 (1982): 545–66.

———. *Red City, Blue Period: Social Movements in Picasso's Barcelona.* Berkeley: University of California Press, 1992.

Katz, Friedrich. "Mexico: Restored Republic and Porfiriato, 1867–1910." In *The Cambridge History of Latin America,* ed. Leslie Bethell, 5:3–78. Cambridge: Cambridge University Press.

Katznelson, Ira. "Working Class Formation and the State: Nineteenth-Century England in American Perspective." In *Bringing the State Back,* ed. Peter Evans, Dietrich Rueschemeyer, and Theda Skocpol. Cambridge: Cambridge University Press, 1985.

Keremitsis, Dawn. *La industria textil mexicana en el siglo XIX.* Mexico City: Secretaría de Educación Pública, 1973.

———. "Del metate al molino." *Historia Mexicana* 33, no. 2 (1983): 285–302.

Knight, Alan. "El Liberalismo mexicano desde la Reforma hasta la Revolución (una interpretación)." *Historia Mexicana* 35, no. 1 (1985): 59–85.

———. *The Mexican Revolution.* 2 vols. Cambridge: Cambridge University Press, 1986.

———. "The Working Class and the Mexican Revolution, c. 1900–1920." *Journal of Latin American Studies* 16 (1984): 51–79.

La Convención. Debates de las Sesiones de la Soberana Convención Revolucionaria. Mexico City: Editorial Jus, 1972.

Lara y Pardo, Luis. *La prostitución en México.* Mexico City: Viuda de C. Bouret, 1908.

Leal, Juan Felipe. *Del mutualismo al sindicalismo en México: 1843–1910.* Mexico City: Ediciones El Caballito, 1991.

Leal, Juan Felipe, and Mario Huacuja Rountree. *Economía y sistema de haciendas en México: La hacienda pulquera en el cambio.* Mexico City: Era, 1984.

Leal, Juan Felipe, and José Villaseñor. *En la Revolución*. Mexico City: Siglo XXI, 1988.

Lear, John. "Workers, *Vecinos*, Citizens: The Revolution in Mexico City." Ph.D. diss., University of California, Berkeley, 1993.

Lira, Andrés. *Comunidades indígenas frente a la Ciudad de México*. Mexico City: Colegio de México, 1983.

Lopez, C. D. *Sociedades y sindicatos*. Mexico City: Tipografía de la oficina de la Secretaría de Hacienda, 1918.

Macedo, Miguel. *La criminalidad en México*. Mexico City: Secretaría de Fomento, 1897.

Martínez, Andrea, and Jorge Fernández Tomás. "Asambleísmo, 'espontaneidad,' huelga y maderismo: Una Ojeada y muchas preguntas sobre las movilizaciones de 1911 en el sector textil." *Historia Obrera* 5, no. 20 (September 1982): 29.

Meyer, Jean. "Los obreros en la Revolución Mexicana: Los 'Batallones Rojos.'" *Historia Mexicana* 21, no. 1 (1971): 1–37.

Meyer, Michael C. *Huerta: A Political Portrait*. Lincoln: University of Nebraska Press, 1972.

Middlebrook, Kevin. *The Paradox of Revolution: Labor, the State, and Authoritarianism in Mexico*. Baltimore: Johns Hopkins University Press, 1995.

Morales, María Dolores. "La expansión de la Ciudad de México en el siglo XIX: El caso de los fraccionamientos." In *Investigaciones sobre la historia de la Ciudad de México*, ed. Alejandra Moreno Toscano et al. Vol. 1. Mexico City: INAH, 1974.

———. "Francisco Somera y el primer fraccionamiento de la Ciudad de México, 1840–1889." In *Formación y desarrollo de la burguesía en México*, ed. Ciro F. S. Cardoso. Mexico City: Siglo XIX, 1987.

Moreno Toscano, Alejandra, ed. *Ciudad de México: Ensayo de construcción de una historia*. Mexico City: INAH, 1978.

———. *Investigaciones sobre la historia de la Ciudad de México*. Mexico City, 1974.

Morgan, Anthony L. "Industry and Society in the Mexico City Area, 1875–1920." Ph.D. diss., Cambridgeshire College of Arts and Technology, England, 1984.

Morgan, Tony. "Proletarians, Politicos, and patriarchs: The Use and Abuse of Cultural Customs in the Early Industrialization of Mexico city, 1880–1910." In *Rituals of Rule, Rituals of Resistance: Public Celebrations and Popular Culture in Mexico*, ed. William H Beezley, Cheryl Martin, and William French. Wilmington DE: Scholarly Resources, 1994.

Mraz, John. "'Calidad de Esclavas': Tortilleras en los molinos de nixtamal, México, Diciembre, 1919." *Historia Obrera* 24, no. 6 (March 1982): 2–14.

———. "Más allá de la decoración: Hacia una historia gráfica de las mujeres en México." *Política y Cultura*, no. 1 (fall 1992): 155–89.

Murga, Gonzalo De. "Atisbos sociológicos." *Boletín de la Sociedad de Geografía y Estadísticas* 6 (1913): 474–97.

Niemeyer, Eberhardt Victor. *Revolution at Querétaro.* Latin American Monograph Series, no. 33. Austin: University of Texas Press, 1974.

Novelo, Victoria. "Los trabajadores mexicanos en el siglo XIX: ¿Obreros o artesanos?" In *Comunidad, cultura y vida social: Ensayos sobre la formación de la clase obrera*, ed. Seminario de movimiento obrero y Revolución Mexicana, 15–51. Mexico City: INAH, 1991.

Peñafiel, Antonio. *Anuario estadístico de la República Mexicana, 1895.* Mexico City: Secretaría de Fomento, 1896.

Pérez Taylor, Rafael. *Un gesto.* Mexico City: Botas e Hijo, 1917.

———. *El socialismo en México, 1913.* Mexico City: CEHSMO, 1976.

Piccato Rodríguez, Pablo. "Criminals in Mexico City, 1900–1931: A Cultural History." Ph.D. diss., University of Texas, 1997.

Quirk, Robert E. *The Mexican Revolution and the Catholic Church, 1910–1929.* Bloomington: Indiana University Press, 1973.

———. *The Mexican Revolution: The Convention of Aguascalientes.* Bloomington: Indiana University Press, 1960.

Radcliff, Pamela Beth. "Women's Politics: Consumer Riots in Twentieth-Century Spain." In *Constructing Spanish Womanhood: Female Identity in Modern Spain*, ed. Victoria Lorée Enders and Pamela Beth Radcliff. Albany: SUNY Press, 1999.

Radkau, Verena. *"La fama" y la vida: Una fabrica y sus obreras.* Mexico: CIESAS, 1984.

———. *"Por la debilidad de nuestro ser": Mujeres "del pueblo" en la paz porfiriana.* Mexico City: SEP, 1989.

Ramírez Plancarte, Francisco. *La Ciudad de México durante la Revolución Constitucionalista.* Mexico City: Ediciones Botas, 1941.

Ramírez Rancaño, Mario. *Burguesía textil y política en la Revolución Mexicana.* Mexico City: UNAM, 1987.

Richmond, Douglas W. *Venustiano Carranza's Nationalist Struggle, 1893–1920.* Lincoln: University of Nebraska Press, 1983.

Rivera Castro, José. "Le Syndicalisme officiel et le syndicalisme revolutionnaire au Mexique dans les années 1920." *Le Mouvement Social* 103 (1978): 31–53.

Robles Gómez, Jorge. *Huelga tranviaria y motín popular*. Toluca: Universidad Autónoma del Estado de México, 1981.

Robles, Jorge, Jorge Jaber, and Jorge Fernández. "Alrededor de 1915: La COM, Los Batallones Rojos, Atl y las Huelgas." In *Memoria del Segundo Coloquio Regional de Historia Obrera*. Mexico City: CEHSMO, 1979.

Rodríguez, Miguel. "Chicago y los charros: Ritos y fiestas de principios de mayo en la Ciudad de México." *Historia Mexicana* 45, no. 2 (1995): 383–421.

———. *Los tranviarios y el anarquismo en México*. Puebla: Universidad Autónoma de Puebla, 1980.

Rodríguez Kuri, Ariel. *La experiencia olvidada: El ayuntamiento de México: política y gobierno, 1876–1912*. Mexico: UAM/Colegio de México, 1996.

Rodríguez Piña, Jaime. "Las Vecindades en 1811." In *Investigaciones sobre la historia de la Ciudad de Mexico*, ed. Alejandra Moreno Toscano et al. Mexico City: INAH, 1976.

Romero, José. *Guía de la Ciudad de México*. Mexico: Porrúa, 1910.

Ruiz, Ramón Eduardo. *The Great Rebellion: Mexico, 1905–1924*. New York: Norton, 1980.

———. *Labor and the Ambivalent Revolutionaries*. Baltimore: Johns Hopkins University Press, 1976.

Salazar, Rosendo. *Del militarismo al civilismo en nuestra revolución*. Mexico City: Libro-Mex, 1958.

———. *La Casa del Obrero Mundial*. Mexico City: Costa-Amic, 1962.

———. *Líderes y sindicatos*. Mexico City: T. C. Modelo, 1953.

Salazar, Rosendo, and José Escobedo. *Las pugnas de la gleba*. Mexico City: Editorial Avante, 1922.

Sánchez Sánchez, Victor Manuel. *Surgimiento del sindicalismo electricista*. Mexico City: UNAM, 1978.

Secretaria de Industria, Comercio y Trabajo. *Monografía sobre el estado actual de la industria en México*. Mexico: Talleres Gráficos de la Nación, 1929.

Semanario de Historia Moderna. *Estadísticas económicas del Porfiriato: Fuerza de trabajo y actividad económica por sectores*. Mexico City: Colegio de México, n.d.

Sesto, Julio. *La ciudad de los palacios*. Mexico City: El Libroa Español, 1920.

———. *México de Porfirio Díaz*. Valencia: Sempere y Compañía, 1910.

Sewell, William, Jr. "Social Change and the Rise of Working-Class Politics in Nineteenth-Century Marseille." *Past and Present* 65 (November 1974): 75–109.

Shaw, Frederick. "The Artisan in Mexico City." In *El trabajo y los trabajadores en la historia de México*, ed. Elsa Frost. Mexico City: Colegio de México, 1979.

Soto, Shirlene Ann. *The Mexican Woman: A Study of Her Participation in the Revolution, 1910–1940*. Palo Alto CA: R & E Research, 1979.

Spalding, Hobart. *Organized Labor in Latin America*. New York: Harper and Row, 1977.

Taibo, Paco Ignacio, II. *Los Bolshevikis: Historia narrativa de los orígenes del comunismo en México*. Mexico City: Joaquin Mortiz, 1987.

Tannenbaum, Frank. *Peace by Revolution: Mexico after 1910*. New York: Columbia University Press, 1966.

Tenorio-Trillo, Mauricio. "1910 Mexico City: Space and Nation in the City of the Centenario." *Journal of Latin American Studies* 28, no. 1 (February 1996): 75–104.

Terry, T. Philip. *Terry's Mexico*. New York: Houghton Mifflin, 1911.

Thompson, E. P. "The Moral Economy of the English Crowd in the Eighteenth Century." *Past and Present* 50 (1971): 76–136.

———. "Time, Work-Discipline, and Industrial Capitalism." *Past and Present* 38 (1967): 56–97.

Thompson, Lanny. "Artisan Marginals and Proletarians: The Households of the Popular Classes in Mexico City, 1876–1950." In *Five Centuries of Mexican History*, ed. Virginia Guedea and Jaime Rodriguez O., 2:307–24. Mexico City: Instituto Mora, 1992.

———. "The Structures and Vicissitudes of Reproduction: Households in Mexico, 1876–1970." *Review* 14, no. 3 (1991): 403–36.

Thompson, Wallace. *The People of Mexico*. New York: Harper, 1921.

Thomson, Guy P. C. "Popular Aspects of Liberalism in Mexico, 1848–1888." *Bulletin of Latin American Research* 10, no. 3 (1991): 265–92.

Trujillo Bolio, Mario. *Operarios fabriles en el Valle de México (1864–1884): Espacio, trabajo, protesta y cultura obrera*. Mexico City: Colegio de México, 1997.

Valadés, José. *Historia general de la Revolución Mexicana*. 10 vols. Mexico: Ediciones Gernika, 1963–65.

Walker, David. "Porfirian Labor Politics: Working Class Organizations in Mexico City and Porfirio Diaz, 1876–1902." *Americas* 37, no. 3 (1981): 257–89.

Womack, John, Jr. "Luchas sindicales y liberalismo social." *Libertad y justicia en las sociedades modernas*. Mexico: Porrua, 1994.

———. "The Mexican Economy During the Revolution, 1910–1920: Historiography and Analysis." *Marxist Perspectives* 1, no. 4 (1978): 80–123.

———. "The Mexican Revolution, 1910–1920." *The Cambridge History of Latin America*, ed. Leslie Bethall, 5:79–154. Cambridge: Cambridge University Press, 1986.

Index